# Global Political Economy

Global Political Economy (GPE) is a broad and varied field of study, drawing from a number of disciplines and approaches. Most International Political Economy (IPE) texts give the impression that the discipline is divided into three paradigms: realism, liberalism and structuralism; this book argues that modern IPE has moved on. Given the bewildering range of debates, students and lecturers need a good clear text which is critical and informative; this book presents an invaluable overview of all the major contemporary debates and approaches now at the forefront of European and American Global Political Economy.

*Global Political Economy* is structured around two basic themes: the first part focuses on the six central concepts of GPE: state, firm, capital, power, labour and globalisation; these concepts have all been subject to recent innovation and debate. The second part of the book considers a select number of theories at the forefront of GPE, from the broad traditions of Marxism, rationalism and hermeneutics/institutionalism. This book provides succinct summaries of these topical, wide-ranging issues and controversies. Given how difficult it is to keep up to date with IPE and GPE, this book represents a compact guide to the wide range of debates in the field and will be ideal for students and lecturers alike in IPE and International Relations.

**Ronen Palan** is Senior Lecturer in International Relations at the University of Sussex. He is joint editor of the *Review of International Political Economy*, co-author of *State Strategies in the Global Political Economy*, and co-editor of *Transcending the State Global Divide*.

# ROUTLEDGE/RIPE STUDIES IN GLOBAL POLITICAL ECONOMY

Series Editors: Otto Holman, Marianne Marchand
(*Research Centre for International Political Economy, University of Amsterdam*) and Henk Overbeek (*Free University, Amsterdam*)

This series, published in association with the *Review of International Political Economy*, provides a forum for current debates in international political economy. The series aims to cover all the central topics in IPE and to present innovative analyses of emerging topics. The titles in the series seek to transcend a state-centred discourse and focus on three broad themes:

- the nature of the forces driving globalisation forward
- resistance to globalisation
- the transformation of the world order.

The series comprises two strands:

*Routledge/RIPE Studies in Global Political Economy* is a forum for innovative new research intended for a high-level specialist readership, and the titles will be available in hardback only. Titles include:

1. **Globalization and Governance**
   *Edited by Aseem Prakash and Jeffrey A. Hart*

2. **Nation-States and Money**
   The past, present and future of national currencies
   *Edited by Emily Gilbert and Eric Helleiner*

3. **The Global Political Economy of Intellectual Property Rights**
   The new enclosures?
   *Christopher May*

The *RIPE Series in Global Political Economy* aims to address the needs of students and teachers, and the titles will be published in hardback and paperback. Titles include:

**Transnational Classes and International Relations**
*Kees van der Pijl*

**Gender and Global Restructuring**
Sightings, sites and resistances
*Edited by Marianne H. Marchand and Anne Sisson Runyan*

**Global Political Economy**
Contemporary theories
*Edited by Ronen Palan*

**Ideologies of Globalization**
Contending visions of a New World Order
*Mark Rupert*

# Global Political Economy

## Contemporary theories

**Edited by Ronen Palan**

London and New York

First published 2000
by Routledge
11 New Fetter Lane, London EC4P 4EE

Simultaneously published in the USA and Canada
by Routledge
29 West 35th Street, New York, NY 10001

*Routledge is an imprint of the Taylor & Francis Group*

Typeset in Baskerville by Taylor & Francis Books Ltd
Printed and bound in Great Britain by St Edmundsbury Press, Bury St Edmunds, Suffolk.

*British Library Cataloguing in Publication Data*
A catalogue record for this book is available from the British Library

*Library of Congress Cataloging in Publication Data*
Global political economy: contemporary theories / edited by Ronen Palan.
p. cm. – (Routledge/RIPE studies in global political economy)
Includes bibliographical references and index.
1. International economic relations. 2. Economic policy. I. Palan, Ronen.
II. Series.
HF1411 .G6469 2000
337–dc21

                                                              00-020054

ISBN 0–415–20488–7 (hbk)
ISBN 0–415–20489–5 (pbk)

To Susan Strange – teacher and friend

# Contents

# Illustrations

## Tables

## Figures

# Contributors

**Shimshon Bichler** teaches political economy in universities and colleges in Israel. His research focus is capitalist development, accumulation and elite dynamics. He is currently working on a book on the global political economy of Israel together with Jonathan Nitzan.

**Lisa J. Carlson** is an Associate Professor of Political Science at the University of Idaho. Her research and publications are in the areas of game theory, international crisis escalation, and trade and conflict. She currently serves on the Executive Council of the Pacific Northwest Political Science Association (1996–99) and will be the Association's President in 2001. She is also research co-coordinator with the University of Idaho's Martin Institute for Peace Studies and Conflict Resolution.

**Philip G. Cerny** is Professor of Government at the University of Manchester. He is the author of *The Politics of Grandeur: Ideological Aspects of De Gaulle's Foreign Policy* (Cambridge University Press, 1980) and *The Changing Architecture of Politics: Structure, Agency, and the Future of the State* (Sage, 1990), and editor/co-author of *Finance and World Politics: Markets, Regimes and States in the Post-Hegemonic Era* (Elgar, 1993). His articles have appeared in a wide range of journals.

**Michael Dunford** is Professor of Economic Geography in the School of European Studies at the University of Sussex and Editor of *Regional Studies*. His publications include *The Arena of Capital* (Macmillan, 1983) written with Diane Perrons, and *Capital, the State and Regional Development* (Pion 1988). He is co-author of *Industrial Change and Regional Development: The Transformation of New Industrial Spaces* (Belhaven 1991) and *Cities and Regions in the New Europe: The Global Local Interplay and Spatial Development Strategies* (Belhaven 1992). At present he is doing comparative research on regional economic performance in Europe and on the determinants of inequality and social exclusion.

**Stefano Guzzini** is Associate Professor in Political Science, International Relations and European Studies at the Central European University, Budapest College. He has published on theories of international relations and international political economy, as well as on the comparative analysis of West European welfare states.

**Anna Leander** is Assistant Professor of Political Science at the Central European University, Budapest College. Her publications cover theoretical issues (theory of the state, feminism and ethics) in international relations and international political economy as well as work on the political economy of the EU and of Turkey.

**L.H.M. Ling** is currently a Senior Lecturer of International Studies at the Institute of Social Studies, the Hague, the Netherlands and an Associate Editor with the *International Feminist Journal of Politics*. Her book, *Conquest and Desire: Postcolonial Learning between Asia and the West* is forthcoming (Macmillan Press/St. Martin's Press).

**Philip McMichael** is Professor and Chair of Rural Sociology, Cornell University, New York. His research focuses on the political history of world capitalism, with an emphasis on states and food regimes. His books include *Settlers and the Agrarian Question: Foundations of Capitalism in Australia* (1984), *The Global Restructuring of Agro-Food Systems* (editor, 1994), and *Development and Social Change: A Global Perspective* (2000, 2nd edition). He is currently President of the Research Committee of Agriculture and Food, International Sociological Association.

**Jonathan Nitzan** is an Associate Professor at the Department of Political Science, York University, in Toronto, and former Senior Editor of the *Emerging Markets Strategist* at the Bank Credit Analyst Research Group. His research focuses on accumulation, capitalist development and power. He is presently working, together with Shimshon Bichler, on a book on the global political economy of Israel.

**Robert O'Brien** is Assistant Professor in the Department of Political Science and the Institute on Globalization and the Human Condition at McMaster University in Canada. His present research focuses on the emergence of a global labour movement. He is co-author of *Contesting Global Governance: Multilateral Economic Institutions and Global Social Movements* (Cambridge, 2000) and author of *Subsidy Regulation and State Transformation* (Macmillan, 1997).

**Henk Overbeek** is Senior Lecturer in International Relations, Vrije Universiteit, Amsterdam (Netherlands). His interests are in international political economy and European integration. His publications include *Global Capitalism and National Decline* (1990), *Restructuring Hegemony in the Global Political Economy* (editor, 1993), *Neo-liberal Hegemony and the Political Economy of European Restructuring* (co-editor, 1998), *Hegemonie und internationale Arbeitsteilung* (forthcoming), and *The Political Economy of European Unemployment* (editor, forthcoming). Henk Overbeek is co-editor of the RIPE series in Global Political Economy (Routledge).

**Ronen Palan** is Senior Lecturer in International Relations at the University of Sussex, and co-editor of the *Review of International Political Economy*. He has been a visiting professor at York University, Toronto and the Hebrew University, Jerusalem. His publications include *Transcending the State–Global Divide*, co-edited with Barry Gills (1994) and *State Strategies in the Global Political Economy*, with Jason Abbott (1999). He is currently researching the offshore economy.

**Richard Phillips** is a doctoral candidate in the department of International Relations and Politics at Sussex University.

**Jan Nederveen Pieterse** is at the Institute of Social Studies in The Hague. He has taught in Ghana and the United States and has been visiting professor in Japan and Indonesia. He is co-editor of *Review of International Political Economy* and advisory editor of several journals. His books include *White on Black: Images of Africa and Blacks in Western Popular Culture* (Yale University Press, 1992); *Empire and Emancipation* (Praeger, 1989), which received the 1990 JC Ruigrok Award of the Netherlands Society of Sciences; and *Development-Deconstructions/Reconstructions* (Sage, 2000).

**Martin Shaw** is Professor of International Relations and Politics and convenor of the graduate programme in Contemporary War and Peace Studies at the University of Sussex. His books include *Dialectics of War* (1988), *Post-Military Society* (1991), *Global Society and International Relations* (1994) and *Civil Society and Media in Global Crises* (1996).

**Hendrik Spruyt** is Associate Professor of Political Science at Arizona State University. Prior to that he taught at Columbia University. He is the author of *The Sovereign State and Its Competitors* (Princeton University Press, 1994) and more than a dozen articles and chapters in edited volumes. He is currently working on a book analysing the interaction of domestic politics and international changes in cases of territorial dissolution. Additionally, he is a co-editor of the *Review of International Political Economy*.

# Series editors' preface

The field of International Political Economy is not only reaching a certain level of maturity – generating its own debates, concerns, schools of thought and gaining increasing recognition – it is also very much in flux. This 'state of flux' is in part a reflection of attempts by IPE scholars to capture the rapidly changing environment of the Global Political Economy. These changes are more profound than – and go beyond – the often signalled transformations in production, finance, labour markets and the state. As observers like Castells, Giddens, and Harvey are arguing, the fundaments of modernity itself are eroding. Within the rapidly expanding field of IPE, changes in the Global Political Economy have resulted in the emergence of a critical, heterodox IPE, which has been labelled New Political Economy (NPE) by Craig Murphy and Roger Tooze. New Political Economy is being characterised by combining various critical strands of thought which challenge statist as well as actor-oriented approaches associated with neorealism and rational actor models. Moreover, a growing group of scholars working within the NPE tradition are focusing on the re-articulation of identities and the growing prominence of culture in the context of the Global Political Economy.

The book *Global Political Economy: Contemporary Theories* provides an excellent illustration of such attempts theoretically to capture and understand the changing Global Political Economy and its ontological and epistemological implications. Bringing together well-known specialists in the field, the volume manages to accomplish three things. First, it provides an excellent overview and discussion of the new ideas and theories imported from other, related fields in the social sciences. As the editor argues, the (re-)introduction of evolutionary economics, Marxian political economy and institutionalism into the heterodox field of NPE serves to break the conceptual boundaries between politics and economics or states and firms and allows us to develop a truly integrated political-economy approach. Second, the contributions in the volume revisit the established categories of IPE and analyse how these need to be re-conceptualised in order to capture current processes of transformation. For instance, it is once again demonstrated how the traditional dyad state/power vs. market/capital no longer holds true. Capital and power are present in both arenas and are so intertwined that we need to think in terms of political-economy. Also, it is increasingly necessary to include 'society' and societal forces such as social movements and non-governmental organisations in our analysis of the Global Political Economy. Finally, the volume pinpoints at a new and important development in the field of IPE, which is the emergence of post-rationalist approaches. This post-rationalist turn – sometimes also referred to as linguistic turn – in IPE is best illustrated by the contributions from Palan and Ling. The emphasis on negotiation, contestation and historical narrative underlines the open-endedness of contemporary processes in the Global Political Economy. It also allows for the introduction of such important dimensions as race, ethnicity and gender which have remained invisible for too long, both in our theorising and our choice of 'key categories' in IPE. Showing how material transformations are intertwined with and embedded in re-articulations of identity and cultural practices is a first step toward expanding the horizons of NPE.

In sum, the editors strongly recommend *Global Political Economy: Contemporary Theories* because it provides a state of the art overview of the debates, issues and new directions in the field of IPE. It is a 'must read' for everyone who wants to stay abreast of the latest developments in a very rich field of study.

Otto Holman
Marianne H. Marchand
Henk Overbeek
Amsterdam, March 2000

# Acknowledgements

The idea for the volume took shape as I was looking for a good accessible text-book for my postgraduate course at Sussex University entitled Contemporary Theories in Global Political Economy. Not only could I not find such text, but it occurred to me that while most students and scholars in the field are comfortable working within the confines of their chosen theoretical and methodological approaches, up-to-date short summaries of other approaches and debates might be a useful teaching tool. The book aims therefore to fill a gap. It consists of sixteen relatively short chapters summarising recent trends in global political economy scholarship, broadly conceived. Special thanks are due to Jeffery Frieden, David Lake and Helen Milner who patiently guided me through the recent developments in the American branch of International Political Economy. The editorial team of the RIPE book series, Otto Holman, Marianne Marchand and Henk Overbeek have read the entire manuscript and made numerous useful comments. Thanks are due also to the three anonymous referees for their useful comments. Finally, special thanks to Victoria Smith, Milon Nagi, Craig Fowlie, Sue Dunsmore, Allison Bell and other members of the Routledge editorial and production team.

# Abbreviations

| | |
|---|---|
| AFL-CIO | American Federation of Labor - Congress of Industrial Organizations |
| BRIE | Berkeley Roundtable on the International Economy |
| CEO | chief executive officer |
| CPN | crossnational production network |
| CTM | Confederacion de Trabajadores de Mexico |
| DOD | Department of Defense |
| EMU | European Monetary Union |
| ESPRIT | European Strategy Programme for Research and Development in Information Technologies |
| FZLN | Frente Zapatista de Liberación Naciónal |
| GATT | General Agreement on Trade and Tariffs |
| GDP | gross domestic product |
| GPE | global political economy |
| HRM | human resource management |
| HST | Hegemonic Stability Theory |
| ICT | information and communication technology |
| IMF | International Monetary Fund |
| INGO | International Non-Governmental Organization |
| IPE | International Political Economy |
| IR | International Relations |
| KMP | Peasant Movement of the Philippines |
| KRRS | Karnataka State Farmers Association |
| LDC | less developed country |
| LED | local economic development |
| MAI | Multilateral Agreement on Investments |
| MNC | multinational corporation |
| MST | Movemento sem Terra |
| MUNS | Multi-lateralism and the UN system |
| NAFTA | North Atlantic Free Trade Agreement |
| NATO | North Atlantic Treaty Organization |
| NGO | non-governmental organization |

| NI | New Institutionalism |
| NIC | Newly Industrializing Country |
| NST | Movemento sen Terra |
| OECD | Organization for Economic Cooperation and Development |
| OPEC | Organization of Petroleum Exporting Countries |
| PGA | People's Global Action |
| PIG | private interest government |
| SAP | structural adjustment programme |
| SRO | self-regulating organization |
| TNC | transnational corporation |
| TRIMs | Trade Related Investments |
| WID | Women in Development |
| WTO | World Trade Organization |

# 1   New trends in global political economy

*Ronen Palan*

The social sciences rarely conform to the public's image of ivory towers inhabited by lightly intoxicated academics engaged in ponderous debates.[1] On the contrary, academic faculties are fractious and argumentative. Yet not everything is disputed: remove the veneer of contestation and inevitably orthodoxy emerges. Orthodoxy cannot be equated with agreement or harmony. Indeed, its power is short-lived and homogeneity is achieved with great difficulty. As Mary Douglas notes (in a different context) 'the inside experience of culture is an experience of choice and decision' (1992: 25). Orthodoxy is experienced in debate and controversies, in those tacit agreements that are masked by overt disagreements. Orthodoxy does not only shape an agenda for research, ensuring academic promotions, research money, and so on, but its powers manifest themselves also in shaping the nature of the predominant forms of its critiques. Thus orthodoxy and its critiques are mutually sustaining, marking between them the subtle and yet surprisingly robust boundaries of a discipline.

Three decades or so after the emergence of International Political Economy (IPE) as a branch of International Relations scholarship (Denemark and O'Brien 1997; Gill and Law 1988), the nature, boundaries and intellectual ancestries of IPE are still matters of dispute. At its launch, the *Review of International Political Economy* invited a number of leading scholars to define IPE as they saw it (Burnham 1994; Hodgson 1994; Krasner 1994; Strange 1994), and their contributions bear testimony to a deeply divided field of study lacking agreement on 'first principles'. Indeed, even the label IPE is under dispute: Gill and Law (1988: xxiii), for instance, prefer the term 'Global Political Economy' (GPE), privileging the global arena over international relationships. Nowadays the two labels are used interchangeably. As will be discussed below, IPE is generally adopted by those who view it as a sub-field of International Relations, whereas GPE is normally the preferred label for those who view it as a transdisciplinary effort, closer to political economy then to International Relations. This book contains the two traditions, hence both labels are used.

But perhaps the will to define close disciplinary boundaries is misdirected. Geographers distinguish between the concept of boundary and frontier: boundaries are lines, frontiers are zones; Ladis Kristof writes:

> [frontier] is outer-oriented. Its main attention is directed toward the outlying areas which are both a source of danger and a coveted prize ... The boundary, on the contrary, is *inner-oriented*. It is created and maintained by the will of the central government. It has no life of its own, not even material existence.
>
> (Kristof 1969: 126–128)

Perhaps we should think of GPE not as a bounded but as a 'frontiered' discipline; an outer-, rather than inner-oriented field of study; its attention is directed towards an outlying area where it overlaps with other 'disciplines'. Its distinct identity is formed not through some shared core assumptions, but in this vague zonal terrain where one discipline meshes with another.

This volume charts this shifting zonal terrain that marks the outer boundaries of contemporary European, American and developmental GPE. Our intention here is not to adjudicate among competing approaches, but to inform and educate the reader who may find it difficult to keep up with the range of scholarship that is relevant to contemporary GPE scholarship. A cursory acquaintance with GPE reveals it to be a broad and somewhat inchoate field of study. While the great majority of GPE texts still give the impression of a field divided into three, so-called 'paradigms': realism, liberalism and structuralism, it is evident that contemporary GPE has by and large moved on to a considerable degree. GPE has absorbed and, in turn, has been absorbed into, the broader trends in the social sciences loosening in the process its ties to the discipline of International Relations. As a result, the *main* division lines in contemporary GPE no longer trail International Relations' controversies, but reflect broader issues and contemporary debates in political economy and the social sciences.

This introductory chapter maps out contemporary debates in GPE. I stress in particular the rising in significance of the methodological debate between, on the one hand, rationalist and methodologically individualist approaches, and on the other, the critical or post-rationalist traditions.[2] The book is divided into two parts. Part I focuses on six of the central concepts of GPE: state, firm, capital, power, labour and globalisation, each of which is increasingly subjected to a rigorous and critical evaluation. These are not necessarily the six fundamental concepts of GPE, but they are the six that have been the subject of the greatest debate and innovation in the past two decades. Part II covers a select number of theories, currently at the forefront of GPE. These theories and approaches are drawn from the three broad traditions of rationalism, Marxism and institutionalism.

## Beyond state and firm

Traditionally, GPE was concerned with two central institutions of the modern world and the relationship between them, the state and the multinational enterprise, or as some have described them, the state and the market. Famously, Gilpin defined IPE in the following terms:

The parallel existence and mutual interaction of 'state' and 'market' in the modern world create 'political economy' … In the absence of state, the price mechanism and market forces would determine the outcome of economic activities; this would be the pure world of the economist. In the absence of market, the state or its equivalent would allocate economic resources; this would be the pure world of political scientist.

(1987: 8)[3]

The implicit assumption in Gilpin's formulation, namely that politics and economics are two separate, indeed, parallel realms, proved to be deeply unsatisfactory. The challenge faced by IPE was to overcome the conventional distinction between politics and economics and come up with a truly integrated political-economy approach. This theoretical challenge, which is not unique to GPE but pervades the entire field of political economy, pointed the way towards the current theoretical realignment discussed below.

Although most academic analysis of GPE remains dominated by states and markets and the relationships between them, a central contention of this collection is that in the past decade or so the substantive content of GPE has moved on considerably. To begin with, the relationship between states and markets has undergone changes due to a profound restructuring of the environment of accumulation through economic globalisation. At the same time, it has become clear that GPE can ill afford to remain aloof towards a set of important debates taking place in fields as diverse as political sciences, economics, human geography, business studies and sociology.

The chapters by Cerny (Chapter 2), Phillips (Chapter 3) and McMichael (Chapter 7), each provide us with an up-dated summary of the recent scholarship on the state, multinational enterprises and globalisation, drawing loosely on the theoretical traditions discussed in Part II. Combined, these chapters provide ample evidence of a world that is changing in dramatic ways. Cerny and McMichael both demonstrate that the more discerning observers in GPE have long abandoned the sterile state versus globalisation debate. These two chapters are concerned in particular with the realignment of forces and new forms of politics that operate in a complex way under the auspices of a changed state. Although drawing on different theoretical traditions, their argument chimes well with the recent developments in neo-Gramscian scholarship (discussed by Overbeek, Chapter 11) and in particular the emergence of new global disciplinary forms which Stephen Gill had dubbed, the 'new constitutionalism' (Gill 1995a, 1995b).

I would like to highlight here in particular the chapter on multinational enterprises, because the dramatic developments that have occurred in that field have largely been ignored in both GPE and IR (Phillips, Chapter 3). Richard Phillips demonstrates that multinational enterprises operate in what they consider to be a global market, fundamentally altering their conception of spatial and economic location, alliances and belonging. More crucially, the traditional image of the capitalist economy as if it consists of independent and fiercely competitive corporations seeking to maximise profit, is seen to be misleading. The diverse forms of what is now branded 'alliance capitalism' challenge not only orthodox conceptions of the market, but also traditional conceptions of the nature and functions of state boundaries. The result of these changes is a re-shaping of the forms of competitive capitalism which generate in turn, as Nitzan and Bichler (Chapter 5) show, new forms of global governance. The far-reaching developments in the area of firm and inter-firm relationships have rekindled interest in institutional economics, arguably the most significant theoretical development in the field in the past decade. The impact of institutional economics on GPE is discussed by Nitzan and Bichler (Chapter 5), Spruyt (Chapter 9), Dunford (Chapter 10) and Leander (Chapter 12).

GPE, however, is looking beyond, state, market and globalisation. As this implies, the relationship between states, firms (the market) and the environment of accumulation (globalisation) is not simply an empirical matter, but raises important questions of interpretation. At each and every point in the discussion we are confronted by three crucial questions, concerning the nature of power, capital and labour. The issue of power is closely linked to that of agency, traditionally associated with politics and the state (Guzzini, Chapter 4). It also, as Nitzan and Bichler demonstrate, lies at the heart of the central structuring agent of the modern world, capital – which traditionally lies in the field of economics or 'the market'. And yet the two chapters by Guzzini and Nitzan and Bichler demonstrate that, on the one hand, the duality of state/power, market/capital, is untenable, as power and capital manifest themselves in both state and market necessitating a truly political-economic form analysis, but on the other hand, perhaps more than any other chapters in this collection, they hold the key to the failure – if that is the right term – of GPE to generate its own unique brand of theory. Power is undoubtedly the central concept of GPE, and as Nitzan and Bichler demonstrate, power does not simply belong to the state or the political side of the equation, but relationships of power are at the very heart of the economy side. And yet, as Guzzini demonstrates, the conceptualisation of power remains elusive as ever. More then any other branch of political economy, GPE centres on power, and yet, it does not really know how to conceptualise power.

Although somewhat abstract, the concept of power is intimately connected to some of the most important questions raised by GPE concerning the relationship between current transformations and prospects for life and work of 'real' people, i.e. often conceptualised under the category of 'labour', arguably the most ignored category of them all (O'Brien, Chapter 6). Labour is, as both O'Brien and Ling (Chapter 16) argue, a 'hidden' substratum most notable for its absence in mainstream IPE. It is not accidental that both the French school of regulation (Chapter 10) and the neo-Gramscians (Chapter 11) originally evolved as critique of contemporary conceptualisation of labour.

The six categories of state, multinational enterprises, capital, power, labour and globalisation, are intimately connected: they inform one another and define in a non-dogmatic manner the intellectual terrain that is the space occupied by modern GPE. None of these categories 'belongs' exclusively to GPE, but by their very nature, they stimulate the sort of interdisciplinary research that characterises GPE.

## The return of political economy

The debates that surround the six categories discussed in Part I of this book, pave the way for the theoretical realignment discussed in Part II and a return to the tradition of political economy. This does not, however, signal the resurrection of another orthodoxy. Orthodoxy is normally viewed in narrow terms to denote what is at any given time the 'mainstream'. But a field of study does not consist only of its mainstream. There are, in addition, certain discursive formations, which, however difficult their boundaries may be to define, one none the less tacitly recognised throughout a given discipline as the boundaries of what is considered by members to be relevant to their subject-matter. This book contends that some significant changes have taken place in the field of GPE in recent years.

The old orthodoxy in IPE was very much IR generated and viewed the field as divided among three schools of thought, realism, pluralism (liberalism) and structuralism. The immediate difficulty with this taxomony is that it consists of a number of misleading appellations built upon a false historiography. To start with, 'realism' or 'political realism' has dominated the discipline of International Relations, and some argue still dominates the field of IPE. This is predicated on the assumption that states are volitional entities (hence often assume 'unitary actors') who pursue their 'egotistic' interest regardless of any moral constraints. Since all states are pursuing their interest, the only mediating factor in international politics is power. On that basis the theory hypothesises that power distribution in the international system defines the main characteristics of the system, including, and that used to be thought of as the IPE portion, the international trading system. Thus, for instance, it is argued that hegemony lends sufficient stability to the system to allow for an international trading system to flourish (for discussion, see Guzzini, Chapter 4).

Realists normally trace their ideas to Machiavelli (or a particular reading of Machiavelli, the cynic[4]) and to Hobbes, by which they mean they view the international system as somewhat akin to Hobbes's concept of the state of nature. But it is clear that the theory of political realism is traceable to the anti-reformation philosophical work of Botero, who coined the term 'reason of state', and to the work of the German thinkers of the nineteenth century like Treistchke, who coined the term 'political realism' and in particular to the German liberal, Friedrich Meinecke.[5] This false historiography of realism may go some way towards explaining why it is so difficult to differentiate between realism and liberalism in IPE.

Liberals or pluralists are commonly understood to be those who do not view the state as a unitary volitional entity but, on the contrary, as an instrument for the achievement of societal goals. Theoretically, the state is disaggregated while normative consideration of system optimisation through the tools of rational choice is advanced. Interestingly, although liberalism is viewed in international relations as a different 'paradigm' to realism, it seems that international relations liberals often arrive to the same set of conclusions as international realists. So for example, Krasner (1982) and Snidal (1985a), among others, demonstrate that hegemonic stability theory has its roots not in the realist theory but in fact in public choice theory, or neoclassically driven political economy. In fact, the fusion between realism and liberalism began as early as the 1970s with the work of Keohane and Nye (1971). What began as an attempt to develop a new approach to international relations then folded back to realism in the 1980s (Keohane 1984). Meanwhile, realists were increasingly interested in questions of identity and interest using the medium of rational choice theory, thus blurring further the distinction between realism and liberalism. Similarly, Robert Gilpin (1987) advanced a combination of a realist theory and neoclassical economics. It was only logical for both realists and liberals to adopt the more rigorous tools of rationalist methodology as discussed in Chapters 8 and 9. As a result, the division lines separating realism and neoliberalism are increasingly difficult to maintain.

Structuralism is yet another misnomer representing a particularly problematic neo-Marxist school more commonly known as the world systems approaches. World systems theory proved particularly useful in developing a political economic interpretation of the international environment that was not wholly predicated on a concept of a pluralist state system. On the contrary, world systems theory conceptualised the capitalist economy as a unified system in which the state system took a decidedly secondary role (Wallerstein 1974). But while the conceptual shift from a state system to the capitalist system has been welcomed by Marxist literature (see Chapters 10 and 11), the over-deterministic, structural and paradoxically ahistorical analysis of history of the world system has given way to more nuanced approaches.

These developments have resulted in the far reaching realignment of GPE from international relations back to its roots in political economy. But the return of political economy is not without its problems. Political economy is deeply divided among at least three schools of thought, each of which survived the traumatic dissolution in the late nineteenth century of political economy and the emergence of the modern disciplines of economics, political science and sociology. These remnants of older political economic traditions are at the heart of the renewal of GPE thought.

The first of these remnants of political economy survived in the tradition of utilitarian thought contributing nowadays to what Hodgson (1994) calls the imperialism of neoclassical economics. Here, neoclassical concepts and methodologies, such as marginal utility, optimisation, equilibrium and rational choice are increasingly used to explain the determinant of international policy-making. As a result, very influential methodological individualist-based IPE schools of thought have flourished in recent years, particularly in the United States. They include strategic interaction and game theoretic approaches to IPE (Carlson, Chapter 8) and the neoinstitutionalist transaction cost economics theories of IPE

(Spruyt, Chapter 9 and Cerny, Chapter 2). This branch is concerned primarily with the inter-state arena and policy-making and still sees itself as operating within a field of study called 'international political economy'.

Alternative traditions, including Marxian economics, evolutionary institutionalism and hermeneutics[6] survive by and large in other academic departments such as geography, business studies, economic history and organisational and sociological theory. In contrast to mainstream economics which 'has evolved primarily an examination of a single set of idealized rules governing market exchange' (Eggertson 1990: 4), the critical wing, which tends to identify itself as GPE, is concerned primarily with labour and institutions such as the family and the firm, the market and the state, and above all, the exercise of power. Among these, this volume highlights in particular the contribution to GPE of the neo-Gramscian/transnational class alliance approaches (Overbeek, Chapter 11), and the French school of regulation and neo-Schumpeterian approaches (Dunford, Chapter 10). In their unique ways, both are concerned with issues such as state/society relations, the formation of global order and transnational hegemonies. Renewed interest in the evolutionary institutionalism of Veblen, Commons and Polanyi (Phillips, Chapter 3, Nitzan and Bichler, Chapter 5 and Leander, Chapter 12) and historical sociology (Leander, Chapter 12 and Shaw, Chapter 14) is beginning to make serious inroads into GPE. Marxian, evolutionary institutionalist and sociological traditions are better prone to define their area of study as 'global political economy' privileging, as Gill and Law (1988: xxiii) suggest the global over the international.

The renewed interest in the philosophical roots of political economy equally raises the question of thematic boundaries. Michel Foucault rephrased the old social democratic slogan, 'knowledge is power' in a novel way. A Foucauldian sensibility (which, of course, precedes Foucault) challenges rationalist discourses and the traditional mode of explanations of truth and their relationships to hierarchies and exclusionary practices. By extension, it challenges not only class hierarchies, but also colonial and hence racist hierarchies, as well as gender hierarchies. As a result, the singularity of the class-based exploitative politics of traditional Marxism is giving way to the multifaceted and sometimes subtle forms of exploitative politics, including the various discursive techniques which are viewed as expressions of power relations (Pieterse, Chapter 13, Palan, Chapter 14, Ling, Chapter 16). The 'new' IPE, as Murphy and Tooze (1991) call this rather eclectic 'post-rationalist' branch of GPE, maintains that power, exploitation and hegemony take many forms, not all of which are purely 'materialist' or of economic nature.

As a matter of fact, GPE does not claim that economics and/or materialist interests are at the heart of each and every event, trend or process in the international or the global arena. GPE does not privilege economics; it privileges a *political-economic* mode of analysis or, analysis that denies the separation between politics, economics and society (for discussion see Nitzan and Bichler, Chapter 5). This places GPE at an analytical advantage but equally at a pedagogical disadvantage. Analytically, GPE is evolving (hopefully) into a heterodox field of study which as a matter of practice as much as matter of principle does not rule out any form of analysis from the outset.[7] But as a result, debates in economics, sociology, geography, political sciences, anthropology, philosophy, business, organisation theory, international relations and even psychology and psychoanalysis, and the whole diversity of epistemological and methodological positions upon which they draw, are considered relevant to the student of GPE. The sheer size and depth of the literature challenge even the most diligent and hardworking student of GPE.

Yet we should not overplay the significance of contemporary dividing lines. The history of economic and social thought teaches us about the subtle but the important linkages, the cross-references, and the shared points of origins that draw together surprisingly diverse arrays of theories and approaches. There is much more to unite the different approaches and the so-called 'paradigms' of GPE than may appear at first sight. In our different ways we all try to make sense of the processes of order and change that shape the contemporary world; we are all aware that technological change combined with the growing integration of the markets and cultural penetration are impacting upon state and society in unpredictable ways. None the less, contemporary GPE is so rich and interesting, diverse and yet informative because it exhibits strong commitment to theoretically informed empirical research. At the core of current theorisation, therefore, are not only those broad theoretical traditions which are the focus of Part II of this book, but also substantive debates centring on practically all the fundamental categories of the social sciences, including the subject (or the individual), the state, the multinational enterprise, the political economic environment, power, labour and capital.

## Economic approaches to politics

In a talk given at the 1996 annual conference of the European Association for Evolutionary Political Economy Paul Krugman defined economics in the following terms:

1  Economics is about what 'individuals' do: not classes, not 'correlations of forces', but individual actors. This is not to deny the relevance of higher levels of analysis, but they must be grounded in individual behaviour. Methodological individualism is of the essence.
2  The individuals are self-interested. There is nothing in economics that inherently prevents us from allowing people to derive satisfaction from others' consumption, but the predictive power of economic theory comes from the presumption that normally people care about themselves.
3  The individuals are intelligent: obvious opportunities for gain are not neglected. Hundred-dollar bills do not lie unattended in the street for very long.
4  We are concerned with the 'interaction' of such individuals: most interesting economic theory, from supply and demand on, is about the

'invisible hand'; processes in which the collective outcome is not what individuals intended.

(Krugman 1996: 2)

If standard economics is about what individuals do, and as Krugman suggests, not classes or 'correlations of forces' (a term by which Krugman probably means what sociologists call the social structure) then, by default Krugman offers a good definition of what political economy is about. Paraphrasing Krugman, we may say that political economy as opposed to standard economics is about social classes, states and 'correlations of forces', not about the individual. Political economy, then, centres precisely on those topics and issues that standard economics ignores, a point for which we find affirmation in no less an authority than John Maynard Keynes. In seeking to defend the science of economics Keynes argued that 'the problem of want and poverty and the economic struggle between classes and nations is nothing but a frightful muddle, a transitory and unnecessary muddle' (quoted in Hardt and Negri 1994: 35). Antonio Negri wryly observes that standard economics is united in the despairing conviction that 'everything beyond the equilibrium – is nothing but the work of imbeciles' (ibid.: 35).

On that basis one would not expect political economists, those 'imbeciles' who seem to find nothing better to do with their time than concern themselves with what Keynes thought were unnecessary and frightful muddles, to find much inspiration in economics. Yet Krugman alludes to a particular tradition of political economy that has evolved out of economics when he talks about 'higher levels of analysis'. The reference is to the fledgling field of economic approaches to politics or as it is sometimes called, 'new political economy' – a very different set of literature to the 'new international political economy' that Murphy and Tooze (1991) espouse. These are sets of theories that adopt in essence a neoclassical methodology to explain the determinants of policy-making. For example, new political economy state theory maintains that government policies can be explained by neo-classical concepts of marginalism, optimisation, equilibrium (Meier 1990: 185). As opposed to conventional International Relations, the new political economy dis-aggregates the state and views it as 'simply another of the myriad institutions contained in any society, owned of necessity by certain individuals and not by others' (Auster and Silver 1979: 1). The state, however, is a privileged institution. Domestically, the state behaves as a 'natural monopoly' and the 'surplus' that the state maximises is a sort of monopoly 'rent' that the sovereign can enjoy. As a result, the surplus that the state garners attracts hordes of office-seekers and other interests anxious to get their hands on it.

The state is viewed therefore as an exogenous factor introducing friction and disequilibrium into the proper functioning of the market. Adam Smith's theory of the invisible hand suggested that when individuals' egotistical advantage-maximising behaviour is allowed a free reign, fantastic energy is released and it fuels economic growth. If channelled inappropriately, however, the individual's egotistical behaviour may turn parasitic and deleterious. As Adam Przeworski

(1990) notes, there is a little irony in that the new political economy seeks, on the one hand, a reduction of the role of the collective arm of society to a minimum, and at the same, requires the state to maintain the appropriate 'rules of the game' to prevent pervasive rent-seeking behaviour.

In any case, the theory of the state as an economic actor presents inter-state relations in a new light. Contrary to conventional political economy, GPE demonstrates that the state is involved in games at two separate levels: internally, the state is involved in the games that the 'new political economy' has identified, but at another level, internationally, the state is involved in another game that has its own set of rules. State behaviour is therefore complex and analysis must be carried out on both levels (Evans *et al.* 1993; Milner 1997). This branch of international political economy is discussed in Chapter 8.

But if the market is a superior mechanism for resource allocation as standard economics tells us, then why do the main agents of modern capitalism, the multinational enterprises (MNE), try to replace market relationship by their own internal bureaucratic hierarchies? They do so either directly by expanding, merging and acquiring competitors, or in more subtle ways, by allying themselves and creating informal relationships with their competitors (Phillips, Chapter 3.) Nitzan and Bichler (Chapter 5) tell us that the paradox is not a paradox at all: the problem is simply that standard economics is wrong; far from having an allegiance to the market (whatever the 'market' might be), multinational enterprises are 'sabotaging' markets in order to raise their profits margins – in fact, the perfect markets of standard economics is anathema to the MNEs! But in contrast to the evolutionary institutionalism of Nitzan and Bichler, a revisionist branch of neoclassical economics argues that in many cases 'exogenous' costs of economic transactions are so high as to render internal hierarchies of the MNE the more efficient mechanism for resource allocation. Without seeking to adjudicate among these competing perspectives, I would only note that we already gain an inkling into three, potentially competing 'core' assumptions in GPE, those founded upon individual rational choice, those founded on profits, and those founded upon theories of logistical efficiency (Chapter 9).

## Marxian political economy

Marxist theory never accepted the conventional dividing lines of academia and certainly never adopted the analytical division between domestic and international politics. If anything, Marxism proceeds from a unified theory of political economy, a *global* political economy. For Marxism, the central institution of the modern world is capital and hence the dominant social institution is that of capitalism. But as Nitzan and Bichler show in Chapter 5, the nature of capital remains a 'riddle'.

Capitalism can be defined as a social system based on the profit motive and the dominance of commodity relations, including the commodification of labour. The rise of capitalism as the dominant social institution entailed a set of profound socio-economic transformations, including the dominance of contractual relationship over familial and coercive relationships, the rise of capitalist law and the capitalist state. One strand of Marxism maintains, rather problematically, that political and 'cultural' transformations are the unwitting results of the rise of capitalism. In other words, societal, political and ideological transformations are merely by-products of the changing 'material conditions of life'. Modern Marxist thought strives, however, to transcend this base–superstructure model with a more nuanced historical and holistic political economic account.

Marx viewed capitalism as a particular 'logic' that imposes itself historically. Capital was first and foremost a self-expanding value. Capitalism expands in a series of waves: at certain historical periods capitalism tends to expand spatially penetrating new and distant markets. In other periods, capitalism deepens its grip on social life. These two types of expansionary tendencies can form the background of an holistic account of diverse developments, from the colonialism of nineteenth-century capitalism, to the formation of the Bretton Woods system in the twentieth century and the rise of globalisation towards the twenty-first century (McMichael, Chapter 7). At the same time, Marxist political economy also accounts for the deepening of capitalist social relations and the extension and commodification of all aspects of social life. With its emphasis on capital, Marxist political economy, therefore, subsumes GPE within a broader theory of society and history. In fact, since the 1930s, Marxist thinkers like Benjamin, Adorno and Horkenheimer, and more recently Deleuze and Guattari and Hardt and Negri were predicating what Lyotard (1984) called the 'post-modern' condition as the furthest extension of subsumption of society under capital.

Marxist GPE analyses institutions in three ways:

1   While new institutionalism views institutions as historically emergent solutions to market failure (Spruyt, Chapter 9), Marxists view institutions primarily as forms of the institutionalisation of power (Poulantzas 1973). According to this theory, social classes entrench their gains by normalising and institutionalising them. Institutions contain therefore layer upon layer of embedded class gains. In time, these gains are so deeply entrenched that institutions such as the state, the family, the firm and the like, appear to be class neutral and are widely accepted as such. We need to reflect carefully upon persistent inequalities and power differentials to begin to unravel the class nature of these institutions and the manner by which they ensure the persistence of power differentials.
2   Contemporary Marxist theory maintains, however, that institutions cannot be reduced exclusively to the above; they are, in addition, representative of the complex manner of the changing nature of the material base. The institutional constitution of the contract, private property, democracy and so on are not directly determined by capital, but *over-determined* by the central institution of capital.
3   In addition, certain key institutions, particularly the state, have an important remedial role to play in class-divided societies. The state cannot be viewed simply as the epiphenomenon of the materialist base, or simply as a tool in

the hands of the ruling class. The state has evolved structures that contribute to the long-term survival of capitalist relationships. So the state entrenches ruling class power and interest and yet at the same time it must remain relatively autonomous of these interests (Poulantzas 1973).

With its emphasis on the complex, class-based nature of institutions, Marxism provides GPE with two strong hypotheses. The first concerns the issue of development, which is central to all branches of political economy. For neoclassical development theory the solution to development is quite simple: let market forces do their job. Considering the relatively low level of industrialisation among the less developed countries, the law of diminishing returns suggests that the bulk of international investment should have been directed towards Third World countries. The law of diminishing returns predicts therefore faster rate of economic growth among the less developed countries. This, of course, has not happened. On the contrary, the post-war world economy continues to exhibit traditional patterns of concentration and centralisation of capital. In one interpretation, the one favoured by the World Bank, the IMF and so on, such disturbing counter-factual evidence does not invalidate the law of diminishing returns or the broader theoretical edifice of 'developmental economics'. On the contrary, the failure of development is due (again!) to 'exogenous factors', namely, the failure of third world countries to develop appropriate political systems. Thus, modernisation theory, which is closely allied to neoclassical economics, prescribes changes in the domestic political system of developing countries combined with open markets and free competition worldwide.

Marxism maintains, however, the centrality of the law of uneven development so that 'imperialist expansion on the one hand, and monopolistic developments on the other, give a new lease of life to the capital system, markedly delaying the time of its saturation' (Mészáros 1995: 34). The ideal of global market equilibrium is delayed and 'sabotaged' in order to ensure higher profit margins. In a number of ways, neo-Marxism introduces then the issue of hierarchy and power into the analysis of the world economy. Thus, in contrast to Keynes's 'frightful muddles', Marxism incorporates into the core of its theoretical edifice precisely those elements that economics treats as 'exogenous' or contingent. As a result, it reaches diametrically opposed conclusions to those favoured by standard economics.

The second strong Marxist hypothesis concerns the issue of transnational or so-called global governance. Marxism reminds us that bourgeois ideology seeks to eliminate labour from the analysis. Growth and economic welfare are attributed to the invisible hand of the market, to the acumen of the modern CEO, to the successful policies of government, to technology, but certainly not to the sweat and toil of the millions upon millions of worker that make up the 'economic system'. But labour is the 'hidden' substructure of the modern economy, both as the true producer of goods and services and the ignored but ever-present face of resistance. Michel Aglietta argues that classical Marxists failed to appreciate that labour-power is not a commodity like all the others

(Aglietta 1979: 46). In contrast to the homogenised or 'fungible' nature of the commodity-form, labour-power can be incorporated into capital as wage-labour only in certain *definite* labour processes. Consequently, society, which includes social and political relationship is pivotal to the organisation of labour and hence cannot be considered 'external' or exogenous to the economic system. The question of global governance, then, is the question of the global *governance of labour* and the maintenance of transnational class hierarchies (see O'Brien, Chapter 6). Indeed, the French school of regulation with its focus on the relationship between capital and labour explains to us why an already transnational capitalism takes a sudden 'national' turn in the 1930s and only from the 1970s has become 'global' again (Palan 1998a).

Marxism, then, provides GPE with a critical and holistic interpretation of the modern economy as a *global political economy*, viewed as a set of structures, patterns and relationships that can only be understood with the aid of a political-economic, as opposed to either political or economic interpretation.

## The return of institutionalism

In 'the legal foundations of capitalism', John Commons distinguishes among three traditions of economic thought: classical economics of Adam Smith, David Ricardo and Karl Marx centred on production and the commodity, the 'hedonist economists' such as Bantham, Senior, Jevons, Clark, who concerned themselves with the subjective side of economic theory,[8] and volitional theories of economics associated with thinkers such as Hume, Malthus, Carey, Bastiat, Cassel, Anderson and, especially, the Supreme Court of the United States. Volitional, or as it is now called, evolutionary economics, he writes, 'start, not with a commodity or with a feeling, but with the purposes of the future, revealing themselves in rules of conduct governing transactions which give rise to rights, duties, liberties, private property, governments and associations' (Commons 1959: 4).

John Commons and Thorstein Veblen are the high priests of this tradition. They argue persuasively that towards the end of the nineteenth century, the law courts in the United States effectively altered the nature of private property and the law of contract, and by doing so instituted a form of capitalism which is quite distinct from the one described by Marx. As a result, private property turned from an exclusive holding of *physical objects* for the owner's private use into a principle of control of limited resources needed by others.[9]

According to Commons, these momentous events took place between the years 1872 and 1897. In a number of important rulings the US law courts effectively altered the traditional meaning of property which meant 'any tangible thing owned' to mean 'any of the expected activities implied with regard to the thing owned':

> comprehended in the activities of acquiring, using and disposing of the thing. One is Property, the other is Business. The one is property in the sense

of the Things owned, the other is property in the sense of exchange-value of
things. One is physical objects, the other is marketable assets.

(1959: 18)

The original meaning of property, the owning of things, did not disappear, but
was relegated to what may be described as the internal 'economy' of a going
concern or a household. Our perception of our personal private property still
corresponds, by and large, to the older, corporeal view of property. Modern
capitalism, however, is concerned almost exclusively with the non-corporeal
property. General Motors's management and shareholders, for instance, are not
particularly concerned with the use-value of GM cars, machine tools and so on,
but with their exchange-value, their marketability. But as Commons (1959) notes,
'exchange-value is not corporeal – it is behaviorist. It is the market value
expected to be obtained in exchange for the thing in any of the markets where
the thing can or might be sold.' The value of one's holding became capitalised
earning capacity (Nitzan and Bichler, Chapter 5).

What is the value of a company, say, IBM? Is it the value of IBM is an aggregation of the values of its machines, real estate, 'knowledge' and managerial
practices? Classical political economy and Marxism appear to suggest so. There
is, however, another way of measuring the value of IBM and that is its valuation
of the company in the stock market. In the stock market 'investors' value IBM as
they purchase and sell IBM shares. What, then, determines the latest market
value of an IBM share? The price is determined by what buyers are prepared to
pay for the share. Buyers reach their decision primarily on the basis of their estimate either of the company's future earning capacity or their perception of
other buyers' perception of the company's future earning capacity. In other
words, the value of IBM is entirely subjective. Consequently, it can very well
happen that a company with a minuscule turnover such as the Yahoo! Website is
valued by the market more than IBM! Yahoo is capitalising on the perception of
its future, indeed, distant future, earning capacity. The value of IBM, therefore,
is an entirely 'subjective' proposition, it is based on aggregate estimates of the
future and not on any corporeal assets. Estimates of the future value of IBM are
then translated into money: 'real' money or as real money as any other money.
So money and 'value' are created and disappear as the 'capitalisation of future
earning'. What does this tell us about the nature of value, capital and money?
How significant is this mechanism to the functioning of the capitalist system?
About power and interest? These are the sort of questions evolutionary
economics seek to address.

These ideas, then, form the theoretical underpinnings of evolutionary
economics, the implications of which are discussed in particular in Chapters 3
and 5. The question that neither Commons nor Veblen sought to answer was
whether the changes in the concept of private property and the concomitant
transformation of capitalism can be described purely in institutionalist terms, or
whether there were some 'exogenous' material interests that determined the sort
of choices that were made. Was it not the case, as Antonio Negri (Hardt and

Negri 1994) argues that jurists were actively seeking to *accommodate* the needs of capitalist accumulation? Is it not the case, after all, that a Marxist political economic theory can accommodate Veblenian institutionalism? This remains an open question. But the perception of the market as an institution has become central to modern GPE.

## Towards post-rationalist GPE[10]

Although different, the three 'residues' of classical political economy share a rationalist epistemology. State or transnational firms are assumed to be rational, calculating 'actors', with clear – usually utility-maximising – preferences and goals (from power to profits). Differences in opinion tend to focus on whether the actors are individuals or institutions and whether the choices are constrained or not by information and knowledge gap or uncertainty. But what of everyday, recurring, phenomena which imply that the world is not a rational order driven by a set of universal rules, iron laws, or systemic logic? There is evidence for a growing interest in post-rationalist (not anti-rationalist) modes of explanations in GPE. Post-rationalism consists of sets of theories that explain order – and disorder – as the product of institutional and historical continuity, formal and informal rules of conduct, social and institutional interaction, common pathologies, consciousness and language, conflict and contest, and so on.

The shift to post-rationalist GPE is represented in this book from Chapters 13 onwards. Broadly speaking, post-rationalist GPE adopts an open-ended historical narrative in which outcomes are not predictable, but negotiated and contested, with each actor-network perpetually frightened of loss or stasis. States and multinational enterprises are viewed no longer simply as instrumentalist advantage-maximising institutions, but as complex organisations which exceed their goals and functions, but in non utilitarian ways. Their language, their scripts, their histories, their techno-structures and artefacts matter; analysis of which reveals them to be trapped in their own evolutionary logic but also constantly at work to renew themselves. Consequently, we have witnessed the 'opening up' of GPE from its economistic and material base to broader questions of history and culture.

For such post-rationalist GPE, which is a truly diverse and broad movement, the significance of Foucault's work in particular cannot be underestimated. Among other things Foucault problematised the concept of agency in a way that places Marxism (after Marx) and mainstream political economy firmly in the camp of 'rationalism'. Foucault's studies of power and discipline have demonstrated that historical change comes about at least in part through collective agencies that cannot be defined as institutions or as social classes, but are contingent forms of alliances and identities emergent in discourse. In *Discipline and Punish* (1977), for instance, Foucault identifies a group of reformers that innovate new forms of discipline and power. These 'regional' studies then provided the basis for his research into the history of subjectivity, or the very historical conditions that have produced the modern subject and modern rationality as the underlying 'infrastructure' of modern capitalism.

Today's critical wing of global political economy is a mixture but not a synthesis of Marxist, institutionalist and post-structuralist thought. Marxism provides us with a strong hypothesis of the long-term trajectories of capitalism. But Marxism has proved particularly weak in predicting or prescribing short- to medium-term trends. The challenge, then, is to bridge the broad social critique of Marxism with the robust empirical bent of institutionalism and post-structuralism.

## Between economics, political economy and global political economy

Since the two traditions of thought, rationalism and the critical tradition, have adopted diametrically opposing views of the nature and purpose of interdisciplinary research, their conception of the nature and boundaries of GPE differs as well. To the rationalist approaches, particularly to methodological individualist GPE, the boundary between GPE and other disciplines is clearer: GPE is a sub-field of International Relations which stands at the intersection between domestic and international politics, on the one hand, and trade and finance, on the other. However, as Carlson (Chapter 8) notes, in recognition of the fact that states do not engage in trade, individuals and firms do, and states only determine the terms of trade, contemporary rationalist GPE has tended to disaggregate the state and encompass 'domestic' determinant of trade policy.

The broadly critical tradition in the social sciences is naturally attracted to holistic interpretations of social relations. The assumption being that there are totalising processes driven by a predominant logic which we call capitalism, and that such totalising processes manifest themselves in all aspects of social life. The critical tradition maintains therefore that there is no point in studying each facet of social life as an independent system of relationships – for the simple reason that they are not independent but interdependent. Consequently, the critical tradition does not accept the analytical legitimacy of formal academic divisions. The critical tradition is then divided between its rationalist and post-rationalist wings.

There is a subtle but important difference between totalising processes and the concept of a totality. Totalising means a system of thought and practices which seeks to universalise and dominate its surroundings; such systems are expansionary but they never truly obtain their goal: they never create a truly total system. In that case there is no one concept, nor one set of dynamics or rationale that can provide a full or even partial explanation for even events. Everything is complex and multifaceted. Consequently, a system of thought that is grounded in the assumption of totalising processes is evolutionary, historicist, non-teleological and often accepting of eclecticism; a system of thought premised on the assumption that the world 'out there' is a totality, a whole, tends to privilege homeostasis, equilibrium and lack of history. Political economy that seeks to incorporate all these variables and more specifically, apply them in a systemic study of the economic system tends to be critical, evolutionary and dynamic.

We can see now how the notion of totalising processes forces a distinct interpretation of the relationship between GPE and political economy. Since there is no one global system (a totality), the international cannot be treated as a separate realm, but as an important ingredient of societal theories. And yet, the uniqueness of the institution of the state and sovereignty should not be ignored. Consequently, political economy in principle is indistinguishable from international political economy, in the sense that good political economy is international in character and vice versa. But if we were to insist on a distinction, then I would argue that while political economy is grounded in a theory of the State, critical GPE supplements it by offering a theory of states, of the plurality of states, or more appropriately, critical GPE seeks to develop a theory of the nature of a transnational economy operating within a system of fragmented political authority. Political economy has tended to concentrate on the analytical as well as prescriptive question of how order and change come about in a 'social formation'. The problem however is that its mode of theorising is predicated on the assumption that each social formation is subject to its own autonomous set of dynamics. In contrast, critical international or global political economy changes the order of the question; it asks how order and change come about in a system of fragmented political authority. Thus, the very discontinuity between the political and economic spaces is treated by GPE as one of major sources of continuing change in the international political economy.

Although deeply divided and heterogeneous, there is still therefore a line threading its way through the fascinating maze of conflicting and multifaceted topography of the social sciences and political economy, a line that can be rightfully described as IPE and GPE. It has to do, fundamentally, with the unique problematic of the operation of the modern economy within a fragmented political system.

## Notes

1  I would like to thank Angus Cameron, Lisa Carlson, Philip Cerny, Sandra Halperin, Otto Holman and Marianne Marchand for their insightful comments on this chapter.
2  'Critical tradition' or 'traditions' does not imply (and often indeed is not) analytical or theoretical rigour. The term critical tradition is generally reserved for those studies that take a critical view of the status quo and *explicitly* seek to replace the predominant power structures, be they capitalism, industrialisation or the prevailing gender and race power relationships with what they see as more just and equitable social arrangements. The term critical tradition should not be confused with *critical theory*, otherwise known as the Frankfurt School tradition of Marxist thought.
3  *States and Markets* is the title of another famous book by Susan Strange (1988). Strange, however, chose this title in irony to convey her criticism of the then reigning orthodoxy in IPE. She deeply regretted her choice as clearly she became associated with the state and market approach to IPE.
4  A reading that Robert Walker (1994) notes is at odds with contemporary interpretation of Machiavelli. See Pocock (1975) and Bettali (1972).
5  Treitschke (1916), Meinecke (1962), for discussion see Palan and Blair (1993), on Treischke, see Metz (1982).
6  For an excellent discussion of the complex and yet overlooked relationship between hermeneutics and economics see Mirowski (1990).

7    The late Susan Strange, for instance, argued persuasively that GPE is not a theory or
     a discipline but 'a framework of analysis, a method of diagnosis of the human condi-
     tion as it is, or as it was, affected by economic, political and social circumstances'
     (1988:16). For discussion, see Palan (1999).
8    For discussion see Nitzan and Bichler, Chapter 5 in this volume.
9    For an excellent analysis see Screpanti (1998)
10   This section draws on Amin and Palan (forthcoming).

**Part I**

# Key categories in the global political economy

# 2 Structuring the political arena

## Public goods, states and governance in a globalizing world

*Philip G. Cerny*

## Introduction: transforming the state-based order

The history of the nation-state as a basic organizational form for politics in the modern world is a complex one. Although the nation-state and the international 'states system' are nearly four centuries old, it is only in the twentieth century that we have come to associate 'the state' – and the politicians and bureaucrats who populate its institutions – with a systematic expansion of the social and economic tasks, roles and activities undertaken by governments, what Karl Polanyi (1944) called *The Great Transformation*. In economic terms, only in the Second Industrial Revolution did the modern nation-state develop the range of socio-economic functions we had become accustomed to expecting by the middle of the twentieth century. Mass production, modern industrial enterprises, the bureaucratic revolution in both public and private sectors and mass politics brought together a range of structural elements conducive to the development of the national Industrial Welfare State.

The institutional coherence and structural effectiveness of the modern state are based on two complementary characteristics. On the one hand, on the endogenous level, it is seen as the dominant *arena of collective action*, i.e. as a set of internal institutions and rules of the game which allow for a substantial range of socially indispensable actors to pursue their political objectives but at the same time permit effective collective decisions to be made. On the other hand, on the exogenous level, it is seen as the predominant (and by some, the only) *source of credible commitments* in the international system, i.e. as a coherent enough structural unit in itself that international treaties and other commitments to other 'like' units (other states) are likely to be kept, thus making it possible to stabilize and order international politics to some extent at least. The central problematic of the era of globalization, therefore, is whether and how complex processes of globalization alter, shape or potentially even undermine the capacity of states to continue to constitute effective arenas of collective action and sources of credible commitments. In effect, we are asking whether underlying structural conditions that made the era of Polanyi's 'Great Transformation' possible are now being fundamentally altered and thus whether (and how) any new great transformation will have to be embedded in processes of globalization rather than in 'the state' *per se*.

Of course, it is almost inconceivable that states and the states system as such will become entirely redundant or disappear. After all, the collapse of feudalism did not mean the disappearance of the nobility or the Church; it merely enmeshed them in a new institutional and political context within which their roles were transformed (Mayer 1981). Today, states as we have come to know them over the past century-and-a-half or so are being increasingly caught up in restructured webs of power that limit or transform their tasks, roles and activities by altering the context within which those states exist and operate – both materially, by leading to 'distributional changes' among competing domestic groups, and ideationally, by leading to new 'social epistemologies' which transform our understanding of how the world actually works. Thus, I argue, a prospect of significant transformation has been opened up since the second half of the twentieth century by what was once thought to be mere internationalization or interdependence amongst states, but which is now a more complex and cross-cutting process called 'globalization'.

This transformation, I suggest, has three main interlocking dimensions. The first and most obvious dimension involves a change in the character of the state's domestic tasks, roles and activities. This basically involves the way so-called 'public goods' are perceived, pursued and provided. In particular, the aim of social justice through redistribution has been challenged and profoundly undermined by the marketization or commodification of the state's economic activities (and of the state itself) and by a new 'embedded financial orthodoxy'. These changes not only constrain the state in its economic policies but also alter people's understanding of what politics is for and challenge the political effectiveness of the national liberal democratic political systems which are supposed to represent what the people want (Cerny 1999).

The second dimension involves a fundamental reorientation of how states interact economically as well as politically with each other. Rather than perceiving the international tasks, roles and activities of the state as stemming from traditional 'inside/outside' distinctions, state actors, by which I mean politicians *and* bureaucrats, are increasingly concerned with promoting the competitive advantages of particular production and service sectors in a more open and integrated world economy. In pursuing international competitiveness, states or, more to the point, a range of state agencies closely linked with those economic sectors most deeply entangled in the world economy, increasingly accept and indeed embrace those complex interdependencies and transnational linkages thought to be the most promising sources of profitability and economic prosperity in a rapidly globalizing world. Given the complexity of both public and private transnational linkages in this environment, the boundaries between state functions and state actors, on the one hand, and private functions and private actors, on the other, are being overlaid, cross-cut and eroded at multiple levels. This process is leading to the crystallization of multilayered and asymmetric institutions and patterns of authority and, within this structural context, the fragmentation and refocusing of actors' identities and objectives.

Thus the final dimension of this transformation process concerns the relationship between structure and agency – in other words, people, i.e. the individuals and groups who actually bring these changes about, directly or indirectly, intentionally or unintentionally. This does not merely concern those global ideologists in business studies, important as they are, who declare that we live in a 'borderless world', nor just the rapid growth of transnational pressure and interest groups like Greenpeace that focus on the problems of 'the planet'. It also involves both public sector and private sector strategies for generating concrete competitive advantages in the world marketplace. In this process, for example, the focus of the economic mission of the state has shifted considerably from its traditional concern with production and producer groups to one involving market structures and consumer groups, considerably reshaping the way political 'publics' and pressure groups as well as state actors see themselves and their own tasks, roles and activities. Unfortunately, there is not the space to deal with this more actor-centered dimension in this chapter; the focus here will be on changes in the structural context. However, it needs to be remembered that structural change does not take place by itself. It needs to be driven by 'agents', i.e., actors operating within previously structured but continually evolving sets of constraints and opportunities, constraints and opportunities which can either severely restrict what actors can in fact achieve, or else enable them to exploit opportunities and even to construct the new spaces necessary to bring about wider changes.

These three dimensions, I suggest, add up to a profound challenge to traditional structures both of the domestic nation-state and of the interstate system, undermining key aspects of the previously symbiotic relationship between the two. But we should not expect the nation-state to wither away; indeed, in some ways it will continue to expand and develop its tasks, roles and activities. The crucial point, however, is that those tasks, roles and activities will not just be different, but will lose much of the overarching, macro-political character traditionally ascribed to the effective state, the good state or the just state.

## Problematizing the state: the shifting structure of public goods

The power structure of a globalizing world inevitably becomes more diffuse – diffracted through an increasingly complex, prismatic structure of socio-economic forces and levels of governance. The underlying governance problematic in such multilayered political contexts is at least twofold: in the first place, it becomes harder to maintain the boundaries which are necessary for the efficient 'packaging' of public or collective goods into coherent policy approaches and, indeed, economically efficient outputs; and, in the second place, it becomes harder to determine what people actually *want* in the way of public or collective goods, i.e., to measure what is the 'preferred state of affairs'. In this context, state actors are crucial in regulating particular economic and social activities. But their actions as such do not necessarily uphold or strengthen the cohesion and 'relative autonomy' of the state. On the contrary, merely by defending their particular policy or institutional 'turf', by pursuing specific policy objectives relevant to their particular issue-areas, and by working within and through particular personal networks and policy communities, state actors often in effect segment or even fragment the state as an aggregate institutional structure. Paradoxically, state actors frequently, even normally, act in routine fashion from within to undermine the holistic and hierarchical character of traditional state sovereignty, a tendency which is multiplied and accelerated in the context of globalization.

In this more complex and diffracted world of globalization, therefore, state actors often act in ways that either consciously or inadvertently open up even more autonomous spaces for their own action. The result is a growing 'privatization of the public sphere', not just in the apparent sense of selling off state agencies or contracting out public services and functions, but in the deeper sense of transforming policy functions that had previously been thought of and accepted as intrinsically belonging to the 'public' sphere (and thus as components of the common good in the philosophical sense) into essentially 'private' phenomena in the wider global context. In this sense, society itself is reduced to an aggregation of competing 'associations of consumers' in which administrators are little more than buyers in competing corporations (Ostrom *et al.* 1961: 839). Whether such changes are good or bad is of course a matter for debate. They are applauded by neoliberals but opposed by those who hold to a more societally constructed or normatively collective view of the public interest.

In this context, our understanding of the meaning of the very term 'the state' may be shifting considerably. In the framework developed by the British philosopher Michael Oakeshott (Auspitz 1976; Oakeshott 1976), the Western state tradition is rooted in the idea that the state is essentially a 'civil association', i.e., that it has no other generic function except to enable people to live together and engage in various activities in common, i.e., to provide some sort of overarching order to stabilize social life; additional, more limited ends are subordinate and secondary, and therefore states *per se* persist and endure over time in ways other forms of association do not. They cannot merely be done away with or go bankrupt unless they break down entirely. In contrast, what Oakeshott calls an 'enterprise association' has particular, more limited ends; both the ends and the association itself can alter and be altered – or even wound up – because they depend upon a specific configuration of power and on the objectives of particular actors. In this sense, the more 'privatized' or 'marketized' state of today might be seen as losing at least some of its character as a civil association and as becoming more of an enterprise association in an inherently more private global sphere.

To understand these trends, we need to reassess the very conception of public or collective goods in a globalizing world. The argument of this chapter is that the key to understanding the shape of new and complex governance structures in the global era lies in the way that economic competition is changing in the world. Many of what were thought to constitute collective or public goods at the time of the Second Industrial Revolution either are no longer controllable by the state because changing patterns of international competition mean that the underlying structural features of such public goods have become effectively transnational, and/or have come to constitute private goods in the wider world marketplace. Today, I argue, the heart of debate over the future of the state is about choosing among competing conceptions of what should be treated as public and what should not, i.e., about the nature of public and private goods in a globalizing world, and the way this debate is translated by state *and other* actors not merely into policy change but into institutional change as well (Evans and Davies 1999; Stone 1999).

Different categories of public goods have different kinds of normative and economic characteristics. I refer to four such categories: regulatory, productive, distributive and redistributive collective goods. Each of these categories has been transformed by the structural changes associated with globalization and the other economic and political trends that are inextricably intertwined with globalization. For example, the Third Industrial Revolution of the late twentieth century, rooted in technological advances in computer technology, communications, robotics, etc., has profoundly altered the conditions of supply of all types of goods, whether public, private or mixed. In effect, production processes, management structures and distributional or marketing processes are all moving away from the era of hierarchically organized mass production and distribution associated with the Second Industrial Revolution (Reich 1983 and 1991). There are several aspects to this – more complex and more flexible production processes, 'lean' management structures and the segmentation of both producer and consumer markets, while the globalization of finance has increasingly divorced financial capital from the state and, some argue, from the 'real economy' of production. In this context, political (as well as economic) control, stabilization, regulation, promotion and facilitation of economic activities have become increasingly fragmented.

The first category, regulatory collective goods, involves the establishment of a workable economic framework for the ongoing operation of the system as a whole, involving the establishment and application of rules for the operation and interaction of both market and non-market transactions and institutions. Typical regulatory goods include the following:

- establishment and protection of private (and public) property rights;
- a stable currency system;
- abolition of internal barriers to production and exchange within the national market;
- standardization of a range of facilitating structures such as a system of weights and measures;
- a legal system to sanction and enforce contracts and to adjudicate disputes;
- a regulatory system to stabilize and coordinate economic activities;
- a system of trade protection;
- various facilities which can be mobilized to counteract system-threatening market failures ('lender of last resort' facilities, emergency powers, etc.).

Real or potential inefficiencies in the provision of such regulatory collective goods can have exceptionally wide ramifications, because their provision in and of itself can be said to constitute a sort of 'collective collective good' – not merely a collective good in itself, but one which involves holding together the system as a whole. Regulation as such constitutes a framework within which not only other collective goods, but also private goods, are produced and supplied. Regulatory collective goods, therefore, are inextricably intertwined with the very foundations of the capitalist state. Regulation, however, is becoming far more complex and difficult to enforce in the global era.

In a world of relatively open trade, financial deregulation and the increasing impact of information technology, for example, property rights and other basic rules are problematic for states to establish and maintain. For example, cross-border industrial espionage, counterfeiting of products, copyright violations and the like have made the multilateral protection of intellectual property rights a focal point of international disputes and were probably the most controversial cornerstone of the negotiations which led to the establishment of the World Trade Organization in 1994. International capital flows, the proliferation of offshore financial centers and tax havens, etc., have made the ownership of firms and their ability to allocate resources internally through transfer pricing and the like increasingly opaque to national tax and regulatory authorities. Furthermore, traditional forms of trade protectionism are both easily bypassed and counter-productive. Currency exchange rates and interest rates are set in rapidly globalizing marketplaces, and governments attempt to manipulate them often at their peril. Legal rules are increasingly evaded, leading to the growing importance of 'soft law' such as private arbitration and the newly rediscovered tradition of private merchant law, and attempts to extend the legal reach of the national state through the development of extraterritoriality are ineffective and hotly disputed. In this context, the ability of firms, market actors, and competing parts of the national state apparatus itself to defend and expand their economic and political turf through activities such as transnational policy networking and regulatory arbitrage has both undermined the control span of the state from without and fragmented it from within.

The second and third categories of collective goods involve various specific directly or indirectly state-controlled or state-sponsored activities of production and distribution – productive collective goods, on the one hand, and distributive collective goods, on the other. Although these two categories often overlap, the differences between them can be quite significant, as can be seen in recent theories of public policy such as the New Public Management and 'reinventing government' literatures (e.g., Dunleavy 1994; Osborne and Gaebler 1992) which are themselves closely linked with discourses of globalization. In line with the narrower economic definition of public goods set out above, then, 'productive collective goods' are defined as involving the production of goods and services whereas 'distributive collective goods' involve the delivery of those goods and services.

With regard to productive collective goods, the validity of the public ownership of politically, economically or militarily 'strategic' industries, along with the establishment and maintenance of state monopolies in a range of public services, have usually been seen to derive from economies of scale and scope as well as transactions cost savings in their production. Nevertheless, normative considerations have also played a major political role, especially for both nationalists and socialists. However, the interaction of the advent of flexible manufacturing systems, on the one hand, and competing low-cost sources of supply on the other, especially from firms operating multinationally, has been particularly important in undermining the viability of state-owned and para-public firms, as seen, for example, in the crisis of public ownership and the wave of privatization of the 1980s and 1990s.

Today, international competitiveness counts for far more in terms of domestic economic growth and prosperity than maintaining an autonomous, self-sufficient national economy; this is increasingly true not only in the civilian sector but in the military sector too (Latham and Hooper 1995). Third World countries too have for some years increasingly rejected Second Industrial Revolution-style Import Substitution Industrialization and embraced Export Promotion Industrialization, thereby imbricating their economies more and more closely with the global economic order (Harris 1986; Haggard 1990). The same can be said for more traditional forms of industrial policy such as state subsidies to industry, public procurement of nationally produced goods and services, or trade protectionism. Even social liberal economists nowadays regard the battle to retain the idea of the 'national economy' to be lost, and see states as condemned to tinkering around the edges (Reich 1991).

With regard to distributive collective goods, we are talking about the supply or provision of products and services to the public (or to potentially distinct 'publics') on a collective basis, whether these goods are produced in the private sector or in the public sector. In contrast to productive collective goods, distributive collective goods are characterized less by their technical indivisibility and more by potential 'soft' criteria like management structures, on the one hand, and what their consumers rather than their producers want – the ideology of shopping, applied to public services as well as private consumption – on the other. In an era when consumer preferences are diversifying, policy-oriented economists have come to consider a much larger range of such goods as appropriate for market or quasi-market provision rather than public provision. This changing perspective has resulted both from a re-evaluation of the nature of demand – the belief that 'publics' are essentially collections of self-regarding consumers rather than embedded in like-minded or homogeneous social collectivities – on the one hand and from a belief that public sector hierarchies are inherently costly and cumbersome superstructures, on the other. Many basic public services and functions such as the provision of environmental health protection, street lighting, garbage collection, police protection, certain kinds of transportation or energy infrastructure, etc., which have until now been at the bureaucratic heart of the modern industrial/welfare state, are being disaggregated and commodified in a range of experimental ways.

Distributive collective goods increasingly overlap with the fourth category, redistributive collective goods, which have always been even more fundamentally political, with their public and collective character deriving more typically from political decisions about justice and fairness rather than from the economic efficiency (or inefficiency) of those public allocation mechanisms which they engender. Many of these goods are only 'collective' or 'public' goods because political decisions have been made (whether or not in response to public demand) to treat them as public for reasons of justice, equity or other normative considerations. Redistributive goods have included health and welfare services, education, full employment policies, systems for neocorporatist wage bargaining, environmental protection, and the like – indeed, the main apparatus of the welfare state. Today, the provision of redistributive collective goods is changing dramatically. Neocorporatist wage bargaining and full employment policies are under challenge everywhere in the face of international pressures for wage restraint and flexible working practices. Although developed states have generally not found it possible to reduce the overall weight of the welfare state significantly as a proportion of Gross Domestic Product, much long-term structural growth in such expenditures has been checked and there has been a significant transformation in the balance of how welfare funds are spent – away from the maintenance of free-standing social and public services and towards the provision of unemployment compensation and other 'entitlement' programs, which are themselves being increasingly means-tested rather than universally provided (Clayton and Pontusson 1998). And the most salient new sector of redistributive public goods, environmental protection, is particularly transnational in character; pollution and the rape of natural resources do not respect borders.

Today, the capacity of states to provide collective or public goods in general is increasingly seen as inherently limited, with governments in danger of both 'overload' and impotence. The focus of public policy has shifted towards the relative capacities of different states to promote a favorable investment climate for transnational capital by providing a much more circumscribed range of public goods described as 'immobile factors of capital' (Reich 1991). These include:

- 'human capital' (the skills, experience, education and training of the work force);
- infrastructure (from public transportation to high-tech 'information highways');
- support for new technology;
- provision of those public services necessary for a good 'quality of life' for new elites and middle managers, such as support for high-quality housing estates in 'edge cities';
- the maintenance of a public policy environment favorable to investment and profit-making by potentially 'footloose' companies (whether domestic or foreign-owned).

Particularly central to this transformation, of course, has been the changing technological and institutional context in which *all* goods are increasingly being produced and exchanged, especially the rapid development of 'post-Fordism', characterized by a wider process of 'flexibilization' (see Amin 1994). At the heart of flexibilization in both production processes and firms themselves has been the explosive development of information technology, which allows management not only to perform routine management and production tasks more efficiently but also to monitor what employees are doing and to control both direct production and transactions costs much more closely. This expanded monitoring capability leaps national borders and brings firms, markets and consumers into a single, global production process in an increasing number of sectors. In addition, as the trade and production structures of the Third Industrial Revolution evolve, they will be increasingly coordinated through the application of complex financial controls, rapidly evolving accounting techniques, financial performance indicators and the like in both public and private sectors (Power 1997). Indeed, the use of such financial controls closely shadows and feeds back into the globalization of financial markets, which increasingly look to financial performance (as embodied, especially, in 'shareholder value') rather than market share as the key criterion of investment decisions.

But these aspects of the Third Industrial Revolution – flexibilization of production, firm structure and monitoring – only represent the supply side of the equation. The demand side involves the development of ever more complex consumer societies and the resulting segmentation of markets – making it profitable to produce not merely large runs of standardized products but also short runs aimed at niche markets and rapidly evolving tastes. The technological capacity to produce flexibly – the ability of business to produce at the appropriate scale – has combined with an increasing differentiation of the class system in advanced capitalist societies. Much of the so called Long Boom from the 1950s to the early 1970s grew out of burgeoning first-time mass markets for such products as cars, so-called 'white goods' (refrigerators, washing machines, etc.) or television sets. Customers coming back a subsequent time looking to buy new models, however, demanded higher specifications and greater choice. Differentiating demand and flexible supply have therefore converged on market segmentation, producing a wider range of variations on a particular product or set of products, with each variation targeted on a particular sub-set of consumers. This process has also created consumer demand for foreign-produced goods and has forced firms to globalize.

More importantly for this chapter, however, is the fact that these pressures now increasingly are seen to apply to the provision of public goods by governments as well, with 'choice' replacing standardized collective provision and with consumers (or 'customers') increasingly replacing producers as the key interest groups. The expansion of the social and economic functions of the state which have for decades been associated with the development of advanced industrial societies is coming under increasing pressure from both above and below, from new transnational economies of scale and from the disaggregation of national culture societies and political 'publics' into associations of consumers. Governance in the future will no longer look so much like 'government'. Structures and processes of governance must adjust to this multilayered reality, although there are still different directions this evolution could take. The discourse of globalization is torn between the simplistic jargon of business management and the desire of state actors to harness globalization for their own political objectives and projects. In this context, the state itself is being transformed from the national Industrial Welfare State of the Second Industrial Revolution into a Competition State – a state which is itself an increasingly important independent variable in the globalization process.

## The Competition State: eroding the 'inside/outside' distinction

The crisis of the national Industrial Welfare State lay in its decreasing capacity to insulate national economies from the global economy and from the combination of stagnation and inflation which resulted when they tried. Today, rather than attempt to take certain economic activities out of the market – to 'decommodify' them as the welfare state was organized to do – the Competition State has pursued increased marketization. This 'commodification of the state' itself is aimed at making economic activities located within the national territory, or which otherwise contribute to national wealth, more competitive in international and transnational terms. In pursuing this path, national policy-makers have a range of potential responses, old and new, with which to work; taken together, these responses turn the Competition State into a driving force for further globalization.

In this context, transnational factors and three-level games have propelled four specific types of policy change to the top of the political agenda:

- a shift from macroeconomic to microeconomic interventionism, as reflected in both deregulation and industrial policy;
- a shift in the focus of that interventionism from the development and maintenance of a range of 'strategic' or 'basic' economic activities in order to retain minimal economic self-sufficiency in key sectors to one of flexible response to competitive conditions in a range of diversified and rapidly evolving international marketplaces, i.e., the pursuit of 'competitive advantage' as distinct from 'comparative advantage';
- an emphasis on the control of inflation and general neoliberal monetarism, supposedly translating into non-inflationary growth, as the touchstone of state economic management and interventionism ('embedded financial orthodoxy': Cerny 1994);
- a shift in the focal point of party and governmental politics away from the general maximization of public welfare within a nation (full employment, redistributive transfer payments and social service provision) to the promo-

tion of enterprise, innovation and profitability in both private and public sectors.

In this context, there have been some striking similarities as well as major differences between leading capitalist countries.

Among more traditional measures is, of course, trade policy, including a wider range of non-tariff barriers and targeted strategic trade policies. The core issue in the trade issue-area is to avoid reinforcing through protection the existing rigidity of the industrial sector or sectors in question, while at the same time fostering or even imposing adaptation to global competitive conditions in return for temporary protection. Transnational constraints are growing rapidly in trade policy, however, as can be seen in the establishment of the North Atlantic Free Trade Area, the Asia-Pacific Economic Cooperation group, and the World Trade Organization. Two other traditional categories, monetary and fiscal policy, are perhaps even more crucial today, and the key change is that relative priorities between the two have been reversed: tighter monetary policy is pursued alongside looser fiscal policy through tax cuts. And exchange rate policy, difficult to manage in the era of floating exchange rates and massive international capital flows, is none the less still essential; however, it is increasingly intertwined with monetary and fiscal policy (Frieden 1991).

Potentially more innovative, combining old and new measures, is the area of industrial policy and related strategic trade policy. By targeting particular sectors, supporting the development of both more flexible manufacturing systems and transnationally viable economies of scale, and assuming certain costs of adjustment, governments can alter some of the conditions which determine competitive advantage, especially:

- by encouraging mergers and restructuring;
- by promoting research and development;
- by encouraging private investment and venture capital, while providing or guaranteeing credit-based investment where capital markets fail, often through joint public/private ventures;
- by developing new forms of infrastructure, especially the so-called 'information superhighway';
- by pursuing a more active labour market policy while removing barriers to mobility.

A third category of measures, and potentially the most explosive, is, of course, deregulation. The deregulation approach is based partly on the assumption that national regulations, especially the traditional sort of regulations designed to protect national market actors from market failure, are insufficiently flexible to take into account the rapid shifts in transnational competitive conditions characteristic of the interpenetrated world economy of the late twentieth century. However, deregulation must not be seen as just lifting old regulations, but also as the formulation of new regulatory structures which are designed to cope with, and even to anticipate, shifts in competitive advantage. Furthermore, these new regulatory structures are often designed to enforce global market-rational economic and political behavior on rigid and inflexible private sector actors as well as on state actors and agencies. The institutions and practices of the state itself are increasingly marketized or 'commodified', and the state becomes the spearhead of structural transformation to market norms both at home and abroad.

Although each of these processes can be observed across a wide range of states, there are significant variations in how different Competition States cope with the pressures of adaptation and transformation. There is a dialectic of divergence and convergence at work, rather than a single road to competitiveness. The original model of the Competition State was the 'strategic' or 'developmental' state which writers like John Zysman and Chalmers Johnson associated with France and Japan (Zysman 1983; Johnson 1982). This perspective, which identifies the Competition State with strong-state technocratic *dirigisme*, lives on in the analysis of newly industrializing countries (NICs) in Asia and other parts of the Third World. However, the difficulty with this approach has been that the scope of control which the technocratic patron-state and its client firms can exercise over market outcomes diminishes as the integration of these economies into global markets and the complexities of third-level games proceeds, as the recent Asian 'financial meltdown' demonstrates. Nevertheless there are distinctions even here; for example, Japanese administrative guidance and the ties of the *keiretsu* system have remained relatively strong despite a certain amount of liberalization, deregulation and privatization (Vogel 1996), whereas in France the forces of neoliberalism have penetrated a range of significant bastions from the main political parties to major sectors of the bureaucracy itself (Schmidt 1996).

In contrast, the orthodox model of the Competition State today is not the developmental state but the 'neoliberal state' or the Anglo-American model. Thatcherism and Reaganism in the 1980s provided both a political rationale and a power base for the renascence of free-market ideology throughout the world. Several factors have contributed to this pre-eminence:

- the flexibility and openness of Anglo-Saxon capital markets;
- the experience of Anglo-American elites with international and transnational business and their willingness to go multinational;
- the corporate structure of American and British firms and their (relative) concern with profitability and shareholder returns rather than traditional relationships and market share;
- the enthusiasm with which American managers have embraced lean management and downsizing;
- the relative flexibility of the US and UK labor forces;
- an arm's-length state tradition in both countries.

Throughout the debate between the Japanese model and the Anglo-American model, however, the European neocorporatist model, rooted in the post-war settlement and given another (if problematic) dimension through the consolidation of the European Community (now the European Union), has been presented by many academic commentators as a middle way (e.g., Hall 1997; cf. Crouch and Streeck 1997). In bringing labor into institutionalized settings, not only for wage bargaining but for other aspects of the social market too, in doggedly pursuing conservative monetary policies, in promoting extensive training policies, and in possessing a universal banking system which nurtured and stabilized industry without strategic state interventionism, the European neocorporatist or 'coordinated' approach (as practiced in varying ways in Germany, Austria and Sweden in particular) has seemed to its proponents to embody the best aspects of both the Japanese and the Anglo-American models. However, in the 1990s the signs of what in the early 1980s was called 'Eurosclerosis' have reappeared; the European Monetary Union project is widely regarded as deflationary; and the liberalizing, deregulatory option is on the political cards again, especially in the context of high German unemployment. This is true for recently elected social democratic parties too, including New Labour in the United Kingdom (Cerny and Evans 2000) and the Schröder Government in Germany.

As John Zysman (1996) has written, '[n]ational developments', i.e., differences in models of state/economy relations or state/societal arrangements, 'have ... driven changes in the global economy'. This has certainly been the case for the Competition State. States and state actors, for reasons of domestic economic and political objectives (including capturing the benefits of globalization for coalition-building purposes), seek to convince, or pressure, other states and transnational actors such as multinational corporations or international institutions to adopt measures which shift the balance of competitive advantage towards their domestic constituents. The search for competitive advantage adds further layers and cross-cutting cleavages to the world economy, in turn increasing the complexity and density of networks of interdependence and interpenetration. Finally, genuinely transnational pressures can develop whether from multinational corporations or from nationally or locally based firms and other interests (such as trade unions) caught in the crossfire of the search for international competitiveness. Such trends not only bring pressure to bear on the state for institutional evolution. They also create strong pressures for the expansion and/or establishment of transnational regimes, transnational neocorporatist structures of policy bargaining, transgovernmental linkages between bureaucrats, policy-makers and policy communities and the like.

In all of these settings, the state is no longer able to act as a decommodifying hierarchy (i.e., taking economic activities out of the market). It must act more and more as a collective commodifying agent (i.e., putting activities into the market) and even as a market actor itself. It is financier, middleman, advocate and even entrepreneur in a complex economic web, not only where the frontiers between state and market become blurred, but also where their cross-cutting structures become closely intertwined and their behavioral modes less and less easy to distinguish. Emerging political and economic structures are closely inter-twined but not yet very clearly demarcated, and the possibilities for alternative equilibria are fluid. Of course, states and markets have always been intertwined and mutually supporting, and indeed, the state still remains the central focus for consensus, loyalty and social discipline. But this role nowadays puts the state into an increasingly contradictory structural location. Not only is it more complicated for the state to act as a genuine 'collective capitalist', as it was called in the neo-Marxist state debate of the 1970s (see Holloway and Picciotto 1978), but states are also increasingly quasi-market actors and commodifying agents themselves. In such complex conditions, the state is increasingly caught up in and constrained by cross-cutting global/transnational/domestic structural and conjunctural conditions – while simultaneously attempting to manipulate those conditions for domestic advantage.

One paradoxical result of the emergence of the Competition State, therefore, is that the actual *amount* or weight of government imbrication in social life can increase while at the same time the power of the state to control specific activi-ties and market outcomes continues to diminish. One example is the way financial globalization and deregulation have intensified pressures for govern-ments to increase monitoring of financial markets, criminalization of insider trading and the like (Helleiner 1998). The growth of competing authorities with overlapping jurisdictions does not reduce interventionism; it merely expands the range of possibilities for 'splintered' governments (Machin and Wright 1985) and special interests to carve out new fiefdoms, both domestically and transnationally, while undermining their overall strategic and developmental capacity. The attempt to make the state more 'flexible' has moved a long way over the past decade or so, not only in the United States and Britain where deregulation, privatization, and liberalization have evolved furthest but also in a wide range of other countries in the First, Second and Third Worlds. In this more intertwined world, the Competition State is at the heart of an ongoing process of competi-tive deregulation and creeping liberalization.

## Conclusions: the future of political globalization, or from structures to actors

In both of these ways – the changing character of the public goods question and the emergence of the Competition State – complex globalization undermines, alters and transforms the state's structural capacity to constitute an effective arena of endogenous collective action and to make credible exogenous commit-ments. The very 'structured field of action' (Crozier and Friedberg 1977) of politics is changing, enmeshing the state and the states system in new sets of opportunities and constraints. These new sets of opportunities and constraints of course have their origin in the internationalization and transnationalization of key aspects of economic life, aspects which constitute an 'exogenous independent variable' (Spruyt 1994) or set of 'preconditions' (Finnemore 1996) for political structuration. At the same time, however, complex state *responses*, rather than merely filtering or mediating globalization pressures, actually internalize those pressures, reinforce them and feed them back into the international environment.

What we have here is not a rigid straitjacket, but a new and more complex playing field. In many ways the game of *political* globalization is still wide open. Indeed, that game is not a one-off; it is an 'iterated' game which continues to be played indefinitely, with strategies and tactics of the players and their epistemological 'shadows of the future' feeding back into an ever-evolving set of opportunities and constraints. Furthermore, this game is characterized by a range of alternative outcomes or 'multiple equilibria', from world government to chaos with a range of diversely structured possibilities in between. Some form of uneven pluralism, or the sectoral hegemony of financial markets and/or multinational corporations, or even the 'durable disorder' that is sometimes called neomedievalism are far more likely scenarios. And the differences among these are immense too.

Thus any overall future outcome will be by its very nature 'path-dependent'. In other words, it will be shaped by historical accidents, conjunctural events and the actions of a wide range of agents – economic, political and social (Cerny 2000) – who will be attempting to navigate through the shoals of this ever-shifting channel. Several factors – new distributions of resources, new patterns of coalition-building, and new attempts to manipulate the discourse(s) of globalization in order to capture the benefits of globalization for particular projects, networks and constituents – will shape the future course of political globalization itself. Therefore, after having focused in this chapter on the structural underpinnings of political globalization, the spotlight must now be turned on the other half of the 'structuration' equation, i.e., the role of those actors who will try to mould that playing field in the future to their own purposes. Only they can determine what form any new 'great transformation' might take.

## Acknowledgements

I am grateful to the Nuffield Foundation and to the Max-Planck-Institut für Gesellschaftsforschung, Cologne, Germany, for financial and logistical support during the writing of this chapter.

# 3 Approaching the organisation of economic activity in the age of cross-border alliance capitalism

*Richard Phillips*

Many scholars agree that contemporary capitalism is undergoing profound transformations. In its earlier stages, nineteenth-century capitalism was undertaken by small, mono-product craft production factories operating in relative autonomy from other firms. Then through the twentieth century, capitalism became more complex. Markets were increasingly organised on national and international scales with the evolution of a new form of multinational corporate organisation – the multidivisional or M-form enterprise (Chandler 1977). Like the prototypical Ford Motor Company, such enterprises organised increasingly diverse facets of production. In the latter stages of the twentieth century, another transformation appeared to be underway. Revolutionary changes in information and communications technology are bringing about paradigmatic shifts in the scope and scale of business enterprise with the result that the variety and complexity of *inter*-firm, rather than *intra*-firm, relations have come to define innovation-intensive economic activity branded *alliance capitalism* (Gerlach 1992; Dunning 1995).

Like changes in the nation-state, the study of international political economy is faced with a challenge rooted in its state-centric legacy (Sally 1994). In international relations, business considerations have been little more than an addendum to a discipline some have characterised as an 'intellectual Procrustean bed, too short to accommodate reality, so that the study of international business is either cut-off altogether, or curled up at the bottom of the bed where it safely can be overlooked' (Strange 1993: 101). But to address the 'new style' MNEs of the 1990s and bring the firm back into the fore of international political economy, we confront an important condition faced by IPE – it must 'import' much of this understanding from more dedicated disciplines such as international business studies and the strategic management literature.

However, IPE is currently between a rock and a hard place. In addressing the institutional environment of interfirm relations, the variety of work is itself embedded in many localised, context-dependent discussions (Storper and Harrison 1991).[1] This problematises multidisciplinary arenas, such as IPE, that strive to explore broader considerations behind contemporary transformations. Faced with this, we equally cannot return to beliefs that the many facets behind interfirm relations can be enclosed within a single approach to the firm. The variety and complexity of interfirm relationships entail many conflicting and contradictory aspects that problematise a mono-causal approach (Osborn and Hagedoorn 1997).

Consequently, right at the outset, the international political economist faces a double problem in tackling the organisation of economic activity in capitalist economies: what theoretical insights to bring in, and how to go about it, given the diversified and context dependent forms of analysis. It is to shed light on these problems and work towards their alleviation that this chapter is conceived.

## Theorising the firm in alliance capitalism

Contemporary scholars now recognise that the organisation of economic activity can stem from a variety of institutional arrangements including decentralised markets, internalised corporate hierarchies, interfirm alliances, and government planning (Crouch and Streeck 1997; Dunning 1997). Although all modes may be in operation to various extents, questions concerning the shift from corporate hierarchies to interfirm alliances have become central. Whether we discuss small and medium enterprises, the multinational enterprise, or even interfirm alliances, we can essentially understand all of them as appendages to a more fundamental conceptualisation of the firm. But as one can view a glass as being half full, or half empty, how we understand the drive for profit is equally dependent upon biases between *efficiency* considerations and *strategic* ones.

The firm is often viewed in terms of efficiency or cost reduction. Since Common (1934) argued for the transaction to be the unit of economic analysis, a long-standing research tradition has sought to identify and operationalise the various limitations and constraints that raise transaction costs between actors promoting the decision to internalise markets or contract with other market actors. Ronald Coase (1937) famously raised the question: why does the firm exist? His answer: the firm represents a form of economic organisation that improves upon market failures. In other words, the internalisation of external markets within the firm is possible because the costs associated with spot-market transactions (arm's length transactions between buyer and seller) could be reduced when controlled internally. Thus decisions to internalise factors of production, or to seek others through external market sources, depended on the efficiency of the firm's internal 'shadow market' relative to prices demanded from transactions in the external market.

Several other authors contributed greatly to the development of transaction cost analysis by further identifying market imperfections. For example, Simon (1955) introduced the concept that economic actors possess a limited pool of knowledge and reasoning in which to make decisions ('bounded rationality'). Thus, decisions to internalise transactions within a firm are not based on a comprehensive consideration of possible alternatives and cost considerations, but bounded by transactional constraints on the ability to acquire information. Another central development was when Knight (1965) highlighted the existence of transaction costs associated with risk and uncertainty. For example, opportunistic behaviour creates uncertainties that raise the cost of the transaction (e.g., costs associated with implementing policing mechanisms, or other precautionary measures). Thus, by bringing market transactions inside the firm, management safeguards and appropriate incentives can reduce opportunistic behaviour and the cost opportunism poses for engaging in contractual market relations.

In synthesising a comparative institutional approach known as transaction cost or 'new institutional economics', Williamson (1975, 1985) included the importance of transaction-specific assets, or 'asset specificity', along with bounded rationality and uncertainty. For example, a firm working in a particular site may have costs associated with the location, as well as costs of acquiring particular physical and human capacities. Where production today often entails large, capital intensive requirements, such costs restrict the ability to both enter and exit contractual relations and affect the decision on whether markets or hierarchies ultimately govern particular domains of economic activity.

As a way of understanding alliance capitalism, transaction cost analysis purports to understand firms such as multinational enterprises (e.g., Rugman 1986), as well as interfirm relations. For example, strategic alliances are seen as constellations of bilateral agreements among firms that improve upon the ability of the price system to coordinate increasingly complex business ventures (Teece 1992). Ultimately, collaborative arrangements (such as joint ventures) may be both devices for minimising uncertainty in the short term, while also minimising transaction costs through trust building and mutual forbearance (Buckley and Casson 1988: 52).[2]

Transaction costs are not the only way to understand the nature of firms in alliance capitalism. In developing the so-called *eclectic approach* or OLI-paradigm, John Dunning (e.g., 1981, 1988) extends upon the internalisation thesis, to cover ownership[3] and locational issues[4] specific to modern multinational enterprises. The eclectic paradigm may be seen as a bridge between an internalisation theory of the firm, and interfirm alliances, by incorporating the cost considerations surrounding international production and distribution. For example, alliances may result from the inability of the MNE to maintain various ownership advantages such as when intangible assets (e.g., knowledge) are learned and copied by other firms over time.[5] With a more strategic twist, alliances could increase the internalised control of market segments between partners and align internalisation advantages against rival corporations or alliances (Mytelka 1995). Or when formed around R&D projects, alliances can be seen as learning experiments aimed at maintaining or creating ownership advantages through new knowledge production (Ciborra 1991). Or equally, alliances may be more generally related to improving locational advantages such as when a lack of knowledge about particular environments promotes alliances as effective means to enter foreign markets (Mitchell and Singh 1992; Murray and Mahon 1993). But despite the variety of 'variables' that could be added to the internalisation thesis, the eclectic paradigm still essentially sees alliances as an extension of the fundamental quest of firms to internalise markets via 'group internalisation' (Dunning 1988: 343).

In contrast to the above, the strategic management literature represents a bridge between seeing the firm as cost efficient on the one hand, and strategically motivated to seek out many ways to achieve profit. First, approaching competitive strategies start with an understanding of the firm not as a single organisational entity, but as a collection of discrete value-adding activities situated within a larger system of value creation. Michael Porter (1980) introduces the concept of the value chain as the analytical tool by which to disaggregate the firm into its strategically relevant productive activities. The firm is seen to consist of two basic functions: primary activities[6] and support activities.[7] Each support activity is required in different degrees and forms for each primary activity such that both together define a value-chain within the firm. Understanding competitive advantage thus requires an understanding of how a firm's primary and support activities are organised in comparison with those of their competitors (Porter 1985: 39).

With these conceptual tools, strategic alliances are seen as key organisational features for configuring value-chains on world-wide dimensions. Coalitions may help configure activities in the value chain that allow firms to reap a variety of benefits: economies of scale or learning; to acquire, pool, or sell access to knowledge; to reduce risk; or to shape competition by influencing who competes and on what basis (Porter and Fuller 1986: 321–325). Whichever benefits are highlighted, coalitions are ultimately seen as 'transitional devices' or responses by firms to compete under the changing conditions of profitability defined by emerging global industrial structures.

The above represents the branch in the strategic management literature associated with the product-based emphasis. For example, the ability to extend 'opportunity horizons' and venture into new markets is seen to stem from companies reacting to rapidly depreciating product life cycles. In another strand of strategic management literature, a competency-based view is emphasised. In that view, increasingly, it is not just the improved organisation of production that enables firms to capture dominant market shares, but their ability to pursue innovations on the future products that usurp present markets. Such authors highlight how corporations now pursue a variety of business ventures. As senior managers cannot meaningfully consider every discrete capability required to pursue business ventures, the need to distinguish between a few core aspects from a variety of non-core considerations becomes important for strategic planning. Recognising this, a second critical branch of strategic management literature has introduced the notion of 'core competencies' (Prahalad and Hamel 1990).

The competence view of the firm (Hamel and Heene 1994; Foss and Knudsen 1996) almost entirely emphasises understanding the firm in a more active, strategic light.[8] Firms are seen to actively seek to accumulate both tacit and explicit knowledge that enhances their ability to integrate a variety of discreet business skills and aptitudes.

In order to see how this helps us grasp changes in interfirm relations, we need to understand the basic assumption behind a competency view of the firm. Such views start by recognising that businesses depend not only on the efficient processing of physical goods, but equally on information, know-how and techno-logical expertise. Thus, the nature of the firm tends to be pursued through concomitant discussions on the nature of knowledge and learning. In such discussions, the notion of *path-dependency* has been adopted from evolutionary theory to highlight the way in which the accumulation of learning tends to depend upon previous experiences. In practice, this means that managers are constrained in the directions of their technological search (Patel and Pavitt 1997). Analytically, firms are thus seen to have distinct 'learning trajectories' available to them (Maskell and Malmberg 1995).

The second key notion concerns the interactivity of the learning processes (e.g., Lundvall 1992; Malmberg and Maskell 1997). Similar or related industrial activities tend to gradually cluster or 'agglomerate' in spatial regions that produce distinct specialisations. The close proximity between customers, suppliers, and a variety of other institutional elements in the local milieu, produces an environment where a variety of resources, knowledge and other capabilities are more easily acquired than when spatially dispersed (Lam 1997). Over time, close face-to-face interactions form durable routines which facilitate knowledge transfer and the cross-fertilisation of ideas, as well as allowing for shared values to develop, reduce uncertainty, and ease communication flows.

Both the path-dependency of knowledge, and the interactivity of learning are important contributions to the argument that modern interfirm relations are conduits that facilitate innovation by helping a group of firms achieve the critical competencies needed to commercialise new products and enter new markets (Teece 1988, 1992; Inkpen 1996).[9] In such arguments, the need for complemen-tary assets underscores the limited resources of individual firms. Merging complementary assets enables the production of more complex sets of products (Hobday 1998).[10] With the rise of complex product systems and the organisa-tional forms required to produce them, we begin to address changes in the nature of innovation in alliance capitalism.

Rather than put all their eggs in one basket as it were, firms are increasingly developing functionally-related products situated within complex product systems. But as Prencipe (1997) reminds us, decisions to outsource production and product development may damage the firm's ability to master the product's evolutionary dynamic. Simple notions of core competencies should be rejected because product systems each have particular characteristics that require a thor-ough understanding of the core, linkage, and peripheral relationships between various technologies. Thus, technological imperatives exist and are required for understanding business activity (Patel and Pavitt 1997).

## Technology and the firm

We now begin to get into a wholly different terrain than an analysis of the firm. Understanding alliance capitalism must also look for insight from the technical environment in which firm innovation is tied. This analytical movement is essen-tial as it is precisely in trying to understand the firm that we are required to look further. For example, applying transaction costs frameworks to explain alliances require authors to address the nature of the transactions specific to particular technical conditions (e.g., Antonelli 1988a; Picot *et al.* 1996).

From a technical perspective, the telematics revolution is a particularly important line of argument to help understand alliances. Many see revolutions in information and communications technologies (ICTs) as the most important cluster of innovations to impact upon economic organisation. For example, such technologies are seen to affect the fundamental conditions of production and distribution for the economic system; namely, the relative supply cost structure for all inputs of production (Freeman and Perez 1988). The rapidly falling relative costs of information processing and telecommunications are seen to provide a broad industrial foundation of relatively limitless supply when compared to the physical resources traditionally consumed by industrial manufacturing. This culminates in a new 'techno-economic paradigm' where diverse technical, organisational and managerial innovations converge to widely affect the way in which productive activity is undertaken across an economy (see discussion by Dunford, Chapter 10 in this volume).

Such paradigmatic revolutions have a 'generic' influence on many products and services; changing the potentials for innovation across numerous economic sectors and thereby affecting the underlying innovation process in an economy. Generic technologies both fuse products and production processes together as well as diversify whole ranges of products and services. These changes are often understood as representing the increasingly systemic nature of innovation. This means that influences come from beyond the purely technical aspects to encompass elements such as the market environment, production facilities, and the broader social contexts under which innovation is organised (Kline and Rosenberg 1986).

For example, generic technologies trigger a sequence of chain reactions and positive feed-back mechanisms that further impacts upon the process of innovation. As firms learn that the process of innovation often lies beyond their individual corporate boundaries,[11] the changing techno-economic paradigm triggers the formation of inter-industry alliances that search for skills and new market presence (Nicholls-Nixon and Jasinski 1995). But equally, such behavioural responses increase demands for rapid knowledge transfers; evoking changes in the process of innovation itself which further exacerbates demand for interfirm relations (Malmberg and Maskell 1995).

With the increasingly systemic nature of innovation, organisational transformations occur in response to the intense interaction required of networked actors. Network organisations represent institutional arrangements evolved to cope with the highly interactive process of innovation. Most arguments here build from the theme that networks represent the 'interpenetration of market and organisation' (Imai and Itami 1984). For example, like the Japanese *keiretsu*,[12] cross-border networks blend strong core ties between firms coupled with weaker ties to other network constellations. In this way, both the 'hierarchy benefits' of centralised strategic management along with 'market benefits' like local responsiveness to change are combined (Imai and Baba 1991). Similarly, changes in

technology also promote such synergies as advances in telematics provide benefits both for small firms as well as for large firms (Antonelli 1988b). With these
opposing tensions, interfirm cooperation allows for an 'organisational balance'
between the integration and association of resources needed for innovative firms
to develop technologies (Foray 1991).

While much of this literature treats inter-organisational changes as enabling
technical change, another often underplayed feature of innovation is the
constraints from technological appropriability (Chesnais 1988; Dosi 1988). In an
economic environment based upon the continuous technical innovation, profitable experimentation gains market share and serves as a guide for the evolution
of innovation down technical 'trajectories' based on particular engineering
paradigms. Such paradigms are tied to the evolutionary role of firms as
'explorers' of partially known developments (from basic research) whose temporary monopoly on the application of such knowledge eventually diffuses back
into the public realm (Nelson 1992). Thus, a key component affecting these
trajectories is constraints on the ability to appropriate aspects of the innovation
process itself as financial incentives are ultimately what motivates private agents.

In adopting the notion of the 'appropriability regime' from innovation theory,
Chesnais (1988) expands upon the insight of Porter and Fuller (1986: 325) that
firm coalitions also shape the nature of competitive relations.[13] In periods of
rapid technological change, a weakened appropriability regime may cause
leading firms to defend oligopolistic technological barriers around clusters of
related industrial activities based upon specific 'core technologies'. Such clus-
tering represents ways for several firms to cooperate for 'the mutual protection of
technological appropriability' (Chesnais 1988: 79).

## Firms, technology and the state

Questions surrounding the catalysts and constraints of innovation lead us to
further embed interfirm networks in an increasingly complex institutional setting.
The role of the nation-state, rather than waning out of the picture, is of
continued importance for its ability to promote or inhibit the evolution of
science and technology within the *national system of innovation* (Lundvall 1992;
Freeman 1995; Metcalfe 1995).[14] Thus, in addressing innovation, we are again
required to shift our intellectual footing. Within this next branch of literature,
governments are positioned as central agents affecting the organisation of
industry through selective or strategic policy decisions surrounding the national
technology infrastructure (Tassey 1991, 1992).

The importance of such an infrastructure is that many crucial developments
in commercial technology stem from basic research funded by national governments. It is now a 'stylised fact' that technological advances increasingly require
scientific progress (Dosi 1988: 229). Underneath this fact lies a subtle but important distinction often conceptually lumped together. 'Science' encompasses basic
research advances that increase the provision of *public* knowledge, where 'technology' represents the private development and refinement of specific aspects of

scientific knowledge applied into the process of production (Pavitt 1993). In understanding their different natures, scientific research is recognised as responding to a complex set of motivations and reward mechanisms largely distinguished from the profit-oriented drive of technological developments (Dasgupta and David 1987, 1988, 1991). Thus, the role of the state is seen as a critical factor in supporting a wide science base that would otherwise go under-developed if left only to private in-house R&D.[15]

In offering such support, the nation-state may even affect interfirm relations more directly as science and technology policies are geared towards integrating basic research with the commercialisation of technology. Increasingly, states are recognising the importance of developing a wide science foundation through pooled R&D resources (Chesnais 1988: 104–113).[16] By pooling R&D resources through cooperative projects, the governments may also serve to stimulate the creation of interfirm networks. A case in point is *ESPRIT* project (European Strategic Programme for Research and Development in Information Technologies) where strategic partnerships were the intended effect of the European Commission (Mytelka 1995).

## Firms, the state and the world economy

Since states are not isolated, autonomous structures, for some authors this means that understanding alliance capitalism requires us to further embed the activities of business agents within a larger, macro-economic consideration of the world economy. This vantage attempts to follow a more general outlook to identify the historical reasons behind why interfirm cooperation has increased in importance and what position they fulfil in the long-term workings of the world economy.

For example, Charles-Albert Michalet (1991a, 1991b) develops a theme that the modern world economy is evolving not as a single operating system but a mixed economy integrating diverse national economies through the rise of global finance and micro-economic governance structures. Interfirm cooperation is seen as a response by micro-economic agents to curtail the instability of global finance and stabilise global economic activity through network and alliance relationships. The 'contractual economy' represents the first expressions of governance evolving at the micro-economic level to offset the unbalanced and potentially devastating effects of global competition.

For example, alliances have evolved their ability to externalise the rising costs associated with globally internalised corporate structures by restructuring industrial activities among several partners. Network organisation pools the necessary resources to pursue a joint activity (e.g., technological development) without necessarily entailing extensive interfirm reorganisation. From this basis, the contemporary economic environment is being organised along cooperative and competitive dimensions based on new forms of cartel-like coalitions where network firms also belong to specific alliances. In this contractual, world mixed economy, market access is seen to stem from both partnerships with specific network firms, and through the position of these network firms in specific alliances.

Manuel Castells (1989, 1993, 1996) brings to the fore the notion that the modern world economy (more preferably called a global economy) now operates on a planetary level in real time. In summary, the informational economy represents changes in state activity, firm behaviour, and industrial and technical change that although having evolved disproportionately and from distinct trajectories, are now converging into a global economy founded upon the creation and application of knowledge. These convergent trends mutually reinforce an *organisational logic* whereby the operating unit is not the firm but the business enterprise itself; projects organised across individual firms or formal alliances into extensive network relations.

The rise of the 'network enterprise' is seen as an organisational logic, distinct from paradigmatic changes in technology, that has enabled the global operation of economic activities. The network enterprise represents the increasing organisation of business activities into an enterprise not run by individual firms or even multinational corporations but by international networks constituted through a variety of actors and institutions continuously adapting to support the environments and markets in which the enterprise itself operates. The transformation of business enterprise into organisational networks, although distinct from technical change, interacts with the revolution in information technology such that both together have historically founded the development of the global informational economy.

Kenichi Ohmae (1990) expanded upon his earlier work to identify three major changes in the conditions faced by corporations in the interlinked, triadic economy.[17] In distinction to both of the previous perspectives, the world economy is approached from the perspective of business managers adjusting to conditions where increased consumer power, the diverse nature of technology, and rising fixed costs place innovation and productivity as the main determinants of sustained advantage. In this environment, strategic alliances are the most effective means to maximise the contribution to the rising fixed costs of production symptomatic of the modern world economy. Thus, successful strategic alliances are about long-term compromises between otherwise independent corporations that enable them to pursue their separate interests while still trying to maximise contributions to the rising fixed costs of innovation. Like *keiretsu* relations in Japan, alliances that will be able to cope with the new conditions of business will maintain a large degree of independence between firms, reducing the managerial emphasis on partner control that comes with equity ownership.

## Firms, industries and the institutional environment

In understanding alliance capitalism, we have seen that the rise of interfirm relations is a complex phenomenon that crosses numerous disciplines. In doing so, the literature encompasses an extensive and often conflicting range of rational motivations as well as a plethora of analytical considerations. Ultimately, what this means is that future work must take on an interdisciplinary character and address the insufficiency of mono-causal theoretical approaches (Osborn and Hagedoorn 1997). But how?

Many approaches have begun to converge on the so-called 'meso-level' of analysis in order to provide an institutional environment to understand changes in competition, industrial organisation, and interfirm relations (Foss 1996). For example, notions of flexible specialisation (Piore and Sabel 1984), development blocks (Dahmén 1988), industrial districts (Becattini 1989), value-chains and industrial clusters (Porter 1990), *filières* (Antonelli *et al.* 1992), innovation systems (Lundvall 1992), production complexes (Scott and Storper 1992), ecosystems (Moore 1993, 1996), business groups (Granovetter 1995), business systems (Whitley 1995, 1998), innovation communities (Lynn *et al.* 1996), industrial complexes (Ruigrok and van Tulder 1996), and business organisations (Yeung 1998) cover some of the recent attempts to embed the firm in a wider institutional environment. But while such analytical focuses are growing, there is still no clear basis upon which to determine when concepts should be used and how they inform transformations in the industrial system (Scott and Storper 1992; Foss 1996; Maskell *et al.* 1998).

To begin untangling the conceptual vagueness that exists, we need to understand that such approaches broadly work within an 'institutionalist' tradition struggling with some basic intellectual divisions. While most would agree that the economy essentially represents a set of inputs and outputs forming a production system, it is how we understand the structure of institutional governance in this system which divides the intellectual community into two basic outlooks. First, there are those which attempt to identify the reasons why certain forms of governance rather than others, exist at given moments in time. While different labels may exist, this *comparative institutionalism* is largely disposed towards identifying how an environment chooses between broad institutional arrangements such as between decentralised markets, corporate hierarchies, government planning, etc. (e.g., Williamson 1975, 1985; Dunning 1997). Second, there are those which try to understand the change in opportunities and constraints that come with particular institutional developments.[18] While both make the claim that 'institutions matter', what distinguishes complex institutionalism from the latter is the view that we are not in a position to use general organisational classifications to address the *complexities of distinctiveness* that give institutional configurations their durability and relevance.

The rise of meso-level focuses should be considered as part of a complex institutionalist tradition attempting to identify how the competitive process is redefining its organisation. Such discussions often study 'governance' institutions to locate the structure of power and decision-making in the coordination of modern industrial activity. But here too there is an underlying tension in how authors try to reconcile the seemingly opposing tendencies in alliance capitalism. For example, we saw in the previous section that revolutions in information and communications technology have redefined the opportunities and constraints of both large and small firms. On questions of power and the governance of industrial activity, initial reactions often stress the historical continuity between previous epochs where large firms dominated the organisation of industries and controlled the output of smaller firms.[19] Thus, there are those that feel that the increase in interfirm networking is not a return to the small, craft producers but a continuation of the capitalist tendency toward the centralisation and concentration of capital represented by competitive processes elevated to rivalries between global galaxies of firms or transnational alliance formations (e.g., Michalet 1991a; Moore 1993; Castells 1996; Gomes-Casseres 1996; Ernst 1997). From this perspective, understanding changes to the competitive landscape entails an elevated shift in the unit of analysis away from the isolated firm and towards networked organisations.

Others find less conflict with transformations in the capacities of large and small firms. The trend of large firms towards outsourcing production can have a positive role in increasing the size of the units within the industry. Rather than conflict, both large and small firms appear as symbiotic. We can see this in some of the fastest-growing sectors in the world information economy (e.g., high technology areas such as electronics and computer sectors) where we have large firms and smaller firms co-existing in mixtures of large-scale internalisation, coupled with links to smaller external economies made up of smaller firms. These enmeshed networks of large core firms and smaller ring firms have developed patterns where small producers tend to only supply up to 20 per cent of their business to a particular large customer (Sturgeon 1997a, 1997b). Thus, we see examples where although Southern California aircraft firms have strong power over the local rings, industrial control is problematic in that with decreasing dependency relationship, many of the ring units are able to sell outside their regions (Scott and Storper 1992).

Thus we have come to a conflict in our instincts concerning industrial domination and the more complex pictures offered by in-depth empirical research. There are far more cases where production networks contain at least some large units than those where none are found. Large firms are central to alliance capitalism. But given network production systems, small and medium-sized enterprises are equally key. How do we understand the nature of control – the organisation and distribution of industrial governance in alliance capitalism – when faced with a complex mixing of small, medium-sized and large firms both territorially agglomerated while also disembedded from regional localities and re-embedded in cross-border interfirm relations? Despite the many attempts to embed the firm in a meso-level environment, what has been largely amiss in the literature is that the search for the correct organisational form to describe the elevated redefinition of competition is ultimately a wild goose chase.

Rather than a new organisational form competing for supremacy, contemporary capitalism is about a plurality of complex organisational formations with distinct institutional histories (Crouch and Streeck 1997). Interfirm networks problematise simple notions of domination which equate size and power. So long as corporate power is viewed simply as a particular firm characteristic, institutionalist analysis will fail to recognise the complex organisational nature of modern competition. Firms, especially large ones, are important. But they are only part of the conflicting picture of alliance capitalism where small is equally beautiful. Ultimately, we need to understand that neither large nor small firms are in the same circumstances as previously, nor are they important features for the same reasons as in previous eras. To understand how they have changed, what has been long overdue is a 'two-level theory' where both the firm level and the interactions between firms are explained together (Foss 1996).

The basic problem is as following: conventional practice proceeds by first developing a framework in which to analyse firms and then selecting the firms to consider. The selection process is provided by an industrial arena such that today industries are most often conceived for statistical ends: product categories which configure the arenas in which firm competition can have a quantified relationship. This can be most clearly seen in relation to anti-trust analysis where competitive conditions are derived from the absence of 'dominant positions' within a definite geographical product market. Such structural approaches to industrial organisation have an extensive history evolved out of the increasing formalisation of economic analysis earlier in the twentieth century. The effective result of this intellectual legacy is that the competitive process is framed between a particular selection of firms and derived by the sale of particular products.

But as industrial products increasingly become concatenated on various degrees and levels, the problem of clearly and consistently isolating industries is left to an analytical design. For example, an unambiguous definition of industry would be possible only if the products involved are fairly homogeneous and have a high degree of substitutability (Ballance 1987). This raises the possibility that outside of the unambiguous conditions of perfect competition or perfect monopoly assumed by many economic frameworks, there may be no theoretical concept to which the term 'industry' can be usefully applied (Berg 1996). Thus, without a consistent match between a set of technical characteristics that make up a product, the various service characteristics that define its usage, and the particular methods used in its production, one cannot uniquely identify an autonomous industrial system (Foray and Garrouste 1993). The all-too-common result of industrial ambiguity is the theoretical withdrawal back onto the level of firm.

Such problems are not new and have been central weaknesses in how competition has been understood (Auerbach 1988). But without an alternative recourse, our intellectual footing falls back onto the firm whether or not the rise of networks and the move toward a meso-level analysis call out for otherwise. Symptomatic of the theoretical deficiency surrounding how we address industries, we increasingly see lots of work that, like Storper and Harrison (1991), find little resemblance between the real boundaries of production systems and the abstractions of product classifications. For example, underlying work on the influential competence view of the firm is the attempt to break away from a product/market share view of firm behaviour towards competition as a multi-layered game (De Leo 1994). In anti-trust cases, authors increasingly find that dated approaches to industrial organisation and market definition reinforce the need for contemporary notions of industry to recognise that competitive arenas and market power are highly unstable features which shift with rapid technological change (Jorde and Teece 1992; Teece 1992).

Most damning of traditional conceptualisations is some recent empirical work implicating that the blurring of industrial boundaries brought with network behaviour is not a problematic categorical by-product of competition, but an essential dimension in the competitive process today (Borrus 1997; Borrus and Zysman 1997a, 1997b; Ernst 1997; Sturgeon 1997a, 1997b). That is, the development of business activities and industrial organisation are a mutually constitutive process that meso-level formulations cannot address with dated conceptualisations of what industries are. The blurring of industries is not a classificatory problem; it is a theoretical one.

## Wintelism and the merchant system of industrial organisation

Earlier I mentioned Foss (1996) who found that a two-level theory is currently missing. As will be argued here, we are not left totally in the dark. There is recent empirical research coming out of the *Berkeley Roundtable on the International Economy* (BRIE) bolstering a two-level theoretical approach. Through a series of recent works on the electronics industry (Borrus 1997; Borrus and Zysman 1997a, 1997b; Ernst 1994, 1997; Sturgeon 1997a, 1997b) an argument is being developed to link the rise of a new competitive form emerging in the US with changes in industrial organisation arising across a number of national and industrial sectors. The new competitive form is referred to as 'Wintelism' where the market dominance of companies like Intel for microprocessors, and Microsoft for Windows operating systems, exemplify the importance of knowledge – specifically in the form of *de facto* market standards for hi-tech components – to modern competitiveness and market success.

Contrary to previous eras in electronics, standards are increasingly designed to be 'open', in the sense that electronic components are made interoperable with other technical systems and digital information networks by early release of technical information into the public domain. But this openness at a technical level is symptomatic of a shift in competitive strategy pursued by large firms. In this strategic shift, standards are increasingly 'open-but-owned' and reflective of the contemporary conditions of competition where dominant companies battle to capture markets through attempting to get proprietary technical standards accepted by the market.

Battles for open-but-owned standards are not just a new addition to competitive repertoires. The rising importance of standards and 'architectural' designs is also intimately connected with both the restructuring of corporate as well as industrial forms of organisation. In the attempt to excel in the research and development required to create and define standards, leading or 'brand-name' corporations are pursuing innovation intensive activity while delinking from production-intensive activity (Sturgeon 1997a, 1997b). The delinking process is fuelled by trends where leading companies increasingly outsource their productive capacity to 'turnkey' manufacturers.[20] This shedding of productive capacity enables brand-name firms to concentrate resources, reorganise firm boundaries and interfirm relations to help pursue innovation at the *product level* – creating, enhancing and destroying the characteristics that define products and how they interact with other products. Thus, market-creating innovative capacity is increasingly hoarded in-house by dominant corporations where market-supplying capacity is allowed to migrate into the 'external economies'.[21]

Reinforcing the delinking process, as 'brand-name' firms increasingly outsource production to concentrate on product-level innovations, this shift has disruptive effects on industrial organisation. The protective barriers once offered by the high fixed costs of production are increasingly being withdrawn. Without traditional protective barriers, leading companies must pursue stable grounds for controlling market positions. This is done precisely through the continual creation and destruction of markets for hi-tech products that result from battles to define the technical standards and architectural designs. But despite shifts in innovation, production is still essential.

Rather than in-house manufacturing, specialised suppliers have become key mediums through which to facilitate the outsourcing of production. The relative benefits offered by an industrial system of specialised suppliers centres on the development of minimal interdependency to avoid exclusive ties to particular contractors. By maintaining dependency levels at or below 20 per cent on any one customer, specialised suppliers help constrain the development of monopoly control over key components and allow production to cater to a wider range of industrial requirements. As well, while no supplier depends upon a particular customer, equally large companies can also outsource production to an array of manufacturers to take advantage of various specialisations. This increase in substitutability between customers and suppliers defines the *merchant* character of industrial organisation.

The importance of a merchant system of industrial organisation stems from the uncertainty of the contemporary environment. As it develops, it creates a feed-back pressure for the continual organisational separation of innovation and production. As merchant forms of industrial organisation develop, brand-name companies are increasingly pressured to further shed production capabilities. This increasingly situates merchant producers as central conduits in the proliferation of electronic products. As capturing *de facto* market standards relies upon the speed at which preference for one system can be 'tipped' away from another, Wintelist competition thus reinforces and is reinforced by an evolving merchant system of industrial organisation based on turnkey manufacturers.

As product systems, like digital information and communication networks, span the globe, Wintelist competition equally depends upon merchant industrial changes beyond national (especially American) industrial systems. Increasingly, turnkey merchant manufacturers operate as production service companies to provide a wide array of global-scale manufacturing and value-added services (Borrus and Zysman 1997b). Such companies manage CPNs for international customers and rival even traditional MNEs in the size and scope of their international production network. Thus, where internal production capacity, international production facilities, and economies of scale, were once key to the dominance of large multinational enterprises, the benefits of scale are being redistributed away from the traditional MNE to external suppliers organised cross-nationally. With the rise of merchant producers and the delinking of innovative capacity and manufacturing, cross-national production networks enable the organisation of global production strategies without innovating companies having to pursue costly foreign direct investment.

The strength of merchant organisation lies in the industry wide distribution of risk (Ernst 1994, 1997). The production of electronics components involves a much more organisationally complex agenda than in previous eras. Firms need to coordinate global operations but under the constraints posed by the globalising electronics industry. Competition for new and emerging international market shares face problems of technical complexity where increasing fixed costs of production and rapidly depreciating assets disintegrate the electronics value-chain into clusters of specialised commodity producers. Capturing new and emerging markets thus requires collective forms of organisation that, under increasingly tight time schedules, must integrate specialised skills located in geographically different localities ('districts' or 'agglomeration economies') into complex international supply chains. It is the need to integrate complex supply chains into cross-national production networks that is driving the character of corporate activity to shift from partial to more systemic forms of globalisation (Ernst 1997). Effectively, underneath alliance capitalism is the rise of 'systemic globalisation' where business enterprise is adopting to the complexity and volatility of high-technology products, and where industrial capabilities are functionally specialised and distributed world-wide.

In returning to the two-level theory raised earlier, the logic behind systemic globalisation provides us with empirical support for the need to develop two-level theorisation. Modern systems competition depends upon the increase in systemic globalisation. With the increasingly systematic organisation of cross-national production networks, uncertainty itself is being exploited by today's leading brand-name companies. As merchant product service companies increasingly take on the task of coordinating cross-national production networks, their operational flexibility effectively reduces the time it takes to get products to the market. The complex manufacturing skills and specialised capabilities required to learn the various aspects of product development are acquired from wherever they may be distributed rather than attempt to comprehensively accumulate capabilities in-house. Today, specialised productive advantages are often located in Asia. This is why the delinking of production from innovation brought by Wintelist changes by mainly American-led companies are tied to changes in Asian production networks which are able to compress speed-to-market for products that help establish *de facto* standards (Borrus 1997).

A subtle but important nuance of the systemic globalisation thesis is that where new market definition and penetration strategies are key to excelling under the volatile conditions of high-technology ventures, systems competition is also pursued in and through the organisation of industrial activity on a world-wide scale. Echoing insights by Sayer and Walker (1992) on the social division of labour, what we see is industry organisation itself becoming a central site of competition and a driving force in the development of alliance capitalism. That is, BRIE research into the electronics industry has directly implicated a two-level theoretical approach to capture the mutually constitutive development of business activities and industrial organisation.

## Conclusion: IPE in the age of cross-border alliance capitalism

In broadly reflecting upon the nature of a two-level theoretical approach to alliance capitalism, we see that such work follows an institutionalist agenda that emphasises the historical specificity and embeddedness of interfirm relations. This is not a crude institutionalism representing little more than an exercise in mapping the relations between firms and their regional, domestic and international settings (e.g., Sally 1994). In dealing only with existing structures, interfirm networks are removed from the dynamic processes surrounding the systemic constitution of industrial organisation where both firms and network relations redefine their boundaries to changing conditions (Sturgeon 1997a). Instead, IPE in the age of cross-border alliance capitalism requires an increasingly 'complex institutionalism' that can grasp co-evolutionary changes in firm and industrial organisation.

## Notes

1   For example, just some of the relevant disciplines might include: economic geography, organisational studies, international business studies, new institutional economics, the economics of technical change and innovation, and strategic management; not to mention the more dedicated alliance research.
2   Mutual forbearance referring to the condition where in learning to trust each other, contracted actors come to refrain from damaging each other's interests.
3   For example, multinational enterprises engage in international production when they possess relatively more ownership advantages in servicing particular foreign markets than do rival firms – usually intangible assets (such as patented knowledge, access to key resources, etc.) that give the MNE the ability to earn revenues in foreign markets that exceed the costs of engaging in international production.
4   In conjunction with owning specific rent-producing assets, MNEs must also be able to manage activities so as to take advantage of distinct social, political and economic factors while also avoiding the potential hazards that come from changing locational circumstances. In evaluating the risk factors of different environments, MNEs weigh various locational elements such as: labour conditions, market size, infrastructure, natural resources, and regulations.
5   Similarly, Maskell *et al.* (1998) identify the process of 'ubiquitification' as a central challenge affecting the competitiveness of firms and regions and thus changing the economic geography of contemporary capitalism.
6   These deal with the input of resources, processing them into a final product, distribution of products to the market, and additional product maintenance or value enhancement services such as marketing and sales.
7   These encompass aspects such as human resource management (e.g., recruiting and training), firm infrastructure (e.g., general management and finance), technology development (e.g., information systems), and the procurement of materials.

52    *Richard Phillips*

8  Sometimes, this view is seen as an extension of the resource-based view of the firm (Wernerfelt 1984; Penrose 1995).
9  Some recent work has brought a precautionary voice warning against blindly following upon this oft-used line of argument. For example, alliances may raise the risk of losing control over core competencies (Lei and Slocum 1992). This is buttressed by work from Mitchell and Singh (1996) who find alliance partners at greater risk of insolvency in situations of environmental shock.
10 Complex product systems are highly customised, engineering-intensive goods which often require several producers to work together simultaneously in project-based organisation forms (Hobday 1998).
11 Changes in the personal computer industry leading to the fall of IBM serve as a good example. See Ferguson and Morris (1993).
12 The *keiretsu* is a long-term affiliation of firms tied together through reciprocal share-holdings, credit relations, trading relations, and interlocking directorships and organised around a core bank or trading company (OECD 1992: 100).
13 The appropriability regime refers to the degree (tight or weak) to which an innovation can be protected by particular firms over others.
14 Metcalfe (1995: 38) describes the national system of innovation as 'that set of distinct institutions which jointly and individually contribute to the development and diffusion of new technologies and which provides the framework within which governments form and implement policies to influence the innovation process'. It is a means of harnessing the numerous facets in which organisational and institutional arrangements and linkages are conducive to innovation and growth.
15 Such as the underlying development of the internet through fundamental break-throughs in distributed communication networking during the 1960s; funded through the Defense Advanced Research Projects Agency (research arm for the US Department of Defense).
16 To see these insights developed into government R&D policy, see the 1996 report '*Endless Frontier, Limited Resources: US R&D Policy for Competitiveness*' published by the Council on Competitiveness (http://nii.nist.gov/pubs/coc_rd/rd_cover.html).
17 Empirical research has shown that over 90 per cent of cooperative agreements in 'core technologies' (information technology, biotechnology and new materials) takes place within the US, Japan and Europe triad (Hagedoorn and Schakenraad 1990: 8).
18 This tradition tends to be far less coherent in terms of an institutionalist method-ology, representing largely context specific accounts with idiosyncratic conceptual developments.
19 Recent empirical work on *differential accumulation* reminds us that the concentration of wealth while on the rise for core industrial actors, appears to be at the expense of a wider industrial body (Nitzan 1998).
20 In a turnkey system of production, innovating companies pursue the design of elec-tronic components and pass their specifications onto merchant manufacturers who purchase component inventories through a turnkey contract; like purchasing the rights to produce products before they have been produced. Only when producers have delivered the finished products do they recoup their initial purchase. As well, turnkey manufacturers often bundle a wide variety of extra services along with the finished product (e.g., product testing and documentation, delivery and distribution, final assembly, etc.), which cement strong market ties by allowing customers to detach from various manufacturing and support concerns.
21 Numerous examples implicate this broader pattern as many hi-tech 'name brand' companies have established dominant market shares while having little in-house manufacturing capacity (e.g., Dell, NCR, Philips, ATT, Hewlett Packard, DEC, Sun Microsystems, Silicon Graphics, and Cisco Systems).

# 4 The use and misuse of power analysis in international theory

*Stefano Guzzini*[1]

Power is ubiquitous. No theory and hardly any explanation in International Relations (IR) or International Political Economy (IPE) can do without it. At the same time, power is one of the most under-researched concepts in the discipline. In IR, conceptual pieces on power barely make it more than every four years or so into our scholarly publications.

This state of affairs is paradoxical. For power is certainly no self-evident or secondary concept. Dictionaries usually cite more than twenty meanings. And also in IR, it has been used in innumerable and increasingly polyvalent ways. For reasons of clarity, one scholar (Rosenau 1980), went as far as to to drop it from his vocabulary and to replace it either by capabilities as a property concept, or by control as actual influence over outcomes.

Moreover, power is a central concept in IR theory, in particular in its long-time dominant school of thought, realism. For Morgenthau (1948), power was the consequence of the drive for domination, the immediate aim of all political action, and the essence of international politics. Yet, whereas he still felt compelled to discuss the origins of the essence of politics as power – origins he found in human nature – this effort has remained unrivalled, and also strangely unattempted (for this critique, see Krippendorff 1977: 36), even in the realist camp.

More generally, power has been of central importance in IR, because it seemed essential for the understanding of two central issues: who (one or more) can be expected to win a conflict? And, related to this, who (one or more) governs international politics? Power, traditionally understood as resources or capabilities has been used as an indicator for the strength of actors, and consequently of the capacity to affect or control events. Likewise, a general capacity to control outcomes has been used as an indicator for the ruling of the international system. In other words, IR assumed a double causal link between these two facets in a way comparable to Robert Dahl's (1961) famous power analysis in *Who governs?* (the city of New Haven). There Dahl assessed power empirically by checking who prevailed in crucial decision-making. In the case of a consistent pattern across issue-areas, he would have deduced a hierarchical power structure. In its absence, i.e. when many different actors prevailed in different crucial municipal decisions, he judged the local government as pluralistic.

This chapter argues that the resurgence of some power analysis in the last twenty years, mainly in IPE and contructivist IR, challenges these tacitly assumed links between resources and control over outcomes, as well as between control over crucial outcomes and general rule. More precisely, the chapter makes two arguments. First, with regard to the link between resources and outcomes, the discussion will show that power cannot play the central role it assumes in both neorealism and neoinstitutionalism. Second, with regard to the understanding of 'rule' and 'governance', different 'structural power' approaches have shown the need to make more encompassing power concepts in order to capture important facets of international rule. These approaches, derived mainly within IPE, run the risk, however, of overplaying the causal strength of their analysis, and of understating the non-materialist aspects of rule or governance.

The argument will be laid out in three steps. To begin with, the realist-dominated power discussion prior to the neoinstitutionalist reformulation of the1970s–80s will be presented. Here it can be shown that power is meaningless, if used as a 'lump' concept as required by balance of power theories. In the second section, I then show that neoinstitutionalist attempts to rescue at least the facet of power concerned with the link between resources and outcomes are caught in a dilemma: either they keep a more generalisable analytical framework, by sacrificing the significance of power, or they keep a causal explanatory role for power at the expense of a parsimonious and generalisable analysis. The third section finally demonstrates the utility of concepts of power derived from structuralist IPE approaches for understanding international rule, but indicates, with the hindsight of constructivist approaches, their overly materialist bias.

## The theoretical uselessness of realist and neorealist lump concepts of power

In his turn to a more scientific theory of realism, Waltz touched neither upon the underlying concept of power, nor on the central place of balance of power theory in classical realist writings. Waltz uses micro-economic theory for an approach which focuses on the systemic level of analysis. Analogous to markets, the balance of power sets the range of options available to actors. In turn, markets and hence the balance of power system, are 'made by actions and inter-actions of its units, and the theory is based on assumptions about their behavior' (Waltz 1979: 117).

Relying on economic theory, Waltz assumes an analogy between the role of power in IR and the function of money in neoclassical economics (for the following, see also Guzzini 1998: 136–137). The striving for utility maximisation which can be expressed and measured in terms of money, parallels the national interest (i.e. security) expressed in terms of (relative) power.[2]

In an astonishingly overlooked argument, Raymond Aron (1962) opposed this very transfer of economic theory to IR theory. First, for Aron, it made little sense to liken the maximisation of security as expressed in power to the maximisation of utility as expressed in terms of money. Aron (1962: 28–29) argued that there are three classical foreign policy goals (puissance, security, glory/ideals) that cannot be reduced one into the other. Having no single aim, no optimal rational choice could happen. In the language of rational choice, foreign policy is indeterminate since alternative ends are incommensurable. If this were correct, then rational choice theorists (e.g. Elster 1989: 31–33) accept that their approach cannot be applied for explanatory purposes (see also Guzzini 1994: 83–86).

Aron's claim is based on the different degree of fungibility of money and power resources. The commensurability of means and aims presupposes a high degree of fungibility of power. The term fungibility refers to the idea of a moveable good that can be freely substituted by another of the same class. Fungible goods are those universally applicable or convertible in contrast to those who retain value only in a specific context. Yet whereas fungibility seems a plausible assumption in monetarised economies, in international relations, even apparently ultimate power resources like weapons of mass destruction might not necessarily be of great help for getting another state to change its monetary policies (see, in particular, Baldwin 1989: 25, 34, 209).

Aron did, of course, recognise that economic theory can be used to model behaviour on the basis of a variety of also conflicting preferences. But for him, with the advent of money as a general standard of value within which these competing preferences can be put on the same scale, compared, and traded-off, economists were able to reduce the variety of preferences to one utility function. In world politics, for reasons of its lacking real-world fungibility, power cannot play a corresponding role as standard of value. With no power–money analogy, there is also no analogy between the integrated value of utility and the national interest (security) (Guzzini 1993: 453). Consequently, (realist) theoreticians in IR cannot use economic theory as a model (Aron 1962: 102).

In a later, indeed very late, response to Aron, Waltz (1990) said that the analogy between power and money is not vitiated by a qualitative difference. Rather, the problem is simply one of measurement. Power, Waltz argued, does none the less function as a medium of exchange. Yet, although diplomats might agree on some approximations for their dealings, Waltz's argument misses the central point: for making the theoretical model work, power needs to be an (objectivised) standardised measure of value, as well (for this punctual reminder, see Baldwin 1993: 21–22).

The critique of the fungibility assumption of power is most damaging for balance of power theories. If power is segmented, if capacities are issue-specific, then the positioning of power in a general balance is guess-work. Therefore, balance of power theorists literally need a lump concept of power which assumes that all elements of power can be combined into one general indicator. Given this central, albeit weak dimension of their theory, even sophisticated theoreticians have resorted to rhetoric instead of arguments to defend their position. Hedley Bull, for instance, after assessing the difficulties to arrive at an over-all concept of power, at some point candidly writes that 'the relative position of states in overall power nevertheless makes itself apparent in bargaining among states, and the conception of overall power is one we cannot do without'

(Bull 1977: 114). His first argument, deriving power *ex post* from its effects, comes close to the usual power tautologies. The second argument, well, is no argument at all (on the level of observation). And yet Waltz (1979: 131) finds it convincing enough, when he asserts that the 'economic, military and other capabilities of nations cannot be sectored and separately weighted'.

It is here, where regime theorists and neo-institutionalists part company with neorealists. Relying heavily on Baldwin's work, Robert Keohane and Joseph Nye (1977) had already argued for issue specific power structures. Later, Keohane (1986: 184) explicitly criticised Waltz's fungibility assumption and argues that power concepts are only useful within circumscribed issue areas where fungibility can be assumed. Waltz remained unimpressed and answered:

> Obviously, power is not as fungible as money. Not much is. But power is much more fungible than Keohane allows. As ever, the distinction between strong and weak states is important. The stronger the state, the greater the variety of its capabilities. Power may be only slightly fungible for weak states, but it is highly so for strong ones.
>
> (Waltz 1986: 333)

Waltz's defence, however, is inconsistent. If power resources were so highly fungible that they could be used in different domains, then one does not need to argue with their variety: economic capabilities can be used for producing political, social or cultural outcomes. If one assumes a great variety of capabilities, one implicitly assumes that a strong state is strong not because it has a lot of overall power, but because it possesses a high level of capabilities in distinct domains. This is still no case for the fungibility of power as desperately as balance of power theories would need it.

As Baldwin a long time ago already showed, a single international power structure relies either on the assumption of a single dominant issue area or on a high fungibility of power resources. Since both are of little avail, it 'is time to recognise that the notion of a single overall international power structure unrelated to any particular issue area is based on a concept of power that is virtually meaningless' (Baldwin 1989: 167).

## Power in IPE: the neoinstitutionalist link between resources and outcomes

The rebirth of power analysis in IR/IPE has to do with what Baldwin called the 'paradox of unrealised power'. In a regional conflict, the major power of the world was apparently unable to lay down the rules and had to accept a humiliating military and political defeat against the Vietcong. Some scholars, in the academic equivalent of the stab-in-the-back theories fashionable among some US military, tried to explain away this paradox by identifying the lack of 'will' on the side of the US to use these resources, i.e. so-called conversion failures. An explanation based on alleged conversion failures implies that the war did not show the relative weakness of the US (in spite of its tremendous capabilities), simply its unrealised strength. Consequently, any event could be explained *ex post* so as to suit any assumption about the distribution of power. In other words, such an explanation had the scholarly implication that power cannot be empirically assessed at all. As so often, the trouble with this type of power analysis was not that it was wrong, but that there was no way it could go wrong.

Neoinstitutionalist analysis has, however, opted for a more sophisticated approach. If power is not a lump concept, but must be understood within specific issue areas, then two different theoretical tracks can be pursued. On the one hand, one could accept the apparent lesson of the Vietnam War and argue that control over resources, even issue-area specific ones, does not necessarily translate into control over outcomes. Power no longer functions as a determining cause. On the other hand, one could try to stick to a strong causal role for power, one in which the link between valued resources and outcomes is not loosened. This can be done by further specifying the situational context that defines which policy instruments can count as actual power resources in this particular issue area.

As I will argue, these two very valuable attempts have problems of their own. They express a dilemma. They can stick to a generalisable explanation in which, however, power plays no longer a central role, or propose a causal, but situation-specific concept of power which is inconsistent with generalisable explanations.

### Non-causal power and prediction

Regime analysis maintains the basic causal approach of realism in which the distribution of power is the main independent variable for explaining international events. It supplements it, however, by including an intervening or, at times, autonomous variable (Krasner 1982), be it called regimes or simply institutions: 'power measured in terms of resources may look different from *power measured in terms of influence over outcomes*. We must look at the "translation" in the political bargaining process' (Keohane and Nye 1977: 18, original emphasis).

This approach, which was meant to supplement realism, paradoxically risks stripping power analysis of its predictive character. Indeed, in *Power and Interdependence*, Keohane and Nye showed that realist explanations were of little use in the context of complex interdependence, whereas they were useful in the context of power politics. But they had no theory that anticipated when which context applied (not that this would be easy, or perhaps even feasible). They offered a typology of explanations, in place of a theory which could explain *ex ante* why in a certain situation one should use one model rather than the other. In that sense, their approach repeated earlier approaches which distinguished different types of actors or different contexts in international anarchy – and their predicament, so masterfully captured by Arnold Wolfers (1962: 86): 'One consequence of distinctions like these is worth mentioning. They rob theory of the determinate and predictive character that seemed to give the pure power politics hypothesis its peculiar value.'

Indeed, Robert Keohane increasingly came to have doubts about the causal role of power. While discussing hegemonic stability theory, he shows empirical anomalies of the 'crude' version, which derives the existence of regimes solely from shifts in the distribution of power. A more sophisticated version needs to rely on an aspect of the unit-level, namely leadership.

> Rather than being a component of a scientific generalization – that power is a necessary or sufficient condition for cooperation – the concept of hegemony, defined in terms of willingness and an ability to lead, helps us to think about the incentives facing the potential hegemon.

> (Keohane 1984: 39)

In his model, the determination in the explanation shifts from interests defined in terms of the distribution of power, to rational choice made on the basis of given interests defined in terms of 'power, expectations, values, and conventions' (Keohane 1984: 75). See Figure 4.1 for a simplified model of Keohane's rational actor approach.

But in this model, only predictions of a very limited kind are possible – with a secondary role for power. Power is assumed to be one of the two primary motivations for rational action. Similarly, the distribution of power is part of the actor's definition of interests of an actor. Yet, we are still far away from

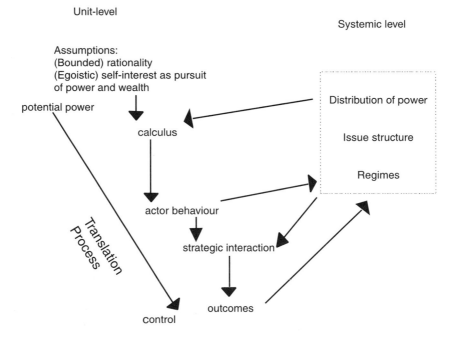

*Figure 4.1*    Keohane's rational actor approach

*Source*: Based on Keohane, R. O. (1984) *After Hegemony: Cooperation and Discord in the World Political Economy*, Princeton University Press.

predicting possible outcomes. In this model, prediction is no longer based on power resources, but on rational choice. But similarly, the rational calculus helps us to predict behaviour in strategic interaction, not its outcome.[3]

### Causal power and educated guesses

Decreasing the causal explanatory value of power as the central link in the translation from resources to outcomes, Robert Keohane emphasises instead the role of rationality and regimes on strategic interaction. David Baldwin, on the other hand, wants to keep a strong causal link between power as control over relationally valued resources and as control over outcomes. The price for this, however, is that power analysis must potentially become very narrowly circumscribed to particular instances, where no prediction is possible. Whereas the first institutionalist move kept, however limited, predictive capacity of a theory, based on rational choice and not on power, this second move saves a central causal role for power at the price of predictability in IR/IPE.

Baldwin defines power as the capacity to get somebody else to do what he or she would not have done otherwise. This effect is not limited to empirical changes in behaviour, but applies also to attitudes, beliefs or the propensity to act (Baldwin 1989: 7). He circumscribes the use of power for three reasons: the already mentioned problem of fungibility, the relational character of power, and the inevitably counterfactual character of power analysis.

Baldwin's conception is shaped by his relational understanding of power. In Keohane and Nye, this relational aspect is present to the extent that power derives from relations of vulnerability interdependence defined by the high cost to be paid for substituting these resources. Baldwin, on the other hand, begins with individual, not collective actors, with relations, not resources. Baldwin's preferred example for the relational character of power might serve as illustration. If a suicide candidate is threatened with a gun to choose between his money and death, he might not feel threatened at all. The gun-bearer has no power over the suicide candidate in this relation.

In other words, power comes not (only) out of the utility attached to resources, but exists through the actual value systems of human beings in their relations with each other. The major difference is that personal value systems cannot be simply assumed in the empirical power analysis, as they can in utilitarian action theories. Instead, the researcher has first to analyse the value systems of the interacting parties in order to establish whether there are power resources in the first place.

For this reason, Baldwin (1985: 285; 1989: 134) insists that one can only study power, if understood as a causal variable, in well circumscribed 'policy-contingency frameworks' (for the following, see Guzzini 1993: 451–456). The context then specifies the scope and domain of power, as well as the norms and values within which interaction takes place. Once circumscribed, power can be defined as a causal antecedent to an outcome. Baldwin follows Lasswell and Kaplan to the extent that a power base 'refers to the causal conditions that gives influence its effectiveness. Thus, by definition, ineffective influence attempts cannot employ "influence bases"' (Baldwin 1985: 23). Keohane, by keeping contextual analysis to a fairly general level, can make probabilistic predictions on behavioural outputs, but not outcomes, leaving power as a secondary variable. Baldwin's attempt to keep power a central causal determinant forces him to include all the necessary information into a contextual analysis, thereby making predictions on the basis of power impossible.

Besides the relational concept of power, the lack of fungibility, and the potential need to have a very elaborate contextual analysis prior to the assessment of power, it is the unavoidably counterfactual character of power which makes Baldwin's approach of power both causal and yet little generalisable. Counterfactuals are no easy matter in empirical sciences. Since power relations involve getting somebody else to do what he or she would not have done otherwise, one can assess power *ex ante* on the basis of what this foregone action would have been. With that move, power analysis stops being a central element of building middle-range theories, but instead appends itself to an action theory to be meaningful (this applies also to Keohane). A good example can be found in Baldwin's (1985: 154) discussion of economic sanctions in the Peloponnesian War. The sanctions failed to deter war. To assess the importance of economic sanctions, one needs, however, to know what would have happened in the case they had not been applied. More precisely, one needs to know whether war was inevitable or not. For realists, war would have been inevitable because the rise of Athenian power had been provoked by the necessity of Sparta's balancing behaviour. Economic sanctions could not have worked. The scholarly assessment of the role of economic sanctions is then dependent on a more general action theory which defines the (*ex ante*) counterfactual expectations against which influence attempts can be judged.

Consequently, Baldwin's approach with its much greater sensitivity to personal and historical idiosyncrasies has little generalising capacity, despite its clear causal character. Indeed, as Keohane warily noted about Baldwin's approach, if 'we defined each issue as existing within a unique "policy-contingency framework", no generalisations would be possible' (Keohane 1986: 187).[4] Baldwin himself faces this problem of prediction in his analysis, when he writes that counterfactual 'discussion may amount to little more than "educated guesses", but this is preferable to ignoring the problem' (Baldwin 1985: 22). What is left is no longer an economistic, but a historical institutionalist approach (see also Leander, Chapter 12 in this volume).

## Rule in IPE: structural power and governance

With the link between resources and control weakened, the second link between the distribution of control over outcome as indicators of international rule might not be worthwhile studying at all. And yet, this is where IPE has made its most important contribution to power analysis. In fact, concepts of structural power redefine the context within which strategic interaction takes place, the resources considered important for assessing capabilities in the first place, and the outcomes that should be included in power analysis. Their common claim is that the sole reference to the first link, as done by neoinstitutionalists, is insufficient, if not biased, for understanding rule in the international system.

But opening up power analysis to political economy comes at a price. Some approaches indulge in some vain hope that by simply retuning the concept of power in a more structuralist way, one could safeguard its central causal explanatory power. And all of them tend to neglect the less materialist part of rule, that part which is now the focus of much constructivist/post-structuralist literature.

### Structural power as indirect institutional power

Shortly after the publication of *Power and Interdependence*, James Caporaso (1978) tried to clarify the difference between a behavioural and structural understanding of power. His critique parallels Bacharach and Baratz's (1970) famous critique of Dahl's power analysis. Caporaso (1978: 4) criticises behavioural approaches of power, on the ground that they neglect 'the ability to manipulate the choices, capabilities, alliance opportunities and pay-offs that actors may utilise'. Here, structural power refers to the conscious manipulation of the institutional setting within which bargaining relations take place. Many important issues are decided before they reach the bargaining stage, indeed, often because they never reach it – hence, Bacharach and Baratz's reference to non-decision-making.

Clearly, intentional agenda setting is an important facet of power analysis. Despite opposite claims, however, it is compatible with behaviouralist approaches. It is still intentional action aimed at changing the context within which strategic interaction takes place. Therefore, it is probably better to express the difference in terms of structural versus relational power, as two facets of the same action theory. In the same year as *Power and Interdependence*, Cheryl Christensen (1977) had already proposed a structural power concept which would take into account the (power) effects of the situational setting within which interaction occurs. Similarly, Susan Strange (1985: 15) distinguishes between relational and structural power, and Joseph Nye (1990: 166–168) between 'command' power and 'soft' or 'co-optive' power.

Consequently, regime theory can coherently integrate this facet of power. Stephen Krasner (1985: 14) distinguishes between relational power and meta-power. The first refers to the 'ability to change outcomes or affect the behaviour of others within a given regime. Meta-power refers to the ability to change the rules of the game'. In fact, what this does is to stress the importance of the feedback effect that action can have on regimes which define the background for rational calculus, a link already present in Keohane's approach (see Figure 4.1).

### Structural power as non-intentional power

A more original contribution of structural power concepts in IPE has been the stress on non-intentional power. The late Susan Strange (1988) suggested that we should think of power backwards from its effects, and not in terms of intended outcomes. Her concept of structural power stresses both the diffusion of the origins of power (and the variety of power resources), and the diffusion of its effects (for a more thorough analysis of Strange's approach, see Guzzini 1998: 176–183). For her, power no longer lies mainly with states or with military capabilities, but with the international control of credit and knowledge, for instance. Similarly, there is no reason to exclude all those crucial effects that might not have been intended from power analysis. Whether interest rate policies of the German Bundesbank were intended to destabilise the European Monetary System is less significant than the fact that only a few players could have affected such an outcome. As an old Chinese saying has it, it makes little difference to the trampled grass beneath whether the elephants above it make love or war.

This analytical shift from intentions to effects diminishes the importance of the neoinstitutionalist approach for understanding power, based on resources, interests and rationality. It focuses on systematic, not on chosen features of power. As I have shown elsewhere (Guzzini 1993: 456–461), such an approach is compatible with an individualist approach, yet not with a behaviouralist one. Economic approaches can include unintended consequences (Elster 1989), but they cannot include them into their concept of power. Should they? This depends on whether the implications of keeping non-intentional power out of power analysis are considered significant. At stake is that such unintended effects are then considered purely incidental and hence irrelevant for the assessment of power (Knorr 1973: 77–78).

We have reached here the heart of a political debate. Power is a concept which has a variety of purposes (Morriss 1987: 37–42). To mention two: power is used in practical contexts in which we are interested in what we can do to others and what others can do to us. It is also important in moral/legal contexts where it functions as an indicator of effective responsibility: if actors could not have done an act (if they had not the capacity to do so), they cannot be found guilty for it. The first indicates the realm of action, power becoming an indicator of politics as the art of the possible. The second assesses possible blame. By limiting the practical context to only those actions with which we intend to affect others, we rule out any moral judgments on those actions that affect others, whether intended or not. Leaving out non-intentional power mobilises a status quo research bias and blinds us for the tacit power of the strong. Hence, it seems that those scholars interested in international rule were right to stress power as the production of unintended effects. As Baldwin (1989: 205) noted, without much developing it himself, 'concepts of power that allow for the possibility of unintended influence may be more useful for the student of dependency and autonomy than other power concepts'.

### Structural power as systematic bias

Caporaso's concept of structural power repeats the ambiguities of Bacharach and Baratz's non-decision-making approach, an ambiguity which has largely passed unnoticed (for an exception, see Debnam 1984: 24). On the one hand,

Bacharach and Baratz talked about (intentional) agenda control. On the other hand, Caporaso (1978: 33) referred to the impersonal 'mobilisation of bias' when he mentioned the 'social structuring of agendas that might systematically favour certain parties'. Such an understanding of power was common currency in dependency writings, both Marxist and non-Marxist (for the latter, see, in particular Galtung 1971). They are still used in IPE in the Gramscian School (Gill and Law 1988, 1989) whose concept of structural power refers 'to material and normative aspects, such that patterns of incentives and constraints are systematically created' (Gill and Law 1988: 73).

Such a conceptualisation can be criticised on two accounts. First, it conflates power with benefits. Here, I would argue that although it is important that systematic bias be part of any *power analysis*, thus contradicting behaviouralist approaches, it should not be collapsed into the *concept of power*. Second, I will argue that a Gramscian theoretical underpinning is too limited to account for forms of impersonal and consensual power.

Structural power as systematic bias has been criticised for deducing power from rewards, the so-called benefit fallacy of power (Barry 1988 [1987]: 315). Nelson Polsby (1980: 208) explicitly mentioned the case of the free-rider who certainly profits from a certain systemic arrangement, but who basically remains at its mercy. One would not necessarily ascribe power to free-riders.

But the benefit fallacy exists only within a causal framework itself. To say that a system benefits certain people does not mean that they caused that benefit or that they control it.

> All one need do is note that a status quo that systematically benefits certain people (as Polsby agrees it does) is relevant in itself ... Yet if the social system performs in such a way as systematically to advantage some individuals or groups, it certainly seems odd not to take account of this.
>
> (Morriss, 1987: 106, 105)

In other words, in terms of the second link between rule and outcome, systematic benefits are relevant.

And here it is very important, within which framework of analysis such systematic interest-furthering is conceived. Rational choice approaches can, of course, account for the privileges and advantages that stem from the social position of actors, but for which they did nothing. They can do so, but then only as 'systematic luck' (Dowding 1991: 137). As a consequence, we have no choice but to live with this fateful polity. Power, understood as an indicator of the art of the possible, is ruled out. By reducing a systematic bias to a question of luck, this approach leaves out of the picture the daily practices of agents that help to reproduce the very system and positions from which these advantages were derived. For this reason perhaps, Dowding (1996: 94 and ff.) rephrases his approach and now explicitly includes systematic luck into power analysis which he very correctly then links to normative debates.

If, on the other hand, we grant that such systematic benefits should be part of a power analysis, it is preferable not to include them in the very concept of power. Instead, I referred to it within the context of the concept of rule (or governance), not power. Elsewhere, I have argued that doing otherwise produces an overload of the concept of power (Guzzini 1993: 468–474), as if adding the word power to structure would suffice to have a structural causal determinacy.

The second ground on which this concept of structural power shows weaknesses, is the theoretical underpinning of consensual rule in Gramsci's concept of hegemony. By presenting their approach, Gill and Law explicitly refer to Steven Lukes' (1974) critique of Dahl. In distinguishing three dimensions of power, Lukes had criticised the overly empiricist approach in Dahl which rules out from power analysis many, although not all, situations in which the behaviour of an actor was influenced without any visible bargaining or conflict. The one exception which can be included into behaviouralist analysis is the 'law of anticipated reactions' in which actors, anticipating reward or punishment, adapt their action accordingly. It thus includes consent in the sense of an obliged behaviour against the original intention of one actor. This exception is still permissible in this framework of analysis because it keeps the causal link between intentions, here imputed, and influenced behaviour. Lukes' third dimension of power, however, stresses those situations in which consent results not from any obligation or threat, but from the internalisation of values and ideas. Whereas in the law of anticipated reactions, consent follows an adaptation process, here nothing of that sort is necessary.

Lukes mentions Gramsci as one inspiration for the third dimension. Gramsci's concept of hegemony refers indeed to the role of ideology in preempting collective action against existing rule. This ideology is considered self-evident and hence is naturalised for the collectivity. Yet, the basis of this ideology is to be found in the realm of production. And here it seems increasingly difficult to define a strict relationship between the sphere of production, particular social classes, and ideologies (for the best application of this approach, see Rupert 1995a). Similarly, the reproduction of structures is not as mechanistic as presupposed in neo-Marxist writings, but can be conceptualised as rituals of power. In other words, although one does not need to leave a materialist context entirely, the more hermeneutical scholars might rely on neo-Weberian approaches such as Bourdieu's field theory (1980, 1982). This theory employs a less materialist background for the establishment (and analytical definition) of social groups whose power is derived from forms of economic, social, and cultural capital (for applications of Bourdieu's power approach to IR, see Ashley 1989 and Guzzini 1994 and 2000).

A final reason to reassess the materialist bias of structural power approaches in IPE is their tendency to objectify or naturalise structures. In this regard they face a similar criticism as levelled against the macro-level of regime analysis. By presupposing intersubjective units of analysis (rules, norms, symbols), these approaches need also an intersubjective ontology (Kratochwil and Ruggie 1986). Whereas neorealism is eventually too individualist for this, structuralist approaches tend to objectify structure. Theories assuming intersubjective units then open up for a social constructivist understanding of power.

Such a constructivist understanding is already implicit in Bull and explicit in Baldwin. When Bull defended the lump concept of power, he said that it is one we cannot do without. In classical diplomacy, with its balancing and band-wagoning, its arbitrations and compensations, diplomats must find a common understanding of overall power. In other words, diplomats must first agree on what counts before they can start counting. Similarly, Baldwin writes that barter exchange is a better approximation for power relations than money. This points to the essential role of trust and, in particular, of social conventions in translating the value between different goods. In this regard, money is not basically different from power: its fungibility is an effect of social conventions, not of some inherent or objective criteria (Baldwin 1989: 26–27; Guzzini 1994: 54–56; Kratochwil 1996: 212; Hall 1997: 593; Guzzini 1998: 231–234).[5]

## Conclusion

This chapter has argued that recent approaches in IPE have challenged the presumed double link in power analysis, that is, between control over resources and control over outcomes, and between control over outcomes and rule/gover-nance. It has argued that the power concept that undergirds balance of power theories is analytically useless. Moreover, it has shown that institutionalist attempts to remedy this problem run into a dilemma: they either maintain a probabilistic predictive framework, but reduce the importance of power therein, or they maintain a strong causal role for power, yet at the price of stripping power analysis of its predictive capacities. Finally, concepts of structural power, mainly developed within IPE, have shown a different understanding of the second link between outcomes and international rule, stressing non-intentional power and the systematic bias of the international system. As such, both links have been thoroughly rethought within IR and IPE.

Unfortunately, this does not mean that the use of power in international anal-ysis has become more precise. Power is still a short cut for understanding international affairs, its undiscussed ubiquity an indicator of intellectual laziness. In other words, power has been a short-circuit for leaving things unexplained despite opposite appearance (Guzzini 1993: 478). Taking the recent power debate seriously could avoid power arguments still being used as apparently sensible answers whose only certainty is to kill theoretical reflection and sensible empirical research.

## Notes

1  For helpful comments on an earlier draft, I am grateful to David Baldwin, Anna Leander, Micheal Merlingen and Ronen Palan.
2  The relationship between power and security is not clear in Waltz (see also Grieco 1997: 186–91). He explicitly stresses that states maximise security, not power. At the same time, neorealists assume states to be rank maximisers or relative gain seekers, hence my formulation. Important for my argument, and consistent with realism, is

that such gain be measured on a common scale (the final rank), which is established with reference to power.

3   Rational choice can predict behaviour under the condition that we do firmly assume egoism as underpinning the maximisation of utility. True, the rationality assumption is perfectly compatible with altruism (Keohane 1984: 74). Leaving this assumption open, however, implies that the very same approach is compatible with any outcome to be explained: only *ex post* it can describe why an actor decided this way – or the other. Consequently, removing the assumption of egoism turns the rational choice approach into a mere taxonomy and robs it of its predictive power (see also Schmalz-Bruns 1995: 354).

4   Baldwin (1989: 137) responds to this charge by arguing that this is not necessarily so. But neither is it to be excluded: the extent of necessary situational analysis is itself an empirical question.

5   This does not mean that fungibility equally applies in economics and IR. The original argument, now correctly phrased in sociological terms, still holds: in real world politics, the social conventions of power translations are much more politically contested than the naturalised use of money in functioning market economies. Fungibility is hence still different in these two spheres and Aron's critique still applies.

# 5  Capital accumulation

## Breaking the dualism of 'economics' and 'politics'

*Jonathan Nitzan and Shimshon Bichler*

Political economy attempts to tie together the quest for power with the pursuit of plenty. But things which need to be linked are assumed separate to begin with, and indeed, the distinction between power and well-being is a fundamental tenet of modern social thinking. The origin of this duality goes back to the emergence of industrial capitalism during the latter half of the eighteenth century. Classical political economists, siding with the rising bourgeoisie against the *ancien régime*, promoted a novel idea: the 'free market'. Their purpose was to separate civil society from the institutions of family, community and state in which it was previously embedded (Polanyi 1944). According to Adam Smith, free markets operated as an 'invisible hand', a mechanism which he claimed automatically allocated resources to their most efficient use. But in order to be effective, the invisible hand had to be left alone. The call for *laissez-faire* was therefore a call for the *depoliticization* of production and well-being.

And so from Smith onward, it became increasingly customary to separate human actions into two distinct spheres, 'vertical' and 'horizontal'. The vertical dimension revolves around power, authority, command, manipulation and dissonance. Academically, it belongs to the realm of politics. The horizontal axis centres around well-being, free choice, exchange and equilibrium – the academic preoccupation of economists. The consequence of this duality was to make modern political economy an impossible patchwork: its practitioners try to re-marry power and well-being, but having accepted them as distinct spheres of activity to begin with, the marriage is inherently shaky.

A principal casualty of this separation is the theory of capital. Academic departmentalization placed it firmly in the hands of economists, leaving political scientists, sociologists and anthropologists with practically no say. The result was emphasis on material considerations and all but complete neglect of power. This did not clear the water, though, for despite having monopolized the concept of capital, economists were still unable to decide what it meant. While all agreed that capital was monetary wealth, figuring out what made it grow proved much harder. In general, economists tried to make the accumulation of monetary wealth a consequence of production, but as the latter grew in complexity the link became difficult to pin down. Moreover, having dispensed with the study of power to begin with, economists were unable to use it as a possible solution for their riddle. There were exceptions, of course, the most noted of which was Karl Marx. As a political economist, Marx tried from the very outset to integrate, not separate power and production. Yet for all its insight, his synthesis remained vulnerable. He insisted on building the concept of capital squarely on the productive labour process, which in turn meant that the broader institutions of power, however prominent in his historical narratives, remained secondary in his *analytical* abstractions.

Although there is an undeniable connection between capital and production, the link is neither simple, nor sufficient as a basis for a theory of capital. Some Marxists, particularly those associated with the social structures of accumulation and regulation schools, have attempted to augment the material concept of capital with cultural and political 'variables' (for instance, Aglietta 1979, Kotz *et al.* 1994, and Dunford, Chapter 10 in this volume). This, though, does not get to the root of the problem. The solution is not to 'add' power, but to integrate it into the very definition of capital. Capital must be understood as incorporating both power and productivity.

Such broader definition could prove important for international political economy. Specifically, it can help us re-interpret state and capital not as separate entities standing against each other, but rather as partly overlapping institutions with intimately intertwined histories. From this perspective, the gradual ascent of global capitalism reflects the changing relationship – both contradictory and reinforcing – between state power anchored in sovereignty and capitalist power rooted in ownership.

This chapter paints the background for such a proposal, outlining the main problems of capital theory, key issues which need to be resolved, and the way in which an alternative concept of capital may affect the future evolution of IPE. Briefly, existing theories of capital can be classified into three groups, based on their relationship to production. The neoclassical paradigm makes output a function of *factor inputs* (the amount of the different factors of production – labour, raw materials and capital goods – used to produce that output). Capital, perceived as one of these factors, is counted in its own technical units. Marxists view production as a socio-material transformation in which capital changes its skin from money, to commodities, to more money. The engine of this transformation is the *labour* process, in which living labour power is converted into 'dead labour' embedded in commodities. Capital, growing directly from this process, is measured in labour time. For the institutionalists, production is a complex *societal* process, whose qualitative intricacies cannot be easily deciphered, let alone quantified. In this latter framework, capital is neither a productive input nor a material output, but rather a symbolic pecuniary crystallization of the power controlling the process. Seen in that way, capital can be measured only in differential terms, relative to other capitals. Conceptually, neoclassical and Marxist theories are built from the bottom up, deriving accumulation from the underlying process of production. The institutionalist view, on the other hand, is constructed from the top down, with production subjugated to accumulation. The troubled history of capital theory suggests that bottom-up explanations are logically vulnerable if not impossible. The top-down view, although largely unexplored, is unlikely to face the same problems. Indeed, by focusing directly on power and on the way it shapes societal reproduction, this route not only bypasses the intractable 'input–output structure' of industry, but also offers a way of integrating politics into our very conceptualization of capital.

## The material basis of capital

Despite their pivotal significance, the definition of capital and the meaning of accumulation have remained unsettled (Schumpeter 1954: 322–327, 625–645; Braudel 1982: 232–249). Historically, the principal contention stemmed from trying to marry two different perceptions of capital: one as an income generating fund, or 'financial wealth', the other as a stock of physical instruments, or 'capital goods' (Pasinetti and Scazzieri 1987). The central question has been whether and in what way 'capital goods' are productive, and how their productivity affects their overall magnitude as 'capital' (Hennings 1987). Mainstream economics has generally tried to show that capital goods were indeed productive, and that this 'positive' attribute is what made capital as a 'fund' valuable.

The marriage did not work well, partly due to a large age difference: the concept of 'capital' predates that of 'capital goods' by a few thousand years, suggesting their overlap is not that self-evident. The older partner, capital, comes from the Latin *caput*, a word whose origin goes back to the Fertile Crescent. In both Rome and Mesopotamia capital had a similar, unambiguous economic meaning: it was a monetary magnitude. There was no relation to produced 'means of production'. Indeed, *caput* meant 'head', which fits well with another Babylonian invention, the human 'work day' (Bickerman 1972: 58, 63; Schumpeter 1954: 322–323).

The younger partner, 'capital goods', was born millennia later, roughly together with capitalism. The growing significance of mechanized instruments captured the attention of pre-classical writers, but initially they referred to these mostly as 'stocks' (Barbon 1690; Hume 1752). The Physiocrats were the first to give 'capital' a productive role, and it was only with Quesnay and Turgot during the latter half of the eighteenth century, that the association between 'capitals' (as monetary advances) and mechanized production started to take shape (Hennings 1987).

Attempts to link capital and capital goods began in earnest with the classical writers, and from Adam Smith onward the productive attributes of capital have finally assumed centre-stage. The classical economists did not have a complete theory of capital, however. They tended to treat the amalgamate of 'capital goods' as a 'fund' or 'advance', whose principal role was to 'assist' the original factors of production – labour and land. Although the general view was that capital goods were valuable due to their productivity, no attempt was made to quantify their 'amount'. The link between capital goods and capital was therefore left unspecified. In hindsight, the principal obstacle was that the classicists still viewed capital goods as a 'secondary' input, and in that sense *qualitatively* different from the original 'primary' inputs. This proved no more than a temporary roadblock, however.

Taking the classical lead but without its associated inhibitions, the neoclassicists followed Lauderdale (1804), making capital goods a fully 'independent' factor of production, on a par with labour and land. Their view of capital, articulated since the latter part of the nineteenth century by writers such as Wicksteed, Marshall, Menger and primarily Clark, emphasised the *distinct* productivity of capital goods, elevating them from mere accessories to requisites. In his book *The Distribution of Wealth* (1899), Clark used this newly-found symmetry among the factors of production to offer an alternative theory of distribution. The theory stipulated a direct mathematical link between income and production, based on two principal assertions. One was that output was a function of quantifiable 'factors of production', each with its own distinct productive contribution. This assumed that labour, land and capital were observable and measurable (so for instance, we can see that production uses 20, 10 and 15 units of each factor, respectively); that the way these factors interacted with one another in production was similarly straightforward (so we know exactly what factors enter the production process and how they affect all others factors); and that we can associate definite portions of the output with each of the factors (for instance, labour contributed 40 per cent, land 15 and capital goods 45). The second assertion was that the income of these factors was proportionate to their contributions, and more precisely, to their marginal contributions (so that the wage rate is equal to the productive contribution of the last worker added to production, the rent is equal to the contribution of the last hector of land, and the profit rate is equivalent to the contribution of the last unit of capital).

Formulated at a critical historical junction, the new theory provided a powerful justification as well as explanation. The need for such a theory became apparent during the latter part of the nineteenth century, when the emergence of US 'big business' accelerated the centralization of capital, raised profit margins and heightened income inequality, much along the lines anticipated by Karl Marx. These new circumstances made earlier profit theories – for instance those based on 'abstinence' (Senior 1872), or on 'waiting' (Marshall 1920, first published in 1890) – look hopelessly irrelevant. According to these earlier theories, capitalists who invested their money were abstaining from current consumption, and therefore had to be remunerated for the time they waited until their investment matured. Yet by the end of the nineteenth century, the huge incomes of corporate magnates such as Rockefeller or Morgan enabled them to consume conspicuously regardless of how much they invested. Moreover, when these magnates chose to be frugal, the reason was usually power, not delayed consumption. Clearly, there was a pressing need for a more robust ideology, and this is where Clark's theory of marginal productivity came into the picture.

Contrary to the Marxist claim, Clark insisted that capital was not in the least parasitic: much like labour, it too received its own marginal productivity, an income which was therefore essential for the growth process. The marginal productivity theory enabled neoclassicists to finally remove their classical shackles. The classicists, whether radical or liberal, were interested primarily in well-being and distribution. Production was merely a means toward those higher ends. Clark helped reverse this order, making distribution a corollary of production. And indeed, since the turn of the century, attention gradually shifted from the causes of income inequality to its ramifications, a subject economists felt could be safely delegated to sociologists and political scientists. With so much going for it, the marginal productivity theory was rapidly endorsed by professional economists and, of course, by their 'captains of finance'. Rockefeller, who donated $45 million to the University of Chicago where Clark taught, later stated 'it was the best investment I ever made' (Collier and Horowitz 1976: 50).

## Some very unsettling questions

Clark's logical foundations, though, were hardly solid. One central problem, identified already by Wicksell (1935: 149), was the 'quantity' of capital. In the real world, capital was usually associated with numerous capital goods. Unlike labour and land, however, these were *heterogeneous*, and therefore could not be aggregated in terms of their own 'natural' units.[1] The only way to 'add' a machine producing aircraft parts to one making shoes, to another making biscuits, is by summing their values measured in *money*. The money value of any capital good – that is, the amount investors are willing to pay for it – is the present value of its expected future profit (computed by discounting this profit by the prevailing rate of interest, so *Value = Expected profit / Rate of interest*). Now, as long as our purpose is merely to measure the money value of capital, this method is hardly problematic, and is indeed used regularly by investors around the world. The difficulty begins when we interpret such value as equivalent to the 'physical' quantity of capital. To see why, suppose that the rate of interest is 5 per cent, and that a given machine is expected to yield $1 million in profit year after year. Based on the principle of present value, the machine should be worth $20 million (= $1 million / 0.05). But what if expected profit were to go up to $1.2 million? The present value should rise to $24 million (= $1.2 million / 0.05), but that would imply that the very same machine can have more than one quantity! Clark's productivity theory of distribution was therefore based on a *circular* notion of capital: the magnitude of profit was explained by the marginal productivity of a given quantity of capital, but that quantity was itself a function of profit, which the theory was supposed to explain in the first place! Another, perhaps more substantive 'social' challenge to the concept of physical capital came from Veblen, to which we turn later. Yet, for almost half a century Clark's theory remained resilient, and it was only during the 1950s that the early criticism against it began to echo.

The first shots were fired by Robinson (1953–4) and Champernowne (1953–4), followed by the publication of Sraffa's seminal work *The Production of Commodities by Means of Commodities* (1960). Sraffa showed unequivocally that the 'quantity of capital' was a fiction, and that productive contributions could not be measured without prior knowledge of prices and distribution (which the theory was supposed to explain). Now, because capital goods were heterogeneous, neoclassicists were never able to *directly* aggregate them into capital. This aggregate could none the less be 'quantified', they argued, if only indirectly, by looking at the rate of interest. The logic was simple: the higher the rate of interest, the more expensive capital becomes relative to labour, and hence the less of it will be employed relative to labour. According to this view, the 'capital intensity' of any productive process, defined as the ratio between the quantity of capital and the quantity of labour, should be negatively related to the rate of interest: the higher the rate of interest, the lower the intensity of capital. Of course, the relationship must be *unique*, with each 'capital intensity' associated with one and only one rate of interest. Otherwise, we end with the same capital having more than one 'quantity'. But then that is exactly what Sraffa found ...

His famous 'reswitching' examples demonstrated that, contrary to neoclassical theory, 'capital intensity' need not have a one-to-one relationship with the rate of interest. For instance, consider an economy with two technologies: process $X$ which is capital intensive and process $Y$ which is labour intensive (i.e., less capital intensive). A rise in the rate of interest makes capital expensive relative to labour, and according to neoclassical theory should cause capitalists to shift production from $X$ to $Y$. As Sraffa showed, however, if the rate of interest goes on rising, it is entirely possible – indeed most likely – that process $Y$ will once again become the more costly, causing capitalists to 'reswitch' back to $X$. This creates a logical contradiction, since if we accept the rate of interest as a proxy for capital intensity, $X$ appears to be both capital intensive (at a low rate of interest) and labour intensive (at a high rate of interest). In other words, the same assortment of capital goods represents *different* 'quantities' of capital .... The result of Sraffa's work was not only to leave profit in search of explanation, but also to rob capital goods, the basis of so much theorizing, of any fixed magnitude.

These writings marked the beginning of the famous 'Cambridge Controversy', a heated debate between Cambridge, England, where Robinson and Sraffa taught, and Cambridge, Massachusetts in the USA, the home of many neoclassical economists (the controversy is summarized in Harcourt 1969, 1972). Eventually, the neoclassicists, led by towering figures such as Nobel Laureate Paul Samuelson, conceded there was a problem, offering to treat Clark's neoclassical definition of capital not literally, but as a 'parable' (Samuelson 1962). A few years later, Ferguson, another leading neoclassicist, admitted that because neoclassical theory depended on 'the "thing" called capital' (1969: 251), accepting that theory in light of the Cambridge Controversy was therefore a 'matter of faith' (1969: xvii–xviii).

Yet faith was hardly enough. The fact that capital did not have a fixed 'physical' quantity set off a logical chain reaction with devastating consequences for neoclassical theory. It began by destroying the notion of a production function which, as noted above, required that all inputs, including capital, have measurable quantities. This in turn nullified the neoclassical supply function, which was built on the basis of such production function. And with the supply function gone, the notion of equilibrium – the intersection between supply and demand –

was similarly made irrelevant. The implication was nothing short of dramatic, for without equilibrium, neoclassical economics failed its two basic tasks of explaining prices and quantities.

Clearly, this was no laughing matter. For neoclassical theory to hold, the belief that capital was a *material* thing, a well-defined physical quantity with its own intrinsic productivity, had to be retained at all cost. The first and most common solution was to gloss the problem over, or ignore it altogether, and as Robinson (1971) predicted and Hodgson (1997) confirmed, so far this seems to be working. Indeed, most economics textbooks (including Samuelson's!) continue to 'measure' capital as if the Cambridge Controversy never happened. A more subtle method was to argue that the problem of quantifying capital, however serious in principle, was of limited importance in practice (Ferguson 1969). Given the abstract nature of neoclassical theory, though, resting its defence on relevance is hardly persuasive. The third and probably most significant response was to embrace disaggregate general equilibrium models. These latter models try to describe – analytically, that is – every aspect of the economic system, down to the smallest detail. The production function in such models separately specifies each individual input, so the need to aggregate capital goods into capital does not arise in the first place. General equilibrium models have serious theoretical and empirical weaknesses.[2] Their most important problem, though, comes not from what they try to explain, but from what they ignore, and that is *capital*. While the 'shell' called capital may or may not consist of individual physical inputs, its existence and social significance are hardly in doubt. By ignoring this pivotal concept, general equilibrium turns itself into a hollow formality.[3]

Of course, ignoring problems does not solve them. This is evident most vividly in empirical neoclassical studies, where production functions are used to explain changes in output. The results of such studies are usually highly disappointing, in that only part of the output – and often only a small part – is explained by the 'observed' inputs, leaving a sizeable 'residual' hanging in the air. As we elaborate later in this chapter, one possible reason for this failure is that production is a holistic process, and hence cannot be made a 'function' of individual inputs in the first place. Neoclassical economists reject this possibility. Instead, they prefer to circumvent the problem by separating inputs into two categories – those which can be observed, namely labour, land and capital, and those which cannot, lumped together as technology. This by-pass, suggested by Marshall (1920) and popularized by Galbraith (1958, 1967), enables mainstream economists to argue that the output 'residual' of empirical production functions is not a theoretical embarrassment, but simply a 'measure of our ignorance'. The problem, they say, is that we do not know how to 'measure' technology. Had we known, and had we incorporated the 'quantity' of technology into the production function, the 'residual' would have most surely disappeared. Unfortunately, this argument is only too convenient in that it can never be verified! Theories that claim to explain reality should be tested on how well they do so – the smaller their 'error' the more convincing the theory. Here, however, the problem is not the theory but the facts, so the error does not matter ...[4]

Neoclassical theory remains an edifice built on foundations of sand. The most questionable of these foundations is the notion that capital is a measurable entity, denominated in some 'physical' units and possessing its own intrinsic productivity. In fact, capital fulfils none of these requirements. The result is that the theory is unable to convincingly explain not only the structure of prices and production, but also the distribution of income which supposedly results from such structure.

## The Marxist entanglement

Throughout *Das Kapital* there is no 'analytical' definition of capital, perhaps for a good reason. In contrast to classical theory, Marx saw capital not as a 'thing', but as a comprehensive social relation whose description was intertwined with its explanation. The context of capital included the production process, the division of labour, technological progress and, above all, the institutional and power arrangements shaping the collective consciousness. According to Wright (1977: 198), the notion that capital accumulation involves merely the tangible augmentation of machinery, buildings, raw materials and alike is alien to Marxist thinking. Instead, he maintains, 'capital accumulation must be understood as the reproduction of capitalist social relations on an ever-expanding scale through the conversion of surplus value into new constant and variable capital'. Emphasising this aspect of Marx's writing, Shaikh (1990: 73) similarly reiterates that 'capital is not a thing, but rather a definite set of social relations', and that in order to understand it, 'one must therefore decipher its character as a social relation'.

Marx started with three fundamental principles. The first was that human history was driven largely by a struggle over economic surplus. The second was that production and redistribution were inseparable: surplus presupposed a class society, whereas classes meant a struggle over how this surplus was created and who was going to get it. The third principle was that, regardless of its particular form, surplus was always generated through the labour process. The analysis of every class society therefore had to begin with the underlying process of production. This latter conviction created the infamous 'materialistic' bias underlying Marx's theory of accumulation.

The consequence of this bias was over-preoccupation with contents, less attention to form. The content of capitalism is the technological fusion of workers and instruments through an ever expanding process of production and consumption. The form of capitalism is capitalist control, that is, the manipulation of human beings via the abstract accumulation of ownership titles. Marx repeatedly emphasized the interdependence of the two; he nevertheless failed to integrate this interdependence into his *analytical* framework of accumulation. When it came to describing accumulation in *abstract* terms, his attention was focused almost solely on production, leaving the dynamics of power practically ignored. The result was that although Marx saw accumulation as an antagonistic social process, in the end his analysis got entangled in the same 'materialistic' trap confounding the neoclassicists.

The main difficulty, known as the 'Transformation Problem', arose in converting production values (conceptualized in labour time) into market prices (measured in dollars and cents). The conversion proceeded in two steps: one from labour values to production prices (which would prevail under hypothetical conditions of competition), and the other from production prices to market prices (as observed in our 'imperfect' reality). Both steps were mired in controversy. In the first stage, Marx's value equation required the equalization of three ratios across the economy: the rate of profit (ratio of surplus value to the sum of constant and variable capital), the rate of exploitation (ratio of surplus value to variable capital) and the organic composition of capital (ratio of constant to variable capital). Competitive forces were thought to equalize the first two, but there was no comparable force to equalize the third.[5] The logical result was production prices which generally deviated (albeit predictably) from labour values. Starting from Marx himself, the history of Marxian economics is marked by attempts to resolve this problem while retaining the 'materialistic' assumption which created it in the first place. The inevitable consequence was to blur the meaning of accumulation, which in turn placed the entire labour theory of value in doubt.

Until the 1950s, discussion of the Transformation Problem was largely confined to Marxist circles. But then external attacks began to mount. In 1957, Samuelson showed that, mathematically at least, the Transformation Problem was simply a 'complicating detour'. Marx stipulated a two-stage analytical process, moving from the conditions of production, to values, to prices of productions. In fact, argued Samuelson, the process required only one step, without any intermediate resort to values. 'Marxolaters, to use Shaw's term,' he suggested triumphantly, 'should heed the basic economic precept, valid in all societies, cut your losses' and dump the labour theory of value (1957: 891–892, cited in Howard and King 1992: 242).

And then came Sraffa's *Production of Commodities by Means of Commodities*. As noted earlier, the immediate casualty was neoclassical capital theory, but that was just the beginning. Based on Sraffa's framework, it became apparent that Marxist theory too was vulnerable to inherent contradictions, going far beyond Samuelson's redundancies. As Steedman (1975, 1977) and others have shown, the value-price transformation was not only a complicating detour, but generally an *impossible* detour. Once the analysis moves from elementary to joint production processes – that is, to processes in which multiple inputs jointly produce multiple outputs – labour contents could be indeterminate, nil, even negative! Needless to say, numerous attempts were made to resolve these inconsistencies, but such solutions came at the cost of complicated formulas and restricting assumptions, further undermining the theory's overall appeal.

In our view, the Marxist entanglement and neoclassical débâcle share the same root, in that they both try to measure accumulation *solely* on the basis of production. Marx (1867: 114) insightfully made the magnitude of value an expression of the 'portion of the total labour-time of society required to produce it'. His troubles began when, in line with the classical political economists before him, he too tried to build this total *from the bottom up* – that is, on the basis of individual labour inputs. In this, Marx not only assumed that production contained the code of distribution and accumulation (which the post-Sraffa controversy put into question), but also that the production processes, including that of 'labour power', could be *objectively* identified in functional, quantitative terms. As it turned out, this was impossible not only in practice, but also in principle.

Interestingly, Marx was remarkably prophetic in anticipating the demise of his own labour theory of value, and for this very reason. His insight is worth quoting at some length:

> As large-scale industry advances, the creation of real wealth depends less on the labour time and quantity of labour expended than on the power of the instrumentalities set in motion during the labour time .... Human labour then no longer appears enclosed in the process of production – man rather relates himself to the process of production as supervisor and regulator .... He stands outside of the process of production instead of being the prin- cipal agent in the process of production. In this transformation, the great pillar of production and wealth is no longer the immediate labour performed by man himself, nor his labour time, but the appropriation of his own universal productivity, i.e., *his knowledge and his mastery of nature through his societal existence* – in one word, the development of the *societal individual* .... As soon as human labour, in its immediate form, has ceased to be the great source of wealth, labour time will cease, and must of necessity cease to be the measure of wealth, and the exchange value must of necessity cease to be the measure of use value .... The mode of production which rests on the exchange value thus collapses.
>
> (*Grundrisse der Kritik der politischen Ökonomie*: 592f., trans. from the German by
> Marcuse 1964: 35–6, emphases added)

This intriguing idea is typical of Marx's search for inherent contradictions: the very development of the forces of production was set to undermine capitalism. In a complex socio-technological setting, he argued, the direct relationship between labour inputs and final prices was bound to break down. When that happens, price setting becomes increasingly arbitrary, capitalists lose their moral conviction, and with their sense of hegemony seriously undermined, their system can no longer be sustained. Marx was of course proven wrong in believing that the demise of his own theory would bring capitalism down. Perhaps, contrary to his conviction, labour values were not a pre-requisite for a functioning capitalism in the first place. His insight into the societal nature of production, however, and into the insurmount- able problems this created for political economy, was prescient.

The difficulty is simple: if production cannot be mapped from the bottom up, neither can distribution and accumulation. Clearly something is missing from the story of capital, and that something is power. This neglect of power, perhaps more than anything else, is the reason why production-based theories of capitalism run into the wall. Indeed, even if we ignore the first phase of the Transformation Problem, there remains the second step of transforming prices of production into final market prices. The main difficulty here is the necessity of perfect competition (Howard and King 1992: 282; Sweezy 1942: 270–274). Specifically, firms and workers must be 'price takers' (unable to individually affect prices and wages), otherwise market prices need not be proportionate to production prices. Moreover, capital and labour must be able to move freely between industries, since this is the process by which the rates of profit and exploitation equalize across the economy.

Yet these conditions of perfect competition do not exist in reality. Indeed, one could argue that such competition is alien to the very idea of a class society. If instead of competition we recognize the myriad of restrictive institutions such as monopolies and oligopolies, redistribution by government, dual labour markets, core and periphery interactions and so on, labour values become practically useless for the study of prices and accumulation. In fact, under non-competitive conditions, with the wage rate deviating from the worker's 'socially necessary' cost of reproduction, the value of labour power itself – the basic input in all production processes – is already 'contaminated' by power relations. (Paradoxically, Marx was the first to predict these deviations from competition, particularly the process of capital centralization and the growth of state power, although he did not explore their detrimental implications for his own labour theory of value.)

The problem of all production-based theories of accumulation – be they neoclassicist or Marxist – is well reflected in their inability to clearly define *what is being accumulated*. The implicit assumption is that accumulation could somehow be measured in *material* terms. In the neoclassical world, where the goal is 'well-being', capital is presumably reducible to some units of pleasure, or 'utils' as the neoclassicists fondly call them. Marxists see the capitalist as driven by the circular goal of accumulation for the sake of accumulation, a principle best understood in terms of power. Their analytical category of capital, however, is measured in terms of 'dead labour', and therefore remains overly entangled in the material intricacies of production.

## Institutionalist critique and reconstruction[6]

Is there a solution? Does this solution involve the recognition of power as a central axis of analysis? And if so, can power be put into the very definition of capital? The answer requires that we re-examine the fundamental relationship between production and distribution. Most economists, while recognizing the growing complexity of production, refuse to accept its implications for distribution which they continue to link to productivity. The earliest and most notable exception was Thorstein Veblen, whose writing coincided with the emergence of large-scale industry and big business in the USA (cf. 1898, 1899, 1904, 1908a, 1908b, 1908c, 1908d, 1909, 1923). In contrast to the neoclassicists who built their theory on *factor* productivity, and to the Marxists who rested it on *labour* productivity, Veblen began where Marx ended, emphasizing *societal* productivity.

A theory of mature capitalism, argued Veblen, must begin from the viewpoint of its principal actor, the businessman. The emergence of large-scale production since the latter part of the nineteenth century, he maintained, has removed capitalists from the immediate realm of production, turning them into 'absentee owners'. Contrary to the earlier 'captain of industry' who both owned and supervised production, the modern businessman was a 'captain of finance', an absentee owner whose activities and interests focused not on production but on the investment of funds. For the absentee investor, capital is finance and *only* finance. It represents neither tangible means of production, nor intangible knowledge, but rather the present value of expected future profit. The key to accumulation lies in what makes such profit grow, and according to Veblen this has to do not with production, but with the *control* of production. From this perspective, capital incorporates power as well as productivity.

Veblen's starting point was a fundamental distinction between 'industry' and 'business'. By industry he meant the *entire* societal process of production. This process comprised the whole fabric of human knowledge, including the sciences, technology and the underlying cultural traits which together – and *only together* – made human endeavour productive. Veblen rejected at the outset not only the notion of factor productivity entertained by the neoclassicists (which indeed no one has thus far been able to observe), but also the very existence of individual factors of production. Productivity, he argued, was an attribute of society as a whole, a feature of 'industry at large'. Machines, raw materials or human muscles were productive only as repositories of societal knowledge. Without such knowledge, they were merely non-economic objects.

The most important implication was that distribution was necessarily political in the wider sense of the term. Since individual factors of production did not exist to begin with, they could not possibly be used to explain the income of different social groups. The secret of distribution lay *outside* industry. And indeed, under capitalism, industry was controlled by 'business', which for Veblen comprised the institution of absentee ownership and the political context in which such ownership was embedded. The goal of business was profit, an undifferentiated claim on the income generated by industry at large. But since business and industry were distinct spheres to begin with, such profit could be secured only insofar as the former limited, or threatened to limit, the free functioning of the latter:

> Plainly, ownership would be nothing better than an idle gesture without this legal right of sabotage. Without the power of discretionary idleness, without the right to keep the work out of the hands of the workmen and the product out of the market, *investment and business enterprise would cease*. This is the larger meaning of the Security of Property.
>
> (Veblen 1923: 66–67, italics added)

The essential contrast, then, is between an industrial realm whose functioning depends on integration, coordination and cooperation, and a business sphere which thrives on antagonistic power. It is the control of the former by the latter which determines, albeit pervertedly, how income is distributed.

From a Veblenian perspective, profit (including interest) is a nonlinear function of production. This is illustrated in Figure 5.1, which depicts the utilization of industrial capacity on the horizontal axis against the capital share of income on the vertical axis. Up to a point, the two go together. After that point, the relationship turns negative. The reason is easy to see by looking at extremes. If industry came to a complete standstill, profit would be nil (bottom left point in Figure 5.1). But profit would also be zero if industry always and everywhere operated at full socio-technological capacity (bottom right point). The reason is that under this latter scenario, industrial considerations rather than business decisions would be paramount, production would no longer need the consent of owners, and these would then be unable to extract their tribute profit.

In a capitalist society, 'business as usual' means oscillating between these two hypothetical extremes, with absentee owners limiting industrial activity to a greater or lesser extent. This limitation is what Veblen called 'sabotage'. When business sabotage becomes excessive, pushing output toward the zero mark, the result is recession and low profit. When sabotage grows too loose, industry expands toward it societal potential, but that too is not good for business, since loss of control means 'glut' and falling profit. For owners of capital, the ideal condition, indicated by the shaded arc in Figure 5.1, lies somewhere in the middle, with high profits being earned in return for letting industry operate, though *only at less than full potential*. Achieving this 'optimal' point requires

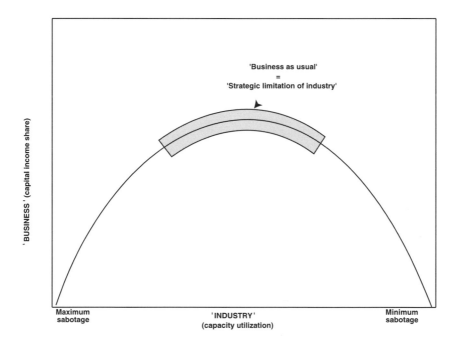

*Figure 5.1*  Business and industry

Goldilocks tactics, neither 'too warm' nor 'too cold'. In the sardonic language of Veblen, it calls for the *strategic* limitation of industry through a 'conscious withdrawal of efficiency'.

This theoretical relationship receives an astounding empirical confirmation from the recent history of the USA, depicted in Figure 5.2. The chart contrasts 'business', measured by the income share of capital on the vertical axis, with 'industry', measured by the rate of unemployment on the horizontal axis (inverted). The data clearly show the negative effect on business of *both* 'excessive' industrial sabotage until the early 1940s, as well as of 'insufficient' sabotage during WWII. 'Business as usual' was restored only after the war, with growing industrial limitations helping capitalists move up and to the left on the chart, toward their 'optimal' income share.

The nature, methods and implications of such limitations are inherently political. Indeed, as capitalism matures, business enterprise comes to incorporate not only private ownership and market exchange, but also larger parts of the legal, customary and ideological codes of conduct, as well as of the institutions and organizations which, taken together, comprise what we call the 'state'. Business limitations rely heavily on tactics such as the manipulation of 'wants', collusion, the erection of entry barriers, or the threat of dumping, but these are only part of a wider picture. Under modern capitalism, the control of industry also

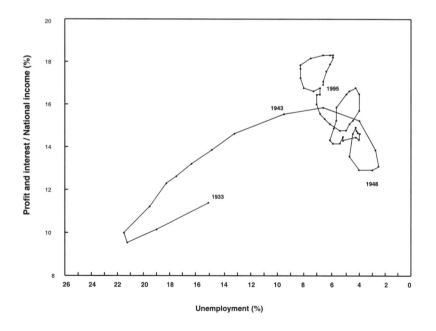

*Figure 5.2*   Business and industry in the USA

*Source*: US Department of Commerce.

*Note*:   Series are expressed as 5-year moving averages

involves – indeed necessitates – a wider set of institutions and actions such as government policies, legal protection for property rights, education and conditioning, policing, bilateral and multilateral international institutions, and the occasional use of military force, to name only a few. Capital, understood as the power to control societal production for business ends, *cannot exist outside this wider political context.*

The institution of absentee ownership, and the notion that profit and accumulation derive from business limiting industry, suggest that all capital is *intrinsically* unproductive. This view contrasts sharply with Marx's 'fraction' taxonomy, which differentiates productive from unproductive capitals. According to Marx, capital accumulates through a circulation scheme, $M–C–P–P'–C'–M'$ *[JN1]*, where financial capital (money $M$), turns into commercial capital (commodities $C$), to be made into industrial capital (work in progress, or productive capital $P$), producing more industrial capital ($P'$), converted again into commercial capital (more commodities $C'$) and finally into financial capital (more money $M'$). Although the circulation of capital is a single process, during the nineteenth century, each 'cycle' (namely, $M–M$, $C–C$ and $P–P$) appeared dominated by a different group, or fraction of the capitalist class. Of these, the industrial fraction was deemed productive, the 'engine' of value and surplus value. The financial and commercial fractions, on the other hand, were seen as largely unproductive, deriving their profit through an intra-capitalist redistributional struggle. There are two serious problems with this view.

The first, theoretical problem, concerns the very link between circulation and accumulation. Marx's circulation scheme describes accumulation in *backward-looking* terms. Profit is earned as a *consequence* of production, making accumulation the *end* of the process, to be measured in units of 'dead labour'. Absentee ownership reversed this order, turning accumulation into a *forward-looking* process. The value of a corporation, measured by its capitalization on the bond and stock markets, reflects not its past profit and interest, but what it is expected to earn in the *future*. This means that accumulation takes place before, not after production.[7] The forward-looking nature of the process is highly significant, since it severs the link between accumulation and circulation. Contrary to Marx's scheme, the corporation's capital in fact never gets into 'circulation' in the first place. Indeed, being merely a symbolic valuation, a present value of future earnings, it *cannot* be circulated. What gets circulated are the resources the firm has at its disposal – money, raw materials, semi-finished goods and depreciated machinery and structures – but the value of these resources is generally unrelated to the corporation's outstanding capitalization. This creates a problem, for with capital delinked from circulation, how could its fractions, embedded as they are in such circulation, be identified?

The second problem is historical. It arises because absentee ownership enables even small investors to achieve extensive diversification, which in turn makes the various 'fractions' difficult to pin down. For example, how are we to classify conglomerates such as General Electric, DaimlerChrysler, or Philip Morris, which operate in hundreds of different sectors across the entire spectrum from finance, through raw materials, to trade, production, entertainment, advertising and distribution? Moreover, diversification has practically broken the functional connection between profit, which is reported by *business firms*, and industrial classification which is based on the *type of production* (US Department of Commerce 1986: xiv). The result is that the very meaning of 'industrial', 'commercial' and 'financial' profit is no longer clear. For instance, in the national accounts, 'manufacturing' profits denote the earnings of firms whose largest *single* line of business, measured in sales, is manufacturing. But if, as often is the case, manufacturing represents only a small part of such sales, the result is that the bulk of 'manufacturing profit' in fact comes from lines of activity *other than manufacturing!* And the problem does not go away even if we limit ourselves to an individual firm. The difficulty here is due to non-arm's-length, intra-firm transactions and 'transfer pricing'. For example, if GE Capital subsidizes GE's jet-engine division by supplying it with cheap credit, the result is to lower profit in the former and raise in the latter, without any change in production and sales. All of this suggests that the fraction view cannot be treated as a universal feature of capitalism. It may have been useful during the pre-diversification phase, but is no longer adequate for the era of absentee ownership and conglomeration.

All capital, including that which is formally associated with 'production', is inherently unproductive. From an institutionalist perspective, the very classification of capitals along lines of industrial activity, even in the absence of diversification and forward-looking capitalization, is misconceived. Production is always a *societal* activity, carried through the *integrated* realm of industry. General Motors does not produce cars. It *controls* the production of cars. But then so do firms such as Mitsubishi Trading and Deutsche Bank. Through different forms of *power*, each company controls key aspects of the production of *cars*, which in turn enable it to command part of the total *societal* profit. The way to differentiate between firms, therefore, is not on the narrow basis of production, but along broader lines of power.

Understood as a power institution, capital could be likened to a 'mega-machine', somewhat along the lines suggested by Lewis Mumford (1967, 1970). Tracing the long historical link between technology and power, Mumford argued that early machines were made not of physical matter, but of humans. In the great deltas of Egypt, Mesopotamia, China and India, the first feats of mechanization were achieved through the formation of giant *social* organizations. The visible output of those early mega-machines were massive public works, such as palaces, citadels, canals, and pyramids. These, though, were largely means to an end. As Orwell put it, 'The object of power is power' (1949: 267), and indeed, according to Mumford, the true purpose of the ruling king and priests was the very assembly, operation and control of the *mega-machine itself*.

Extending this concept to the contemporary business world, we can argue that the earlier elite association of kingship and priesthood has now been replaced by a coalition of capitalists and state officials, overseeing a new mega-machine named capital. The visible 'output' of this new mega-machine is profit, but that is merely a code of power. What is being accumulated is neither future utility nor dead labour, but *abstract power claims on the entire process of social reproduction*.

Although driven by a similar quest for power, capital is qualitatively different from the ancient mega-machine. Older forms of power, for instance those institutionalized through bureaucracy, gender or race, are usually uni-dimensional and relatively inflexible. Capital, in contrast, is multi-dimensional and highly supple. There are four main reasons for this.

First, the process of commodification, when extended to capital, makes power itself vendible. Given that buying and selling capital is the very essence of investment, the result is not only to 'normalize' the expansion of power, but also to remove all intrinsic barriers on such expansion short of a world monopoly.

Second, in contrast to other, socially unique codes of power, profit is measured in common monetary units and carries more or less the same power prerogatives all over the world. This universality makes the geographical expansion of capital power far easier than that of other, more unique forms of power.

Third, the focus on profit enables power to expand indirectly as well as directly. The ancient mega-machine was a relatively well-defined organization. Power was exercised over the organization itself and was therefore 'labour augmenting': to have more of it meant to have a larger organization. The capitalist mega-machine is much broader. It consists not of the corporation, but of the entire scope of capitalistic production. Capitalists struggle to control portions of this totality, with their success measured in terms of profit. Like their earlier counterparts, they could do so directly by making their corporate organization bigger in terms of employees. But they can also do it indirectly, by raising their profit per 'unit of organization', or profit per employee. In contrast to the ancient kings, therefore, capitalists could become 'lean and mean', expanding their power through smaller, 'labour-saving' organizations.

Finally and perhaps most importantly, *any form of power which systematically affects the future flow of profit is automatically capitalized* (non-systematic effects are usually ignored by investors). In this way, male domination reducing the wages of women, environmental policies lowering the legal penalty for pollution, the use of military force affecting the price of raw materials, the impact of television on labour docility, the pacifying of indigenous populations through religious missionary, and so on, all have an impact on the flow of profit. Once 'systematized', they become facets of capital.

Absentee owners exert their power over society. They measure it, however, *relatively to other owners*. Under modern conditions, capitalists are driven not to maximize profit, but to 'beat the average' and exceed the normal rate of return. This *differential* drive suggests a way to embed both production and power within the concept of accumulation (Nitzan 1998). In a nutshell, command over profit, and hence capitalization, represent business power to limit societal production. Differential capitalization, the ratio of one's own capitalization to the average capitalization, therefore represents the relative social power of an owner. Finally, the rate of differential accumulation, the extent to which one's own capitalization expands faster than the average rate of capitalization, measures the change in capitalist power. Achieving differential accumulation implies particular power to limit social production.

This differential nature of capitalist power is anchored in the need for exclusion. In non-capitalist systems, exclusion is usually embedded in relatively rigid customs, such as those preventing serfs from growing into kings, slaves from turning into masters, and untouchables from becoming Brahmins. Capitalism does not have similar customs. Commodification makes upward mobility possible, and in principle there is nothing to prevent a son of a wandering vendor of quack medicine from assembling the Standard Oil of New Jersey, or a university dropout from starting Microsoft. This, though, does not imply that capitalism has done away with exclusion. Far from it. Indeed, for John D. Rockefeller and William Gates to have acquired their own power, others had to give it up. Because of the constant threat of 'equal opportunity', such exclusion requires relentless formation and reformation of 'distributional coalitions', somewhat along the lines articulated by Olson (1965, 1982). The difference therefore is largely one of form: whereas in other power systems, exclusion is largely *static*, built into the social code and resulting in relatively stable groupings, under capitalism it must be *dynamically* recreated, through ever-shifting alliances.

The upshot is that the accumulation of capital in general depends on the accumulation of capital at the centre. It is 'dominant capital', the large coalitions of big business and state institutions at the core of the process, which are crucial. The periphery of capital, the many capitals outside the core, are in fact a constant threat to the viability of capitalist development as a whole. Subject to the strong centrifugal forces of competition, their behaviour is forever undermining the collusive essence of business 'sabotage', without which accumulation is impossible. Only to the extent that dominant capital is able to retain and augment its *exclusive* power against these other lesser capitals (existing or potential), keeping them 'out of the loop', can the capitalisation process be sustained.

The institutionalist perspective allows us to see capital as a strategic concept whose essence is not production, but *power over production*. From this viewpoint, accumulation involves two inter-related processes. One is the progressive commodification of social relationships, centred around the commodification of power itself in the form of capital. In this sense, capital is a *quantification of power*. The result not only makes capital the most flexible, dynamic and efficient form of power, but also enables it to incorporate other forms of power. The historical ascent of capital is manifested in the emergence of the 'normal rate of return' as a principal regulator of social relations. The belief that capital has, and should have, a 'natural' pace of expansion, now dominates the decisions not only of business people, but increasingly also of state officials and international institutions. The ups and downs of this rate affect the flow of private capital and public funds, the employment or unemployment of resources, and the good or ill fate of entire nations. How this 'normal rate of return' comes into being, the way it spreads around the world, the reason for its fluctuations, and the impact it has on the lives of billions are perhaps some of the more important political-economic questions of our time.

Part of the answer is undoubtedly routed in the second process of accumulation, namely the centralization of corporate power. An orderly flow of profit is contingent on the strategic limitation of industry by business, a process which was first normalized by the giant corporation, and which has since been sustained by ever more complex corporate alliances, backed by state institutions, organizations and policies. The 'normality' of profit in general, therefore, reflects the extent to which dominant capital has been able to consolidate, sustain and enhance its differential power to control and shape the process of societal reproduction for its own advantage.

Finally, it should be noted that capital is a ruling-class ideology *par excellence*. Its differential essence is inherently antagonistic, serving those who own it largely by undermining those who do not. Indeed, even proponents of this ideology, from Adam Smith onwards, admit that the engine is the quest for profit, and that the bettering of human lives is merely an assumed consequence. Yet any ideology emphasizing prowess and control can never be truly universal. A theory of capital can tell us volumes about society as seen from above, but relatively little on the view from below. It can certainly not form a basis for universal emancipation. The current hegemony of capitalism is therefore necessarily partial, and in no way does it mark the beginning of the 'end of history'.

## Bringing capital into IPE

How does all of this bear on international political economy? So far, much of the IPE literature has centred around the state. With the exception of a few writers, such as Cox (1987), Gill and Law (1989) and van der Pijl (1984, 1998), the general sentiment, echoed by Underhill in a recent IPE reader, is that 'Understanding the state is in a way *the* problem of international political economy' (1994: 34–35, original italics). The purpose of IPE is usually expressed along two dimensions – to integrate politics and economics and to link the international with the domestic. These two dimensions, so it is argued, converge in the state, the principal theatre where the clash of human agency and social structure generates historical change.

The institutionalist view opens an alternative route. Instead of associating states with 'politics' and capital with 'economics', it allows us to recognize both state and capital as power structures towering over the organization of societal production. Moreover, these two institutions do not simply stand against each other, but are rather intertwined in an evolving symbiosis. Historically, capital emerged from within the state, eventually growing to transcend it (transnational corporations such as DaimlerChrysler or BP-Amoco are not only larger than some developed economies, but can no longer be associated with a particular 'parent' state). That has not made the state irrelevant, though. Indeed, capitalist power is impossible unless embedded in the wider political context created by states. From an institutionalist perspective, therefore, the central question of IPE should focus not on the state *per se*, but more specifically on the development of capital as an increasingly central moment of the state. Such 'capital-centred' IPE can evolve along numerous trajectories. The following briefly outlines several research agendas worth pursuing.[8]

### The corporation

How does capital power get 'packaged' through legal incorporation? Why is it internalized and how is it quantified? What are the boundaries of 'dominant capital'? In what ways can dominant capital grow differentially, that is, relative to the average? Can we identify qualitatively different paths, or 'regimes of differential accumulation'? What are the broader political-economic causes and consequences of each such regime? For instance, how do such regimes relate to the formal political process, the pace of economic growth, or inflation? How and why does capital, an association of individual owners, 'spread' progressively from the corporation itself, through the industry, to the sector, to the nation-state, and now to the entire world? Is this progressive breakdown of 'barriers' necessary for the viability of dominant capital, and if so, what will happen once dominant capital becomes truly transnational with no further barrier to transcend?

### The state

Against the ascent of capital, what are we to make of the state? How has its relationship with capital changed? How and to what extent do state and capital 'overlap'? How has their 'symbiosis' changed over time? For instance, could we see the state as being initially a 'cocoon' for capital, which is gradually shed off, or turned into a supporting limb? If the impact of a given state policy – for instance the effect on profit of military spending or intellectual property rights – can be capitalized, what does that imply for the locus of power? How do we decide where this power resides? What aspects of capital power, if any, can exist without the support of state institution? Is the state necessary for accumulation?

### IPE

How has the multiplicity of states, with the associated layers of differential power, affected the formation and accumulation of transnational corporations? Could a global state play a similar role? What does this imply for the future of the nation-state and the inter-state system? In what way has the ascent of transnational firms shaped the structure and behaviour of states? Is there any discernible historical pattern here, and could it be theorized? Does the power essence of capital necessitate *both* universalization (globalization) and interconnectedness (and thus separate states)? How has the changing interaction of capital and state power affected the formation of elites and dominant ideologies?

### Contradictions, ideology and hegemony

What are the points of conflict between the needs of capital to limit societal reproduction, and its position as a dominant ideology? How could capitalist ideology reconcile the conflicting drive for power by the few with the pursuit of Lakshmi by the many? Can an ideology of commodification and private property become universal in its own right? What additional, non-capitalist ingredients are necessary to build a hegemonic bloc around what neo-Gramscians call the 'transnational capitalist class'? How can these extra-capitalist factors be sustained against capital's limitless quest for power? Can a truly transnational class exist in the absence of a global state? Does the emergence of such class mark the coming of a global state, and could this state paradoxically become the beginning of the end of capital?

## Acknowledgements

We wish to thank Stephen Gill, Don Goldstein and Ronen Palan for their instructive comments. Research for this project was partly supported by a grant from the Social Science and Humanities Research Council of Canada (SSHRC).

## Notes

1   Although labour and land are not homogeneous either, their heterogeneity is fundamentally different from that of capital goods. The quality of labour could be moulded through education, whereas land could be improved through cultivation. Capital goods, on the other hand, are not at all supple. Once made, they can rarely be converted for tasks other than those for which they were originally designed.

2   First, the production theatre becomes infinitely complex, making identification and quantification impossible. Second, without aggregation some input complementarity is inevitable, so the corresponding marginal products cannot be derived, even on paper. Third, because rationality and utility maximization alone do not guarantee downward-sloping excess demand functions, general equilibrium models need not be 'stable' (Rizvi 1994). And fourth, the theory is inherently static, and hence can say little on the dynamic essence of accumulation.

3   Aware of the inherent circularity of 'tangible' marginalism, the 'Austrian' economists sought to circumvent the problem altogether by substituting *time* for capital goods. Following Jevons (1871), who formulated his production function with time as an input, writers such as Böhm-Bawerk (1891), Wicksell (1935), and later Hicks (1973), reinterpreted capital goods as 'stages' of a temporal production process. Capital was counted in units of the 'average period of production', itself a combination of original inputs and the time pattern of their employment. In general, it was believed that 'roundabout' processes (which are longer, more mechanized and indirect) were more productive, and that lengthening the average period of production was therefore tantamount to raising its 'capital intensity'. The Austrian theory had two main drawbacks. First, its emphasis on original inputs – to the exclusion of tangible capital goods – was dangerously close to the classicists and to Marx, something the neoclassicists were more than eager to avoid. Second, its focus, including its link to the time preferences of consumers, remained exclusively materialistic. It tried to establish a positive relationship between an aggregate quantity of capital on the one hand, and productivity/utility on the other. Its route was therefore not that different from Clark's, and indeed it too fell into the 'reswitching' trap (see Hunt 1992, ch. 16).

4   Consider two hypothetical production functions, with physical inputs augmented by technology: (1) $Q = 2N + 3L + 5K + T$ and (2) $Q = 4N + 2L + 10K + T$, where $Q$ denotes output, $N$ labour, $L$ land, $K$ capital, and $T$ 'technology'. Now, suppose $Q$ is 100, $N$ is 10, $L$ is 5 and $K$ is 4. The implication is that $T$ must be 45 in function (1) and 10 in function (2). Yet, since technology cannot be 'measured', we would never know which function is correct, so both can safely claim validity....

5    The basic value equation is Value $= c + v + s$, with c being the value of constant capital, v the value of variable capital and s denoting surplus value. The rate of profit is given by $\pi = s / (c + v)$, the rate of exploitation by $\varepsilon = s / v$ and the organic composition of capital by $\theta = c / v$. Dividing both sides of the rate of profit equation by v we get $\pi = (s / v) / (c / v + 1) = (\varepsilon) / (\theta + 1)$. Clearly, if $\pi$ and $\varepsilon$ are equalized across the economy, so must $\theta$.

6    This section draws partly on Nitzan (1998).

7    'Robber Barons' such as Cornelius Vanderbilt and Jay Gould were often accused of 'watering' or 'diluting' their companies by issuing stocks whose value far exceeded their tangible property. But in so doing, they were in fact 'the innovators of modern corporate tactics: the capitalization according to *earnings* rather than in ratio to actual assets' (Josephson 1934: 72, original emphasis).

8    Some of these ideas are developed theoretically and empirically in Bichler and Nitzan (1996a and 1996b, 1999), Nitzan (1992, 1998, 1999) and Nitzan and Bichler (1995, 1996, 1997).

# 6  Labour and IPE

## Rediscovering human agency

*Robert O'Brien*

In her introduction to the 1984 edition of *Paths to International Political Economy* Susan Strange (1984: ix) praises the emerging field of International Political Economy (IPE) for being an open and unenclosed corner of social science. In the same text Roger Tooze (1994) charts the rise of IPE as a discipline and records its spreading appeal. This chapter argues that although IPE has continued to expand its vision and increased its popularity since that time, it retains a serious blind spot because it ignores the agency of non-elite groupings of people.[1] This exclusion is regrettable for two reasons. First, by focusing on abstract entities such as states and firms the field loses sight of many of the crucial issues such as the impact of the global economy on life chances and survival. Second, ignoring the activity and fate of social groups can contribute to misleading analysis as key actors are overlooked.

The general argument will be illustrated by examining the case of labour in international relations. Workers are largely invisible in the study of IPE. While the field has expanded its vision from the study of foreign economic policies to incorporate markets and firms (Doremus *et al.* 1998; Stopford and Strange 1991; Eden *et al.* 1991), it has generally ignored, with a few exceptions (Harrod 1997; Enloe 1989; Cox 1987), the role of social forces, social movements or other non-elite collectivities of people. This chapter argues that such an omission is a mistake both theoretically and empirically. In particular, the neglect of workers and labour issues hinders thorough analysis because they are intrinsically connected to issues of transformation and stability.

The chapter is divided into four sections. The first section investigates the omission of labour studies in IPE. After examining the degree to which labour is neglected in the field, three explanations are put forward for this neglect. These include the general biases towards statist and institutional analysis, the association with Marxist thought and the seemingly unproblematic role of workers in the early years of IPE. The other sections of the chapter examine recent developments in the global political economy (GPE) which will make it increasingly difficult and mistaken to continue avoiding serious analysis of labour issues. The first development is the problem created by labour shock as millions of new workers are integrated into the global economy. The increasing globalization of economic activity is bringing more and more people into competition with each other. This raises the possibility of increasing social tension in developed states. The second development is the changing position of US labour in the GPE. US labour has been expelled from the post-war growth coalition and is in the process of reassessing its role in the globalization process. This raises new issues and concerns about the future of US foreign economic policy. The third issue concerns the development of workers and peasant organizations as the primary opposition to the neoliberal globalization project. For differing reasons, and with varying strategies, workers are increasingly posing a threat to neoliberal projects and the creation of international regimes. In addition, the role of unorganized workers in the informal, and particularly the peasant, sectors of the workforce is an area of increasing unrest and opposition. Attempts to understand the process of globalization and its trajectory must take these forces into account. The chapter concludes by considering the implications of focusing upon labour for theory in IPE.

In this chapter the term labour refers to groups of people who rely upon their own physical work to provide themselves with the resources necessary for existence, it goes beyond wage labour to include informal sector workers, peasants and subsistence farmers. Unions are a form of organization which represents elements of labour, but they are only one part. Most labourers are not represented by unions, yet they still play a key role in the functioning of the global political economy (Harrod 1987). The action of labour as a broad and diverse social force in unionized and non-unionized forms is the subject of this chapter.

## Neglected labour

The study of work, workers and peasant organizations is not of much concern to the field of IPE. In a mid-1990s survey (Denemark and O'Brien 1997) of IPE at over 200 UK and US universities, not a single respondent offered a course dedicated to labour issues. The only indication that labour might be an issue in US courses was the occasional reference in reading lists to Robert Reich's (1992) study *The Work of Nations*. This book reflected an unease about transformation in the US political economy, but did not broaden out into a concern about workers in general.

To update this analysis I reviewed the degree to which labour issues have featured in two leading International Relations/International Political Economy journals. *International Organization* claims to be one of the leading scholarly journals in the field of International Relations. It does not confine itself to IPE work, but does take IPE as one of its main interests. From 1994–97 *International Organization* published eighty-one articles. Reference to labour was restricted to two articles dealing with immigration policy in advanced industrialized countries (Money 1997; Haus 1995). Occasionally, labour also made an appearance as a special interest group in broader studies of trade policy (Nollen and Quin 1994). In the field of IR as represented by *IO*, labour is nearly, but not quite, invisible.

The *Review of International Political Economy* has set itself up as a heterodox IPE forum (Amin *et al.* 1994) and, as a result, has given more attention to labour issues. Of seventy-six articles published between 1994–97, approximately 10 per cent (seven) articles examined labour issues. More significant than the number of times labour was examined was the place that labour took in the studies. Fordist approaches (Lipietz 1997, 1996) put labour relations at the centre of considering IPE and the European Union. Other articles examined the impact of the changing nature of work on firms and political authorities (Hoogvelt and Yuasa 1994; Dassbach 1994). Some studies explored the role of class in international policy (Cafruny 1995) while others speculated upon how the globalization of economic relations was changing worker and citizen views of the state and traditional political alliances (Rupert 1995b). One raised the question of peasants in the IPE (McMichael 1997).

Among scholars working or educated in the British tradition of IPE, the study of the financial system has taken centre stage. Recent noteworthy studies include subjects such as the relationship between monetary order and long-term credit (Germain 1997), the nature of the global financial order (Underhill 1997), the role of states in the emergence of global finance (Helleiner 1994), and a second look at the notion of Casino Capitalism (Strange 1998). Academic papers presented to the IPE section of the British International Studies Association meeting in December 1997 were dominated by discussion of the financial system. Of twelve papers sponsored by the IPE section, five dealt with the subject of finance or financial interests.

Casting an eye over the publication of recent books, journal articles, contents of IPE courses and papers presented at academic conferences one would have to conclude that the study of labour is on the fringes of the discipline of IPE. Some work is being done on the subject, but it is not seen as being central to the field. There are three factors which help to account for this neglect. Firstly, the study of workers suffers from the same neglect as the study of other groups of people in IPE. IPE in the work of scholars such as Krasner (1994) continues to focus upon states. Disputes may rage about the conditions under which states cooperate, but the focus is clearly upon states. Feminists' work which has studied women in the global political economy (Enloe 1989; Mies 1986) has not made a significant impression in the field. Recent work on the activity of social movements (Thiele 1993), NGOs and advocacy networks (Keck and Sikkink 1998) is starting to make a dent in mainstream IPE. To the degree that such scholarship is accepted, there may be increasing room for a discussion of labour issues in IPE.

Second, the study of labour issues may be harmed by guilt of association. Interest in labour issues is often associated with Marxist analysis and Marxists have not been prominent in mainstream IPE. Non-Marxist analysis finds it difficult to focus upon workers as a significant variable. Within the Marxist tradition, many international relations studies have focused upon the role of elites rather than workers (Gill 1990; Kees van der Pijl 1998). There has been much more interest in the activities of a transnational ruling class (Sklair 1997) than with other classes.

A third explanation may lie in the fact that during the years when IPE was emerging as a distinct field of study, the role and influence of workers' organizations were largely unproblematic. IPE emerged as a response to increasing turbulence in the international economic system in the 1970s (Strange 1984). Chaos in the monetary system, upheaval in the oil regime and trade frictions were the subjects of interest. Despite the crisis of governability described in national political science literature (Rose 1981), workers were not one of the factors causing problems in the field of IPE. Indeed, as Cox (1977) noted, US workers were a key element in system maintenance.

Despite previous obstacles to studying the activity of workers as an important part of IPE, there are good reasons to do so. The role of workers should be of interest even for those scholars who do not put the relations of production at the centre of their analysis. Workers are significant not because of a prior theoretical commitment to the relations of production, but because they exercise influence in the global political economy and are shaping the structure of global order. This case will be advanced by examining three areas where labour is crucial to the evolution of the global political economy. The first case is the labour shock thesis which links the integration of labour in developing countries to social distress in developed states. The second is the changing position of US labour in the global economy and its possible transformation into an oppositional force. The third factor is the growing opposition of industrial and peasant workers in the developing world to the neoliberal globalization project.

## Labour shock thesis

Neoliberal globalization is bringing an ever-increasing number of workers into the global workforce. A series of GATT trade rounds have greatly reduced tariffs and the World Trade Organization (WTO) is now addressing non-tariff barriers. The WTO is also extending its liberalizing mission into the areas of services and agriculture. The 1980s' debt crisis resulted in the death of the nationally based development project as countries scrambled to integrate themselves into the global economy (Hoogvelt 1997; McMichael 1996). Export-oriented industrialization is the strategy of choice from Mexico to Poland to China. Yet, what is the likely effect of a flood of products onto the world market and the global proletarianization of hundreds of millions, if not billions of workers?

By global proletarianization I mean the process whereby workers or peasants engaged in local or nationally based economic activity are incorporated into production processes that have an international reach. The percentage of labour around the world engaged in such activity is relatively small, but is growing rapidly. For example, it has been estimated that in a 10-year period 5–6 million workers in the Pearl River Delta of China have been hired into new factories (Castells 1996: 235).

The answer to this potentially significant question is a matter of much controversy in political economy. A parsimonious liberal trade theory once suggested that a likely result is that wages in developed states will plunge. In 1948 Paul Samuelson developed the factor price equalization theorem. It stated that under certain conditions of international trade (as laid out in the Hecksher–Ohlin model), there would be a tendency towards the price of factors in each country to come closer together (Grimwade 1989: 10–15). Furthermore, the owners of the scarce resource would suffer, as it becomes less scarce with the opening of trade. A country with high labour costs engaging in trade with a country with a large labour surplus could expect to see the wages of workers in the traded sector decline.

On the surface of it, such a theorem would suggest that globalization is a threat to wages in some sectors of Western economies. Most liberals deny that such a threat exists. They stress the benefits of comparative advantage and the restrictive set of assumptions behind the Hecksher–Ohlin model which make such a scenario unlikely. Analysis which suggests that unskilled workers in developed countries lose out from international trade (Wood 1995) has been vigorously challenged by articulate opponents claiming that trade is a minor influence on wages levels (Krugman and Lawrence 1994). There are three difficulties in trying to clarify this argument. The first is that the data available for analysis is often incomplete and can be misleading. The second is that we are witnessing a dynamic process as globalization accelerates. This may mean that small effects in the past are simply a precursor to greater effects in the future. The third is that the debate is intensely ideological, as well as being one of empirical investigation. The majority of economists are wedded to a vision of liberal trade and are reluctant to publicize theories or data that might be 'misinterpreted' by the public and serve as a justification for protectionism.

Lambert and Caspersz (1995) have argued that Asian industrialization threatens to greatly expand the number of workers in global competition. Building upon World Bank forecasts of economic growth they foresee the growth of Asian countries and labour forces dramatically undercutting wages and the standard of living in developed countries in the absence of international labour regulation. World Bank (1995: 9) figures estimate that by 2025 another 1.2 billion people will join the world's labour force. The effect of this surge in labour supply is difficult to predict. Liberals foresee movement to equilibrium, critics on the left and right make predictions of social discontent in the developed world. The increasing number of workers entering into global competition (as opposed to just national) do so in an environment of existing widespread unemployment and underemployment.

The recent financial crisis in Asia suggests that earlier predictions of exponential growth were mistaken. Nevertheless, a rapidly growing global workforce is still likely. In addition, the increased competitiveness of Asian goods following the devaluation of Asian currencies combined with slower world economic growth is likely to increase pressure on Western workers.

Scholars from different approaches may at least agree that a massive expansion of the number of workers competing in a global economy, at the minimum, poses a serious adjustment problem for Western societies. The prescriptions for adjustment vary from making labour markets more flexible, to the provision of minimum income levels or wage subsidies, to international agreements on labour standards, to strengthening unions or weakening unions, to liberalizing economic activity, to protection of key industries. What should not be in dispute is that there is a problem, and that if it is mishandled the political support for continued liberalization in developed states may evaporate. This leads us to examine the case of US workers in particular.

## US labour in transition

The second reason to suggest that increased attention should be given to the study of workers' organizations is the changing role of workers in the US political economy. In the past thirty years US labour has moved from being an unquestioning ally in the spread of US hegemony to being a growing obstacle to further liberalization and internationalization. US labour has not abandoned the US state for worker internationalism, but it is rethinking its position. This raises doubts about the social base in the US for maintaining leadership in the liberalization process.

In the immediate post-war era, US labour was firmly engaged in the politics of productivity (Maier 1977). The politics of productivity involved subsuming class conflict by ensuring growth and productivity gains were distributed across the economy. It reflected a belief that proper technical management of the economy would create the conditions for prosperity which would eliminate the need for harmful distributional battles. It was a method of neutralizing labour opposition by integrating unionized workers into a division of economic spoils. Internationally, organized labour played a crucial part in laying the groundwork for today's process of neoliberal globalization. US labour took a leading role in marginalizing radical workers' organizations in Latin America, Asia and Western Europe (Cox 1977; Radosh 1969). This ground-clearing work facilitated the expansion of US business and resulted in labour becoming an agent in the globalization process (Herod 1997).

However, the rise of neoliberal governments in the United States and Britain, accompanied by a business offensive against workers, led to the ejection of labour from the governing coalition (Rupert 1995a: 167–207). This marginalization of moderate worker organizations corresponded with a movement by US elites to separate their destiny from the rest of the nation (Lasch 1995; Reich 1992). As the polarization of US society continues and the revolt of the elites is clearer, it becomes more practical for workers to look to the international realm for solidarity and assistance. In the US context, Rupert (1995b) has argued that the NAFTA debate may be a watershed in organized labour's acceptance of the dominant brand of liberalism. Not only did labour break with US corporations over the issue of linking workers' rights to regional trade agreements, but it also openly opposed a Democratic Party leadership and a sitting Democratic President. A second notable change in the policies of organized labour was the attempt to work with environmental and consumer groups to forge a common position on this element of economic policy. Finally, the AFL-CIO was forced to cultivate relations with the emerging independent Mexican unions rather than rely on the Mexican government-sponsored CTM union. The CTM proved adequate for US workers' interests in the Cold War when the fight was against Communism, but allies in the fight against transnational exploitation would have to be found in unions controlled by their members.

US workers are in the process of re-evaluating their interests in relation to US corporations and the US state. They can no longer be counted upon to unquestionably back expansion of US capitalism. Yet, national interests can and do still motivate workers' organizations. In the recent debate about limits to pollution at the Kyoto climate change conference some US unions stood side by side with US corporations in resisting measures which might increase costs of production. The AFL-CIO urged President Clinton not to sign the Kyoto Protocol because it did not put limits on the greenhouse gas emissions of developing countries (AFL-CIO 1998). Earlier union analysis (AFL-CIO 1997) stressed the possible threat of a climate change treaty to the US industrial base. In another example, the United Mine Workers of America sponsored a resolution in the Alabama state legislature protesting against the climate change treaty because it was more demanding of developed than developing countries (WIP 1998).

In addition, the pressure upon US workers to reject a broad-based social unionism in favour of corporate unionism or individualized employment contracts remains substantial. Wells (1998) has described this as a contest between an internationalism based upon a coordinative unionism and a new feudalism based upon firm level labour – management productivity alliances. Workers, threatened with unemployment or job insecurity, are encouraged to identify with their company against other workers in rival companies. The thrust of modern Human Resource Management (HRM) is to bind workers to the corporation and to undermine collective worker identity. Similarly, a strategy of the modern competition state (Palan and Abbott 1996) is to use labour as an asset to attract investment. Workers can be educated or suppressed in an effort to attract high or low value added investment. In either case, the intention is to place the workers of one country into competition with the workers of another country. As a result of these countervailing pressures it is prudent to exercise caution about claims of large-scale transformation in the attitudes and activity of US labour.

In what ways might a more oppositional US labour movement influence the global political economy? One method is by changing the agenda for international institution building. At the multilateral level labour organizations have complicated the WTO's plan to extend liberalization into new sectors and regions as they press for inclusion of core labour standards (O'Brien 1998; Leary 1996). Labour organizations are pushing the IMF and the World Bank to revise the neoliberal content of their structural adjustment lending (ICFTU 1995). In the case of the World Bank lending to South Korea, this has resulted in provisions aimed at offering unprecedented (if limited) protection for workers (World Bank 1998). At the regional level, an alliance of convenience between labour and right wing populism has stalled US approval for the expansion of NAFTA. A second method is shaping the international economic environment through influencing corporate policy. In concert with other social groups labour has increased pressure on multinationals to change their investment locations or method of conducting business. This is particularly evident in the campaigns for company codes of conduct to temper poor labour and environmental practices (Forcese 1997; Compa and Hinchliffe-Darricarràre 1995).

The recent, hesitant, transformation of US labour may be part of a new internationalism for a broad spectrum of groups concerned with labour issues. A number of authors (Waterman 1998; Moody 1997) have raised the possibility of a new internationalism based upon transnational networks of labour activists inside and outside unions. These networks would form alliances with other social movements in the north and south to offer an alternative prescription for economic, political and social order.

## Resistance strongholds

Earlier sections have argued that turbulence in the labour market created by neoliberal globalization and the repositioning of US labour in the political system are two reasons for paying increased attention to workers and their activity in the study of IPE. Moving away from workers in the developed world we can see that labour in the developing world also plays a significant role in influencing the trajectory of globalization. Two central challenges to an expansion and stabilization of a liberal global economy are workers in Newly Industrializing Countries (NICs) and peasants in developing countries.

Let us begin with workers in the NICs. The recent financial crisis in East and Southeast Asia places the issue of workers' rights and activities firmly on the analytical agenda. The Asian development model sometimes sympathetically described as paternalistic authoritarianism (Pye 1988), was thought to prosper because, in contrast to Latin American authoritarian models, development was more egalitarian. Workers were often coerced, but they shared in the benefits of growth (in this view). Stability was ensured by growth. Suddenly, economic growth is gone, at least temporarily. Workers in South Korea face the prospect of unemployment in a welfare-less state; notions of loyalty and community may be loosened under the strain of structural adjustment. At the time of writing Korean unions are participating in a fragile joint strategy with government and employers in response to the financial crisis (IHT 1998b). In Thailand and Indonesia the crisis is more serious and the fallout for the local population is catastrophic.

The social chaos arising from the financial meltdown in Asia and the reaction of workers to that chaos will be a large factor in determining regional and global stability. Even the World Bank has recognized the danger of social disintegration. In a February 1998 interview, World Bank President James Wolfenson announced that approximately 60 per cent of the $16 billion it has promised in financial assistance would be directed to 'protecting the poor and providing a social safety net' (IHT 1998a). Social unrest is now viewed as an imminent danger to internationally backed plans for financial restructuring. The threat to the IMF's and World Bank's rescue packages does not come from the political and economic elites of the target states, but from those who will bear the costs of such restructuring – the working population.

As important as the role of workers in Asian states may be, there is another significant labour issue confronting the global political economy. To use McMichael's (1997) terms, it is the 'agrarian question'. Put somewhat crudely, the agrarian question concerns the implications of replacing peasant-based agriculture with capitalist agriculture. Although this was a subject of grave concern in Western states in the nineteenth century and attention to peasant affairs was also raised during social revolutions in China, Cuba and Vietnam in the middle of this century, the agrarian question has not been posed again until very recently. It has re-emerged in response to the threat liberalization of agriculture poses to billions of peasants around the world.

Slowly, but surely, a global peasant alliance is emerging to challenge the dominant notions of liberalization, consumption and environmental destruction. The most dramatic event has been the peasant and aboriginal rebellion in the southern Mexican state of Chiapas (Reding 1994). Although the rebellion draws upon a historical legacy of oppression, it was clearly linked to steps taken by the Mexican government to liberalize agricultural land holdings in the run up to the NAFTA. Local concerns were linked to broader developments in IPE. The Zapatistas have been quick to exploit modern technology to broadcast their cause world wide and have begun the task of forging links with similarly minded groups in other parts of the world (www.ezln.org).

The Peoples' Global Action against 'Free' Trade and the World Trade Organization (PGA) is another example of a peasant based anti-imperialist grouping. The PGA is an instrument for co-ordination which brings together people's movements to oppose trade liberalization (PGA 1997). The PGA organizes conferences approximately three months before the biannual Ministerial Meetings of the World Trade Organization. Conferences are used to update the PGA manifesto and to co-ordinate global and local action against free trade. The conference committee for the February 1998 event included groups such as the Frente Zapatista de Liberación Naciónal (FZLN) from Mexico, Karnataka State Farmer's Association (KRRS) from India, Movemento sem Terra (NST) from Brazil and the Peasant Movement of the Philippines (KMP). The PGA is committed to non-violent civil disobedience and a confrontational attitude in pursuit of its opposition to free trade. It represents a constituency firmly in opposition to dominant trends in the global political economy.

This analysis is not arguing that workers or peasants in the developing world will serve as the basis for a revolutionary movement to overthrow capitalism. There are certainly many peasants in the world, but the power they face in economic and military terms is immense. It is possible, however, to identify these groups as offering potentially significant resistance to the liberalization project. They represent a key force in world politics, but it is one usually hidden from view because of the standard IPE analytical categories. Analysis of international order that ignores them would be incomplete and flawed.

## Conclusion

This final section of the chapter seeks to clarify the argument and suggest some implications for theory. We can begin with stressing what the chapter has not argued. It has not argued that the financial system, firms or elites are unimportant. They are crucial to our understanding of the global political economy. Yet, they are not the whole story. Groups of people who act in the context of their relationship to the productive process also have a significant influence on the functioning of the global political economy.

This brief chapter has suggested that in at least three areas (labour shock, position of US labour, developing world labour and peasant organizations) there is a critical relationship between workers and international order. There is a relationship between the workplace and world order (Harrod 1997: 112). If one accepts the argument that people organized around their identity as workers and farmers have a potentially significant role to play in international relations, then one is forced to consider the implications for theorizing in IPE.

Here we run into a difficult problem. Mainstream international relations is about relations between states. Much of US-based international relations and IPE literature continues to work in a state-centric regime approach (Hasenclever *et al.* 1997). IPE has broadened this outlook to include firms, but has not gone much further. Neither field is able to address the question of a discussion paper from the United Nations Development Programme which asked *Rival States, Rival Firms: How Do People Fit In?* (Grunberg 1996). The question of human welfare is hidden when one focuses upon corporate and state interests. Moreover, the agency of people is obscured by the state–firm dichotomy.

Murphy's (1994) work has highlighted how forms of international organization have adapted to economic change and how such organization is dependent upon social organization within and across states. If it is correct that the roots of global order are in specific locations, the study of IPE needs to be grounded in the life of everyday people. Particular forms of order offer possibilities and constraints for action, institutions shape the way in which politics is channelled and the state remains a centre of authority, but agency does not lie in these quarters. People act and it is people's actions that shape the world.

Unless one looks at the activity and agency of workers and farmers, it is difficult to understand the changing principles, rules and norms of global order. For example, why was it that liberalism was embedded in a particular social purpose following the Second World War? What will determine whether the powerful 'Washington consensus' (neoliberalism) of the 1980s and early 1990s is tempered or replaced at the turn of the century? The answer to these questions involves determining *whose* principles, rules and norms are triumphant and this forces one past a focus on states to considering the role of social forces and human agency.

One method of rediscovering the importance of human agency would be to link the conduct of international relations with domestic politics where the activity of interest groups is more visible. Keohane and Milner (1996) have brought together a number of authors who have undertaken this task in a variety of ways. Milner (1997) has gone further to outline how domestic institutions and interest groups shape the possibilities for international cooperation. These are steps in the right direction, but they hardly seem to catch the global contest over the restructuring of production that is a central feature of global political economy.

Analytically, we need some method of integrating the study of social forces with the study of institutions (both international and national) and world order. Robert Cox (1981) proposed one such method which put the relationship between social forces, forms of state and world order at the centre of the study of international relations. More recently Harrod (1997) has suggested that IPE might benefit from an interchange with those areas of industrial relations not subsumed in human resource management. Traditionally, industrial relations was concerned with the interplay of social forces that emerged from the organization and control of work. It may be fruitful to bring these two traditions together to generate a synthesized approach to IPE.[2]

An integration of human agency and attention to social forces would allow IPE to come to terms with the development of a vast range of transnational social activity which is of increasing importance. Labour groups (Waterman 1998) are following the lead of environmental and feminist activists to influence policy in what Castells (1996) calls the networked society. The activity of what has variously been dubbed global civil society (Lipschutz 1992), global society (Shaw 1994), world civic politics (Wapner 1995) and transnational advocacy networks (Keck and Sikkink 1998) is playing a role in changing the structure of the global economy. Prominent examples of the importance of this activity include the mobilization of opposition to the negotiation of a Multilateral Agreement on Investment at the OECD (Strom 1998), the negotiation of an international convention banning the use of landmines (Cameron *et al.* 1998) and the interaction between multilateral economic institutions and global social movements (O'Brien *et al.* 2000).

Many people in the world face life-threatening problems of environmental degradation and economic deprivation. To date IPE has been woefully inadequate in turning its attention to such issues. Part of the explanation lies in the relative youth of IPE as an area of investigation. However, another part of the explanation lies in a conscious choice of the appropriate issues and actors for scholarly study. The first shortcoming may be remedied by time, the second requires deliberate action. Unless more attention is diverted to the study of non-elite collectivities in IPE (especially labour), existing blind spots will cripple the field's potential. Strange's (1984) praise of the field may prove to have been premature.

## Notes

1 Thanks for useful comments go to participants at the International Political Economy Group workshop 'Pathways to IPE: 15 Years On', University of Newcastle, 21 February 1998. Subsequent helpful criticism was also given by Randall Germain, Ronen Palan and Don Wells.
2 A workshop funded by the International Studies Association undertook this task in Washington, DC, in February 1999.

# 7 Globalisation

## Trend or project?

*Philip McMichael*

## Introduction

Globalisation is on practically everyone's lips. Or so it would seem. One of the distinguishing features at the turn of the century is the powerful apparatus of communication dedicated to the image of a world unified by global technologies and their universal appeal. And yet we know that while 75 per cent of the world's population has access to daily television reception, only 20 per cent of the world's population has access to consumer cash or credit. We may see TV commercials depicting the world's peoples drinking Coca-Cola, but this is part of the symbolic and sanitising dimension of the image, rather than the reality, of globalisation. The seduction of 'globalisation' involves the belief that we are living in an unprecedented era. Are we at a new stage in social history, or does global integration merely extend previous developments? Available data is overwhelmingly national, which privileges territorial space at a time when it is apparent that cross-border flows of capital, and people, constitute an important ingredient of current global restructuring dynamics. Not only are the measures conventional, but they obscure the relational networks and flows that operate above and below nation-states.

Some would say that globalisation is inherent to capitalism, that, as Marx argued, the history of capital presumes a world-embracing commerce. This is a theoretical proposition, proven in practice as the world capitalist economy has expanded to embrace much of the social world (at least via the establishment of a state system that regards all territory as potential market space). But the key issue is how, and with what effects, this world-embracing commerce is now instituted.

Interpretations differ – ranging from accelerating economic integration which erodes national differences (Radice 1998) and undergirds an emerging transnational class (Sklair 1997; Panitch 1998), through discursive or cultural integration via multicultural interactions or global 'McDonaldisation' (Koc 1994; Ritzer 1996), and social integration via time/space distanciation (Giddens 1990), to expanding forms of supranational governance (Cox 1992; Gill 1992) and/or crisis management (Amin 1997). Common to each interpretation is the unification of distinct regions, political entities and cultures, whether through a process

of homogenisation or through the principle of 'unity in diversity'. While interpretations differ, most assume the existence of a singular or dominant process
that is either continuous or discontinuous. That is, either globalisation is the
mature phase of capitalist, cultural or political integration, or globalisation is a
threshold in which *extant* social and political arrangements are undergoing a
fundamental reformulation.

In addition, there is a perspective that views globalisation as an incomplete or
even multiple phenomenon constituted through the juxtaposition of different
principles and scales of political and social organisation (see, e.g., Jessop 1997;
Mann 1997; Shaw 1997). Recently, in context of the global financial crisis triggered
by the 1997 meltdown in East and Southeast Asia, some commentators are charac-
terising globalisation as market expansion now halted by non-/anti-market
practices in non-Western cultures. Thus:

> spreading capitalism is not simply an exercise in economic engineering. It is
> an assault on other nations' culture and politics that almost guarantees a
> collision. Even when countries adopt some trappings of capitalism, they
> may not embrace the basic values that make the system work.
>
> (Samuelson 1998: 42)

In other words, globalisation has stalled, or is in remission.

In short, globalisation has many dimensions and interpretations. This chapter
is concerned to delineate some of these dimensional and interpretive perspectives, recognising of course that they are inter-related. I shall consider each
through evaluation and synthesis of some of the major debates. The four
perspectives are:

1   The self-regulating market.
2   Social geographies.
3   Geopolitical relations.
4   Governance and regulation.

Discussion of each of these perspectives will concomitantly address this chapter
title, namely, is globalisation best understood as a trend or a project?

## Perspectives on globalisation: the self-regulating market

Is the global market more powerful than individual states? A central theme
running through debates about globalisation is the question whether and to what
extent the nation-state is disappearing or failing in the context of global
economic integration. Common policy shifts across the world of states include
closer integration with flows of trade, investment and finance, rendering macro-
economic policy weaker and contributing to the process of 'shrinking the state'
via declining social expenditures. Within this perspective of the de-centring of

the nation-state, the transnational corporation plays a key role in its ability to relocate production as a competitive, cost-cutting strategy, compelling national and municipal jurisdictions to adopt policies that reduce friction for capital, and enhancing the market's role in investment decisions. Palan (1998b) has referred to this transactional movement as 'the new sovereignty'. Whether and to what extent this is a zero-sum situation, where markets or capital undermine states, is part of this perspective (see Castells 1997; Sassen 1996).

Perhaps the best known exponent of the 'powerless state' is Ohmae (1990), who depicts the global economy as a 'borderless world'. He argues that the 'region-state' (e.g., the San Diego/Tijuana zone, the Growth Triangle of Singapore, Johore of southern Malaysia and the nearby Riau Islands of Indonesia) is the natural economic zone in a borderless world. In theory, Ohmae's perspective describes the purest form of 'flow governance', where the region–state can ignore the legitimation pressures that states, and indeed macro-regional free trade agreements, face in legislating market rule. But in practice states themselves coordinate such zones and administer to the populations and social conditions included in and exploited by the zones.

The 'powerless state' perspective offers a logical/historical view of capitalist markets superseding states in organising economic activity. In many ways this perspective *mirrors* the neoclassical theory that markets are compromised by state 'intervention', by definition, that they are more efficient with less state regulation. The opposing view portrays the 'powerless state' perspective as a myth. Weiss, for example, argues:

> rather than counterposing nation-state and global market as antinomies, in certain important respects we find that 'globalisation' is often the by-product of states promoting the internationalization strategies of their corporations, and sometimes in the process 'internationalizing' state capacity.
>
> (1997: 4)

She suggests that the notion of the powerless state stems from the differential capacity of some states to exploit the global market, especially distinguishing the East Asian 'robust state capacity' from the 'relatively weaker developmental capabilities of states in the second-generation NICs – that is, the Southeast Asian economies' which 'rendered these economies more vulnerable to external pressures than their northern counterparts' (ibid.: 4, 5).

Weiss deploys an international relations perspective, in which (differentiated) states are counterposed to markets, or international economic exchanges. The concept of differential state capacity critiques the powerless state thesis as over-stated and overgeneralised, emphasising variety rather than convergence of state capabilities, and arguing that national differences may be more pronounced in an internationalised environment. Certainly, to the extent that global processes are embedded in (and expressed through) national institutions and cultures, which are historically distinct, then one would expect to find difference crys-tallised. But the real question is what 'difference' expresses, as it is by no means primordial. 'Difference' is constituted through historical relations, which must themselves become the point of analytical departure.

Weiss also observes that economic integration does not enfeeble states, so much as specific policy instruments (e.g., macro-economic strategies of fiscal and monetary policy). Thus states like Singapore can adapt to changing global markets with new industrial/technology policy to generate higher-value activities (Weiss 1997: 19). Drawing on the pre-1997 East Asian 'miracles', explained by unique institutional arrangements such as 'embedded autonomy' (Evans 1995), Weiss concludes: 'rather than attributing the current proclivities for macroeconomic adjustment to "globalisation", one should look in the first instance, domestically, to a country's governing institutions, and thus to differences in national orientations and capabilities' (1997: 20). But national institutions and policy regimes cannot be isolated from their world-historical context, which now includes the global financial crisis.

What emerges from this debate is a stand-off, where each side portrays the other as exaggerating the power of states, or markets. The point really is that markets themselves are political institutions, embedded historically in states and the state system at large (McMichael 1987). That is to say, commercial bureaucratic states and the capitalist world economy were mutually conditioning. Initially, the early modern states instituted a world market built on mercantilist principles. Commercial policy institutionalised the monopolising tendencies of merchant capital as a means of enlarging national wealth. In the nineteenth century, industrial capitalism transformed the state/market nexus. States increasingly instituted markets built on the principles of free trade, imposed on the world by the British state through its naval, commercial and financial supremacy. Polanyi (1957) observes that the 'self-regulating market' initiative originated in an institutional act engineered by British capitalists to promote machine production, and its need for expanding inputs and market outlets. The 1834 Poor Law Act, by eliminating local parish support for the working poor, and promoting labour mobility, instituted the labour market. The Bank Act of 1844 instituted central banking, establishing fiduciary money to manage currency values relative to the gold standard and stabilise business conditions. And the Corn Law repeal in 1846 stimulated cheap grain imports from the 'New World' to reduce the cost of wage foods. Together, these measures *instituted* the markets in labour, currency, and land that underpinned Britain's prodigious commercial expansion on a global scale.

While British measures to institute commodity markets opened up the ninteenth-century world to the dynamics of industrial capitalism, they also generated a protective cycle of market regulation across the world of constitutional states. In this movement lay the various national forms of regulation: land markets and agricultural trade generating agricultural tariffs (and early conceptions of national food security); labour markets generating social democratic responses (in domestic labour legislation and early import-substitution industrial strategies); and money markets generating constitutional forms of currency management to stabilise conditions for private accumulation. This broad protective and regulatory movement framed the state formation process. In fact, the moral of this story is that states and markets are mutually conditioning, and that this relationship is socially mediated.

We need only to consider the civil unrest on all continents arising from the current restructuring of states in an attempt to stabilise world markets to confirm the proposition that states and markets are inseparable social complexes. Debates about globalisation that ignore this proposition repeat the abstractions of neoclassical theory and its belief in the self-regulating market. By extension, world markets are embedded in international institutions that constitute an additional site of power relations between (unequal) states on the one hand, and states and international institutions on the other. Hence the historical role of the Bretton Woods institutions (e.g., the IMF, World Bank) in shaping global financial and trade conditions is a critical dimension of global political economy.

## Perspectives on globalisation: social geographies

One of the dimensions of the changing nature of state/market relations is the juxtaposition of two different principles of social organisation: spaces and flows. Space normally refers to social geographies, especially political jurisdictions or territories. Flows refer to the circulation of information, people, money, technology and goods and services. States formed historically to govern space, and to mediate the 'space of places' (Tilly 1975; Castells 1997: 123). States also have governed flows, which, apart from smuggling and high finance, have been predominantly state-to-state in form (e.g., trade). The concept of a 'space of flows' refers to the rise of increasingly de-regulated exchanges, especially of money, but increasingly of commodities – whose prices are manipulated across space to minimise taxation. States are not well suited to governing this 'space of flows', which is a growing dimension of the global political-economy. Arrighi (1994) suggests this may be cyclical, where the 'capitalist' principle (financial liquidity) overrides the 'territorial' principle in an unstable post-hegemonic world order, eroding the centre of accumulation (e.g., the US home market), and heightening speculation on an unknown financial future.

In the meantime, however, the intensification of flows threatens the social foundations of territorialism. Democratic politics have hitherto been based on social relations grounded in the governance of territories. Recently Guéhenno has argued that the 'territorial foundation of political modernity ... is under attack from new forms of economic modernity' – namely, networks of information, or flows. The territorial basis of taxation, which is the substance of the national state's governing capacity, is called into question today by three dynamics: the mobility of [certain] people, capital, and the attribution of added value in the internal transfer accounting operations of transnational corporations (TNCs) (Guéhenno 1995: 10).

Castells perceives in the 'network society' a fundamental opposition between two spatial logics, the space of flows and the space of places (1997: 123). He argues that the concentration of power, wealth and information occurs in the space of flows, whereas most human experience and meaning concentrate locally, in the space of places. And Hoogvelt observes that (from Marx) the annihilation of space through time (via circulation of money and information) re-orders economic activities into two kinds: 'real-time' economy 'where distance and location are no longer relevant', and 'material' economy 'where there is still some "friction of space" that limits choice of location' (1997: 121). Money has become a 'real-time' resource, permitting an unprecedented degree of global mobility (ibid.: 121).

Both Castells and Hoogvelt develop Harvey's notion of time/space compression being the essence of globalisation (1989). In a world reconfigured by flows of money and information the core economic, symbolic and political processes are increasingly removed from places where people construct meaning and exercise power (the realm of civil society). Castells argues that the disembedding of power from place generates a legitimacy crisis undermining the meaning and function of institutions of the industrial era (e.g., the nation-state, class politics, citizenship, the patriarchal family). It is in this contradiction that he finds social movements emerging to restore local systems of power and identity, or to refashion power and identity on a transnational scale. Either way, his message is that the techno-economic process of globalisation is not going unchallenged and will be transformed 'from a multiplicity of sources, according to different cultures, histories, and geographies' (Castells 1997: 3).

This perspective parallels Weiss' point that globalisation crystallises difference, which in turn informs the kinds of adaption or resistance by social groups and institutions. But it promises more in the sense that it suggests that globalisation, as a grid of multiple networks, is not simply dismantling the nation-centred social system, but conjuring up a melange of new subjectivities that express combinations of spaces, flows, and their dynamic interrelationship (cf. Appadurai 1990). Arguably, it is the source of 'postmodern identities' in which subjects negotiate the opposition between historical time (represented in space) and real time (represented in the instancy of global communication in the 'space of flows'). In other words, this perspective suggests that globalisation is the politics of culture, expressed in the replacement of the politics of citizenship by the politics of differential identity (ethno-politics, sexual politics, environmental politics, etc.).

This line of inquiry is fruitful insofar as it grounds global integration in its social manifestations, where emergent movements express the new contradictions associated with the attempt to reinstall the self-regulating market in a world scale. While movements vary in composition, scale, and mission, they share a context of failure or erosion of states and national political projects under the pressure of 'market rule'. Not all movements articulate this context, but most respond to the shifts in political authority and market conditions (whether unemployment, labour casualisation or abuse, intensification of sweatshop or export production, environmental stress, ethnicisation of economic or political opportunity, and commercialisation of forests). Polanyi (1957) characterised the dialectic of market rule and social countermovements as the source of 'the great transformation', whereby society was 'discovered', in the form of the welfare state. Arguably, globalisation constitutes a replay of this dialectic, on a global scale.

As Bienefeld (1989) reminds us, the late twentieth-century 'self-regulating market' initiative stems not from Polanyi's English manufacturers seeking a hospitable commercial environment at home and abroad, but from global financial interests seeking to de-regulate all national institutions and impose market rule. Countermovements have emerged to challenge or resist market integration, sometimes with considerable effect precisely because of the greater sensitivity of capital circuits (integrated flows) to political instability. For example, the 1994 *Zapatista* uprising expressed a concerted (historically and culturally-based) challenge to the Mexican government's collaboration in market rule through NAFTA. The uprising destabilised the Mexican, and subsequently, Latin American, financial markets. It also appealed for a strengthening of Mexican civil society, connecting to other minority communities.

The politics of globalisation is not, then, something completely different. It concerns the active reformulation of global power relations in material and discursive ways, but the reformulation implicates existing historical (uneven time/space) relations. Nevertheless, globalisation can be viewed as an era in the making, producing an intermingling of peoples and cultures, especially via informational technologies, and new forms of resistance and utopic movements.

Informational technologies also reconfigure production relations. Castells characterises 'the new industrial space' as geographically discontinuous, because of 'the technological and organizational ability to separate the production process in different locations while reintegrating its unity through telecommunications linkages, and microelectronics-based precision and flexibility in the fabrication of components' (1996: 386, see also Phillips, Chapter 3 in this volume). Unlike the commodity chain approach to global industrial organisation, which focuses on a geo-politically derived hierarchical division of world labour in the conception and fabrication of products (Gereffi 1989), Castells' 'space of flows' situates hierarchies of innovation and fabrication in global networks. Here the 'direction and architecture of these networks are submitted to the endless changing movements of cooperation and competition between firms and between locales, sometimes historically cumulative, sometimes reversing the established pattern through deliberate institutional entrepreneurialism' (Castells 1996: 393).

Hoogvelt offers a complementary perspective, of corporations adopting a 'loosely confederated network structure' in order to survive in and negotiate an environment where markets and technologies are in constant flux. Informational technologies facilitate this, but are both expensive and rapidly obsolescent, 'placing an ever greater premium on access to financial resources, multiplant production and extensive marketing networks' (Hoogvelt 1997: 110). The consequence is that companies (high-tech industries such as automobile, aerospace, computers, and telecommunications) enter increasingly into strategic alliances and joint ventures, giving rise to the 'networked' or 'virtual' firm. The virtual firm is governed by financial mergers and speculation, and a lack of responsibility for labour force reproduction in any particular place (ibid.: 111, 113). In this config-uration, social rather than geographical hierarchies (as understood in the classic international division of labour between north and south) organise a global production landscape that is fluid, unstable, and characterised by 'jobless growth', overproduction tendencies, and recurring outbreaks of financial crisis – quite similar to one scenario portrayed by Marx.

## Perspectives on globalisation: geopolitical relations

The geopolitical perspective focuses on the illusion of universality. The logic of this position is that the world was once divided unequally along geographical lines, and that globalisation eliminates geographical divisions. Thus the International Forum on Globalisation analysts critique the multilateral institutional establishment proposal to end global poverty by fostering a 'free trade regime' (Mander and Goldsmith 1996). They argue that there is no such thing as a 'level playing field' in the international trade and investment arena. Furthermore, the emerging global regime subordinates governments and states to global flows of money and commodities, privileging corporations that are predominantly northern. The new trade rules elaborated by global institutions such as the World Trade Organization, are viewed, like the Chinese perspective on the Opium Wars settlements, as 'unequal treaties', appropriate to colonial relations (Khor 1997: 10). The focus of this kind of perspective is on geographi-cally-based inequality, understood in north–south terms. This geopolitical division of the world underlies the powerful development paradigm, where some states and societies were and are considered historically more equal than others (Rist 1997).

The focus of contention is the newly established World Trade Organization (WTO), as the institutional arm of the 1990s' free trade regime. The formal content of WTO rules conceals the substantive differences among supposedly equal members, because some wealthy states are relatively immune from trade sanctions arising from the dispute settlement mechanism. Power relations are embedded in universal rule-making. The WTO representation of the world evidently dovetails with the ideology of economic liberalism espoused by the United States, which frames the outlook of the G-7 powers, even if they do not always agree on particular policies.

Market rule, and its institutional framework, are anchored in a powerful state. Under the nineteenth-century system, Britain anchored the gold standard with sterling and a superior navy that opened world trade channels. In a post-hege-monic, multipolar world, the United States has sought to extend the fruits of its hegemony by using multilateral enforcement mechanisms to institute a global free trade regime (McMichael 1995). The dollar continues to play the role of *de facto* international reserve currency, allowing the US to export its deficit. However, as Arrighi claims, 'although the US state still has some privileged access to its services and resources, the main tendency of the last 30 years has been for most states, including the US, to become the servant rather than the master of extraterritorial high finance' (1998: 69). Under these conditions, the structure of global power has quite unstable underpinnings, which have been exposed as global financial arrangements have become more fragile.

Market rule rests on institutionalised coercion in a world of unequal states. George has referred to the World Bank–IMF debt management strategy as 'financial low-intensity conflict', confirmed by the Presidential Commission on Integrated Long-Term Strategy, which stated in 1988:

> We … need to think of low-intensity conflict as a form of warfare that is not a problem just for the Department of Defense. In many situations, the United States will need not just DoD personnel and material but diplomats and information specialists, agricultural chemists, bankers, economists … and scores of other professionals.
>
> (quoted in Ismi 1998: 11)

In short, the geo-political perspective adds a necessary power dimension to globalisation. It is an important corrective to the techno-economic, network and market perspectives that focus on integrating mechanisms at the expense of the historical and political relations of world capitalism.

A more elaborated version of the geo-political perspective is the concept of the 'globalisation of poverty' (Chossudovsky 1997). Chossudovsky argues that IMF structural adjustment programmes (SAPs) have generated a global cheap-labour economy through the decomposition of the national economy of indebted states, especially through currency devaluation and wage de-indexation. The WTO, in turn, is a vehicle for generalising the 'free trade zone' to the entire country – a phenomenon that is extensive in Mexico, for instance, where wages are about ten times lower than equivalent wages in the US. Accordingly, the northern countries increasingly approximate the 'rentier economy', centred in services such as intellectual property (patents, licences) and finance and marketing, which facilitate the appropriation of profit from the south. In short:

> material production takes place off-shore in a Third World cheap-labour economy, yet the largest increases in GDP are recorded in the importing country … [where]… cheap-labour imports [in primary commodities and manufacturing] generate a corresponding increase in income in the services economy of the rich countries.
>
> (Chossudovsky 1997: 86)

As many commentators (e.g., Hirst and Thompson 1996) will point out, the bulk of global investment and trade concentrates in the wealthy zones of the world, making globalisation a questionable proposition. The geo-political perspective, however, addresses a more profound aspect of the dynamics of the project of globalisation. Twenty per cent of the world's population consumes 86 per cent of the world's resources, and we have reached the age of 'indifferent imperialism', where the wealthy states 'have so greatly increased their technological advantages that they do not *need* to exploit the whole world, just some of it' (Schaeffer 1995: 267). Nevertheless, southern states are constrained to attract capital and offer advantageous conditions at the expense of the sustainability of their labour forces and natural resources. To identify globalisation only with the zones of advantage and wealth repeats the fallacy of developmentalism, which sees (selective) material progress as a universal standard, ignores its entropic consequences, and misconstrues the unequal control and consumption of planetary resources as a temporary condition (cf. Rist 1997). Globalisation is selective, and yet it threatens the survival of the natural world and, by extension, the human species.

## Perspectives on globalisation: governance and regulation

Cohen (1998) argues that governance is shared between states and market forces (the invisible hand of competition). Hoogvelt develops this perspective by arguing that competition certainly imposes a global market discipline, but 'it is time/space compression that creates the shared phenomenal world that supports and reproduces this discipline on a daily basis' (1997: 125). Like Sklair (1997), she posits a global capitalist class that governs by institutionalising structural power via the general adoption of cultural values and a legitimating ideology, under the banner of deregulation of markets and privatisation of previously state-owned industries via structural adjustment programmes (Hoogvelt 1997: 138). Restructured states internalise new regulatory modes and goals, expressing the paradox of re-regulation in increasingly powerless states.

The paradox of re-regulation can be untangled by viewing the market in formal and substantive terms. The formal institution of market rule is symbolised in the rhetoric of 'free trade' and the construction of an international regime comprised of multilateral institutions, free trade agreements, international codes of market behaviour, and the like. Substantively, the market annihilates space by time (and time by space), that is, market relations and discourse discount historical relations. Where the formal dynamic enlists the jurisdictional parameters of market rule, the substantive dynamic transcends territorial space and operates through flows in 'real time', which is oblivious to geography.

The contradiction arises in the selective impact flows have on territorially-based social relations (rather than the image of flows superseding spaces). Thus, when a national government enters into a free trade agreement, a segment of its population, or a social tradition, may be marginalised through exposure to a global marketplace dominated by more powerful economic actors. Thus Mexico's embrace of NAFTA threatens its progressively less subsidised small maize farmers by exposing them to subsidised imports of corn from Iowa.

From another angle, the contradiction is *internal* to the formal institution of market rule, insofar as the market de-nationalises, or produces a 'destatization of the political system' (Jessop 1997: 574). Arguably, this is the intent, or consequence, of structural adjustment, where indebted states are bailed out by the IMF under conditions that 'open' their economies and implement social austerity measures to privilege powerful global economic actors. Viewing the market as a de-nationalising movement does not imply a borderless world, rather it implies transformed states. In my view, this transformation involves a shift from states managing national economies, to states managing the global economy – in two senses: facilitating global circuits of money and commodities, and resolving the contradictions of global capitalism. The concept of the 'globalisation project' interprets this transformation, emphasising the changing institutional arrangements which purport to manage the global economy (McMichael 2000).

Globalisation, as a political project, concerns the attempt to institutionalise the neoliberal agenda of market reform by removing public constraints on economies. The premise is an ideological assertion that markets are 'self-regulating', and that the visible hand of the state is a recipe for inefficiency. The nineteenth-century attempt to install the 'self-regulating market' focused on the formation of markets in land, labour and money, via nation-state building. The current attempt focuses on the freeing of such markets by subordinating nation-state policies to the authority of financial orthodoxy, as institutionalised in multilateral agencies and agreements. Here the emphasis is on substituting global forms of governance of market practices for national forms of government. Government (i.e., national developmentalism) is viewed as a constraint on global flows of capital and commodities and on the formation of global markets for money, labour and natural resources (to optimise conditions for speculators and investors).

Market rule is simultaneously crisis management (see Amin 1997). The financial turmoil of the late 1990s revealed that financial markets overshadow productive investments. That is, money now reproduces money rather than social labour, since the value of money is no longer governed by the effective command of wage labour, rather by credit-mongering and speculative circuits of financial capital (Marazzi 1995: 74). Consequently, global regulation concerns avoiding financial collapse. The global regulators have two goals: to underwrite and reschedule debt, on a decidedly *ad hoc* basis (and with apparently increasingly frequent occurrence); and to use debt rescheduling as a lever to liberalise national financial systems, even though government compliance is quite variable, and in some cases agencies continue to extend credit to stimulate debt repayment (Kanbur 1998). These goals are and were exemplified in the emergency financial bail-out of beleaguered Asian Pacific national banking systems in late 1997, by IMF packages supplemented with northern financial assistance. The IMF's role is to extract financial adjustment in the assisted states to sustain global capital flows.

The globalisation project involves a profound reformulation of money, and states. Under the nation-state system over the past century or so, central banks controlled and adjusted national currencies in accordance with their exchange values (Ingham 1994). At this historical juncture, citizens and governments (except perhaps the US) no longer control national currencies, which have become objects of speculation. The evaluation of currency values occurs in real time, via the 'information standard'. The integration of computer and telecommunications technologies compress space into instant time, abstracting the determination of value from territorial and social space.

Money is no longer only a means of payment and medium of commodity circulation, but also a commodity, where currencies (and hence countries) are brought directly into competition with one another. The effect is to force states to adopt competitive market policies in order to defend their national currency. As Altvater and Mahnkopf argue: 'When interest and currency rates are no longer determined politically by legitimate institutions of the nation-state but rather are formed by global markets ... Politics does not disappear, but its rationality is synchronized with the economy' (1997: 463). It is therefore not surprising that Malaysia's trade minister, Rafidah Aziz, should request increased bailout money from the West at ASEAN's thirtieth meeting (December 1997) in the following way: 'Forget politics. It is pure survival of the global economy' (quoted in Mydans 1997: 6).

States today embrace a new (ideological) rationality in a disembedded world (money) market, and this centres on the legal regulation of monetary relations: the substitution of regulatory policy for process politics (Altvater and Mahnkopf 1997: 464). And it is not unusual for regulatory policy to be administered externally by the Bretton Woods institutions acting on behalf of the international creditor banks (Chossudovsky 1997: 183). In fact, the Asian crisis revealed that while all states yield power to anarchic global financial markets, states at the base of the currency pyramid are compelled to pay for the casino-like movement of short-term funds in search of quick profits, under IMF 'trusteeship'.

The need for market credibility has a near universal hold, delegating public functions to semi-autonomous technocratic bodies such as central banks, utilities regulators and social service coordinators that function as market regulators (Picciotto 1998: 3). The substitution of market for social criteria in the evaluation of need governs the movement from welfare to workfare in northern states (Teeple 1995). However, this movement is not uncontested, as suggested by the progressive electoral victory (among others in Europe) of the German Social Democrats over the conservative Christian Democrats in September 1998, on a platform of preserving German, and European, welfare state foundations.

Under conditions of recurring financial instability, the global managers perceive states in instrumental terms: as rationalisers of global financial circuits and of global financial crises. This is evident in the standardised conditions imposed, and continuing to be imposed, on indebted states by the IMF, with little regard for the specific circumstances of each country, and in the application of financial, rather than social criteria. The severe depletion of social capital under the austerity measures of the SAPs lies behind the World Bank's new interest in 'state effectiveness', as part of a broad strategy of stabilising seriously deteriorating social conditions. But, consistent with the rationale of financial viability and hospitality towards global capital circuits, the Bank continues to sustain the myth of globalisation as the path to economic well-being, as illustrated, for example, in its 1997 *World Development Report*.

The Bank's stance highlights the inextricable connection between global integration and the reformulation of governance. The World Trade Organization (WTO) embodies the mature version of the 'new constitutionalism', whereby the political and bureaucratic elites responsible for managing global economic flows do so with growing insulation from popular scrutiny (Gill 1992). The formal power of the multilateral institutions structures policy discourses across the debtor states. A more far-reaching, substantive, power is presaged in the negotiation over the terms of the WTO. In particular, the current dispute over the reach of the WTO regarding investment is central to instituting a global property regime. This has involved separate negotiations within the OECD regarding a Multilateral Agreement on Investment (MAI), to formulate global investment rules under the slogan: 'A level playing field for direct investment worldwide'. While the WTO is as yet only empowered to rule on 'trade-related investments' (TRIMS), the MAI strategy would relax restrictions on foreign investment into, and out of, any member state, and grant the legal right for foreigners to invest and operate competitively in all sectors of the economy (Clarke and Barlow 1997).

As yet only proposals, these proposed rules indicate the direction the global political and corporate elites favour. Of the world's largest 500 TNCs, 477 are based in OECD countries and are organised into various corporate lobby groups involved in constructing the MAI. Their target is global, especially having access to southern resources, and the urgency follows a rising share of world GDP controlled by TNCs: from 17 per cent in the mid-1960s through 24 per cent in 1984 to 33 per cent in 1995, and a growing concentration, where just 1 per cent of the world's corporations are responsible for 50 per cent of all global foreign direct investment (Hoedeman *et al.* 1998: 159). The new rules, however, are proving to be contradictory, as liberalisation destabilises and deflates the global economy, reducing profitable investment possibilities at the same time as capital concentrates and centralises in one financial merger after another.

## Conclusion

The present world conjuncture is represented (and justified) by globalist discourse as a transition towards a more efficient and bountiful future. Because we are taught to think about the world in positivist (causal or evolutionary) terms, globalist discourse is compelling: if not as a utopia, certainly as a tendency subject to empirical confirmation. Arguably, this way of seeing the social world is deeply embedded in the 'development' episteme, by which world history is naturalised as a process of endless material growth modelled on the European experience (Cowan and Shenton 1996; Rist 1997). Recently, however, the profound instability of the global economy has generated a growing recognition of the 'limits of globalisation' among the financial and development establishment (e.g., Rodrik 1997; Soros 1997).

The globalisation project is simultaneously a project of crisis management and a blueprint for continuing development through private means. Like the development project, the globalisation project is an attempt to construct a stable hegemonic ordering of the world. Whereas the vision of the development project offered an alternative to the politics of anti-colonial movements and socialism, the globalisation project targets public policies of welfarism and developmentalism, portrayed as undermining market efficiencies, and therefore economic growth. It is evident in the imposition of conditions and the elaboration of rules geared to 'opening' economies in the name of the market: enlarging the domain of transnational enterprise and resource access, and instrumentalising states as crisis managers. In this sense, states are not being eliminated, rather they are facing pressures to restructure institutionally to secure global credit, and circuits of money and commodities, legitimised by 'consumer citizens'. This includes the European initiative to establish a single currency via the centralisation of monetary policy.

Finally, the globalisation project is governed by the fetishism of the money commodity. The post-Bretton Woods monetary relations of integration, securitisation and unsustainable fictitious capital creation compel the financial agencies to attempt to manage the global political-economy in order to preserve money. Preserving this virtual form of capitalism requires managing power relations within states and across the state system. As such, the globalisation project is a movement to institute market rule by a powerful global managerial class. Its historical specificity is expressed in its increasingly *ad hoc* form of crisis management, caught in a financial web of its own making. Preserving money means sacrificing social goals, and the rest of the world routinely bears the burden of adjustment. But the rest of the world is catching on, and it is in the dynamics of the emerging counter-movements that the question of 'globalisation: for whom?' will be resolved.

## Acknowledgement

I am grateful to Rajeev Patel for reading and offering insightful comments on an earlier draft of this chapter.

# Part II

# Theoretical innovation and contemporary debates

# 8 Game theory

## International trade, conflict and cooperation

*Lisa J. Carlson*

Rational choice analysis is one of several theories used to explore questions in international political economy (IPE). As Crane and Amawi (1997: 22) point out, some consider rational choice a theory in and of itself, while others view it as a tool or analytic technique to be employed within a larger theoretical system. Either way, rational choice analysis has been used to generate new insights on questions dealing with issues in IPE. This chapter is intended to provide the reader with a broad introduction to the rational choice approach and identifies some of the ways in which the theory has contributed to our understanding of issues involving international trade, cooperation, and conflict.[1]

International trade theory operates on the premise that free trade leading to higher real incomes is desirable for individual countries and the world as a whole. From this presumption, we predict that a great deal of free economic exchange would occur, and yet, we observe that conflict over trade has been endemic in the international system for hundreds of years (Conybeare 1987: iv). Thus, one important question to be addressed is why states fail to pursue the Pareto optimal course of action by imposing tariffs on their trading partners' goods and services (Frey 1997: 232). A logical extension to the issue of protected trade involves identifying the conditions under which the imposition of tariffs escalates to the level of a trade war or leads to the removal of trade barriers altogether. Some have addressed the latter issue by identifying the political correlates of a stable world trade system and/or the enforcement mechanisms necessary to sustaining cooperation (Gowa 1989a: 307).

Rational choice analysis, and game theory in particular, has attempted to answer the questions posed above in at least four different ways. Free and fair international trade is a public good; trade is a simple Prisoner's Dilemma game and only under certain conditions is it a public good; trade generates security externalities (the relative gains argument); and trade is best understood as the result of domestic (and international) bargaining games. Before we discuss how rational choice analysis has addressed the foregoing issues, a brief discussion of the theory is in order.

## Decision and game theory

Rational choice analysis grows out of a single theory – decision or utility theory.[2] Dacey (1999) offers the reader an insightful introduction into the core assumptions and concepts of decision theory. He states that:

> decision theory provides a prescriptive analysis of the process of human cognitive decision making based upon an unfolding of decision problems. The theory assumes two actors are involved in the decision problem. The first actor is a cognitive and rational human decision maker who is endowed with a set of actions [A] under her control. The second actor is a non-cognitive, metaphorical actor called Nature who randomly selects from a set of states of nature [S] beyond the control of the decision maker. A decision problem is represented as a pair [S, A] composed of a set S of states of nature and a set A of acts.
>
> It is assumed that the decision maker can infer the outcome of every act in each state. A decision maker faces a decision problem under certainty if and only if there is a unique outcome associated with each act. If the decision maker knows there is a set of outcomes associated with each act and knows (or does not know) the probabilities of the outcomes in each set, the decision problem is properly characterized by risk or (uncertainty). Each act-state pair determines an outcome. The decision maker resolves the decision

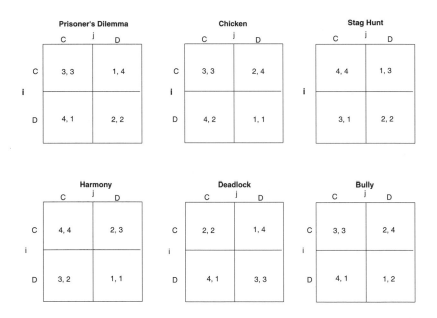

*Figure 8.1*　Games

i, j = nation-state actors; C = cooperate (do not impose a tariff); D = defect (impose a tariff); preference orderings for i and j: 4 > 3 > 2 > 1

problem by inducing a consistent and transitive preference ordering over the set of acts and then by selecting the most preferred act.

Game theory is an extension of decision theory in that it presumes a minimum of two cognitive rational decision makers.[3] In contrast to decision theory, a game is being played by a group of individuals whenever the fate of an individual depends not only on his own actions but also on the actions of others (Binmore 1990). The essential elements of a game are players, actions, information, strategies, payoffs, outcomes and equilibria. The players, actions and outcomes are collectively referred to as the rules of the game and the modeler's objective is to use the rules of the game to determine the equilibrium (Rasmusen 1989: 22).

Game theory is a useful way to model strategic interactions between actors in situations of conflicting objectives. Because the international trade game involves two or more rational actors, game theory – not decision theory – is the proper theory to model interstate interactions. As Frey (1997) notes, one of the strengths claimed for the theory is its parsimony and level of abstraction. Those characteristics of game theory provide modelers with the tools necessary to gain insight into complex political problems. Moreover, because game theory is based on a rigorous and a well specified theory of human behavior, the theory produces empirically relevant hypotheses that can explain and predict cooperation and conflict within a single logical axiomatic structure (Kratochwil and Ruggie 1986).[4]

## *Games*

'A theory is supposed to reduce a potentially infinite complexity to a perceivable structure' (Rapoport *et al.* 1976: 7). Toward that end, game theorists have developed a class of games for the purpose of analyzing different strategic bargaining situations in the international system. The most common 2x2 games are shown in Figure 8.1.

The structure of a 2x2 game in normal form is completely contained in the information provided by the payoff matrix (Rapoport *et al.* 1976: 7) and one game is distinguished from another on the basis of the actors' preference orderings of the payoffs. According to Conybeare (1987), the games of Prisoner's Dilemma (PD), Stag Hunt, and Chicken can be derived from the pure theory of trade and therefore play an important role in understanding the conditions under which free trade or trade wars take place. In general, 'these three games have attracted a great deal of attention precisely because cooperation is necessary to the realization of mutual benefits but it is by no means automatic' (Oye 1996: 81).

## International free trade is a public good

Many consider the basic international trade game to be an instance of Prisoner's Dilemma (Krugman and Obstfeld 1991; Conybeare 1984).[5] Starting with this presumption, some argue that the establishment and maintenance of free trade are made more difficult by the fact that free trade is an international public good. Economists distinguish between public and private goods on the basis of rivalry and excludability. Rivalry exists if two individuals cannot consume a good at the same time. Excludability exists if those people who do not pay for a good or service can be excluded from consuming the good or service. If the claim is that the benefits of cooperation in a fair trade system are non-rivaled and the benefits of defection (imposing a tariff) are non-excludable, then international trade has the properties of a pure public good (Sandmo 1989).

The problems associated with the provision of a public good are well known. Since the benefits of any action an individual nation takes to provide a public good also goes to others, individuals acting independently do not have an incentive to provide optimal amounts of such goods. Furthermore, when the group interested in the public good is very large, and the share of benefit that goes to any one individual is very small, usually no individual will have an incentive to 'purchase' any of the good (Olson 1965).

The lack of an incentive to pay for the provision of the public good is known as the 'free-rider' problem. Free riding exists because an individual will receive the public good even if s/he does not pay for it. And since the contribution of any one individual is so small, no one will notice the free-rider and so the possible costs associated with being detected and punished can be avoided (Abrams 1980). The key point is that in large groups (such as the nation-state trading system) public goods will not be provided voluntarily unless some form of coercion or special incentive is provided to induce individuals to bear their share of the costs.

As noted, the standard game-theoretic model used to characterize the international trade game is Prisoner's Dilemma. The simple PD game is based on the following set of assumptions. There are two actors, states i and j, who are unitary rational state actors that seek to maximize national income. Each state has one of two acts available to them: cooperate (C) or defect (D). To cooperate means not to impose a tariff (contribute to the public good) and defect means to impose a tariff (refuse to contribute to the public good). The game is non-cooperative (binding agreements are prohibited), each player selects one act and the players choose their acts simultaneously (they select an act without observing the act chosen by the opponent). Four different outcomes can result based on the combination of acts chosen: CC (free trade); DD (protected trade); CD (the cooperating player is unilaterally exploited); DC (a player unilaterally exploits the cooperating opponent).

Both players' preference ordering over the outcomes in the game are assumed to be: DC > CC > DD > CD. This ordering is consistent with the presumption of international trade theory that nations are better off under free trade (CC) than mutual tariffs (DD). However, what is good for the world is not necessarily the best outcome for an individual nation (Conybeare 1987: 23). If one nation can raise its tariffs while its trading partner retains low tariffs (DC), then the first can shift the terms of trade in its favor. This shift in the terms of trade can make the exploitative actor better off than under free trade (Morrow 1994: 263).

The predicted outcome in the one-shot PD game is DD or protected trade. The reason this holds is that a player is always made better off by defecting irrespective of whether the opponent chooses to cooperate or defect (a dominant strategy) and neither player can improve their position by switching strategies and moving to a new outcome (a Nash equilibrium). What makes the Prisoner's Dilemma unique is that while DD is an equilibrium outcome neither player has an incentive to alter, this outcome is not Pareto optimal. There is another outcome, CC, which both players prefer to DD (Abrams 1980: 307). Thus, PD has been considered the archetypical example of the disjuncture between individual and group rationality (Snidal 1985b: 926). The problem is that both sides would be made better off pursuing free trade had each not behaved in their own best interest.

The simple version of the PD public goods game neatly accounts for why cooperation can fail even though it is in states' best interests not to pursue protected trade. But note the difficulty that is generated with particular formulation of the problem. Whereas the pure theory of international trade predicts that states will always pursue free trade, the one-shot PD game predicts that states will always pursue protected trade. Neither extreme holds up under empirical scrutiny. Clearly, there are conditions under which states will or will not opt for free or protected trade. The question thus becomes what factors account for the disparity between the game's prediction and the empirical world and how can we construct a proper model that accounts for both conflict and cooperation in trade?

## Leadership and hegemony

One answer suggests that a very powerful nation, called a leader or a hegemon, must exist in order for states to escape the public goods PD dilemma. Since the provision of the public good is deemed so valuable to the hegemon, the hegemon will bear the full cost of providing the public good in order to maintain a system of fair trade and induce political stability (Kindleberger 1973; 1981). This view, which Lake (1993) calls leadership theory, assumes that a benevolent leader with free trade preferences is a necessary condition to overcome the free rider problem in order to induce stability in the system.

A variation on this theme, known as Hegemony Theory (Lake 1993), relies on the interaction of states' national trade policy preferences to explain patterns of open or closed trade in the system. In Lake's (1988) version, it is assumed that a hegemon's preference ordering is not consistent with PD but with the game called Harmony: CC > CD > DC > DD. Note that the hegemon's most preferred outcome changes from unilateral exploitation to mutual cooperation or free trade. In PD, to be exploited (CD) represents an actor's worst outcome which is now the hegemon's second best outcome, and so on. In this version of the international trade game, the hegemon is playing against other states whose preferences over the outcomes in the game are determined by their economic position in the system. Non-hegemonic actors' preferences may be consistent with the games of Harmony (CC > CD > DC > DD), Prisoner's Dilemma (DC > CC > DD > CD), or Deadlock (DC > DD > CC > CD).

Note that all actors in each of the games have a dominant strategy. Harmony actors always cooperate and Prisoner's Dilemma or Deadlock players always defect, i.e., choose protectionism. Obviously, universal free trade is the outcome when the hegemon is playing against actors with a Harmony preference configuration. Explaining free trade in this case is trivial. The equilibrium outcome that results when a hegemon plays against PD or Deadlock players is not universal free trade since some actors are exploiting the hegemon's cooperative behavior. Since the absence of universal free trade is in equilibrium for the latter two cases, the question becomes how a hegemon induces players to switch their strategy from defection to cooperation.

One answer is that the hegemon must impose negative sanctions on defectors or offer positive side payments to induce the switch (Lake 1988: 50–51; Conybeare 1984).[6] Both of these actions might change the payoffs associated with defection in such a way that cooperation now becomes the optimal act for PD and/or Deadlock players. In effect, the hegemon is using its power to change the preference orderings of the actors in order to change the game itself. If successful, free trade is thus established.

These theories have come under serious attack on both theoretical and empirical grounds (Gowa 1989a). One important criticism charges the literature with the failure to establish that a hegemon is either a necessary or a sufficient condition for establishing and maintaining international free trade (Keohane 1984; Conybeare 1984). First, the notion that free trade is a public good has been called into question. Conybeare (1984: 11–12) for instance argues that free trade is both excludable and rivaled. Since free trade is not a public good, then the rest of the system has no need for a hegemon to provide it. However, public goods problems can develop in large $N$ games since it becomes more difficult to detect, exclude and punish defectors.[7]

Second, some contend the attribution of free trade preferences to a hegemon violates the principles of standard international trade theory (Gowa 1989a: 311). In other words, there is no justification for assuming that a hegemon always prefers free trade (a dominant strategy to cooperate).[8] Dacey (1994, 1995) establishes that the hegemonic trade negotiation game is an instance of the game called Bully or Called Bluff (Snyder and Diesing 1977). Bully is a game composed of PD preferences for the bully (the hegemon) and Chicken for the conciliatory player (DC > CC > CD > DD). Under Bully, the hegemon receives its best outcome and the conciliatory player is guaranteed its second worst.

The prediction derived from the Bully game is consistent with the claim that if a nation were a hegemon, then it would use its power to establish terms of trade favorable to itself. Therefore, a hegemon would not engage rationally in free trade (Conybeare 1984). Given the lack of publicness in trade, the first best policy for the hegemon is predation for the purpose of extracting or extorting monopolistic rents from the rest of the world (ibid.: 11).

While predation may be a hegemon's first preference, it is also recognized that maintaining an open trading system may be made more difficult if other countries can credibly follow suit and impose an optimal tariff of their own. Under this scenario, the Bully game evolves into two-sided Prisoner's Dilemma when the conciliatory nation reverses the order of its worst and second worst payoffs. Imposing an optimal tariff may lead to retaliation followed by counter-retaliation until a new sub-optimal tariff equilibrium is established making countries worse off than had they pursued free trade (Conybeare 1984: 10).[9]

## Iterated Prisoner's Dilemma

But note that with this view, we come full circle. If we accept the view that international free trade is generally not a public good but states' preferences are consistent with a PD structure, then why would we ever observe free trade in the system if a hegemon is a neither necessary nor sufficient to promote cooperation? To find an answer derived endogenously from the PD game itself, we must re-conceptualize how the game is played. International trade, unlike the one-shot PD game, has a future (Morrow 1994: 263). If we assume that the PD game is played repeatedly and indefinitely (as trade games actually unfold in the empirical world), then there may exist conditions under which mutual cooperation is rational, i.e., where CC is in equilibrium (Taylor 1976; Axelrod 1981, 1984; McGinnis 1986: 142; Morrow 1994). The reasoning is as follows.

What makes it possible for cooperation to emerge is the fact that the players might meet again. As Axelrod (1984: 12) points out, the future can cast a shadow back upon the present and thereby affect states' behavior in the current situation (Axelrod and Keohane 1986; Oye 1996; Powell 1993). A high probability of future play, however, is a necessary but not sufficient condition for cooperation to emerge. The reason is that future payoffs are normally discounted or valued less than present payoffs. Thus, the discount parameter must be of sufficient value to make the future loom large enough in the calculation of total payoffs and thereby overwhelm a state's temptation to defect on the present play (Axelrod 1984; Oye 1996: 88).

Even a highly valued future does not determine the most successful strategy to employ in a PD supergame. An optimal strategy – a complete description of a player's choices in all conceivable circumstances (McGinnis 1986: 145) depends on the strategy employed by others in the game (Gowa 1986: 170). For example, if a player's strategy is all D (defect on every move), then the opponent's optimum strategy is also all D. As Morrow (1994: 264–266) points out, the strategies all D (and all C) are independent of the history of the game. However, an iterated environment provides states with an opportunity to condition their moves in the game on the opponent's behavior and this may improve the prospects for cooperation (Oye 1996: 88).

One well-known reciprocal strategy is tit-for-tat. A tit-for-tat player cooperates on the first round of the game and then does whatever the other player did in the previous round (Axelrod 1984: 13). For example, if player j cooperates in round one, a tit-for-tat player reciprocates that cooperation in round two. If j defects in the second round, a tit-for-tat player reciprocates that defection in round three, and so on. The tit-for-tat strategy is important in that it offers insights into how free trade can be established and maintained in the international system.

The strategy indicates that tariff reductions can be supported by the threat of reciprocal punishments. Because tit-for-tat is based on immediate punishment in the next round triggered by defective behavior by j in the previous play, mutual low tariffs can be enforced when both sides place sufficiently high value on trade in the future relative to the gains from cheating in the present. The tit-for-tat strategy is more likely to lead to cooperation when the value players place on future payoffs increases, the reward from cheating decreases, the punishment gets more painful, and the cost of restoring cooperation increases (Morrow 1994: 266).

Cooperation can emerge under the conditions identified above but the effectiveness of strategies of reciprocity in sustaining cooperation hinges on other factors as well. First, it is assumed that states can reliably distinguish between cooperation and defection so that states can respond in kind (Oye 1996: 89). Suppose the following. Prior to the commencement of the trade game, State i places a 10 percent tariff on j's wool exports to i and j places a 10 percent tariff on i's beef exports to j. In round one of the game, both sides maintain their 10 percent tariffs. In round two, i increases its tariff on j from 10 percent to 11 percent. The question for j is whether to consider that 1 percent increase a defection or not. If i's act is deemed a defection, then j must decide whether to ignore, reciprocate or escalate the level of defection. The ability to discriminate between acts is an important one since states may find themselves committed to non-cooperative policies that were generated by misperceptions making both sides worse off.

Another complicating factor involves the tit-for-tat player's willingness to punish j for defecting. In the PD supergame, this is not at issue since players simply implement their strategies automatically. In the empirical setting, however, a state may prefer not to retaliate because the punishment might, for instance, harm domestic interests whose welfare is deemed important to the state. This possibility raises the issue of the credibility of retaliation. If j believes that a tit-for-tat player faces domestic constraints and is unwilling to follow through with punishment, then j may impose a tariff hoping to shift the terms of trade in its favor.

Conybeare (1985, 1987) too finds through an analysis of trade wars that iterated PD games played by large states in the system may develop 'norms' of cooperation but this cooperation is very fragile and may collapse easily (1987: xiii). The Anglo-Hanse trade wars from the 1300s to 1700s and the 1960s Chicken War between the US and the European Economic Community (EEC) are examples of iterated PD games in which both sides maintained their strategies of non-cooperation. Conybeare (1985, 1987) goes on to cite a myriad of factors that account for failure of cooperation to emerge even under iterated conditions.[10]

The key theme and insights that emerge from these studies are that likelihood of cooperation primarily depends on the number of players, the probability of repeated iteration and the preference orderings of the players (Oye 1996).

Cooperation is more likely to occur when the trade game is symmetric, i.e., played by two small states, or asymmetric, i.e., played by a small and a large state (Conybeare 1987). Again, cooperation can emerge among large states but it may be trickier to induce and maintain.

## Absolute vs. relative gains

All of the foregoing models presume that states are primarily concerned with absolute gains and are indifferent to the gains made by others. While this assumption seems reasonable enough, it has become an extremely contentious issue in the field of international relations. On the one hand, neoliberal institutionalist theories pursue their understanding of topics related to international political economy by accepting the assumption that states define their utility in terms of absolute gains (Gilpin 1981; Keohane 1984). On the other side of the debate, neorealist or structural realists assert that states are forced to be concerned with relative not absolute gains, and as a consequence, a state's utility must also be a function of other variables such as power (Waltz 1979; Gowa 1986; Grieco 1988a, 1988b).

For the structural realists, one of the main defects of both the public goods and prisoner's dilemma approaches in explaining the likelihood of free or protectionist interstate trade is the failure to recognize that economic exchange does not occur in a political vacuum (Gowa 1989b: 1246; Gowa and Mansfield 1993). The political environment that states operate in is characterized by anarchy. This means that the system lacks a central authority that can enforce agreements among states and where the threat of force is omnipresent (Powell 1993: 126). Anarchy thus implies that the system is one of self-help and one that generates state insecurity.

Given this environment, if states remove their trade barriers they will not only affect the real income of their trading partners but their security as well. The reason is that gains from trade result in increased efficiency with which domestic resources can be employed, and this in turn can free resources for military use thereby increasing a country's potential military power. As a consequence, states will be less concerned with increases in absolute income than with the relative power effects of trade since each knows that others will seek to exploit the wealth of others to enhance its own power (Gowa 1989b: 1247).

Herein lies the problem with the standard Prisoner's Dilemma formulation of the problem of international trade: It neglects the most crucial aspect of trade in anarchy – the production of security externalities. The model advanced by Gowa and Mansfield (1993) to reflect this argument is a simple extension of the traditional Prisoner's Dilemma game. The actors' PD payoffs are modified with the inclusion of a parameter, $w$, which captures the marginal social costs from trade.

It is surmised that trading with an adversary produces a negative externality while trading with an ally produces a positive externality. These externalities make the enforcement of trade agreements easier when externalities are positive because they raise the long-run value of trade (making defection less likely) and agreements are harder to enforce when externalities are negative (Morrow 1997: 30). Thus, security externalities inhibit free trade because of states' concerns with relative gains.

The systemic theory on relative gains, however, has also been called into serious question (Powell and Dimaggio 1991; Powell 1993). For instance, Morrow (1997) demonstrates that a concern for relative gains should not block trade even between rivals because the gains from trade cannot be turned into a military advantage quickly. Security externalities exist but they are unlikely to be large enough to lead adversaries to suspend trade since additional allocations to the military are likely to be smaller than the gain from trade (Morrow 1997: 31, 33). If this argument is correct, then relative gains approach offers an inadequate explanation of protection in the international system.

## Domestic factors

One of the difficulties with all of the foregoing game-theoretic models is the presumption that the state is the trading entity and we therefore need not give consideration to the domestic determinants of tariffs and trade-induced conflict and cooperation. Simply put, individuals, firms, and corporations engage in trade; states do not. States determine the terms of trade; individuals, firms and corporations do not (Dacey 1999). Here the argument is that protectionism in trade is the result of bargaining among domestic interest groups. There is a domestic 'political market' for tariffs with a demand side – the industry, and a supply side – the government (Crane and Amawi 1997).

This view holds that the unitary rational actor assumption is simply not viable empirically. More importantly, by retaining this assumption in our models, we tend to obfuscate the real dynamics that produce international trade policies. To be sure, the unitary rational state actor assumption has been useful in facilitating our understanding of a variety of issues in International Relations and IPE. But scholars are beginning to give greater attention to the links between domestic and international politics in order to determine how these levels interact to affect the way that states behave in the global arena (Pahre and Papayoanou 1997: 4).

This 'level-of-analysis' problem has been recognized in some of the game-theoretic literature that relies on the unitary state assumption and 2x2 games to analyse international trade. In cases where the prediction of a 2x2 game is inconsistent with empirical observation, e.g., free trade is expected but protected trade results or vice versa, the disparity is frequently explained away by the influence that domestic rent-seekers exert on states' trade policies. The problem here is that these are *ad hoc* explanations for trade policy since they are not and cannot be derived from the foregoing 2x2 game-theoretic models. The question is whether we can jettison the use of game theory as merely a metaphor or analogy (Snidal 1986), and construct rigorous game-theoretic models that specify the mechanism that explicitly links internal influences to external behavior.

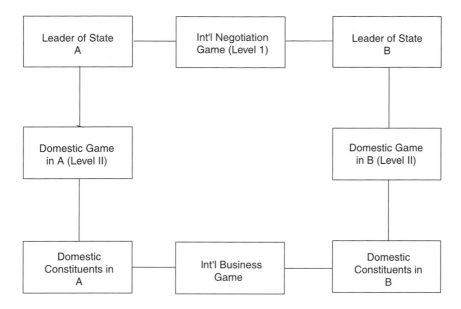

*Figure 8.2* Two-level game

## Domestic–international politics and two-level games

The theory of two-level games, which is still under development, provides a logic for analysing the mechanism that links international trade to domestic or societal influences. The theory, introduced by Putnam (1988) and elaborated by others (Evans, Jacobson and Putnam 1993; Iida 1993; Mo 1994) treats the game in one of two ways. The first approach assumes that domestic politics affects the utility that a government receives from its international strategies. The point here is to make the government's preferences endogenous to the game itself and then determine how this affects a government's choice among strategies (Grossman and Helpman 1994, 1995; Fearon 1997; Pahre and Papayoanou 1997).

In the Grossman and Helpman versions of two-level games (1994, 1995), it is assumed that politicians behave in such a way as to maximize their own political welfare. The government has an objective function that is a weighted sum of the two domestic actors (the contributions made by lobbies and the welfare of the voters) and a government selects tariffs and subsidies in order to maximize the objective function and thereby their political welfare.

The second approach models a domestic bargaining game between governments and their societal actors and an international game played between two governments. Two individuals, or heads of state, serve as representatives of their distinct constituencies and are engaged in a negotiation that must be ratified by domestic bodies. Each individual is engaged in two bargaining games. The first game, called the Level I game, involves the two individuals. The heads of states are negotiating the terms of trade (tariffs, a trade agreement).

Recall that in the one-shot (or even repeated PD game) states will (or might) pursue the non-cooperative Nash equilibrium, which is not welfare-maximizing. If they coordinated their trade policies, they could achieve welfare gains. The problem facing political leaders is to reach a pair of tariff levels closer to their optima, and this involves international negotiations (Milner and Rosendorff 1997: 123–124).

The second game is called the Level II game. The Level II games involve the respective heads of state and their domestic constituents, including the individuals, firms and corporation who are engaged in trade and voting. At Level II, the game begins with dissatisfaction among domestic actors, resulting from the international business game. These grievances are brought to the attention of the head of state. The heads of state attempt to resolve these concerns in the Level I game. The key point is that the two levels are strongly linked. Any solution to the Level I game must be a solution to each of the two Level II games (Dacey 1999). An illustration of the two-level game is provided in Figure 8.2.

With this view, a government's decision to pursue freer or more protectionist trade is a function of the domestic constraints and pressures placed on the leader. The logic of two-level games has been used to analyse the role of interest groups on trade policy (Dacey 1995), the impact of legislatures on the conditions for the ratification and terms of trade agreements (Milner and Rosendorff 1997; Pahre 1997), and the role of public opinion on peace agreements (Trumbore 1998), among others. As Putnam (1993: 437) points out, however, deriving analytic solutions to two-level games will be a difficult challenge for modelers. But this method seems to provide a promising avenue for those interested in investigating how international and domestic factors jointly determine outcomes.

## Conclusion

This broad overview of the various attempts to model questions pertaining to trade and conflict using game theory, while certainly not exhaustive, does reveal that the approach has made important contributions to IPE and produced new insights into interstate behavior. While many of these issues remain open questions, game theoretic analyses have generated a healthy debate regarding the causes of conflict and cooperation. By focusing on large $N$ collective action problems, the conditions for and limitations of repeated play, and the problems associated with security externalities/relative gains, game theory has shed new light on why cooperation can sometimes fail to emerge even when it may be in states' interests to pursue the cooperative path.

Traditional economic analyses emphasize that protectionism results from a political failure – the state adopted policy that was not welfare maximizing for the society or state. Clearly, however, that very protectionsim represents a political success by some group within society to enrich itself at someone else's expense (Brawley, 1998:155). Here, the logic of two-level games provides a mechanism for examining the influence of domestic actors on state trade policy. These theories provide a promising beginning for exploring the interconnections between trade and politics by making endogenous several key independent variables that affect trading relationships. The key point is that game theory will advance our understanding of questions in IPE only if we continue to develop models designed to address relevant puzzles which lead to the derivation of interesting and empirically testable hypotheses.

## Notes

1 The substantive focus of this chapter concentrates on the application of game theory to a narrow set of questions that pertain to the interaction between state power and international trade. Therefore, this essay deliberately excludes a great deal of the game-theoretic work in International Relations and Economics that is not designed to explore these questions specifically.

2 The foundations of modern utility theory can be found in von Neumann and Morgenstern (1947); Marschak (1950); Savage (1954) and Luce and Raiffa (1957).

3 The foundations of modern game theory can be found in von Neumann and Morgenstern (1947); Nash (1951) and Kuhn (1953).

4 Clearly there is not universal consensus on the value of rational choice theory as a tool to shed light on and/or resolve interesting substantive puzzles. For a recent critique of rational choice theory, see Green and Shapiro (1994).

5 Not all trade-related games, however, are Prisoner's Dilemma games. One of the key determinates of a state's preferences over the outcomes of a trade game is a state's relative size (wealth). Small states, who are unable to affect their terms of trade and unable to tolerate the imposition of tariffs, are more likely to have preferences consistent with a combination of Stag Hunt and Chicken (Conybeare 1987). Other key variables that may prevent the development of a PD trade game are the opportunities for bargaining, linking trade issues to political issues, and offering side-payments (ibid.: 14).

6 All that may be required to enforce cooperation is for other actors to believe that there is a sufficiently high probability that the hegemon will punish (see Alt *et al.* 1988).

7 Others have countered this by arguing that even if free trade is not presumed to be a public good, the enforcement of trade rules – such as most favored nation trading status – is a public good. It is therefore subject to the same kinds of collective action problems outlined above (Gowa 1989a; Lake 1993: 463). From this view, the creation of institutions or regimes such as GATT, function as coordination mechanisms to avoid these collective action problems.

8 The debate is over whether hegemons are benevolent, as is sometimes claimed, or whether a hegemon simply acts in its own self-interest to establish the order it prefers (Krasner 1976; Stein 1984; Snidal 1985a; see Alt *et al.* (1988) for an attempt to unify these two assumptions into one model). Critics have argued persuasively that a hegemonic preference for free trade cannot be simply assumed (Gowa 1989: 322). Moreover, many have challenged the assumption that domestic constituencies in hegemonic countries must provide international stability or liberal institutions as is predicted (Moravscik 1993: 13).

9 A hegemon may also opt for free trade for purely political reasons (Conybeare 1984).

10 Some of the most important variables include: attempts to link the trade game to larger political issues; the presence of rent-seekers with no interest in cooperation; transactions costs which make bargaining back to cooperation and monitoring those agreements costly; preferences which change over the course of the game; and decision-makers' misperceptions over the game they are actually playing.

# 9 New institutionalism and international relations

*Hendrik Spruyt*

Under the influence of discussions about the limitations of neoclassical economics, political science has engaged in some relatively novel approaches to the study of institutions. The older neoclassical paradigm was only marginally concerned with institutions and focused instead on the efficiency of outcomes in markets. Social outcomes were presumed efficient, provided market distortions did not occur.

New institutionalism (hereafter NI), by contrast, while sharing some key assumptions with neoclassical economics, challenges the efficiency of social outcomes, and problematizes the nature of institutions. It seeks to explain how institutions emerge, which functions they perform, and how institutions impose particular constraints and opportunities on individual behaviors within those institutions.

This chapter proceeds in three parts. I first clarify some key assumptions that underlie the research program. Subsequently, I discuss some key theoretical questions that have attracted the attention of scholars working within the new institutionalist approach. The second part turns to a more explicit discussion of how NI has influenced topics in political economy, and how it has influenced the study of a comparative political economy of institutions. While not claiming to be comprehensive, that section suggests how NI has fruitfully contributed to new approaches on a broad range of research topics within the study of comparative politics and international relations. The chapter concludes by discussing some of the critiques and potential weaknesses of the new institutional approach, and suggests certain amendments to earlier strands of new institutionalist theory.

## New institutionalism: key assumptions and core theories

### The neoclassical paradigm

Neoclassical economics is based on three core assumptions. It operates on the premise that individuals are the primary unit of analysis. Social outcomes are reducible to, and explainable by, individual choices. It is thus methodologically individualist. It, furthermore, assumes that actors are rational and utility-maximizing. Finally, it presupposes that collective outcomes are efficient and optimal. They are equilibrium outcomes (Moe 1984: 741). These are a minimal set of assumptions and arguably neoclassical economics depends on several more assumptions (Winter in North 1990: 19). But for our intents and purposes, a discussion of the limited set of assumptions suffices to draw out the key differences with NI.

New institutionalist theories, sometimes also called the New Economics of Organization, while sharing some of the key assumptions of neoclassical economics, may be seen as a set of critiques and refinements of the latter approach. Like neoclassical economics, the new institutionalist paradigm is based on methodological individualism. Institutions and governance structures, or even larger macro-level processes, are essentially reducible to the calculations and behaviors of individuals. Individuals purposefully create institutions to serve their interests, and they behave strategically within the confines of already existing institutional structures to achieve desired ends. It also assumes that individuals behave rationally and is avowedly utilitarian in scope.[1]

NI, however, differs from neoclassical economics on the nature of the rationality assumption, and on the premise that outcomes are efficient. Influenced by behavioral theories and studies of organizational behavior, it challenges the notion that rationality may be modeled as straightforwardly as classical economists suggest. Scholars of individual behavior have long noted that individuals, in fact, do not maximize their utility and often do not seek full information. Instead they satisfice (Simon 1947). But if information is imperfect, and choices are suboptimal, then collective outcomes cannot be assumed to be optimal either.

Organizational studies similarly challenge the notion of equilibrium outcomes. Human beings and organizations not only satisfice but they often work according to prescripted behavioral routines. Rather than re-assess new information, and new environmental constraints and opportunities, organizations simply run according to standard operation procedures, again, precluding any necessity of an optimal outcome (Allison 1972).

Douglass North, one of the founding fathers of the approach, similarly critiqued the strong rationality assumption of neoclassical economics. Particularly in his later work, he has drawn attention to the many facets of individual and collective behavior that are not well explained by wealth-maximizing behavior, but rather by altruism, ideology, and self-imposed constraints (North 1990: 20). There is some room for discussion whether North's explanation of ideology is itself based on particular assumptions about rationality and functionality, but it is clear that NI differs from the strong neoclassical assumptions in this regard.

Despite these differences, NI does adhere to a version of rational choice arguments, even while admitting for imperfections not recognized by earlier economic theory. In the strong version of rational choice theory, interests and preferences are deduced *a priori*. Borrowing from the economic literature, one attributes similar preferences to all individuals, and explains subsequent behaviors and outcomes as the functional result of the pursuit of such preferences. The weaker version remains agnostic about ultimate preferences. Instead it seeks to clarify the process through which individuals pursue their interests, whatever they may be, within the structural constraints that the individual faces (Elster 1989, Chapter 1).

Perhaps the most critical difference with neoclassical economics is the focus on institutions. Traditionally, economists had neglected institutional analysis. The older assumptions led to the conclusion 'not only that institutions are designed to achieve efficient outcomes, but that they can be ignored in economic analysis because they play no independent role in economic performance' (North 1990: 16). NI, by contrast, makes institutions the centerpiece of its analysis.

## *New institutional theory: structural aspects that govern contracts*

Structural arguments tend to explain the particular types of institutions and governance structures by the particular features of the transactions in which individuals engage, rather than by individual choices. One direction in such structural arguments focuses on the particular features of the goods for which individuals contract, and on the uncertainty involved in the contracting situation. The works of Ronald Coase and Oliver Williamson have been critical in this strand of research.

Another direction in the study of institutions has been pioneered by Herbert Simon and others (Simon 1947; March and Olson 1989). This research program, sometimes called the 'garbage can' perspective of organizations, emphasizes path dependency and randomness in organizational choice. Agent choices and organizational behaviors are thus inherently unpredictable and follow largely from pre-existing routines or the larger environment in which they are embedded. But while Simon's arguments certainly influenced the critiques of the neoclassical approach, such an approach is not usually classified as part of the contemporary NI paradigm. Consequently, I focus on the first structural approach, and more specifically, on three questions that have exemplified this research angle.

One key focus in the NI research program has been the study of hierarchy. How does one explain that some individual transactions and contracts are subsumed under formal governance structures (either political in nature or within a firm), while others are not? The starting point for such analyses has been the collective action literature, pioneered in economics, and imported to political science by Mancur Olson (1965). The now classical argument states that goods that are non-exclusive and non-rival will tend to be under-provided, or not provided at all, due to free rider problems. In the absence of a dominant actor, or a small group of privileged actors, collective goods provision will fail. Hierarchical governance structures are required where such failure occurs.

A second body of literature that has played an important role in this genre emanates from Coase's insights. Neoclassical economic theory held that individual bargaining could lead to efficient outcomes, even in the absence of hierarchical governance structures. Taking Coase's example of a polluting factory and an unwilling recipient of such pollutants, neoclassical approaches would argue that producers and polluters both have incentives to bargain towards the most efficient solution to the problem. Leaving aside questions of morality and norms, either the producer could offer side payments to the victim, or the victim could pay the polluter to diminish the negative externalities of his behavior. Either way the most efficient solution would emerge. In order to achieve such an outcome, however, neoclassical economics assumes that transaction and information costs are low and that property rights can be clearly assigned. (Transactions costs are the costs of preparing, negotiating and concluding agreements.) But in fact they seldom are. Information barriers usually exist and property rights can be ill defined (who is doing the polluting?). Transactions costs may be high (hiring lawyers, the time spent in brokering a deal). Formal institutional structures are thus necessary to reduce such information and transaction barriers and to achieve more efficient outcomes.

A third strand of literature, emanating from economics and the business literature, has also influenced new institutionalism. Oliver Williamson, in particular, has focused on the degree of vertical integration in certain industries. Why do some relations between producers become hierarchical, that is, why are various producers incorporated within the decision-making of an integrated firm, whereas others retain greater independence among producing units? The answer, argues Williamson, lies in the frequency with which producers interact, and in the asset-specific nature of the transaction. Goods are asset-specific if the cost of their alternative deployment is high. Such goods can thus not easily be deployed in another relationship, and, consequently, the opportunity for hold-up increases (Williamson 1975, 1985, 1986; Ouchi 1991). When transactions are frequent and assets are specific, the individual firms involved in the transactions will demand greater formal governance structures. Given the intention of actors to continue the business relation, incidental redress through litigation will not suffice.

### New institutionalist arguments: the interplay of structure and agents

Another major strand in the new institutional literature concentrates particularly on the interplay of agent choices and institutional structure. Institutions can be treated as independent variables in explaining particular agent choices, behaviors, or policy outcomes. Conversely, institutions can be treated as dependent variables. The particular features of the institution in question are explained by the deliberate choices by agents to create institutions that best serve their interests. Both approaches work under the assumption that individuals are rational entrepreneurs. Particularly prominent among scholars of American politics has been the assumption that individuals have a particular interest in maximizing their chances at retaining office.

The literature that focuses on institutions as independent variables seeks to explain how individual behaviors are strategically affected by institutional structures. Different electoral systems affect the behavior of candidates and parties in variant ways. Such systems affect not only the calculations of candidates for office but also of voters who seek to maximize the payoffs for voting. For example, electoral systems with low electoral thresholds, multiple members per district, and proportional representation will tend to generate multiple party systems (Lijphart 1994). In such systems candidates may have more incentives to cater to narrow interest groups than in two-party systems. Voters, conversely, know that voting for such special interest candidates will not diminish their chances to see their votes translated into policy outcomes, since they know that the candidates of small parties may well gain a seat, and will reward such candidate behavior. One can thus compare and contrast the various strategic incentives in two-party and multi-party systems, strategic constraints and opportunities in presidential systems and parliamentarian types, and so on. Recent scholarship is thus bringing together rational choice arguments and the traditional comparative analysis of electoral systems (Cox 1997).

An important subset of this literature focuses on the incentives for individuals to adhere to the hierarchy in the organization. Often the preferences of individuals in the organization may differ from those of the higher echelons. A subset of problems – shirking, principal–agent relations, moral hazard, and adverse selection – may result (Moe 1984). Shirking occurs because the benefits of collective performance do not correspond to the level of individual input. Workers may contribute little to overall firm performance, and yet be amply rewarded. The converse, of course, may occur as well. In such a situation the rational individual will tend to under-perform, given the lack of commensurate reward.

Shirking is a subset of the general problem of principal–agent relations. Given that principals (the hierarchy in the organization) can only imperfectly monitor the agent, the agent will be induced to engage in behaviors that may be counter-productive to the best interest of the principal. Such a situation may particularly arise when the agent possesses privileged information or expertise, or when monitoring is costly or impossible (Jensen and Meckling 1976; Miller 1992; Pratt and Zeckhauser 1985; Stiglitz 1987).

Adverse selection may occur because institutional incentives tend to attract individuals who are not necessarily best suited for a given task. For example, certain organizations (police forces) might reward individuals for high risk behavior (the amount of high profile arrests they make). Yet at the same time the reward structure might attract individuals who tend to be more confrontational than the general population.

Finally, moral hazard refers to the re-direction of individual behavior in an unwanted manner following the conclusion of a contract. Insurance may thus precipitate the very behaviors the insurer would like to minimize in the insuree. Banks, for example, when insured by a federal government (the American case) or by international lending authorities (the IMF), may engage in higher risk taking than would otherwise be the case.

One can also take institutions as dependent variables. In that case one seeks to explain institutional designs by individual preferences. Assuming that elected officials seek to maximize their chances at re-election, while at the same time using their resources efficiently, they will create institutional routines that best achieve such objectives. For example, committee design in the American Congress, or the use of fire alarm systems to control bureaucratic output rather than prospective oversight over such organizations, can be explained by instrumental choices of legislators (McCubbins and Sullivan 1987).

## New institutionalism and international relations

### Governance structures

Collective action theory provides a first clarification of why the international system sometimes demonstrates relative order and adherence to particular rules of behavior, while at other times violations and conflictual behavior prevails. The argument holds for both security and economic issues but has particularly been explored in the latter issue area.

Starting from the liberal premise that low barriers to trade and open market regimes are beneficial to all participants, liberal trade regimes must be understood as collective goods (at least for the members to such liberal associations). Liberal trade creates incentives to utilize comparative advantages and minimizes efficiency losses. As with all collective goods, however, individual incentives may lead actors to freeride and thus undersupply the collective good.

In game-theoretic terms, the situation is similar to a Prisoner's Dilemma. While all would benefit from mutually cooperating to create, maintain, and adhere to a liberal trade regime, the individual might be tempted to defect unilaterally. When all actors are motivated by such calculations the end result will be mutual defection, and a suboptimal outcome for all (Hardin 1982; Oye 1986, Introduction).

The solution to the problem thus lies in the presence of one dominant actor, the leading economy of the world (however measured), to create such a liberal trade regime. Great Britain played such a role in the nineteenth century, while the United States did so in the wake of World War II. Conversely, the lack of British economic strength in the inter-war period, and the lack of American will to lead, led to economic closure and economic depression (Kindleberger 1973). Small groups of leading economies might play a similar role as a dominant hegemon, but only under particular conditions (Lake 1988).

While adhering to the key components of Hegemonic Stability Theory (HST), and treating states as rational, calculating, individual entities, new institutionalists have diverged on some of the key causal claims and consequences of HST. They have done so partially because HST seemed ill suited to explain regime persistence in the face of relative American decline, and HST seemed vulnerable to certain theoretical critiques. For example, were liberal regimes really analogous to collective goods? Was the British regime indeed similar to the American?

Influenced by Coase's argument on transaction and information costs, Robert Keohane (1984) argued that international regimes do not require a leading state to create such a regime, nor do they require a hegemon for its maintenance.

Regimes serve to reduce information and transaction barriers to efficient interaction. Once established, regimes may continue to function as such a solution, even if the hegemon has declined. The liberal trade and financial regimes, sparked by US hegemony, thus continued even while the American share of international trade and finance diminished. Private actors may even create international institutions to diminish transaction and information barriers even in lieu of state action. The oil regime thus consists of a patchwork of measures largely instigated by private actors. Institutional functions that facilitate the ability to contract explain the prevalence of international regimes, not the distribution of power in the international system.

Beth and Robert Yarborough (1987, 1992) explain the nature of international regimes by another set of variables: the frequency of transactions and the asset specificity of international trade. Like Williamson, they argue that frequent transactions and high levels of asset specificity should correlate with more formal institutional hierarchy. British trade in the nineteenth century was largely non-asset-specific. Consequently, there was little need for formal governance, and hence active hegemonic management of the system was low. Few opportunities existed for hold-up and defection. Conversely, post-war international trade is highly asset-specific and the frequency of transactions has increased immensely. In such a situation formal governance structures and active management on the part of the hegemonic economy are imperative. In contrast to the informal British liberal regime, the US institutionalized financial and trading arrangements with formal specification of conditions for compliance, as well as regularized arbitration procedures.

An extension of this argument suggests that in some cases of extreme asset specificity, the demand for formal governance over all aspects of production might even lead to the extension of political rule over other polities. Jeffry Frieden (1994) thus suggests that imperial extension correlates directly with the level of asset specific investments in particular areas. Where private and public actors had investments that could easily lead to hold-up (through seizure and destruction), they would demand that the imperial government step in. High levels of investments in plantation or raw material extraction thus correlate with empire.

Inter-state agreements, hegemonic regimes, and empires are all different solutions to how governance structures and markets interact. With cross-border governance essentially absent, states and public authorities will try to create stable rules at the behest of their respective citizens so as to minimize risks. Hegemonic orders privilege the private actors of the dominant state, but potentially benefit others as well, as long as hegemonic leadership is benign rather than mercantilist (Gilpin 1987). Empires internalize market insecurities by striving to incorporate the major economic spheres of interaction under a single governance structure.

In the absence of international regimes, hegemonically imposed rules of behavior, or extension of imperial oversight, private actors must fend for themselves. One such solution to uncertainty and risk relies on private networks to disseminate information, lower transaction costs, and diminish the inherent risks of international trade and cross-boundary economic interaction. Such networks may be based on family ties or kinship structures (Curtin 1984; Greif 1992). Larger extensions of inter-private associations are also possible as with the trading association of city-leagues. Hendrik Spruyt (1994) argues that the sovereign state system is itself a solution to the problem of creating stable patterns of interaction in the absence of hierarchical governance structures.

## Strategic behavior in institutions

### *Principal–agent problems and security policy*

The literature in international relations has incorporated the principal–agent literature particularly by examining how different institutional structures have led to variant military practices. Deborah Avant (1994) thus argues that the nature of the delegating institution (the principal) influences the ability of the agent to circumvent the principal's wishes. The principal is that group of civilian leaders authorized to conduct foreign and military policy, while the military is the agent, presumed to act under civilian oversight. Divided principals will allow more room for agent defection because agents can bargain with different groups among their civilian superiors. In the US, the divided nature of civilian government allows the military to use Congress against the Presidency and vice versa. In doing so it has greater ability to pursue its preferred policies (in Avant's analysis non-innovation in peripheral wars, as Vietnam). In more unified civilian governments, as in parliamentarian Britain, oversight is more rigorous and effective, and one should expect closer civilian control over military policy.

Peter Feaver (1998) analyses civil–military relations along similar lines. He argues that the model is particularly relevant in democracies where the question of principal and agent is settled. That is, the military recognizes civilian oversight as legitimate. The question then becomes under what conditions the agent can act autonomously or even contrary to civilian demands. The declining ability of civilian leadership to punish and the incentives among the armed forces to shirk, explain why the American military's preferences today might be less attuned to following civilian dictates.

While the principal–agent literature has particularly made inroads in the analysis of security policy, there is no reason why it should not hold equal relevance to other spheres of policy-making in which bureaucracies exercise considerable autonomy. Particular issue areas that rely on high levels of expertise will enable organizations, to whom such issues are delegated, to exercise considerable influence on final policy outcomes. Monitoring will be difficult, and the principal will have to rely on the agent's best judgment and advice. Moreover, private interest groups will have incentives to capture such agents to push for their preferred policies.

## The comparative economy of institutions and territorial integrity

Institutional structures can also determine whether individuals in the polity have incentives to remain loyal to the government or secede. Federalist forms of government, specifically, are a double-edged sword. On the one hand, they give local elites and ethnic minorities considerable latitude in running their own affairs. This will tend to reduce the dissatisfaction with the federal government. Preferential treatment of a particular area will further enhance individual incentives to remain in the federation. At the same time such institutions also create local institutions which can easily be appropriated by native cadres. By establishing fixed territories with local institutional arrangements, the federal government in essence lowers the barriers for potential secession. Such territories serve as focal points of identity, and spatial segregation from other territories enhances local institutional distinctiveness.

Moreover, they create principal–agent problems, similar to the ones discussed above. By giving local elites considerable autonomy and resources, they also create the possibility that such elites will defect from the central hierarchy, and start a polity of their own. This is the classical problem not only for federations but empires as well.

New institutional arguments have been applied with particular fruition to the break-up of the Soviet Union. On the one hand, the Soviet system led to a very rigid formalization of electoral procedures. Ascending to the highest office required the support of a selectorate within the lower party ranks and bureaucracies. Once in office, however, the newly minted leaders could then turn the tables. Principal and agent would thus reverse roles. Consequently, the selectorate institutionalized constitutional procedures maximizing the predictability of the leader's future behavior (Roeder 1993). Such rigid institutional procedures were counter-productive when more adaptive responses were required.

The asymmetric nature of Soviet federalism also created variant incentives for leaders to defect or remain loyal (Laitin 1991; Solnick 1996, 1997). The declining ability of the center (the party) to monitor and punish, combined with the ability of titular elites to mobilize local resources and capture rents from their patronage networks, induced local elites to defect (Nee and Lian 1994).[2]

## Institutions and economic policy

Institutional incentives have also been used as explanations for domestic economic liberalization, as well as foreign economic policy. Much of the literature focusing on the recent trend to market liberalization has focused on the implications of globalization and international organizations. The increasing interdependence of advanced economies and the growth in international financial flows and world trade necessitate domestic liberalization, so the argument goes. In order to tie into this new economic environment, private investors and already liberalized countries demand the opening up of previously protected markets. In addition, international organizations, such as the IMF and World Bank, demand market reforms in order to be eligible for distributions and loans.

While not denying the importance of such broad systemic trends, NI also emphasizes the importance of domestic institutions. Domestic institutions affect whether political rulers have incentives to adopt liberalization programs, and they affect the degree to which certain countries can credibly commit to international agreements.

Authoritarian governments are particularly prone to catering to private interests. In the absence of broad public electoral controls, the ruling oligarchy will seek to maintain itself by giving in to the demands of powerful groups in the ruling coalition. Authoritarian governments create strategic incentives for political entrepreneurs to cater to private interests rather than provide public goods.

But democratic governments may show similar tendencies, although these probably constitute less dramatic distortions from the public interest than authoritarian governments. Democratic regimes with proportional representation, low electoral thresholds, and multiple members per district create greater incentives for political rulers to cater to private interest groups. In contrast to the winner-take-all nature of some two-party parliamentary systems, such as Great Britain, multi-party systems encourage elites to cater to niche groups in order to be (re)elected. Two-party systems create greater incentives for politicians to cater to the general electorate and thus be more concerned with the provision of public goods, rather than more narrow private goods.

For example, the lack of effective public oversight in the authoritarian Spanish system under Franco created incentives for politicians to cater to well-organized groups that opposed financial reform. Institutional changes, following in the wake of Spanish democratization, favored larger parties over small ones and diminished the strategic incentives to cater to this old constituency (see Lukauskas 1997).

Domestic institutions also affect a country's propensity to engage in external liberalization. In the previous Japanese electoral system, multi-member districts effectively led to a division of labor among candidates of the same party. Candidates would thus cultivate specific constituencies in order to gain a loyal base of support. Without a change in electoral system, political entrepreneurs thus had little incentive to forego protectionist platforms in favor of liberalization and the provision of public goods, which would cause their traditional constituents to withdraw their support (Cowhey 1993).

## Developments within new institutionalism

### *Critiques*

While NI has provided useful new insights into some important research questions, the NI approach is not without its critics. One set of critiques has to do with the methodological assumptions of rational choice theory that inform new institutional arguments. Critics challenge the assumption that individuals'

140    *Hendrik Spruyt*

preferences can be narrowly defined and posited *a priori*. Preferences and interests are instead informed by the social context in which individuals are embedded. Variant social contexts will thus spark different sets of preferences, choices, and behavior. Such preferences must be examined inductively not deductively.

Similarly, the idea that agents engage in calculative behaviors to achieve their goals in a utilitarian manner does not hold. Critics point to a multitude of behaviors which seem antithetical to self-interest maximization. How to explain, for example, the virtually suicidal behavior of some military units, or, on a more mundane level, the propensity to vote, even when the marginal benefits of doing so can be discounted as infinitesimally small contributions to the final outcome (Barry 1978).

Rational choice arguments also run the risk of *post-hoc* explanation because of the functional nature of their explanations. As careful analysts who work in the NI vein themselves note, if one argues that actors create institutions to serve their interests, then it is tempting to explain the existent institutions by the actions and preferences of individuals who now benefit from such institutions. To do so is incorrect (Keohane 1984: 81; Yarborough and Yarborough 1990: 252). The actors who benefit from existing institutions may have had nothing to do with their formation. And when actors set out to create institutions to pursue their interests, the ultimate outcome might be due to political compromises, serendipity and accident.

What holds true for critiques of rational choice arguments at the individual level also holds for ascribing such behavior to institutions and states. As with individuals, one cannot posit preferences or interests *a priori*. Constructivist and post-structural theories thus argue that interests and preferences are social constructs, and must be treated endogenously rather than exogenously.[3]

New institutionalism, at the macro-level, also tends to aggregate individual choices, and treats such aggregate choices as ontologically similar to those at the individual level. States thus choose for certain policies and governance structures the same way as individuals. But this treats states as ontological primitives, whereas they are in fact composites of various individual preferences, divergent coalitions, and contending institutions. One needs, therefore, to 'unpack' the state.

### Amendments to new institutionalist arguments

One can try to meet some of these critiques in several ways. First, one might retain the basic methodological orientation of explaining aggregate outcomes by individual purposeful action but surrender the narrow assumptions about individual human behavior. Admittedly this requires greater inductive analysis of particular preferences and motives but there are two benefits of doing so. For one, it avoids the fallacies of institutional explanations that are based on *post-hoc*, efficiency claims. Clarifying preferences and objectives sacrifices deductive parsimony for greater empirical accuracy. Moreover, it avoids the critique that theories based on flawed as-if assumptions cannot generate accurate models.[4]

Second, treating aggregate state level choices as ontologically similar to individual choices needs to be justified. Under which conditions is such an assumption warranted? When might we treat the state as a unitary calculating actor, rather than as a forum with various groups and individual preferences in competition with each other? For example, even if one accepts that international regimes exist to reduce transaction and information costs, not all domestic groups and sectors will have similar preferences on that issue. Consequently, in order to understand why states have dissimilar policies on these issues, domestic analyses will be critical. Martin and Simmons make a similar claim: 'Institutionalists have generally neglected the role of domestic politics. States have been treated as rational unitary actors and assigned preferences and beliefs' (1998: 747).[5]

Finally, one could expand the new institutionalist approach that political science has adopted from economics, with the sociological understanding of new institutionalism. Unlike the economic literature, it sees institutional choices as structured within pre-existing organizational fields. Institutions emerge and spread within a universe of other organizational types. Their relative success must be explained by their position in the field of institutions in which the emergent type is embedded. Some fields may be dominated by one or several actors, not unlike international regimes dominated by hegemonic states. Institutional spread or duplication will depend on the support of the dominant player for that new type.[6]

Institutions may also spread on grounds of appropriateness. Existing norms and rules of behavior will dictate which institutions will survive. Individuals and groups will create certain institutions simply because doing so identifies oneself as a member of a particular club, with all commensurate benefits and obligations. For example, new emerging states tend to create similar scientific organizations and utilize similar symbols of statehood as older and more established polities (Finnemore 1993).

Over time the preferences of individuals for certain institutions might be predetermined by an already existing set. Certain solutions will be taken for granted and not even subject to scrutiny. Alternatives are not even considered within the realm of the possible. In this sense, preferences can thus not be deduced *a priori*, but are socially contingent and must thus be inductively derived.[7]

## Conclusion

This chapter has argued that the new institutionalist research program emerged out of dissatisfaction with the neglect of institutional analysis in neoclassical economics. New institutionalism itself has many incarnations across the various subfields of political science. Without claiming any comprehensiveness, I have suggested several venues in which NI has been applied with some success. The program, however, is not without its critics, which range from disagreeing with the fundamental assumptions of NI, to advocating greater sensibility to domestic politics and sociological approaches that share affinities with NI. The last part of this essay identifies some of these critiques and suggests responses within NI to such arguments.

## Notes

1   Also see the discussion in Eggertsson (1990, Chapter 1)
2   For a new institutional argument focusing on eastern Europe and the Soviet Union, see Stone (1996).
3   For examples of constructivist and post-structural arguments, see for example Wendt (1987), Ashley (1986).
4   For a rebuttal of Milton Friedman's argument that the empirical veracity of assumptions does not matter, see Blaug (1980: 104–128).
5   Similarly, Helen Milner (1997) argues that international and domestic politics are inextricably linked.
6   For a range of essays in this tradition, see Powell and DiMaggio (1991).
7   Actors will respond to each other depending on mutually assigned roles and expectations, see Abercrombie (1986).

# 10 Globalization and theories of regulation

*Michael Dunford*

The ambition of theories of regulation is to explain the trajectories of capitalist economies. The object of analysis is not the political economy of the international system, though, as I shall explain, these theories have had to address phenomena associated with processes of globalization, and, as a result, do intersect with the literature on global political economy. The aim of this chapter is to outline the main characteristics of regulation theory, to explain why historically it operated with a conception of the world economy as a mosaic of national social formations, and to outline the ways in which it has sought to explain the trajectories of capitalist societies since the crisis of the Fordist model and in particular how it seeks to analyse globalization. I agree that insufficient attention is paid to the nature and role of international institutions (Palan 1998a). I shall suggest, however, that the insistence on the centrality of national economies in the post-war 'golden age' and the addition of a concept of insertion of national social formations into an international order were largely warranted. I shall also argue that the more recent transition to a new global-finance dominated regime of growth raises anew the core questions that theories of regulation seek to answer concerning the speed and regularity of growth and social progress. This transition also requires, however, a fundamental re-assessment and revision of earlier ways of analysing the role of the international order and implies an internationalization of the mediation mechanisms that are essential if accumulation is to be reconciled with social progress.

## Theoretical foundations

At the outset regulation theory rested on a critical assessment of Marxist political economy. More specifically, it grew out of a critique of the empirical and conceptual adequacy of some aspects of Marxist theories of value, distribution and growth and, in particular, of the view that these theories were incompletely specified, over-generic and insufficiently concrete. Michel Aglietta's *Régulation et crises du capitalisme* (1976), which founded this approach, rested on a recognition of the fact that capitalist economies sometimes function well, in particular reconciling capital accumulation with rapid growth and/or social progress, and sometimes experience phases of turmoil and crisis. The fundamental question that Aglietta asked was, why do capitalist economies sometimes function well and why are they sometimes crisis-ridden. The essence of the answer is implicit in the title of his study. Capitalism functions effectively when a set of mediations, called a mode of regulation, is put in place which ensures that the distortions and contradictions created by competition and the accumulation of capital are kept within limits that make them compatible with social cohesion and growth in each nation-state. As the sets of mediations and the trajectories that reflect the compatibility/incompatibility of accumulation and social and economic progress are context-dependent and specific to particular places and particular historical moments, the analysis of social change requires the inclusion of intermediate determinations excluded from more abstract economic theories.

As Boyer (1996) has indicated in a paper entitled 'The seven paradoxes of capitalism', the underlying question is one with deep roots in social, political and economic thought. For several centuries social scientists and philosophers have asked a simple question: why do societies founded on competition and conflict not lead to chaos? Essentially there are two sets of answers to this question.

The first is rooted in the work of political philosophers who concentrate on the role of the state in governing the interaction of human individuals. Hobbes, for example, argued that human beings were naturally selfish and self-interested. In their quest to acquire new power and prestige and to guard what they already possess, he argued, they would do anything. The 'state of nature' in which human life is not guided by external authority is a 'state of war', a 'war of all against all', in which life is 'solitary, poor, nasty, brutish and short'. These precepts underpin Hobbes' justification of the 'great Leviathan' or omnipotent state: individuals must transfer or give up their liberty to a 'sovereign' which will guarantee social and economic order. Hobbes also felt that nations were selfishly motivated and were in a constant battle for power and wealth. This conception of the state of nature was taken up by Kant in his essay on *Perpetual peace* in which he seeks to identify the nature of the national and international frame-work necessary for the attainment of perpetual peace (though states in a state of nature with each other differ from individuals in a similar situation). In a similar way, Locke argued that human beings start in a state of nature in which all are equal. A competitive struggle for existence subsequently gives way to the creation of a civil society (a social contract) to 'protect unequal possessions, which have already in the state of nature given rise to unequal rights'.

In the political economy tradition the answers were somewhat different. Adam Smith starts with the view that human acquisitiveness entails a propensity to truck and barter and that in the pursuit of their own interests individuals are led by the invisible and anonymous hand of the market to contribute unintentionally to outcomes which are mutually beneficial and in the social interest. Subsequent economic theorists have addressed Smith's proposition by asking whether and under what conditions a competitive equilibrium exists, is stable, is unique and in particular is Pareto efficient. If a competitive equilibrium is Pareto efficient, there is no reallocation of resources and goods that can make one individual better off without making someone else worse off. (This definition of welfare does not permit increasing the welfare of the poor by taking resources away from the rich.) Modern micro-economic theory shows that the conditions required for this welfare theorem to hold are extremely restrictive. The models used suppose that the distribution of wealth and income are completely independent of resource allocation, and that perfect competition prevails. All information about prices and the quantities of resources and goods offered and demanded is centralized, and equilibrium prices, which set all excess demands equal to zero, are established by an omniscient Walrasian auctioneer. Markets must exist for everything (current and future goods, services, risks, and so on). There are no collective goods or non-pecuniary externalities. (Traditionally the existence of externalities and collective goods was seen as creating a case for collective action.) All technologies, finally, are common knowledge and exhibit constant returns to scale.

In real life these conditions do not prevail. (This argument was made very forcibly by Nicholas Kaldor (1972) in a paper entitled 'The irrelevance of equilibrium economics'.) Markets are therefore not necessarily efficient at solving coordination problems. Collective action taken in the face of market failure may, however, introduce new distortions, so there is often not a first best solution. Critics of interventionism argue that government action to correct distortions may itself lead to political and governmental failure. What is important, however, is the fact that real markets do not satisfy the conditions required to make sustainable the claim that competitive markets are self-equilibrating and efficient.

Theories of regulation seek to answer similar questions. These theories start with the view that individuals and groups have goals, that these goals are expressed in their pursuit of individual interests and that these interests may be antagonistic or may complement and reinforce one another, depending on the social relationships that underpin them (as humankind is viewed as naturally social). Capitalism has enormous potential to mobilize human energy and translate it into economic growth. Capitalism cannot, however, create all the preconditions for its emergence and reproduction. As it develops, it generates conflicts and tensions which can obstruct its further development. Capitalism lacks 'the capacity to convert the clash of individual interests into a coherent global system' (Aglietta 1998: 49), and 'is a force for change which has no inherent regulatory principle' (ibid.: 62). Capitalism can destroy the conditions on which it depends, as the nineteenth and twentieth centuries have demonstrated so clearly. Capitalism must therefore be hemmed in by constraining structures, which are not a product of rational individual calculation or competition, but which

> emanate from the creation of social institutions, legitimized by collective values from which societies draw their cohesion. This cohesion is the product of social interactions that take a variety of forms: conflicts, some of which may be violent; debates that find their way into the political arena; associations that lend collective strength to groups of employees; and legislative provisions that institute and enshrine social rights.
>
> (ibid.: 50)

The underlying view that capitalist economies while potentially dynamic are also potentially self-destroying is rooted in an analysis of its fundamental social relations: the commodity relation, and the wage relation. What is the nature of these relationships and in what ways do they lead to conflict?

In market economies money is the main link between individual and society. Individuals do not have to coordinate their actions through the establishment of equilibrium prices but can pursue their own ends. To act, individuals must draw on social resources to invest, creating a debt or obligation to society. Through their activity the same individuals can earn an income which they can use to settle their debts and to pay for the goods and services they need. The settlement of debts and repayment of credits presupposes the existence of a system of payments (see Figure 10.1). A credit and monetary system comprising a series of commercial banks and a central bank to compensate for recurring disequilibria among commercial banks is therefore the first requirement of a market economy.

Money is also, however, a measure of value. Value is the anonymous judgement of social worth passed by all the members of a market society on the economic actions of each individual. (This social expression of the value of an individual's contribution to society, which is ratified by the system of payments, may, however, differ quite significantly from individuals' judgements of their contributions.)

To limit compatibility problems in such a system of decentralized exchanges, a market must be constituted to centralize information about demands and supplies and to enable assessments of the quality of goods, the creditworthiness of customers, the efficiency of delivery, etc. (see Figure 10.1). Market competition

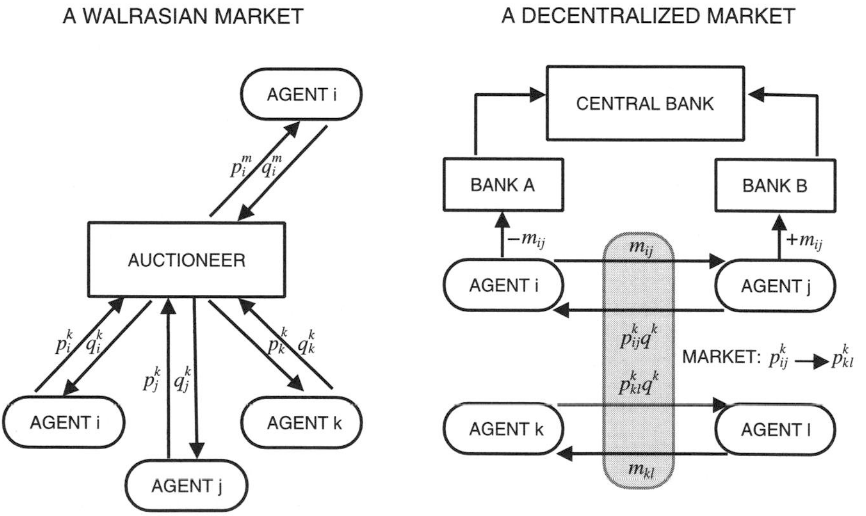

*Figure 10.1*   Walrasian and decentralized markets

*Source*: Based on Boyer (1996)

also depends on a framework of rules governing conditions of entry, rules of competition policy, and so on.

A second fundamental feature of capitalism is the wage relation and the associated social division between those who are able to advance money as capital with a view to the accumulation of money wealth and those whose access to money depends on the sale of their capacity to work. Capitalists cannot accumulate without incurring debts and without submitting the results of their initiatives to the judgement of society. Wage earners are free to change employers and spend their income as they see fit. None the less the employer–employee relation is a class relation. On the one hand, it makes it impossible for a group of free individuals lacking sufficient property rights and money wealth to become private producers in a market economy. On the other, wage earners must accept the hierarchical authority of their employer in return for a wage. The wage labour nexus is therefore a second fundamental institutional form governing wage setting and the organization and intensity of work.

To settle their debts to society and earn profits, capitalists collectively depend to a significant but varying extent on the consumption expenditure of their employees. The wages capitalists pay to their employees are simultaneously a cost and an element of the income on which the sales of their products and those of other capitalists depend. The ideal solution for any individual capitalist is to pay wages that are as low as possible to his/her employees, while all other capitalists pay high wages to sustain high levels of income and demand. The implication is that the individual interests of capitalists and their collective interest differ. As Aglietta (1998: 47–48) argues, the conflict inherent in the wage relation can be resolved if the capital accumulation also improves the living conditions of the labour force and furthers the social development of a wage society. Its resolution depends, however, on the putting in place of mediation mechanisms that place constraints on the cost reduction strategy.

Individually capitalists compete with each other. Competition involves attempts to reduce costs beneath the social average to earn surplus profits, to open up new markets or to invent new products. Increased competitiveness can therefore involve an intensification of work and related strategies of cost reduction, an extension of an enterprise's geographical field of operation, and product and process innovation. Expansion into new areas and innovation often require access to sources of credit and imply investments in projects whose outcomes are uncertain. These facts render the financial system a fourth (alongside the payments system, the market information system and the nexus of employer–employee relations) critical structure of mediation. As Aglietta argued:

> the debts incurred by capitalists are wagers on the future which are not mutually compatible ... To accumulate capital each capitalist tries to [modify] ... the existing division of labour, [making] ... capitalism a dynamic force ... As it takes some time for society to validate or invalidate these wagers, the evaluation of capital at any given moment includes a specific process of buying and selling debts and rights to capitalist property.

> The capital owned by individual capitalists is evaluated by financial markets. The evaluation amounts to speculation on the future[:] ... wagers on the success or failure of the gambles taken by each individual capitalist. [This] ... financial evaluation of capital introduces ambivalent solidarity between industrialists and financiers ... The incoherence of the capitalists' wagers on the future [lead to] ... doubts about solvency, [and] ... drastic revisions in these evaluations of capital, which trigger financial crises.
>
> (Aglietta 1998: 49)

Could all these institutions and systems of mediation be self-implementing? Some economists say yes. Most accept that a political and legal order is required to establish the underlying conditions for accumulation and to establish these institutions. Up to this point in time, viable monetary regimes, rules of competition and market discipline, effective financial systems, functioning labour markets and the establishment and protection of capitalist property rights all depend on the actions of public authorities. At present it is therefore impossible to conceive of a capitalist economy without an explicit role for state.

The legitimacy and coercive power of state are, however, confined to a particular territory. The contemporary nation-state is defined by internal political processes associated with the creation of a domestic constitutional order and its external recognition and establishment of relationships with other nation-states. Each nation-state is therefore inserted in an international regime or configuration.

## Conjunctural, cyclical and secular phases in the development of capitalism

Theories of regulation draw on these underlying ideas to explain the trajectories of capitalist societies. Historically, the development of industrial capitalism has been punctuated by three or four enduring crises. The first occurred after the Napoleonic Wars and saw, depending on the industrial or agrarian character of the country, the first crisis of industrial capitalism or the last (Malthusian) crisis of the *ancien régime*. The second occurred in the Great Depression of the late nineteenth century. The third occurred in the period between the First and Second World Wars. The fourth started at the end of the 1960s.

Throughout the long periods between these phases of turmoil, developed capitalist economies were reasonably dynamic and stable. At the root of stable growth was, it is argued by theories of regulation, the emergence of a sequence of new development models often centred on fundamental transformations of the preceding economic and social order.

These new development models took shape in phases of crisis when older socio-economic orders failed on the economic front and were rejected on the political and social fronts. At the root of these phases of regular macro-economic development were *regimes of accumulation* which involved the establishment of a significant degree of compatibility between accumulation and social progress due to the implementation of evolving institutional architectures and *systems of mediation* (also called *modes of regulation*) that managed temporarily to regulate the conflicts, tensions, imbalances and contradictions capital accumulation unleashes and to translate accumulation into social and economic progress. The development models that underlie phases of growth depend on a *political compromise* between social forces and on the widespread acceptance of particular world views. Thus, the roots of the Fordist model lay in the inter-war struggle between social democratic and New Deal politics, Stalinism and Fascism each of which sought to resolve the contradictions of a liberal order that had failed. (The dominance of market rationality was, as Polanyi (1944) argued in *The Great Transformation: The Political and Economic Origins of our Time*, one of the major causes of the savagery characteristic of the first half of the twentieth century.)

The capacity of mediation mechanisms (structural and legal constraints, collective agreements, and systems of values, shared expectations and rules of conduct) to regulate contradictions and stabilize development is, however, limited for several reasons.

> First, the effectiveness of organisations lies entirely in the stability of their internal rules, but these [rules] allow them limited scope to respond to variations in the conditions governing the accumulation of capital. Second, the institutionalised compromises between interest groups ... only reduce uncertainty by virtue of their rigidity.
>
> (Aglietta 1998: 62)

The stability of regulation presupposes a certain inertia of structures and institutional arrangements. But stability is only relative. The process of regulation itself engenders permanent movements which continually modify the character of social relations, the intensity of conflicts, and the relations of strength. A critical moment can arrive when these institutions and modes of conduct are no longer able to regulate the changes in the framework of the existing regulatory system. Constraints formed to channel growth can become fetters, opening up the question of new forms of overall reproduction.

In the 1970s there was a crisis of Fordism/Keynesianism. This crisis was a crisis of a particular compromise and of the ideologies and social forces that underpinned it. Similarly, subsequent debates about the restructuring of economic and political life are aspects of a search for a new compromise as elites and their supporters seek to establish new world views and development models capable of securing wide acceptance.

## The Fordist model

At the root of the Fordist model was the diffusion of a new techno-economic paradigm centred around the mass production of standardized industrial goods and services and the associated rise of a range of new consumer and producer goods industries. The core of the regulation mode was the reconciliation of the increasing returns and the rapid increases in productivity, which the resulting productive principles potentially permitted, with the growth of real income and stability in its distribution. First, real wages and consumer demand increased regularly, as real wage growth was linked to productivity growth. Second, the division of value added into wages and profits remained stable as increases in money wages were linked to the general level of prices. As the efficiency of capital was relatively steady, improvements in the standard of living of the work-force were reconciled with a steady rate of profit and a rapid rate of accumulation of capital (see Figure 10.2).

At the root of the connection between the growth of income, demand and productivity were the core elements of the wage-labour nexus and state economic management. Nationally differentiated collective bargaining arrange-ments ensured that wages grew in line with productivity and the cost of living. The redistributive functions of the welfare state, comprising the social security and taxation systems which redistribute wealth and income and finance collec-tive services, helped achieve greater social justice and granted nearly everyone the possibility to consume, even in cases of temporary or indefinite incapacity to earn money from work due to illness, unemployment or retirement, without

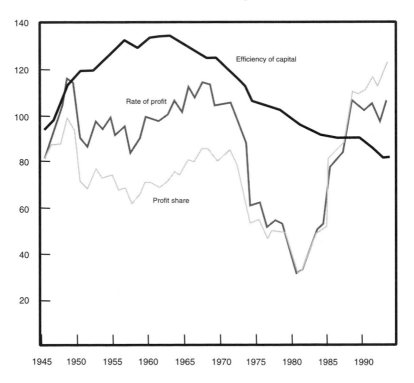

*Figure 10.2*   Trends in profitability: the French case

*Index*: 1924 = 100

encroaching too far on the market-determined hierarchy of wealth and incomes. Keynesian macro-economic management gave the state active responsibility for fine-tuning economic expansion and ensured that incomes and demand grew in a regular manner. In these ways the proto-socialist elements of the post-war social compromise paradoxically created the conditions for the most successful phase of expansion in the history of capitalism.

In this context inequalities diminished (see Table 10.1). Equity was an important dimension of the reconciliation of capitalist interests with social progress. On the one hand, it increased the share of the population enjoying sustained increases in standards of living. On the other, it encouraged the widespread adoption of modern lifestyles and the development of markets for mass consumer goods, which served as an engine of accumulation. Alongside the growth of the consumer goods sector, there was also, however, in several countries (especially in the USA and UK but also in France) a parallel growth of a warfare state underpinned by state expenditure on substantial defence programmes. Interestingly, productive performance was most impressive in those nation-states that committed fewer resources to defence programmes (Kaldor 1990).

To this first pillar, connected essentially with the distribution of wealth, was added another. The rapid rate of accumulation and investment led to steady increases in the size of the employed population, relatively stable employment structures and low unemployment rates. On the one hand, new activities were created to absorb the wage earners made superfluous by productivity growth and shifts in the sectoral profile of employment. On the other, the expanded reproduction of capital permitted and required the large-scale movement of people from agriculture to industry, of women into the workforce and of migrants from less developed countries into employment in the core metropolitan areas of the world economy. The consequence was a transformation of the structure of employment involving the movement of increasing shares of the workforce into paid employment and a stratification of the workforce into socio-professional categories often within large organizations. (Continued growth

*Table 10.1* Trends in US inequality: cumulative growth of average annual real income by quintile in the US, 1947–92

| Quintiles | *Average annual percentage growth of mean family income* | |
|---|---|---|
| | *1947–73* | *1973–92* |
| First (lowest quintile) | 2.99 | -0.69 |
| Second | 2.65 | -0.18 |
| Third | 2.76 | 0.19 |
| Fourth | 2.79 | 0.50 |
| Fifth (richest) | 2.46 | 0.93 |

*Source*: Council of Economic Advisors (1994).

depended, however, not just on an elastic supply of labour but also on the continuing availability of cheap raw materials and energy, especially oil and gas.)

As Aglietta (1998: 58–59) has recently indicated, the financial system and government monetary policies were:

> a second line of defence to guarantee the durability of growth. ... banks could administer interest rates so as to safeguard their profit margins ... [and] competed with each other over credit volumes. The credit system was a buyer's market with rigid interest rates and high elasticity of supply ... [enabling] companies to invest in growth and technical progress at minimum financial cost.

The economic and the institutional configurations differed significantly from one country to another: economic structures and mediatory institutions took on national hues, allowing the development of national varieties of Fordism. Boyer (1996: 26–29), for example, identifies market-led, meso-corporatist, state-led and social democratic variants of Fordism, which themselves reflected different economic and political cultures and varying national political compromises.

The general result, however, was growth that was self-sustained and subject to relatively small cyclical fluctuations. G7 growth rates averaged 4.8 per cent per year in 1960–73, while manufacturing productivity increased at 5.2 per cent per year (see Table 10.2). In contrast to the past domestic markets for consumer goods constituted the engine of growth: in OECD countries in 1960–73 exports accounted for 10.8 per cent of GDP compared with 15.0 per cent in 1974–79 and 15.5 per cent in 1980–89 and 1990–95. Comparable figures for imports were 10.2, 15.0, 15.8 and 15.4 per cent (see Table 10.2). Figures on the importance of trade for the individual EU15 economies were significantly larger.

Growth was therefore to a significant extent internally-oriented in the more advanced countries. Of course there were significant exchanges of goods and factors across national boundaries, and national economies were parts of a hierarchical international order involving a stable set of intergovernmental institutions that had emerged out of the General Agreement on Trade and Tariffs (GATT) and the Bretton Woods fixed exchange rate system. The modesty of the share of trade in GDP, the limited degree of financial integration that stemmed from restrictions on capital movements, and the capacity of nation-states to devalue their currencies in a system of fixed but adjustable exchange rates none the less permitted a significant degree of national autonomy. Aglietta (1998: 60) has argued that the national institutions and in particular the national wage relation and wage standard in their dual role as determinant of national production costs and domestic consumer spending power were the lynch-pins of the Fordist mode of coherence. For all of these reasons national economies were viewed as the building blocks of the international order into which they were integrated through their participation in a range of international institutions.

Table 10.2 Output, employment and productivity growth in the G7, USA, EU15 and Japan: average annual percentage rates of growth

| | G7 | | | | US | | | | EU15 | | | | Japan | | | |
|---|---|---|---|---|---|---|---|---|---|---|---|---|---|---|---|---|
| | 1960–73 | 1973–79 | 1979–89 | 1989–95 | 1960–73 | 1973–79 | 1979–89 | 1989–95 | 1960–73 | 1973–79 | 1979–89 | 1989–95 | 1960–73 | 1973–79 | 1979–89 | 1989–95 |
| Real GDP | 4.8 | 2.8 | 2.6 | 1.7 | 4.0 | 2.6 | 2.4 | 1.9 | 4.7 | 2.5 | 2.2 | 1.5 | 9.7 | 3.5 | 3.8 | 1.9 |
| Real GDP per head | 3.8 | 2.1 | 2.0 | 1.0 | 2.7 | 1.6 | 1.5 | 0.9 | 4.0 | 2.1 | 2.0 | 1.1 | 8.4 | 2.4 | 3.1 | 1.6 |
| Civilian employment in manufacturing | 1.3 | -0.3 | -0.4 | -1.9[1] | 1.5 | 1.1 | -0.4 | -3.1[1] | 0.5 | -1.0 | -0.9 | -3.0[1] | 3.3 | -1.3 | 1.1 | -0.3 |
| Civilian employment in services | 2.4 | 2.6 | 2.2 | 1.3[1] | 2.8 | 3.2 | 2.5 | 1.3[1] | 1.8 | 1.8 | 2.0 | 1.1[1] | 2.7 | 2.2 | 1.9 | 1.6 |
| Real GDP per person employed | 3.7 | 1.5 | 1.5 | 0.7 | 2.0 | 0.2 | 0.7 | 1.3[1] | 4.4 | 2.3 | 1.7 | 0.7 | 8.2 | 2.8 | 2.6 | 1.1 |
| Real value added in manufacturing per person employed | 5.2 | 3.8 | 2.6 | 1.9 | 3.3 | 0.3 | 2.3 | | 5.9 | 3.7 | 2.5 | 1.8 | 10.3 | 3.8 | 3.4 | 2.1 |
| Real value added in services per person employed | 2.8 | 1.3 | 0.8 | 0.4 | 1.6 | 0.5 | 0.4 | | 3.3 | 1.9 | 0.7 | 0.4 | 6.3 | 2.5 | 1.9 | 0.7 |
| Exports of goods and services as a percentage of GDP | 10.8 | 15.0 | 15.5 | 15.5 | 5.5 | 8.5 | 8.6 | 10.5 | 19.6 | 25.4 | 27.9 | 27.3 | 10.2 | 12.6 | 12.9 | 9.8 |
| Imports of goods and services as a percentage of GDP | 10.2 | 15.0 | 15.8 | 15.4 | 5.1 | 9.0 | 10.6 | 11.6 | 22.9 | 26.2 | 29.3 | 29.7 | 9.4 | 12.2 | 10.9 | 8.1 |

Source: Elaborated from OECD (1997) and OECD (1995). Note: [1] = 1989–93

# The crisis of Fordism and after

In the 1970s there were increasing signs of an exhaustion of the Fordist growth regime. These signs of a growth slowdown heralded the start of a new period of uncertainty, crisis and change. Among the first symptoms was the sharp downturn in rates of profit itself stemming from the fall in the efficiency of investment and the increase in the share of wages in national income (see Figure 10.2). These signs suggested the existence of malfunctions in the core systems of mediation (the relationships underlying the wage relation, and the market, money and financial systems) and in particular in their capacity to absorb and regulate the effects of change in the underlying structure of accumulation and growth. What were these changes in the underlying structure of accumulation? In this section I shall consider five: the slowdown in the growth of productivity and the efficiency of capital; the internationalization of production; financial globalization; the increase in individualism and the associated erosion of solidarity; and the erosion of the autonomy of nation-states. These five changes were connected with what I shall call the dual crisis of Fordism.

The crisis of the Fordist economic order was twofold. In the first place, there was a 'supply-side' crisis of the Fordist wage relation (which involved a combination of Taylorist principles of work organization, centred on the separation of intellectual and manual work, and rigid forms of employment and wage determination, which underpinned the regular growth of income and demand). In the second place, there was an acceleration of the globalization of economic life which added a 'demand side' crisis to the earlier supply-side crisis.

At the root of the supply-side crisis there were two factors. First, the diffusion and deepening of Taylorist principles reached certain social and technical limits, narrowing the scope for further innovation and intensification of work which together contributed to the significant slowdown in rates of productivity growth and the efficiency of capital (the value of output divided by the value of plant, machines and equipment). Among the social limits was a popular revolt against hierarchies, against the alienation of work and against 'wasting one's life earning one's living in a one-dimensional society' (Lipietz 1989). Second, the rigidity of wage contracts and substantial increases in the share of wages in national income squeezed profitability (at the same time as inflation made real interest rates negative). This second factor was related to the first in that the increase in the wage share also stemmed in part from the combativeness of trades unions and a range of other social movements active in the late 1960s and 1970s.

In the face of the crisis of the Taylorist productive model, capitalist enterprises responded in several different ways. On the one hand, there was an acceleration of automation and a rapid development of information and communication technologies (ICT). Subsequently, this ICT revolution was seen as heralding a third industrial revolution, involving a Schumpeterian process of replacement of one productive system by another. On the other, there were a range of experiments with new principles of work organization and wage determination (variously referred to by the phrases job enrichment, flexible specialization, lean production and dynamic flexibility), new intra-firm organizational arrangements and management models, and a redefinition of relationships between firms and their subcontractors and markets. These new technologies and new principles of work organization were often put forward as a way out of the crisis of Taylorism and as the foundations of a new productive order (Boyer and Durand 1993). To others these new technologies were less radical. For these critics the new technologies and management principles permitted an adaptation and refinement of the principles of Taylorism rather than their replacement, and involved in particular an increase in the ease and speed of reaction of firms to changes in their external environment, an emphasis on the mass production of quality goods at low cost and the widespread use of information technology, and a reinforcement of the control of capital over production rather than an increase in the autonomy of the workforce and a humanization of work (Boyer and Durand 1993). These innovations did not, however, stem the decline in the efficiency of investment. The reason why lay in part in the fact that the investments that firms undertook in automated machines were expensive relative to the increases in output they yielded. The high costs associated with the design and development of new systems was in turn a consequence of the fact that their development involved the employment of large numbers of well-paid engineers and technicians.

The increase in the wage share was a further constraint on competitiveness, profitability and the financing of investment. To reduce costs and restore profitability, companies sought to rationalize employment, increase employment flexibility and reduce the share of wages and salaries in value added. As Figure 10.2 shows, in the French case it was the reduction in the wage share, rather than increases in the efficiency of capital, which resulted in a restoration in the 1980s of profit rates to their 1960s' levels. Throughout the period after 1965, the efficiency of capital fell. Overall it declined by 45 per cent. This restoration of the rate of profit was therefore to a significant extent a consequence of a sharp increase in the share of profits and a dramatic reduction in the share of wages in national income permitted by a combination of increasing the work done and paying less for it. As Lipietz (1996) points out, French workers produced more each year. Indeed, productivity increased by 30 per cent in 12 years. Yet their hours of work remained the same, and their real wages hardly increased. In France, however, as in a number of other continental European Union Member States, unemployment rose sharply. In the US and to a lesser extent the UK, the fear of unemployment and weak social protection enabled employers to chart another course involving much greater wage flexibility. In the US annual hours of work have increased by one month since the start of the 1970s, while for manual workers and clerical and secretarial staff the average real wage has fallen by 10 per cent since 1973. To maintain his/her 1973 standard of living an American worker must do an additional 245 hours work per year.

The restructuring of productive activities that stemmed from this crisis also involved an accelerated internationalization of production and markets, at first as runaway industries sought to reduce wage costs through investment in low wage locations. The fact that this process of internationalization was designed to escape national wage bargaining systems and took place without an international harmonization of the Fordist wage compromise added a second 'demand side' to the crisis. With internationalization, cost competitiveness emerged as the over-riding concern of governments and elites. Yet, as attempts to increase competitiveness involved reducing the rate of growth of the mass of wages and salaries, there was a decline in the rate of growth of domestic demand, of domestic markets and of economic growth. A key determinant of this slowdown was the internationalization of government austerity programmes. As Lipietz (1989) has argued, in order to reduce its balance of payments deficit, each nation-state sought successively larger wage reductions than its rivals. In order to improve its capital account, each nation introduced yet higher interest rates to attract international deposits. Wage reductions and increased interest rates had depressive effects on aggregate demand and investment. Accordingly, the growth slowdown spread and was reinforced in a war of competitive recessions.

To the earlier supply-side problems were accordingly added the demand-side difficulties of the 'double-sided' crisis of Fordism. This demand-side crisis gener-ated further difficulties. Slower growth tied up large sums of money in stocks of goods and materials. In addition, instability increased, making it difficult to adjust output to changes in the composition and level of demand, and giving further importance to production flexibility.

Greater internationalization of production and international interpenetration of national capitals in industry, finance, services and commerce reduced national economic independence and sovereignty. One consequence was a decline in the scope for Keynesian reflation; any increase in national demand not matched by corresponding increases in demand in other countries would lead to a large inflow of imports and balance of payments deficits as the initial economic poli-cies of the first Mitterand government in France (June 1981–82) showed. Any sustained reflation, it seemed, would have to be organized at an international level. As this experience showed, the scope for the implementation of effective systems of mediation at a national scale was far more limited than in the past.

## Globalization and post-Fordism

In the years since the start of the 1980s there have been profound changes in the structure and trajectories of the advanced capitalist countries and in their rela-tions with the rest of the world. Included were a sharp increase in the degree of global economic integration and the rapid development of a new international division of labour, a radical financial markets regime change and a major restructuring of the scope and limits of state action.

As far as the economic trajectories of advanced economies was concerned, the sluggish growth of the domestic market was associated with a much greater orientation towards external markets and externally-oriented models of develop-ment. As paid employment spread and as capitalism penetrated formerly Communist and Third World societies, trade and international investment were increasingly seen as a source of profit and an engine of growth. A consequence was the emergence of a new international division of labour, increased rivalry between the major economic blocs (North America, Europe and East Asia) and an associated redefinition of the strategic and security interests of the most advanced capitalist countries. (The expansionist and imperialist impulses of the late nineteenth and early twentieth centuries seemed to reassume their earlier significance as the advanced countries set out unchallenged to mould emerging markets in their own image and as the collapse of Communism seemed to permit a much more aggressive international stance.)

The initial driving force was an internationalization of virtually all of the activities of multinational corporations. There was an internationalization of processes of production, of markets, as attempts were made to sell similar products throughout the world, of the sourcing of finance, which was raised increasingly on global markets, of research and development activities, which were located in a greater range of countries, and of management, with the recruitment of managers of many nationalities to create a worldwide management system. Different countries none the less played different roles in this new international division of labour. In the developed world, in those sectors producing traded goods and services, there is an increasing specialization on the skilled, intellectual work performed by what Reich (1991) calls symbolic analysts or problem solvers who work on ideas, concepts and symbols and whose activities (design, technical and financial consultancy, information and communication, marketing, advertising, accountancy and legal services, etc.) involve the appropriation of large shares of the value added created in global production chains. In developing countries, increasingly called emerging market economies, the scale of capitalist activity is increasing with the production of capital and intermediate goods, the growth of a range of processing industries and the expansion of financial and other market services. To paraphrase Morgan and Sayer (1987), development is occurring in these countries, without necessarily promoting a development of these countries.

Associated with this process of internationalization were a decomposition of a number of national oligopolies and an internationalization of the spatial arena in which competition takes place, though it was not the case that markets were made more competitive, as there is a wave of a wide range of agreements, partnerships, mergers and takeovers whose result was the creation of transnational oligopolies. An important component of this aspect of the restructuring process was the internationalization of privatized enterprises operating in areas of economic life that were traditionally a part of the public sector, including public transport, telecommunications, television and the media, and energy. In the Fordist era, these enterprises were largely shielded from international competition, but in the 1980s and 1990s they were often sold off to private owners, usually for sums that fell well short of their economic value, opening up new areas for profitable investment, shifting the dividing line between markets and public services, and altering the status of their employees.

Taken as a whole, this new phase of globalization has significantly weakened the connection between corporations and their territories of origin. In the

Fordist era, internationalization amounted principally to the international exchange of goods. The exchange of the products of one country's labour for those of another did not have a significant impact on domestic price systems, permitting the setting of national wage profiles in national systems of bargaining. 'Cyclical adjustment of economic policies, discretionary devaluations and exchange controls were sufficient to reconcile the national autonomy of ... [the collective bargaining systems] with international trade' (Aglietta 1998: 66). The internationalization of production and the establishment of globally inte- grated production chains alter this situation in several ways. Collective bargaining is no longer the linchpin of developed wage societies. The connection between corporations, their structures of production and the distribution of value added and their territories of origin weakens, as capitalist enterprises more generally have escaped from the national constraints that formerly shaped the path of accumulation, and increasingly are able to set the agenda, 'without any longer being subject to the constraints that formerly channelled ... capital accu- mulation in the direction of social progress' (ibid.: 67). As Aglietta continues, their fundamental concerns are with their overall competitiveness, their global profitability and the global centralization of finance. Their competitiveness and profitability depend on their capacity to organize flows of resources, know-how, finance and goods throughout the world. Strict financial criteria compel them to maximize short-term equity values and to bear down on employment and wages. In these circumstances, the setting of wages takes place in the light of suprana- tional market conditions.

The restructuring of work and employment and wage setting that results is creating a new division of the workforce in developed economies (see, for example, Lipietz 1996). At the top of the hierarchy lies a modern petite bour- geoisie, made up of executives and managers or cadres comprising Reich's (1991) class of 'symbolic analysts'. In the middle are found two groups. First, there is a group of secure workers, made up of middle managers, technicians and public servants, that includes welfare professionals. Second, there is a group made up of clerical and manual workers that includes personal service sector workers and operatives in the service sector and whose employment is insecure and low-paid. At the bottom lies a fourth group comprising those who are excluded from the workforce. The first group gains from globalization, whereas the fourth group tends to lose. What happens to the second and third groups depends on whether they can gain from the prosperity of the first group or suffer from the deflationary competition from the fourth.

In the Fordist era there was a hierarchy, yet society was held together as the individualistic pursuit of social advancement; social distinction and wealth took place on a social escalator which guaranteed a steady increase in each indi- vidual's real income and low levels and short durations of unemployment. To describe this situation and in particular its characteristic distribution of income Lipietz (1996) coined the term 'hot-air balloon society'. Globalization and the weakening of systems of collective bargaining along with an associated reinforcement of individualistic attitudes have ruptured the solidarity on which this model rested.

In the western half of Europe the European Union has sought to channel these processes of globalization by increasing the degree of economic and financial integration (first, with the establishment of the Single Market and, second, with the steps towards economic and monetary union). Fundamentally, the aim was the creation of a unified economic space as a platform for the reinforcement of European companies in European and global markets and not the creation of a set of mediation mechanisms (other than those of the market) capable of channelling accumulation in directions compatible with universal social progress. At the same time as there was no intention to create a new Europe-wide welfare state model, European economic integration added to the destabilization of an economic framework made up of relatively autonomous national systems of prices reconciled with one another by means of exchange rate adjustments. The aim of the integration project is to replace this system with a set of relatively homogeneous national price systems constrained by fixed exchange rates. Adjustment in such a framework could occur either through a European system of fiscal transfers, through high rates of workforce mobility, or through wage flexibility. As there is strong resistance to the idea of a European welfare state and the establishment of social rights as constituent elements of European citizenship, and as workforce mobility in the EU is relatively limited, only wage flexibility remains. At present wage flexibility is weakly developed due to the persistence of earlier principles of wage bargaining in many Member States. In the short term the outcome is a deeper unemployment crisis. In the medium term wage flexibility is a likely area of confrontation between governments and trade union movements and is indeed one of the reasons why some sections of the European class of employers favour the current model of integration.

Alongside and stemming from the globalization of capital and the increase in the degree of global economic integration, financial deregulation and financial innovation permitted a globalization of financial markets. Two groups of factors explain this trend. The first is the mobilization of global financial resources by international enterprises, on the one hand, and the increasing disconnection of national savings and investment, on the other. The former was a result of the internationalization of activities, while the latter stemmed from differences in national growth trajectories and associated differences in the demand for and supply of savings, with, for example, the US emerging as a net borrower (debtor) and Japan as a net lender (creditor). Together this group of factors contributed to a dismantling of controls on movements of capital. The second group was associated with the relative decline in the role of bank deposits and banking oligopolies and the rise of a system of market finance dominated by institutional investors. Institutional investors insist, on behalf of their investors, on the satisfaction of ambitious performance criteria set and evaluated by financial markets. The aim is to secure high returns involving the maximization of short-term equity values, one of whose consequences is an obsession with cutting wage costs and shedding jobs to boost share prices (Aglietta 1998: 67–69). In contrast to the bank oligopolies, which usually held claims until they fell due, this new market finance system introduced innovations in the management of risks leading to a dramatic expansion in the trading in securities and currencies and the explosion of markets for derivatives. As Aglietta (ibid.: 69) indicates, the outcome is 'a complex web of financial interdependence ... woven through arbitrage of interest rates, currency speculation and international creditor and debtor positions'.

This restructuring of the financial sector was accompanied by a major shift in economic policies in favour of creditors and the holders of financial wealth, creating a new set of financial constraints which had a profound impact on national state action. In the 1970s, to encourage economic growth, real interest rates were allowed to fall (as the rate of inflation was allowed to exceed the nominal rate of interest). To protect the real value of the financial assets of creditors and rentiers, the financial sector developed a range of new investment instruments to counter the effects of inflation. As a result new financial markets developed in which interest rates were more sensitive to inflation rates (Aglietta 1998: 75–76). It was in this context that, at the end of the 1970s and start of the 1980s, there was a much more forceful switch to a monetarist agenda, involving the introduction of extremely restrictive monetary policies in the United States and the United Kingdom. This reinforcement of a course of action already observable in the mid-1970s led to a dramatic increase in interest rates, a deep recession that spread throughout the world, sharp increases in unemployment and a profound debt crisis in developing countries that had borrowed recycled oil revenues in the 1970s to fund industrial investment programmes. (Developing countries borrowed to fund industrial investment expecting exports of the resulting industrial products to enable the repayment of debt. Monetarism forced up interest rates, reduced the rate of growth of demand for industrial output and encouraged protectionsim in advanced countries, crippling the debtors.)

By the middle of the 1980s inflation rates had subsided, yet real interest rates remained high, often exceeding the rate of growth. High interest rates, combined with the need to adapt quickly to a rapidly changing economic environment, encouraged investments in liquid assets guaranteeing high short-term returns, such as currencies, shares, land and real estate. Conversely, these conditions discouraged productivist strategies which tied up wealth in fixed, productive assets whose use could not easily be switched from one set of ends to another.

As indicated earlier, the productivity, profits and investment slowdowns of the 1970s and early 1980s entailed a reduction in the rate of growth of output and value added, which the pursuit of restrictive monetary policies and increase in interest rates reinforced. Slower growth put downward pressure on public fiscal revenues and social transfers, as did competitive downward pressure on tax rates. At the same time the transfers required under existing welfare state arrangements increased due to the increase in unemployment and poverty, along with the ageing of the population and the increasing real cost of collective services.

Governments at all levels consequently faced mounting financial pressures and difficulties in raising the revenues commensurate with the increasing demands for public services. A combination of downward pressures on revenues and constant or increasing expenditures creates public sector deficits and increases public debt and debt–GDP ratios, while higher interest rates raise the costs of debt service. (Governments are encouraged to offset these unfavourable trends through asset sales.) The more restrictive monetary policies are and the longer restrictive policies last, the greater, other things being equal, the increase in debt. As financial markets 'dislike' public sector deficits, the credibility of public policy declines, and long-term interest rates go up to incorporate a risk premium (increasing the attractiveness of state debt as profitable placements for financial wealth).

Combined with the increase in individualistic values, these powerful financial constraints have reduced the capacity of governments to finance public services and have provoked a crisis of the welfare state, threatening the cohesion of advanced societies. Essentially, the universal welfare state was developed to cope with low rates of unemployment and not the mass unemployment of the late 1970s and 1980s with its repercussions in the shape of lost output, a narrower tax base and greater social security expenditures. The consequence is an erosion of the principle of social insurance, changes in eligibility, a reduction in the real value of welfare benefits, and a move to more selective modes of intervention. An important aspect of this reform process is the increased role of new non-governmental organizations which step into the breach to mend some of the fissures in the social order. Necessarily, these associations abandon the principle of universality, exercise discretion in choosing who to help and who not to help and function as competitive interfaces and lobbyists between funding agencies (the World Bank, national Ministries of Housing and Health, the European Commission, charities, etc.) and poor people. The result is a slow transition to a national/international neoliberal social state in which social entrepreneurs organize the people they serve as groups of clients and engage in a struggle with other associations for support from potential financial backers (see Lipietz 1996).

## Economic performance: growth and inequality

In the last section I identified a number of inter-related processes that are transforming the societies of the developed and developing world (the globalization of production, the globalization of finance and the erosion of the capacity of nation-states to secure social cohesion) and I suggested that so far there has been a failure to develop new mediation mechanisms capable of channelling growth along lines compatible with universal social progress. The new trajectories of capital accumulation and the new international division of labour are, in other words, neither self-regulating nor hemmed in by the type of mediating mechanisms capable of establishing a new regime of growth. In this section I shall seek to defend this argument by outlining some of the repercussions of the resulting development trajectories. Three phenomena will be briefly highlighted: the degree to which globalization has led to economic convergence of less developed countries with more developed; the growth record of the more developed world; and the inequality crisis in advanced countries.

To appreciate the impact of the new international division of labour on relative living standards throughout the world it is important to place global development in its longer-term perspective (see Table 10.3). Table 10.3 shows GDP per head in a number of countries in each of a series of world regions relative to that of the United States: it shows how the US and other new countries (Canada, Australia and New Zealand) pulled ahead of the rest of the world until 1950, though the Soviet Union did close the gap somewhat in 1929–50. As Table 10.3 suggests, international inequality is largely a result of this concentration of nineteenth- and early twentieth-century industrialization in the western half of Europe and the new countries settled by Europeans. In the period from the Second World War until 1973, Western Europe, Eastern Europe and from the 1960s Southern Europe and Asia experienced rapid catch-up. The group of Latin American countries that had adopted strategies of import substituting industrialization also closed the gap, while Africa stood still in relative terms. In short, the post-war golden age was a period of significant decreases in international inequality. After the mid-1970s Asia continued its rapid catch-up until the recent currency crisis, and Western and Southern Europe continued to close the gap on the United States but at a much slower rate. Conversely, Eastern Europe fell behind, with its slow relative decline turning into a calamitous collapse with the start of the transition from Communism in 1989, as did Latin America and Africa. Catch-up was, therefore, faster up to the mid-1970s, and in the past twenty-five years a number of parts of the world have failed to participate further in the catch-up process. Africa is the most striking case, though in many other countries there is evidence of an economic crisis on an unprecedented scale leading to rapid impoverishment of large sections of the world population and sharp regional conflicts.

Without doubt there are striking recent cases of catch-up. The most remarkable examples are Japan and, more recently, Hong Kong, Singapore, South Korea and Taiwan (see Table 10.4). As Table 10.4 shows, however, Asian growth in the twenty years up to the early 1990s was a product of 'perspiration' (a high savings rate and increased capital and labour inputs) rather than 'inspiration' (technological progress). None the less, in the light of this experience it is frequently argued that these economies illustrate the ways in which investment in education and capital equipment in a context of global free trade can lead to strong convergence. What is more, it is claimed that the accomplishments of the Asian NICs can be replicated, opening up the possibility of catch-up and reductions in global inequality on a hitherto unparalleled scale.

As I have suggested, however, the recent past is characterized not by generalized catch-up but by the existence of winners and losers and by sharply differentiated national development records. There are differences within the group of semi-industrialized Third World countries, with relative decline in Latin America, and South Africa, and advances in East Asia. There are differences within the group of non-industrialized Third World countries, with advances at some points in time in OPEC countries, yet decline in sub-Saharan Africa. There are also differences within the group of former socialist countries, with advances in China, and decline in the former Soviet Union. Most of the dynamic East Asian economies have, however, suffered dramatic recent reversals in their economic fortunes with the financial crisis, initiated in mid-1997 with the collapse of the exchange values of their currencies.

So far the developed world has largely insulated itself from the effects of the instability of global financial markets. Over the last thirty years, however, its growth record has fallen a long way short of that of the 'golden age' that followed the Second World War. In the period since the mid-1970s there was a spectacular fall in output and productivity growth rates, especially in Europe. Table 10.2 records growth rates. In the EU15 average annual rates of growth were just 2.5, 2.2 and 1.5 per cent per year in 1973–79, 1979–89 and 1989–95, respectively. Manufacturing productivity increased at just 3.7, 2.5 and 1.8 per cent.

Alongside the accelerated development of some developing economies and the growth slowdown in the developed world there have been dramatic increases in inequality. The inequality crisis within advanced countries assumes two different forms. In the United States it assumes the form of wage inequality and the rise of the working poor (what Krugman calls 'moneyless America') and in continental Europe it assumes the form of unemployment ('jobless Europe'). In each case the main victims are those people who lack skills. In the United States the real wages of the unskilled fell by 30 per cent in 1973–93. Indeed, in that period just 20 per cent of population gained from an increase of nearly one-third in the wealth produced (see Table 10.1). In France, to take just one European example, unskilled unemployment has risen from 3 to 20 per cent.

As indicated earlier, the erosion of collective bargaining and of the stable wage structure and regular wage growth it promoted, a decline in unionization and the deregulation of job market all weaken the capacity of unskilled workers to secure high wages. Most economists argue, however, that this increase in inequality is a result of a fall in the demand relative to the supply of unskilled labour and an increase in the demand for skilled labour.

Of the factors that reduce the demand for unskilled labour, globalization and increased trade and competition from developing countries are frequently identified as prime causes. As Cohen (1998) has argued in *The Wealth of the World and the Poverty of Nations*, however, there are strong reasons for not attributing the inequality crisis in developed countries to trade. Trade can damage those sectors in which the advanced world ceases to specialize, substituting imports for domestic production. At the same time, however, there are gains in those sectors which make intensive use of skilled labour and in which the advanced world specializes. These gains accrue first and foremost, however, to 'symbolic analysts' who figure prominently in these sectors. If the losses and the gains are compared, it is clear that $100 of extra exports creates fewer jobs than $100 of imports, as the traded goods sectors in which advanced countries cease to specialize are relatively labour-intensive. Most economists argue, however, that

Table 10.3  Comparative economic development: arithmetic average real GDP per head at purchasing power standards as a percentage of USA

| | GDP per head as percentage of USA | | | | | | | | | | | GDP multiplier | | | |
|---|---|---|---|---|---|---|---|---|---|---|---|---|---|---|---|
| | 1820 | 1870 | 1900 | 1913 | 1929 | 1938 | 1950 | 1973 | 1979 | 1989 | 1992 | 1820–1913 | 1913–1950 | 1950–1973 | 1973–1992 |
| Western Europe | 98[1] | 86 | 76 | 70 | 63 | 77 | 54 | 74 | 76 | 78 | 81 | 0.71 | 0.77 | 1.38 | 1.09 |
| New countries | 98[2] | 99 | 98 | 99 | 96 | 97 | 97 | 97 | 97 | 97 | 97 | 1.01 | 0.98 | 1.00 | 1.00 |
| Southern Europe | 67[3] | 56[3] | 30[3] | 33 | 31 | 31 | 21 | 36 | 36 | 36 | 38 | 0.49 | 0.64 | 1.72 | 1.06 |
| Eastern Europe | 55[4] | 39[5] | 23[5] | 24[6] | 23 | 32[12] | 27 | 35 | 34 | 31 | 21 | 0.43 | 1.14 | 1.27 | 0.62 |
| Latin America | 40[7] | 22[8] | 28 | 29 | 28 | 32 | 27 | 29 | | 24 | 25 | 0.72 | 0.96 | 1.05 | 0.86 |
| Asia | 41[9] | 22[10] | 16[11] | 14 | 12[11] | 14 | 8 | 10 | 69[14] | 13 | 15 | 0.34 | 0.54 | 1.33 | 1.49 |
| Africa | | | 3[13] | 5[13] | | | 8 | 8 | | 6 | 6 | | 1.71 | 0.93 | 0.80 |

*Source:* Elaborated from data in Maddison (1995), 110–266.

*Notes:*
1  Excluding Switzerland
2  Excluding New Zealand
3  Excluding Greece and Turkey
4  Czechoslovakia and future USSR
5  Czechoslovakia, Hungary and future USSR
6  Excluding Poland and Romania
7  Brazil and Mexico
8  Argentina, Brazil and Mexico
9  Bangladesh, China, India, Indonesia and Pakistan
10  China, India, Indonesia and Thailand
11  Excluding Burmah
12  Excluding Bulgaria
13  Egypt, Ghana and South Africa
14  Japan

just 2–3 per cent of the labour force is affected by competition from poor countries: in France 300,000 jobs were perhaps lost due to trade-related factors, yet there are 3 million unemployed (see Cohen 1998). On the supply side immigration increases the supply of labour and the competition for jobs and may harm unskilled workers, but its scale is limited and is far from sufficient to account for their recent relative impoverishment.

To explain the increase in the demand for skilled labour (which is outstripping the increase in the supply of skilled labour as a result of mass education) and the fall in demand for unskilled labour there is a second explanation: an upgrading of production tasks in every sector, itself reflected in increases in the proportion of expert or managerial occupations. To explain why there have been such marked changes in the importance of skilled labour, Cohen (1998) focuses on changes in industrial organization, drawing first on Kremer's O-ring theory which suggests that the strength of any activity is equal to the strength of its weakest link and that as a consequence economic activities will increasingly be organized into smaller, more professional and mostly more homogeneous entities.

A further important implication of recent trends in economic organization is that the performance of most enterprises is to a significant extent a result of the cooperative efforts of skilled collectives. In this situation the contribution of individual members of each collective can seldom be identified separately, and there is often no common yardstick with which to compare collectives in different spheres of activity. Any link between the productivity of an individual and individual earnings is increasingly tenuous, leading to a disintegration of salary scales. At the same time the deep-seated uncertainty and changeability surrounding the fate of companies and of particular innovations and strategies

*Table 10.4*  Determinants of growth in East Asia

|  | Annual percentage rate of growth of | | | |
|---|---|---|---|---|
|  | Output | Weighted capital | Weighted labour | Total factor productivity |
| Hong Kong (1966–91) | 7.3 | 3.0 | 2.0 | 2.3 |
| Singapore (1966–90) | 8.7 | 5.6 | 2.9 | 0.2 |
| South Korea (excluding agriculture, 1966–90) | 10.3 | 4.1 | 4.5 | 1.7 |
| Taiwan (excluding agriculture, 1966–90) | 9.4 | 3.2 | 3.6 | 2.6 |

*Source*: Computed from data in Young (1995): 657–661.

cause sharp oscillations in the demand for labour, in wages and in the career paths of individual employees. As Aglietta (1998: 72) argues: 'employees who have undergone identical initial training may end up with entirely different pay levels and careers, depending on the companies or collective activities into which fortune or misfortune has led them'. Fractal inequality is affecting every occupational group.

> No longer do qualifications, seniority or hierarchical responsibility guarantee recognized positions in organisations. A patchwork of individual destinies is emerging as unforeseeable changes plunge one person into redundancy, another into precarious employment, and yet another into work for which he or she is overqualified.

The consequences are identity crises, a frequent sense of social helplessness and widespread exclusion as the integration of the labour force ceases to be a core part of the agenda in capitalist societies.

## Conclusion

In the last section I outlined a number of symptoms of crisis which strongly suggest that contemporary processes of accumulation are leading in the direction of relatively slow growth and an intensification of inequality. I have not discussed the environmental or a number of other qualitative implications of growth. What is clear is that the link between capital accumulation and social progress is comparatively weak. I have argued that the reason why is that the new trajectories of capital accumulation and the new international division of labour are not hemmed in by the type of mediating mechanisms capable of reconciling growth and social progress. In the recent past social and political movements seeking to constrain accumulation sought to do so through the actions of nation-states. Today, the relationships between corporations and their territories of origin are far weaker, and there are important constraints on the autonomy of national state policies of which the most important are financial and are connected with high interest rates, the cost of servicing public debt and the negative impact of slow growth on government revenues. Nation-states still dispose of enormous volumes of resources, and with political will could do far more to solve problems of poverty. Its absence suggests, however, that international constraints are far more pervasive than in the past, and that in future theories of regulation will have to pay far more attention to scales beyond those of the current mosaic of nation-states.

At the centre of the events of the last twenty years is not just the globalization of financial systems and of a range of productive activities but also the triumph of the allegedly superior market over any managed economic system and an associated thesis of convergence of all economies and societies on a US model of capitalism. Implicit in the thesis of this chapter is a critique of these claims. What I have documented is the way in which the Vingt Douloureuses (1977–97) of slower growth, instability and increasing inequality succeeded the Trente Glorieuses (1947–76) of fast growth, stability and diminishing inequality. (The phrase Trente Glorieuses was coined by Fourastié to refer to the thirty glorious years of the post-Second World War 'golden age'. A number of French writers have used the phrase Vingt Douloureuses to refer to the twenty sorrowful/painful years that followed it.) At the centre of the 'golden age' model was not the liberation of market forces but strict controls over finance and money, the assertion of the primacy of collective over individual interests and the political and economic integration of the overwhelming majority of the population certainly in developed countries.

Democratization and the establishment of a set of national and international mechanisms of mediation were a consequence of the shifting balance of political forces after the Second World War and the challenge of Communism. With the erosion of these movements, the triumph of market ideologies and the collapse of Communism, is capitalism returning to its preferred formation and are imperialist impulses reasserting themselves? To what extent is it constrained by the social rights established in the post-war era, and to what extent therefore is the social progress they permitted irreversible and potentially transformational? The answers to these questions are not yet clear. What I have argued is that the crisis of the model of the Trente Glorieuses was the crisis of a specific mode of democratic control and not of any control, that the results of the last twenty years fall far short of the promises of neoliberal ideologists and that growth and equity will depend on a re-establishment of democratic control over accumulation.

# 11 Transnational historical materialism

## Theories of transnational class formation and world order

*Henk Overbeek*

All that I know is that I am not a Marxist.

(Karl Marx, quoted by Engels 1890)

In the field of International Political Economy, there has been a growing widespread recognition over the past two decades that the world has entered a phase of fundamental restructuring which is usually denoted with the term 'globalisation'. This new awareness of the global character of our politico-economic order was also reflected in the birth of *neo-Gramscianism* or what I will call for the purposes of this chapter *transnational historical materialism*.[1] Transnational historical materialism can be defined as the application of the historical materialist method to the study of transnational social relations.

It comprises:

*   a materialist philosophy of history (to be found particularly in such classic texts by Marx and Engels as *The German Ideology* and the Preface to *Contribution to the Critique of Political Economy*) which leads to the ontological primacy of 'social relations of production';
*   a rejection of the separation between subject and object which is characteristic of 'positivist' social science and the adoption of a dialectic understanding of reality as a dynamic totality and as a unity of opposites: in the words of Lucien Sève, 'when the attempt to grasp the essence of things leads us invariably to contradiction, it is because contradiction is the essence of things' (Sève 1975: 676 , author's translation);
*   the method of abstraction as outlined by Marx in the Introduction to the *Grundrisse*.

Transnational historical materialism departs from mainstream approaches to International Political Economy (IPE) on two fundamental terrains. First, it breaks with the state-centrism that remains a core assumption in most writings on IPE from a mainstream perspective. In the debate between neorealist (or neomercantilist) and pluralist (or neoliberal) approaches about the relevance of non-state actors, the ontological primacy of the state is not in question. In that sense both these currents of IPE thinking can be said to be state-centric. In contrast, transnational historical materialism identifies state formation and inter-state politics as moments of the transnational dynamics of capital accumulation and class formation. This also implies that the national–international dichotomy (so central to mainstream theories of IPE) is seen as subordinate to the dynamics of social relations.

Second, transnational historical materialism rejects the reductionism implied in structuralist as well as in actor-oriented approaches. It advocates a historically grounded conception of the *dialectic totality* of structure and agency. This position also leads to a rejection of the positivism that underpins much of mainstream theory in IPE. To be sure, recent developments within broadly conceived main-stream IPE theory show increasing movement away from a straightforward positivist epistemology, in particular by such authors as Wendt (1987, 1995) and Ruggie (1998), towards 'social constructivism' which addresses many of the same concerns characteristic for transnational historical materialism.[2]

There are, however, very few examples of any serious engagement of neorealist, pluralist or constructivist authors with the contributions of transnational historical materialism. In fact, only Robert Cox has ever been paid attention going beyond disparaging comments in a footnote, and then really only by Robert Keohane. The major textbooks in international relations and international political economy by and large ignore transnational historical materialism.[3]

In order to situate transnational historical materialism in the context of a longer tradition, therefore, this contribution will first briefly trace its antecedents from the days of classical theories of imperialism to the late 1970s. In the following section we will highlight the main themes that have emerged in the writings of transnational historical materialism in the 1980s and 1990s. In the final section we will briefly identify some newly emerging themes in transna-tional historical materialism.

## The archaeology of transnational historical materialism

Transnational historical materialism brings back to life themes that were central to the debates on imperialism in the early years of the twentieth century. The global dimensions of the processes of capital accumulation and of class forma-tion, and the changing roles that national states play in these processes, were central in Marx's own understanding of capitalism: 'The world market itself forms the basis for this mode of production' (Marx 1979: 451). By the end of the nineteenth century, however, it was the struggle between rival imperialisms rooted in the various European nation-states that diverted attention away from the transnational dynamics.

### Classical theories of imperialism

The scramble for Africa, the rivalry in China among the European imperialist powers, and of course the rivalry in Europe itself (culminating in the First World

War) prompted a range of contributions to the theory of imperialism.[4] These contributions clearly recognise that the dynamics of capitalism are international. Bukharin's book is organised around the dialectic between 'internationalisation' and 'nationalisation', reverberating in Lenin's characterisation of imperialism as entailing both the division of the world market between associations of capitalists and the carve-up of the globe into spheres of influence among the major imperialist powers. However, to reread these studies will bring disappointment if the purpose is to find clues which transnational historical materialism can claim as support for its emphasis on transnational relations. For most of them, including Lenin, the global dimensions of imperialism are clearly subordinate to the tendency towards 'nationalisation' or the coagulation of organised capital within the nation-state with its inevitable periodic wars. Only Kautsky (the 'renegade') recognised the possibility of joint international co-operation in what he called 'ultra-imperialism'. But ironically Kautsky's article appeared in the very month in which war broke out.

In the years after the Bolshevik Revolution, and certainly after Stalin consolidated his position *vis-à-vis* Trotsky, the interests of building 'socialism in one country' pushed aside the interests of the international socialist revolution, and with it any original theoretical work on the global dynamics of capital. The process of turning inward was reinforced by the effects of the Great Crash of 1929 and the ensuing collapse of the world market in the subsequent years of Depression and war. Only with the gradual reconstruction of an open capitalist world economy after 1949 and the relative relaxation of Soviet predominance in the international communist movement after the Twentieth Party Congress in 1956 could conceptions of the global reach of capital again come to the fore.[5]

### Debates in the 1960s and early 1970s

The suppression of independent thinking of course was never total: Marxist political economy has always been practised by creative theorists who kept their independence from the dictates of the Comintern and Cominform (e.g. Sweezy 1942; Mandel 1962; Baran and Sweezy 1966). The study of the political economy of imperialism and (under)development also produced important contributions from a Marxist perspective (Baran 1957; Emmanuel 1972; Frank 1967; Magdoff 1969).

And particularly in the late 1960s and 1970s, in the wake of the Cuban Revolution, the Sino-Soviet split, the US *débâcle* in Vietnam, and the rise of Eurocommunism, original contributions to a general Marxist political economy abounded (Althusser and Balibar 1968; de Brunhoff 1976; Mandel 1972; Miliband 1973; Poulantzas 1968). The authors in question, however, were almost without exception caught up in, if not imprisoned by, the fierce ideological struggles of the period between social democrats, Stalinists, 'eurocommunists', Trotskyists of various persuasion, and Maoists (each of them passionately hated by all the others) which explains why they found very little response outside their own circles.[6]

For our purposes the most important debate was that about the nature of the relations between the major imperialist powers and the possible role of the emerging European Community. The all-pervasiveness of American dominance in the 1950s and early 1960s explains the prevalence of the theory of American *superimperialism* as expounded by Paul Baran and Paul Sweezy (1968).[7]

These views were opposed by adherents of the theory of inter-imperialist rivalry whose antecedents go back to the classical theories of imperialism of Hilferding, Bukharin and Lenin. Basing themselves on the 'law of uneven development', Rowthorn (1971), Mandel (1968) and others expounded the view that capitalist development was unequal and uneven and would inevitably produce a new challenge to American hegemony. Mandel in fact saw in the process of interpenetration of European capital (via inter-European mergers such as Hoogovens-Hoesch and Agfa-Gevaert) and in the success of the European Community proof of the rise of renewed inter-imperialist rivalry.

Finally, in response to the rise of multinational corporations as the main institutional forms of capital in the post-war world, theories dealing with the 'internationalisation of capital' in France (Palloix 1973; Andreff 1976) and with the *Weltmarktbewegung* (world market movement) of capital in Germany (von Braunmühl 1973; Busch 1974; Neusüss 1972; but also Mandel 1972) raised an issue that had long been suppressed in Marxist theory: the centrality of the world market for an understanding of the dynamics of capital accumulation.[8]

The debate about the EU–American relationship took a decisive turn with the intervention by Nicos Poulantzas (1974). Poulantzas argued that the dominant trend was not interpenetration of capital within Europe but penetration by American productive capital of the European economies. This penetration had far-reaching effects for the competitive position of European firms and for the European class structures. Poulantzas pointed to a process of reconfiguration of class forces in Europe reflecting the fundamental dependence of European capital on American, and leading to the reproduction within Europe of 'American' relations of production. With this analysis, Poulantzas introduced for the first time a conceptualisation of *transnational relations* that became one of the foundations of transnational historical materialism.[9]

A second crucial foundation was the reception in the 1970s of Gramsci's work, facilitated by the translation in English of selections from the *Prison Notebooks* appearing in 1971. Gramsci's influence in France had become considerable in the wake of *1968*, but references to Gramsci do not appear in the work of the 'founding fathers' of transnational historical materialism until 1977 (Cox) and 1979 (van der Pijl). Gramsci's emphasis on the role of ideas in the reproduction of bourgeois hegemony and on the consensual aspects of rule in developed capitalist societies was like music to the ears of the revolutionary generation of the 1960s because it offered an explanation for the passivity and acquiescence of the working class.

With Poulantzas' understanding of the dynamics of transnational class formation and the rediscovery of Gramsci's analysis of bourgeois hegemony, the stage was set for the emergence and consolidation of transnational historical materialism as a relatively coherent approach to the study of social relations at the international level.

## Main themes

As with any other theoretical tradition, there are almost as many variations of transnational historical materialism as there are authors. It is hardly possible to present a simplified categorisation, or to draw clear boundaries identifying who is an insider and who is an outsider to the tradition.[10] It is nevertheless possible to identify a number of key themes that play a role, albeit in varying proportions, in all transnational historical materialist analyses.

### *Commodification and the deepening of capitalist relations of production*

From the standpoint of historical materialism, any analysis of the world we live in must be grounded in an understanding of the way in which human beings have organised the production and reproduction of their material life. This in fact is what Marx understands by 'social': the totality of all activity undertaken by human beings towards the (re-)production of their existence.[11]

The most explicit attempts to construct a theory of the contemporary global political economy based on this departure point are to be found in the works of Robert Cox (1987), Kees van der Pijl (1984, 1998) and Mark Rupert (1995a). In his study of class formation at the Atlantic level in the years between 1945 and 1973, building on earlier work on European integration published in Dutch (van der Pijl 1978), Kees van der Pijl organises the analysis around the 'successive levels of decreasing abstraction' (van der Pijl 1984: 1), i.e. the *labour process*, the level of *circulation relations* and the level of the *profit distribution process* at which concrete class fractions form. It is in the labour process where the real subordination of labour to capital takes place, the precondition for extended capital accumulation. Van der Pijl assigns special importance to the shift from the production of absolute surplus value to the production of relative surplus value as a result of the introduction of new management techniques and production technology to improve the productivity of labour, first in the United States in the early decades of the twentieth century. In a similar vein Mark Rupert (1995a) also analyses the rise of mass production ('Fordism') in the United States as a necessary first step in the analysis of the extension of American global power.

Robert Cox presents us with the most extensive discussion of 'the concrete historical forms of the ways in which production has been organised – into modes of social relations of production' (Cox 1987: 1).[12] Each society is characterised by a specific hierarchically ordered configuration of these modes, conditioning in this way a particular configuration of social forces, which in turn conditions (and is conditioned by) the form of state and the insertion into the international division of labour and the global state system. Cox emphasises that the relationships involved (i.e. between relations of production, state forms and world order) all have material, institutional *and* ideological dimensions, and that moreover there is no predetermined hierarchy between these dimensions: production relations may be logically prior, but are not in any way historically prior. 'Indeed, the principal structures of production have been, if not actually created by the state, at least encouraged and sustained by the state' (ibid.: 5).

The question, however, is to what extent it is possible to identify the under-lying dynamics involved. In other words, if we argue that change is the essence of the historical process, then what drives this change? What generates the contradictions that produce historical change?

In van der Pijl's later work (1997, most elaborately in his 1998 book) the dynamics of contemporary social relations are traced to the contradictions engendered by two processes, *commodification* and *socialisation* (or *Vergesellschaftung*). Commodification entails the incorporation of more and more dimensions of the lives of ever more people into 'tendentially world-embracing market relations' (van der Pijl 1998: 8). Socialisation is the process (driven by the division of labour and the extension of commodification) in which individual 'integral' labour is transformed into functionally differentiated specialised labour and in which individuals are drawn out of closed self-sufficient kin-ordered communities into wider circles of social interdependence and 'imagined' communities.

### The political articulation of class interests

For the sceptical reader there is little in the above passages to warrant the claim that transnational historical materialism breaks with the established 'orthodoxies' of classic Marxism. This is different when we consider the question of the trans lation of 'class' into politics. An instrumentalist understanding of the *Communist Manifesto*, on the one hand[13] (e.g. Miliband 1973), and a structuralist one, on the other (e.g. Poulantzas 1968), have long dominated the Marxist debate. Both of these views in their own way were rather deterministic, allowing little autonomy to the political and ideological spheres.

This is where the adoption of Gramsci becomes of crucial importance.[14] Gramsci was concerned to rethink political strategy in light of the very different experiences of the Russian and the West European revolutions of 1917–19. It is really in the context of this project that all the concepts that have come to serve as keys to recognising 'neo-Gramscian work' were developed (civil society, hege-mony, historic bloc, organic intellectuals, passive revolution, *trasformismo*, war of manoeuvre and war of position).[15] In the West, the political power of the ruling class does not rest (exclusively or primarily) on the control of the coercive appa-ratus of the state, but is diffused and situated in the myriad of institutions and relationships in civil society. This form of class rule, hegemony, is based on consent, backed up only in the last instance by the coercive apparatus of the state. Ideological and moral elements play a crucial role in cementing the historic bloc, in Cox's words, it is 'a configuration of social forces upon which state power rests' (1987: 105 also 6, 409 n. 10) and its hegemony in wider society (Gramsci 1971: 161, 168). Organic intellectuals of the dominant social groups formulate and disseminate these intellectual and moral ideas, transforming them into 'universal' ones which bind subordinate groups into the existing social order (e.g. Gramsci 1971: 181–182).

The question that to some extent divides the two strands of transnational historical materialism is what determines the content of the hegemonic ideology, or at least the overall strategic orientation of the historic bloc of any particular period. The most systematic attempt to develop an understanding of the relationship between the substance of hegemonic ideas and the underlying dynamics of capital accumulation from a non-deterministic standpoint is the 'capital fractions approach'.[16] The starting point for this analysis is found in Volume 2 of *Capital* in which Marx considers the different functional forms capital assumes in the circuits composing the overall reproductive circuit of capital: commodity capital, money capital, and productive capital. In terms of concrete firms, merchant houses, financial firms, and industry approximate these fractions.[17]

In turn, this process of fragmentation of capital shapes class fractions which share common orientations, interest definitions, and collective experiences providing ingredients for a coalition of interests aspiring to represent the 'general interest'. These formulations of the 'general interest' are called comprehensive concepts of control (van der Pijl 1984, 1989; Overbeek 1990). Concepts of control are constituted around two prototypes, the money capital concept and the productive capital concept. The latter reflects the particularities of the productive process and its social context. Usually those groups assert themselves most effectively whose specific group interests at a given juncture most closely correspond with the prevailing objective state of capital accumulation and class struggle (van der Pijl 1984: 33–34).

Comprehensive concepts of control express the ideological and in Gramsci's sense hegemonic structure of particular historical configurations of capital, and function to organise and direct bourgeois hegemony. The notion of 'concepts of control' thus provides a clue to understanding the nature of the relation between structure and agency. The structure is defined by the process of the accumulation of capital, the agency is that of the concrete social forces originating from the sphere of production relations and struggling continuously over the direction of the accumulation process, over the role and nature of the state, and over the world order. To put it another way, concepts of control capture the strategic element in the construction of a historic bloc by linking the construction of politico-ideological projects in a non-reductionist manner to the structural underpinnings of the social order.[18]

### Forms of state

The next theme in transnational historical materialism is that of the various types of state–society configurations to be found in the world, both in terms of the variety to be found at any time in history (synchronic) as well as in terms of the variety over time (diachronic).

The need to organise bourgeois hegemony, i.e. to effect the rule of the historic bloc mainly through consent, is most typical for highly developed capitalist formations with a strong civil society. In societies where the process of socialisation is not as deep, power is based more strongly on coercion, and effected directly through the state, as Gramsci understood pre-Revolutionary Russia.

Following Cox, we may start with identifying 'hegemonic state–society complexes'[19] where political power is based on consent rather than on domination. The economic basis of the state is a self-regulating market, social relations are subject to the rule of law, and the state plays a facilitating rather than a leading role in social and economic life. Van der Pijl calls this type of state–society complex Lockean (van der Pijl 1998: 64–97).[20] The first hegemonic state–society complex came into being in England, with the Glorious Revolution of 1688. From the very start, its essence was transnational: the sphere of its essential features was not restricted to the territory of England proper, but was expanded by the transnational extension of the English historic bloc through emigration and colonisation.

In non-hegemonic states[21] the state–society complex is based on mobilisation by one single dominant class. The 'Hobbesian' state–society complex is characterised by a fusion of ruling class and governing class into a single 'state class' which is constrained in its capacity to articulate its interests in the transnational space dominated by the Anglo-Saxon ruling class (cf. van der Pijl 1998: 78 ff.). Hobbesian states are thus forced to a continuous catch-up drive through *revolution from above*.[22]

Cox has also distinguished as a separate state–society configuration the redistributive party-commanded state (or the state form of 'real socialism'), which van der Pijl subsumes under the category of Hobbesian states as well. Finally, both Cox and van der Pijl (who borrowed Cox's terminology here) distinguish proto-states, states which more or less control a territory without having either the social basis or the administrative capacity to formulate and implement effective socio-economic policies (Cox 1987: 218).

### Transnational hegemony

How to analyse the relations between states in the global system? This is, after all, the specific area that International Relations Theory and IPE study. Transnational historical materialism maintains that relations among states are, as it were, embedded in the wider context of evolving transnational social relations.[23] Consequently, international hegemony should also be approached from this same vantage point, namely as a form of class rule based on consent more than on coercion, and on accommodation of subordinate interests rather than on their repression (Gramsci 1971: 161). In Cox's words:

> The hegemonic concept of world order is founded not only upon the regulation of inter-state conflict, but also upon a globally-conceived civil society,

i.e. a mode of production of global extent which brings about links among social classes of the countries encompassed by it.

(1983: 171)

Hegemony in the global system is a form of class rule, and not primarily a relationship between states as it is in neorealist theory. Hegemony, moreover, is not primarily 'economic', or 'political': 'World hegemony is describable as a social structure, an economic structure, and a political structure; and it cannot be simply one of these things but must be all three' (Cox 1983: 171–172).

The liberal world order of the nineteenth century (*pax Britannica*) was in fact the expression of the internal hegemony of the financial and commercial aristocracy in Britain. This historic bloc projected its social hegemony outward through its control over the British state and its overwhelming military power, and through the promulgation of its liberal internationalist concept of control around the globe. The liberal order of the mid-nineteenth century, however, was not without its own internal contradictions. First, the operation of the free market system created social inequalities of both national and global dimensions which strengthened the call for one or another form of social protection.[24] Second, the operation of the gold standard reinforced these same inequalities, and thus also deepened the dialectical contradiction between the free market and the principle of social protection.[25]

The reconstructed liberal world order of the decades after World War II reflected and reproduced on an enlarged scale the hegemony of the corporate-liberal bourgeoisie, not only in the United States (where its cradle stood) but in Western Europe too. The successive steps in the construction of the *pax Americana* have been extensively analysed by the authors of transnational historical materialism and need not be recounted here.[26]

The analysis of hegemony at the global level raises a number of conceptual problems and challenges. It does represent a crucial step in overcoming the limitations of the state-centric discourse in a way which theories of 'complex interdependence' and regime theory have been unable to. However, it is not self-evident that Gramsci can be read in such a way that his core concepts can be applied to the analysis of global politics. Doubt as to the acceptability of such a reading has inspired many critiques of transnational historical materialism.[27] And although neo-Gramscians do have convincing replies to such an essentialist critique (Rupert 1998; Murphy 1998), it is nevertheless necessary for transnational historical materialism to complement its theoretical defence of the transnational position with concrete historical work to substantiate its claims. The work on the internationalisation of the state (*v*) and on recent tendencies towards the extension of global disciplinary neoliberalism (*vi*), as well as on possibilities for building counter-hegemony in 'global civil society' (*vii*), is quite crucial in this respect.

## Internationalisation of the state

In 'Social forces, states and world orders' (1981) Cox introduced the concept of 'the internationalisation of the state' to explain the mechanisms for maintaining hegemony in the era of *pax Americana*. The 'machinery of surveillance' used for that purpose was primarily made up of the Bretton Woods institutions supplemented by structures for the harmonisation of national policies in such fields as defence (through NATO's annual review procedure) and macro-economic policy (through the OECD).

Most elaborately, Cox reformulated his definition in a section (1987: 253–265) entitled the internationalising of the state (without explaining why 'internationalisation' has changed into 'internationalising'). There, he notes that 'the nation state becomes part of a larger and more complex political structure that is the counterpart to international production' (ibid.: 253). The process can be expressed in three points:

1   a process of interstate consensus formation regarding the needs or requirements of the world economy that takes place within a common ideological framework;
2   participation in this consensus formation is hierarchically structured;
3   the internal structures of states are adjusted so that each can best transform the global consensus into national policy and practice, with 'state structure' both referring to the machinery of government and to the historic bloc (the alignment of dominant and acquiescent social groups) on which the state rests.

(ibid.: 254)[28]

The emphasis on the mutual interests and ideological perspectives of social classes in different countries is important. This aspect is characteristic not only for the work of Cox, but also for Stephen Gill's study of the Trilateral Commission (Gill 1990; also see his later work). In the focus on the rise of a transnational historic bloc and the emergence of a transnational managerial class in command of the global economy there is a strong resonance of the notion of ultra-imperialism as formulated on the eve of World War I by Karl Kautsky.

The 'fractionalist' approach is less susceptible to Kautskian tendencies. In van der Pijl's work, the process of class formation, explicitly understood as a transnational process, is structured by the fragmentation of capital. Crucial in van der Pijl's view on the internationalisation of the state is his concept of a Lockean 'heartland'. The first Lockean state–society complex came into being in England: its essence, however, was transnational. Emigration and colonisation projected 'English' civil society across the seas, and the coherence of this emerging transnational civil society was cemented by the rise of cosmopolitan banking families such as the Rothschilds and transnational elite networks such as the Round Table Society. Through this gradual expansion there emerged a hegemonic 'core' of the state system, or a Lockean 'heartland'. The infrastructure of the heartland has two crucial features: the transnational spread of civil society, and the establishment of a single state, or a group of states with quasi-state structures, serving as the world's banker and providing the power to safeguard capitalist relations of production around the globe.

The Lockean heartland is the sphere where comprehensive concepts of control circulate:

> The struggle for hegemony between fractions of the bourgeoisie, through which the general tendency of the transnational ruling class asserts itself nationally, and between different states within and outside the Lockean heartland, replaces the traditional forms of world politics ever more by 'global domestic politics'.
>
> (van der Pijl 1989: 19)

The expansion of the heartland has historically taken place in confrontation with a variety of 'Hobbesian' contender states where the state–society complex is based on mobilisation by one single dominant class. The 'Hobbesian' state–society complex is characterised by a fusion of ruling class and governing class into a single 'state class' which is constrained in its capacity to articulate its interests in the transnational space dominated by the Anglo-Saxon ruling class (van der Pijl 1998: 78–83). Hobbesian states are thus forced to a continuous catch-up drive (*revolution from above*) that mostly ends in failure, collapse, or violent defeat by the Lockean heartland. This defeat is followed either by gradual incorporation into the heartland (as with Germany after 1945) or by disintegration (as has so far been the case with the Soviet Union).

Van der Pijl calls this incorporation 'hegemonic integration' in the context of an analysis of how the dynamics of capital accumulation, institutional developments and ideological processes combine to produce a truly transnational society.

## New Constitutionalism

The concept of 'internationalisation of the state' is perhaps slightly misleading when attempting to analyse the newly emerging structures of authority in the global political economy. The inescapable connotation after all is state-centric. This explains perhaps why since the collapse of the Soviet Union the emphasis has shifted to other aspects of the governance structures in the global economy. The first signs of this are to be found in pieces by Cox on 'global perestroika' (1994) and Gill on the internationalisation of authority (1992).

Stephen Gill has taken the task of re-thinking this question farthest, not least thanks to his creative incorporation of many insights of Michel Foucault's work on discipline and power (cf. Gill 1995b). The collapse of the Soviet Union and the subsequent transformation of the global state system have eliminated many obstacles to the further expansion of markets through the enhanced global reach of transnational capital. The priorities of economic and social policies worldwide have been recast to reflect the new dominance of investors.[29] International institutions (such as the OECD, IMF, World Bank and WTO) and groupings of dominant states (G7) are engaged in the legal and political reproduction of this *disciplinary neoliberalism* and ensure through a variety of regulatory, surveillance and policing mechanisms that neoliberal reforms are *locked in.* The erosion of democratic control that is implied in this process is called by Stephen Gill 'New Constitutionalism', 'the move towards construction of legal or constitutional devices to remove or insulate substantially the new economic institutions from popular scrutiny or democratic accountability' (Gill 1992: 165).

The (announcement of the) creation of the Economic and Monetary Union (EMU) in Europe has produced a stream of analyses in the tradition of transnational historical materialism. EMU, at least in the neoliberal mould which overlays it, is generally interpreted as the European manifestation of these tendencies. The disciplinary effects of monetary unification under the supervision of an independent European Central Bank – entrusted with the constitutional responsibility to eliminate inflation and deficit financing in the EU – have been clearly recognised by transnational capital throughout the Union.[30]

The movement towards New Constitutionalism has had a deleterious effect on the United Nations system. Robert Cox and Yoshikazu Sakamoto have directed an important project sponsored by the United Nations University on 'Multi-lateralism and the United Nations System' (MUNS), the aims of which were to draw on the insights and expertise of like-minded academics around the world in order both to analyse the background to the crisis of multi-lateralism and the prospects for reviving it in the face of global disciplinary neoliberalism (see Cox 1996: 494–536).[31]

## Counter-hegemony

Like all the writings of transnational historical materialism, even the products of the MUNS project are much stronger in the analysis of the process of global restructuring and the rise of global neoliberalism than in the analysis of possibilities to resist the power of transnational capital. In this sense the approach suffers from an elitist bias, which most authors realise and acknowledge without actually overcoming it.[32]

Van der Pijl concludes from his analysis of transnational class formation that it is the cadre class, the embodiment of transnational socialisation in the contemporary epoch that might represent the best hope for transformative action. However, van der Pijl's final words in the end do not give much strategic guidance:

> the concrete history of our present world and the development of its ruling classes to global unification under a neo-liberal concept, teach us that such a community [i.e. a classless society, a planetary community of fate] cannot come about in a single act. Only through the cumulative momentum of a series of particular, largely contingent episodes, can we hope that the forces capable of imposing limits on the capitalist exploitation of people and nature can prevail, and the suicidal drive of neoliberalism be reversed.
>
> (van der Pijl 1998: 165)

For Cox, resistance must take the form of patiently building up a counter-hegemonic historic bloc, 'a long-term task for organic intellectuals working in constant interaction with the groups whose dissent from the established order makes them candidates for inclusion' (1987: 390). This is too vague for some. In the words of Drainville, for instance, this project must now 'give way to more active sorties against transnational neo-liberalism, and the analysis of concepts of control must beget original concepts of resistance' (1994: 125).

Not only have critics addressed the lack of sophistication in transnational historical materialism with regard to political strategies directed to transform the existing order from below. It has also been argued that notwithstanding the refined analysis of globalisation processes (or perhaps as a result thereof) transnational historical materialism tends to take on board the assumption of growing uniformity and homogeneity that is central to many less critical analyses of globalisation. Instead, it is argued, globalisation produces *hybridity*, fragmented identities, and therefore open-ended and non-ordered change (cf. Ling 1996).

## Conclusion

The transformations that the global political economy has gone through in the past three decades have fundamentally uprooted traditional theories of international politics. For one thing, these changes have opened up the space for efforts to revitalise the Marxist tradition and particularly to introduce non-dogmatic and non-deterministic historical materialism into the discipline of International Relations Theory and its offspring, International Political Economy. Transnational historical materialism (however difficult it is to establish the precise boundaries of this tradition) offers a relatively coherent framework for the analysis of the contemporary global political economy. In this framework the analysis of the organisation of the social relations of production provides the basis for an understanding of transnational class and state formation.

Although it is primarily of Anglo-American origin if looked at in a narrow sense – and to be found almost exclusively in English-language literature – it has strong roots in the traditions of European Marxism. The role of the Dutch 'branch' in particular has been important as a transmission point between the continental European (especially French and German) and the Anglo-Saxon traditions. And recently, transnational historical materialism is making inroads into the Japanese and German language areas in particular.[33]

Simultaneously, under the impetus from constructive critiques, transnational historical materialism branches out into new fields of empirical enquiry and new terrains of theoretical work. One theme that is receiving increasing attention is that of the role of culture and civilisation diversity in the global political economy (cf. Cox 1994, 1995b, 1996, 1999; van der Pijl 1996b). The role of ideology not just among elites and the dominant classes, but among various non-hegemonic and oppositional groups and social forces will also be more intensely studied in the coming period (cf. Rupert, forthcoming). Finally, in acknowledgement of the need to pay more attention to hybridity and to modes and moments of resistance, we will see an increase in the number of studies within the tradition that will tackle issues of transnational identity politics, gender, citizenship and people's mobility.

Whether 'really existing' transnational historical materialism, i.e. with its inherent bias towards elitism, will survive as an intellectually coherent and relatively consistent approach in the wake of attempts to accommodate its critics remains to be seen: *trasformismo* is not always a successful strategy.

## Notes

1   No label can wholly satisfactorily capture at once what is common to the set of approaches to be discussed in this contribution and what sets them apart from other approaches. Several labels have been proposed, among them 'open Marxism' (cf. Drainville 1994), 'Coxian historicism' (Mittelman 1998) and in particular 'neo-Gramscianism' (see Germain and Kenny (1998), for a critical survey of 'neo-Gramscian' approaches, and Murphy (1998) as well as Rupert (1998) for 'neo-Gramscian' responses). The debates engendered by the Germain/Kenny article highlight very clearly why it is confusing at best to identify a broad and living theoretical tradition with the name of any single individual (alive or dead). It is preferable to do, as Stephen Gill (1993) and Kees van der Pijl (1998), and indeed Robert Cox (1981) have done, namely to adopt the more generic conceptual label of *historical materialism*, prefaced by 'transnational' to distinguish the characteristic concerns of the global political economy to which these authors apply historical materialism in the late twentieth century.

2   In the summary of Ruggie, social constructivism raises four types of questions that neorealism and neoliberalism cannot answer: how are the identity and interests of states shaped (or socially constructed), what conception of causality is adequate to recognise 'ideational causation' (or the real and material impact of, again socially constructed, ideas and beliefs); what are the constitutive (as opposed to regulative) rules that make organised social activity possible at all, and finally, how can we account for systemic transformation (Ruggie 1998: 13–28). See further, Palan, Chapter 14 in this volume.

3   Cf. Keohane (1984, 1986); this point is also emphasised by Mittelman (1998: 74). A blatant example can be found in Risse-Kappen (1995: 288). In his introductory and concluding chapters to a book on 'bringing transnational relations back in' (more than 60 pages, 119 footnotes, many more titles referred to) Risse-Kappen succeeds in mentioning Cox (and only him) once in a side comment. Critical text books in IR/IPE have a better record: see, for instance, Burchill and Linklater (1996), Halliday (1994), or Palan and Gills (1994).

4   See Bukharin (1917), Hilferding (1910), Hobson (1902), Kautsky (1914), Lenin (1917), Luxemburg (1913), Schumpeter (1927); for good overviews, see Brewer (1980) and Kemp (1967).

5   For an account of developments within the 'official' communist world in these years, see Claudín (1975).

6   Specific applications of Marxist thinking to the discipline of international relations remained very sparse. For exceptions, see Berki (1971), Tomaschewski (1973), and especially Krippendorff (1975). Later contributions on, or discussions of, Marxism and IR theory include Brucan (1978), Gills (1987), Kubálková and Cruickshank (1980), Linklater (1990), Maclean (1988) and Rosenberg (1994).

7   In terms of intellectual pedigree Baran and Sweezy were inspired not so much by the Hilferding–Lenin line, but saw more relevance in Rosa Luxemburg's work on imperialism and in particular the role of the armaments industry (cf. Luxemburg 1913).

8   The German discussants in particular claimed that their work actually took up a theme that Marx had intended to deal with in a subsequent volume of *Capital*, namely the world market.

9   The term 'transnational relations' was in fact introduced into the discipline by Keohane and Nye in their 1971 special issue of *International Organization*. However, their understanding of 'transnational' is primarily actor-oriented, while Poulantzas focuses on structures and processes rather than 'actors'. 'Transnational', moreover, must be distinguished from inter-national, supra-national, and global: it refers to processes that are simultaneously (sub-)national, inter-national, *and* global, i.e. that take place within, across and beyond national borders.

10  There is a number of edited volumes bringing together contributions from various quarters of the transnational historical materialism field. See in particular Cox (1997), Gill (1993, 1997), Gill and Mittelman (1997), Hettne (1995), Mittelman (1997), Overbeek (1993), van der Pijl (1989) and Sakamoto (1994). The main mono- graphs in the tradition are Augelli and Murphy (1988), Cox (1987), Gill and Law (1988), Gill (1990), Holman (1996), Murphy (1994), Overbeek (1990), van der Pijl (1984, 1996a, 1998), Röttger (1997) and Rupert (1995a). Particularly noteworthy, finally, is the collection of many of Cox's articles edited by Timothy Sinclair (Cox 1996). Contributions from the field of political geography incorporating elements of the transnational historical materialist approach include Agnew and Corbridge (1995), and Taylor (1996).

11  This is brought out very clearly in *The German Ideology*:

>   The first presupposition of all human history is of course the existence of living human individuals ... [Human beings] begin to distinguish themselves from the animals as soon as they begin to *produce* their means of existence ... The creation of life, current life through labor and new life through procreation, immediately reveals itself as a social relation – social in the sense that it implies the collaboration of various people, irrespective of the conditions, the manner and the objective.
>
>   (Marx and Engels 1974: 21, 30; author's translation)

12  Cox distinguishes twelve, ranging from subsistence farming to central planning and state corporatism.

13  This view is based on the famous description by Marx and Engels of the state as the 'executive committee of the whole bourgeoisie'.

14  Gramsci's work was 'rediscovered' in France, particularly after 1968. In the English- speaking world the *New Left Review* published a series of articles by Tom Nairn and Perry Anderson in 1964–65 making use of Gramsci's work to reinterpret British history, but it was not until the appearance of the translation of the *Prison Notebooks* (cf. Gramsci 1971) that the wider dissemination of Gramsci's thought picked up pace (see also Anderson 1977). Of course it is not possible in this chapter to go into the debates that the discovery of Gramsci has engendered, and to which Germain and Kenny (1998) refer extensively in their critical assessment of the contribution of the 'new Gramscians' to international relations theory. The references throughout this chapter are intended to enable the readers to find their own way into how the 'neo-Gramscians' understand Gramsci.

15  The first coherent exposition of these concepts, particularly in terms of their rele- vance to understand international politics, can be found in Cox (1983). More extended discussions are Cox (1987), Augelli and Murphy (1988), Gill (1990, 1993) and Rupert (1995); see Tooze (1990) for a review of Augelli/Murphy and Gill.

16  The approach is often associated with the 'Amsterdam Group' (cf. van der Pijl 1989, Overbeek 1993 for some collections of papers adopting this perspective).

17  Cf. van der Pijl (1984: 1–20); ibid. (1998: 49–63); also Overbeek (1990: 23–29, 176–181).

18  Peter Burnham has critiqued this claim: 'The neo-Gramscian analysis ... simply offers a pluralist analysis of global capitalism which overemphasises the role of ideology in economic policy and regime formation, illegitimately invokes the domi-

nant ideology thesis and fails to specify its implicit fractionalist theory of the state' (Burnham 1991: 90–91); see also Clarke (1978) for an early critique of fractionalism. Rather than extrapolating Gramsci, Burnham tells us that we must understand that 'the culmination of "scientific political economy" is to be found in a critical reading of the work of Marx' (Burnham 1994: 222).

19  Liberal (nineteenth-century Britain), nationalist-welfare (developed capitalist, first half twentieth century), neoliberal (1950s–1970s), state capitalist (1980s and 1990s).

20  The terms 'Lockean' and 'Hobbesian' of course refer to the political philosophers John Locke and Thomas Hobbes. Hobbes's *Leviathan* (1652) paints the picture of a strong centralised state imposing its will on society (the only way to avoid a struggle of all against all). Written shortly after the Glorious Revolution, Locke's *Two Treatises of Government* (1690) in contrast sang the praises of self-governing civil society.

21  Fascist corporative before 1945, mercantilist-developmentalist thereafter in Cox's words, 'Hobbesian' contender states in van der Pijl's terminology.

22  Gramsci's concept of revolution from above (and the *passive revolution* which might be seen as the gradual accumulation of the unintended social transformations resulting from the revolution from above) is crucial in understanding the process of late development in the capitalist era, cf. Cox (1983); van der Pijl (1998: 78–83). Interesting analyses in which these concepts are central include Amineh (1998), van den Berg (1995), Cox (1989), and van der Pijl (1993).

23  This is something that Gramsci was quite outspoken on: 'Do international relations precede or follow (logically) fundamental social relations? There can be no doubt that they follow.' (Gramsci 1971: 176).

24  For the dialectic of the 'double movement' of *laissez-faire* vs. social protection, see Polanyi (1957).

25  For representative accounts of the nineteenth-century hegemonic order, see Cox (1987: 11–150); Murphy (1994: 13–152); Overbeek (1990: 35–58); van der Pijl (1984: 35–49).

26  Cf. Augelli and Murphy (1988: 58–74, 138–153); Cox (1987: 211–267); Gill (1990: 57–121); Murphy (1994: 153–259); van der Pijl (1984: 76–243); Rupert (1995: 167–207).

27  See the argument by Randall Germain and Michael Kenny (1998).

28  Picciotto (1991) argues that transnational corporations favour weak rather than strong transnational regulatory structures, and instrumentalise the existence of different national regulatory systems. The two positions are not mutually exclusive, as the one is framed in terms of objectives, while the other analyses (at least partially unintended) outcomes.

29  Interesting analyses of the ways in which investors and credit rating agencies reproduce disciplinary neoliberalism both globally and in everyday life can be found in the work of Timothy Sinclair (1994) and Adam Harmes (1998).

30  See van Apeldoorn (1999), Bieler (1998), Gill (1998), Holman (1992, 1996), Holman and van der Pijl (1996), Holman, Overbeek and Ryner (1998).

31  Publications coming out of the MUNS efforts include Cox (1997), Gill (1997), Hettne (1995), and Sakamoto (1994).

32  This is the main thrust of André Drainville's critique of what he calls 'open Marxism' (Drainville 1994).

33  In Japan, the efforts of Yoshikazu Sakamoto and others have made the approach better known, resulting among others in the translation of Gill's book on the Trilateral Commission into Japanese. The efforts of Frank Deppe and Leo Bieling at the University of Marburg have done much to broaden the appeal of transnational historical materialism in Germany (e.g. with translations of some of Cox's articles (cf. Bieling and Deppe (1996), Bieling *et al.* (1998), Cox (1998); also van der Pijl (1996a) and Röttger 1997). The work of Cox, Gill, van der Pijl and others has also been noticed and discussed in countries outside the core of the global political economy, e.g. in India (cf. Harshé 1997: 149–191).

# 12 A nebbish presence

## Undervalued contributions of sociological institutionalism to IPE

*Anna Leander*[1]

In the fiftieth anniversary issue of the journal *International Organisation*, the editors state that International Political Economy (IPE) has been little touched by the constructivist turn in International Relations (Katzenstein *et al.* 1998: 675). This chapter argues that their assessment is misleading. Even if its presence continues to be timid and often grossly undervalued, sociological institutionalism occupies a growing space in IPE and raises issues and claims consonant with those made by the 'constructivists' in IR. This chapter argues that much stands to be gained from making the presence of sociological institutional more visible and assertive in IPE.

Institutionalism is pervasive in contemporary IPE. Economic/rational choice institutionalism has become central to mainstream research in IPE; regime theory (Keohane 1984), European integration (Moravcsik 1998), trade policies (Rogowski 1989) and foreign investment (Dunning 1988) are some of the subjects that have been studied with the help of economic institutionalism. Similarly historical institutionalism is referred to in the discussion of the state (Halliday 1987; Krasner 1988; Hobson 1997). By contrast, with few notable exceptions, sociological institutionalism is rarely explicitly discussed except as it relates to other forms of institutionalism.

The neglect of sociological institutionalism in IPE is regrettable. However innovative IPE may be compared to international relations and international economics, frustration is growing among IPE scholars with the apparent incapacity of the discipline to develop further (e.g. Hobson 1997; Keohane 1997). Meanwhile, IPE is chastised by outsiders for its supposed lack of theoretical rigour and adequate theoretical frameworks. IPE scholars are said to overstate their points (Wade 1996), to adopt simplistic interpretation of globalisation (Esping-Andersen 1996; Huber and Stephens 1998), and focus exclusively on globalisation to the detriment of other (possibly more important) factors of change (Andrews and Willett 1997). Unfortunately, in these criticisms, theoretical rigour is often equated with economic approaches and hence the importance of preserving IPE as a 'space of openness' (Helleiner 1994), rather than turning it into a Procrustean discipline, is (Strange 1998) brushed aside.

In this context I would argue that sociological institutionalism offers IPE an excellent opportunity to develop without compromising neither its interdisciplinary nor its theoretical openness. I develop this argument in three steps. The first section introduces sociological institutionalism and shows how it can deal with two central theoretical problems in IPE: the relationship between different spheres of social life and the conceptualisation of diverging spatial levels, global, national, local and international. The following two sections illustrate the contribution of sociological institutionalism to two specific issues: the changing nature of states and of firms.

## Sociological institutionalism: assumptions, concepts and frameworks for the study of IPE

Sociological approaches to economics, also called economic sociology (Swedberg *et al.* 1987), centre on the social embeddedness of economic activity. The term embeddedness derives from Polanyi (1957), who, contrary to the economic (objectivist) tradition, argues that market relations are by no means natural or present in all societies, but rather remain contingent on the social context. The vast majority of current work in this tradition draws on neoinstitutionalist perspectives, hence the label sociological institutionalism.

The core of neoinstitutionalism consists of an interest in how institutions shape, and in turn, are shaped by different social spheres, including the economy (Immergut 1998: 25. See also Phillips and Spruyt, Chapters 7 and 9 in this volume). Beyond this, the different strands of neoinstitutionalism diverge sharply in their interpretations of the nature of institutions, the relationship between institutions and their environment, and the relationship between institutions and actor behaviour. Broadly speaking, there are three traditions of neoinstitutionalist thought: economic or rational choice, symbolic or socio-logical, and historical (Hirsch *et al.* 1990; Powell and DiMaggio 1991; Hall and Taylor 1996). Rational choice theories which centre individual choices and preferences (see Carlson, Chapter 8 in this volume) are often the target of explicit criticisms by the second and the third groups who contest its ahistorical, utilitarian materialist, and/or individualist bias.

Sociological institutionalism has much more in common with historical institutionalism – often synonymous with historical sociology (for discussion see Spruyt and Shaw, Chapters 9 and 15 in this volume) – than with rational choice institutionalism.[2] Sociological institutionalism and historical institutionalism both adopt neo-Weberian methodologies and approaches. They are interested in themes such as path dependence, organisational bias and rule that structure the context of decision-making. Compared with historical institutionalism, however, sociological institutionalism places greater emphasis on non-materialist aspects of institutions, viewed not only as socially, but also as intersubjectively constructed. Research on intersubjective meaning focuses specifically, if not exclusively, on the common sense or shared understandings and practices that inform human action in society. Consequently, 'institutions' in sociological institutionalism include world-views, cognitive maps, code of behaviour, discourses, symbols and mental frames. Sociological institutionalism is particularly interested in questions such as: how institutions develop and change, how do they shape identities, interests, behaviour, firms' strategies, systems of production, states and politics. Contrary to the individualism of choice theoretical approaches, in sociological institutionalism social reality is seen as logically and empirically prior to behaviour: it gives the reasons for action, as opposed to constraints or causes; it defines identities and hence actors' interests (Ruggie 1998: 22). As opposed to materialist approaches, sociological institutionalism stresses that behaviour, identities and interests are emergent through shared understandings of social reality and are not mere epi-phenomena of some underlying material reality.

## Theorising political economy in IPE: conceptualising the relation between social spheres

IPE is confronted by the question of how to relate different social spheres. More specifically, how to avoid the Scylla of 'over-embedding' the economy by seeing it as only socially/politically determined and the Charybdis of 'under-embedding' it by downplaying the influence of social institutions on economic relations. And it is precisely here that sociological institutionalism has something to offer. For the relationship between the economy and other social spheres is at the heart of sociological institutionalism. This, in fact, is the essence of embeddedness (Swedberg *et al.* 1987: 178).

Bourdieu's influential theory of social fields may serve as a good illustration for the contribution of sociological institutionalism.[3] Bourdieu's starting point is that social practices form a unity. His ambition is the understanding of social power and stratification through 'a general theory of the economy of symbolic goods and its relation to the material economy' (Brubaker 1985: 87). Even practices that are usually considered devoid of direct material purpose, such as life styles, music and food tastes, are viewed by Bourdieu as 'economic' in that they are part of the strategy of capital accumulation in a broad sense. In a Weberian vein, Bourdieu insists that not only (material) capital is determining of power relations, but also capital based on symbolic (social and cultural) resources. Concretely, this leads him to study rules governing different spheres of social life and the resulting 'strategies' for accumulating different forms of capital (economic, social and cultural) which are partly and imperfectly transferable from one 'field' of social life to another.

Bourdieu defines fields as a set of (normal, habitual, routine) practices which, in turn, can be understood on the basis of a set of socially and historically informed and shared dispositions, or what Bourdieu calls the 'habitus'. These dispositions translate past experiences into schemes of perception, thought and action that inform individual behaviour (Bourdieu 1980: 91). Fields are interlinked, and individuals are part of several fields at any given time.

The concept of the 'habitus' helps Bourdieu to explain diverse strategies of capital accumulation and allow him, in turn, to paint a rich picture of social stratification and power relations. Similarly, accumulation strategies are not conceived in terms of calculated interdependent sets of decisions, but as behaviour positively sanctioned within the practices of a field and internalised by the individual: it is strategy 'without strategic calculation'. Consequently, rather than provide a theory in the sense of a set of causal propositions that specify the conditions under which certain links occur, Bourdieu (again the heir of Weber) offers a conceptual framework for identifying the links between different social spheres and for studying them empirically. He does not believe in the possibility of a more general theory. According to him, there is no *a priori* given hierarchy among different forms of capital. Their relative value differs from field to field and from society to society.

The relationship between different forms of capital can therefore only be determined empirically. Thus, in *Distinctions* (1979), Bourdieu provides a detailed description of the relationship between economic, social, and cultural capital in different fields of French society and shows how they fit together to form a social hierarchy. In *Homo Academicus* (1984, for the university system) and *State Nobility* (1989, for the state elite) he shows how within a single field, the relative value of different forms of capital have changed and how actors have adapted their strategies to cope with these changes. This open-ended view on embeddedness is very useful for IPE scholars. It allows for a contextual approach to embeddedness which seems particularly important since IPE purports to study political economic realities spanning a great number of contexts.

## Theorising the 'international' in IPE: vertical and horizontal levels of governance

Sociological institutionalism also grapples with a second key theoretical issue for IPE: the link between different 'levels' of the global political economy and the artificial dichotomy between the state and the global (Palan and Gills 1994). The 'two-level games' solution (Putnam 1988; Evans *et al.* 1993) is clearly unsatisfactory, for its focus on the relations between policy-makers and their different constituents leaves no room for structural forces. Moreover, since the theory treats the international and the local as separate and independent realms, it can account only for international phenomena; not for 'global' ones. Needless to say, the two-level game theory does not provide any convincing way of accounting for the (sub- or supra-national) regional level.

Sociological institutionalism provides useful insights into the debate, mainly through the (French) regulation school (see Dunford, Chapter 10 this volume) and the (American) studies of governance. Both conceptualise governance in a way that makes it possible to understand the complex relationship between the transnational (or global), state and regional in shaping the regulation of the economy.[4] The shared aim of scholars from both traditions is to develop an understanding of the economy in terms of the 'rules of the game' as set by the social institutions which govern economic life. It merits underscoring that both schools of thought are part of sociological institutionalism because of a shared 'constructivist' view of social institutions. Both are increasingly focusing on discursive practices, the construction of identities and of interests in the economic spheres (Boyer 1990). Similarly, the interest in linking local and global does not stem from abstract theoretical concerns, but from the obvious fact that the economic sectors, sub-sectors, regional clusters or production networks operate at different levels concomitantly. This has left scholars with no choice but to integrate 'global' and 'local' in their study of regulation/governance.

This has not resulted in a general theory, but in frameworks of analysis for the study of the global and the local. Indeed, the link between the global and the local is neither uniform nor unidirectional. The different levels are 'articulated' with each other: they influence each other but continue to display a certain degree of independence. Moreover, the weight of different levels of governance/regulation varies between sectors, sub-sectors, production-networks and countries (Mytelka *et al* 1985; Hollingsworth 1998). One illustration can be found in Lynn Krieger Mytelka's (1988, 1993) studies of the changing regulation of international production and their effects on different industries. She has analysed how changes in the textile industry, which are largely global in nature, impacted upon individual countries and their policies where differences in national institutions have played a considerable role.

These frameworks make the integration of different spatial levels an inevitable part of the analysis, avoiding the pitfalls of both an artificial separation between national and global realms, and of pretending that the regional and national levels are of no consequence.

## The changing nature of the state and the globalisation of legitimate economic practices

Sociological institutionalism is central to the move in IPE away from sterile questions about 'the end of the nation-state' to the more fruitful ones about the ways in which globalisation is changing political practices. I will make this point with reference to two research tracks of sociological institutionalism which are directly overlapping with IPE.

Applied to IPE, sociological institutionalism examines the social embeddedness of the global political economy. The global political economy, in turn, is viewed not simply as a system of more or less well governed and efficient markets, but as consisting of a number of overlapping sets of practices which rely on a certain self-understanding and which distribute different forms of capital among social actors, hence empowering some over others. Applied to the central relationship between the state and the global political economy, concrete research programmes in this tradition therefore have at least two aspects. First, they focus on shared or taken-for-granted understandings of the nature of the global political economy. Here, sociological institutionalism follows lines similar to those who investigate the so-called 'Washington consensus' in IPE. Second, they examine the practices of those groups of actors empowered (i.e. legitimated) by such shared understandings. At this point sociological institutionalism overlaps with the literature on 'epistemic communities' in IPE.

### Research Track 1: The normative setting of economic practices: exploring the Washington consensus

The 'Washington consensus' is shorthand for the conventional wisdom about the most efficient government action in the present global political economy. IPE scholars are increasingly aware that this kind of shared 'common wisdom' is of crucial importance. Constructivist scholars have argued convincingly that the impact of common wisdom cannot be reduced to the constraints posed by the institutions that embody it. Rather, facts (about e.g. the global economy) and interests (defining e.g. the strategies of states) are themselves intersubjectively constructed. Consequently, one strand of IPE research centres on the extent to which changes in the ideas about what is feasible and sound have shaped 'globalisation' and state strategies (see Cerny, Chapter 2 in this volume). A few examples will illustrate the point.

To begin with, there is considerable research on the ideological and organisational origins of such transnational consensuses. This is important for understanding why change in normative settings takes place as well as to clarify who benefits and loses. In contrast to much of the work in the constructivist tradition, explanations deriving from sociological institutionalism usually venture beyond the realm of discursive constructions into the economic and social structures. This is no doubt the reason for which they have been readily integrated in IPE.

The work of Evans (1997) and Dezalay and Garth (1998) reflect this strategy. Dezalay and Garth explain the emergence of the 'Washington consensus' in terms of the construction of economics as a neutral, technocratic, mathematical science where 'it takes a model to kill a model'. They explore the interests and the strategies of economists who have managed to carve out a niche that secures jobs, funding and status. The shift to neoclassical economics grounded in econometrics is understood as one such possible niche in a context which has been predominantly Keynesian and largely 'verbal'. Dezalay and Garth show how this niche was carved out and developed within US academia through a reliance on media, links to business-life as well as through the control of academic institutions. Similarly, Evans (1997) explains the Washington consensus by the parallel development of neoliberal economics, neoutilitarian state theories, and 'civil-society' centred theories of politics. An unsophisticated neoutilitarian state theory combined with the focus on the new civil society has complemented the neoliberal turn in economics, serving to de-legitimise state intervention in the economy and politics at the state level more generally. As Evans underlines, these theories tend to turn into self-fulfilling prophecies as they tend to result in an exclusive focus on state failures and to deprive the bureaucracy of its economic and social status.

Both accounts move beyond the focus on academic debates to underscore that the impact of these ideas can be explained only by reference to their place in a wider context. Dezalay and Garth (1998) place these shifts in the broader context of the changing nature of the economy – the globalisation of finance and production – and the related increase in the political clout of the

Washington institutions (the IMF and the World Bank). These changes made private business, with an interest in models for reducing uncertainty as well as in further deregulation and state withdrawal, more influential both in academic life and in politics.[5] They also point out that the replacement of Keynesianism with liberalism as the dominant view within the Bretton Woods institutions themselves was all the more significant as the conditionality and reports of these institutions were immediately reflected by private markets. Likewise, Evans sees the immediate, though possibly not long-term, interest of international economic actors (MNCs and financial market operators) in supporting further deregulation and liberalisation as a fundamental reason for the establishment of the Washington consensus. In fact, he considers possible limits to state decline to stem from the risk that if this decline goes too far, the stable predictable, law-abiding environment which is essential for business will disappear and business consequently will cease to support further liberalisation, deregulation and state withdrawal.

Once established, the Washington consensus informs both the identification of problems and their solutions. This shift to a 'market civilisation' legitimises a set of practices whose ideological effect has been a central theme of Gramscian IPE (Gill 1995a) as well as the late Susan Strange (1990). The Washington consensus constrains policies directly through the pressure of international and national financial markets, central banks, credit rating agencies, or conditionality. There seems to be what Gill refers to as a 'new constitutionalism'. That is, the explicit or implicit conditionality imposed by international actors is regulating and constraining politics in much the same way as national constitutions (Gill 1997: 215). The consensus, however, is not only felt as a constraint, it alters the way actors conceive of their interests, what is feasible, what is a problem and what is not. Hirschman has repeatedly pointed out the significance of underlying understandings for the polices adopted, and the implications in terms of incapacity to solve problems (see Hirschman 1967, on inflation in Chile) or of even thinking about solutions (see Hirschman 1981 on the debilitating effect of dependency theory). It is increasingly common in IPE to explain policy choices partly in this way, i.e. with reference to the changing worldviews of actors. Thus, the repatriation of US-trained economists with different worldviews has been used to explain fundamental shifts in policy orientation such as the opening up of the Swedish financial markets (Korpi 1992) or the closing of the Korean Central Planning Board (Weiss 1998).

By the same token, changes in the dominant understanding of the relationship between the state and the economy affects who is a legitimate political actor and what legitimate politics are about. And this leads us straight onto the second research track where sociological institutionalism has been of consequence for IPE.

### Research Track 2: The social setting of economic practices: exploring the diffusion of politics

Shared worldviews empower actors 'in the know' and disempower others. In examining this process empirically, sociological institutionalism joins IPE scholars concerned with the bearers of ideas, their organisation and institutional setting. In the case of the establishment of the Washington consensus, the two groups which have been most studied are those policy-makers and private actors who pushed for the turn to neoliberalism and who have acquired increasing political clout as a result of it. In studying the first group, sociological institutionalism clearly overlaps with IPE scholars' interest in 'epistemic communities' and the role of norms in policy-making. In working on the second, it overlaps with IPE studies of the 'diffusion of power' and the increasing importance of private, often corporate, actors in politics.

First, in the shift to a new dominant understanding of the role of the state in the economy, the focus of much recent research has been on policy-makers, or more precisely the networks of experts and policy-makers usually referred to as 'epistemic communities' in IPE (Haas 1992). The question here becomes which networks of policy-makers carry a particular set of ideas and how they manage to impose these in a given situation. Such studies invite investigation of policy-making practices and, in particular, of the role that norms play. In returning to these issues, IPE scholars (Trentmann 1998) have thus joined IR scholars more generally (Finnemore and Sikkink 1998) and have moved closer to sociological institutionalism.

Sociological institutionalism has contributed to this literature by demonstrating the way ideas are 'imported' and adjusted within national fields of economics and of the economy. Consonant with a sociological approach, the analysis does not de-link the analysis of ideas from the social groups who share them. Lebaron (1997), for example, analyses the 'field' of the professional economists in France in the 1990s showing the role imported ideas, funds, and positions in the international scientific community play in the field of French economics and in the 'strategies' of French economists. In particular, he emphasises the importance of an international status for those French economists who are not well linked up with national networks, that is those who do not come from the Parisian faculties and lack prominent positions on editorial boards and other scientific institutions, and who need to establish themselves from the outside. He further shows the weight of international ideas and institutions in his study of the reform of the legal status of the French Central Bank (in 1993) aimed at making the bank more independent from government. Here 'new constitutionalism' was central. A key impetus for the reform came from the Maastricht Treaty. But beyond this, the pressure of international markets and the changing reference points of central actors who 'only place themselves on the transnational level' (Lebaron 1997: 89) played a central role. Similarly, in her study of the ruling elite of Brazil, Loureiro (1998) shows how foreign education is fundamental both in constituting identities and networks and as a symbolic resource for imposing politics (for a similar study in the French context, see Lezuech 1998). Finally, it merits underlining that the integration of the international consensus can also be negative as in the cases where the policy expert network defines itself in opposition to the dominant consensus, as is often the case with Islamic economic strategies.

As these examples illustrate, sociological institutionalism is closely related to and in effect overlaps with the concerns in IR and IPE about policy-making networks and tends to study them much in the same manner. In fact, it is difficult, if not impossible, to separate work in IPE and in sociological institutionalism on this topic.

The same goes for the study of the second group of actors which is empowered by neoliberalism: the private actors. Indeed, as Strange has repeatedly insisted (including in her last piece, see Strange 1998), it would be a serious mistake not to account for the increasing role non-state actors play in politics. In part, this role is adopted simply by virtue of the changes that are taking place in the international economy. As pointed out by numerous IPE authors, including Strange (1996: Part II), private actors such as accountants, credit rating agencies, banks, or for that matter organised crime or drug dealers, play an increasing role in determining politics. They do not have a popular mandate for such powers, yet the changes in the way that the international economy is operating have made them extremely influential. Sinclair (1994), for example, shows how credit rating agencies dominate private and corporate policies simply because of the enormous importance of their evaluations. The aspect of this privatisation, or diffusion, of power which sociological institutionalism is best equipped to deal with, is how it is accepted and legitimated.

Indeed, in parallel with the structural shift which has conferred *de facto* new political roles on private actors, a privatisation of policy-making which is increasingly placing politics either in the grey zone between the private and the public sphere or purely in the private sphere has taken place. What is new about this privatisation is the legitimacy and official sanctioning of private policy-making. Sociological institutionalists have been concerned with how this has developed.

Two examples can illustrate this point. First, sociological institutionalists have examined the emergence and increasing importance of private regulatory institutions, that is institutions where public policy-making and the setting of rules are mandated to the private actors involved. PIGs (private interest government), or more respectfully SROs (Self-Regulating Organisations), play an increasing role in a number of economic sectors (Streeck and Schmitter 1985; Boyer and Hollingsworth 1997). In a study of the emergence and increasing dominance of SROs of financial markets, Coleman (1994) stresses the importance of the changing perceptions of what is legitimate regulation. In particular he underlines the significant difference between the UK tradition, where state interference continues to be considered as illegitimate, and the US where 'a [state] shotgun behind the door' is considered necessary. In looking at the spread of the 'Anglo-Saxon' model of finance, he stresses the importance of international market pressures and the changing consensus among policy-makers. He further underlines the significance of national traditions for the concrete ways the model is copied and implemented.

Second, sociological institutionalism draws attention to the emergence (or existence) of governance practices consisting of a mixture of public and private actors. Again, conceptions of legitimacy have evolved and play a crucial role in the success of such forms of governance. Thus, in their study of economic policy-making in Russia, Sabel and Prokop (1996) stress the importance of the flexible, decentralised and private sector oriented policy-making usually associated with post-Fordist or flexible production forms. They argue that this is crucial both for creating competitiveness and because this is the policy both national and foreign firms consider legitimate. Similarly, in exploring the role of 'deliberative associations' in Central Eastern Europe, Stark and Bruszt (1998) underline the importance that these institutions be recognised as existing forms of economic activity and as legitimate sites of policy-making.

To sum up, this section has shown how sociological institutionalism has contributed to one specific aspect of the debate about the evolving role of the state in IPE: the role shifts in world views (the establishment of the Washington consensus) play in bringing about changing roles for the state. The overall contention is that sociological institutionalism can provide important insights for understanding exactly how, and if, politics is 'uncaging' from the nation–state in different contexts (Mann 1993) and what, if any, of the traditional 'functions' of the state are disappearing and becoming illegitimate in the process (Ferge 1999).

## A less economic understanding of firms

Although themes consonant with sociological institutionalism have already been addressed in the discussion of political (state) phenomena in IPE, economic actors, such as the firm, are still observed primarily through economic institutionalist lenses. Yet, as the remainder of this chapter will argue, that neglect leads to an unduly restrictive understanding of the power relationships involving firms at the heart of IPE.

In a world where production is increasingly organised in global 'webs' over which states have imperfect control, at best, firm motivations and behaviour is of fundamental importance (Reich 1991). Firms play a central role in determining crucial political questions concerning jobs, income redistribution, taxes, welfare provisions, research and development, or environmental policies. Understanding the firm therefore is a central part of any analysis that purports to ask political questions about the economy (Stopford and Strange 1991; Strange, 1970, 1991, 1995).

That said, IPE scholars have chosen, on the whole, to examine firms through the lenses of economic approaches and particularly institutional economic approaches. The approaches to the firm, and the behaviour of multinationals, most commonly referred to in IPE, centres on oligopolistic market conditions, market imperfections, and strategic behaviour (Gilpin 1975; Kindleberger 1979), on neoinstitutionalism (Dunning 1988) and on product cycle arguments (Casson 1987). As argued by Sally (1994), approaches deriving firm behaviour from their embeddedness in a social and political context have by and large been ignored.

The adoption of an economic approach leads to a concentration on questions of efficiency. These questions are no doubt important but they tend to downplay the distributional, political and social aspects both of firm strategies and of their consequences. Also, they tend to misread the actual behaviour of firms in strictly economic terms, a shortcoming particularly relevant for a discipline like IPE which started with the purpose to overcome exactly such a bias.

Sociological institutionalists reject both the traditional economic view where firm behaviour is analysed solely as a response to external market conditions *and* institutional economic analysis where transaction costs are determining. Instead, sociological institutionalism stresses the social construction of firm identity and behaviour. Firms are viewed primarily as social institutions. Firm strategies and structures are shaped by the internal social context of the firm: firm behaviour is a consequence of firm history, traditions, culture and internal power relations (e.g. personal rivalry, competition among divisions). Moreover, sociological institutionalists link their analysis of the firm as an institution to the environment in which the firm is embedded. And this environment must be considered in terms of the social, political, and cultural relations – not only in terms of markets and economic factors, as neoclassical economics and rational choice institutionalism would have it. As a result sociological institutionalism is better than conventional economic analysis at treating questions such as: why firms behave differently in similar contexts, why some firms adapt well to changing circumstances while others do not, why different firms have different structures and strategies in different contexts, and what are the distributional consequences of firm behaviour.

In his critique of transaction costs economics, Granovetter (1992) provides a succinct statement of the difference between the sociological and the economic institutionalist approaches. Williamson (1975, 1985) contends that the transaction costs (the costs due to the combination of bounded rationality, uncertainty, opportunism, and small numbers) involved in any transaction explain whether the transaction will take place through markets, hierarchies or networks (for a fuller development of transaction cost economics see Spruyt, Chapter 9 in this volume). In his critique, Granovetter points out that Williamson overstates the uncertainty of most market transactions by ignoring the role of social relations and networks in which they are embedded *and* conversely overstates the smoothness of transactions within firms (hierarchies) by understating the problems of transparency and uncertainty in a bureaucratic institution. In some cases the importance of social ties for regulating exchange is obvious, as e.g. in sectors dominated by family firms, minority groups or migrant workers (Ben-Porath 1980). But Granovetter contends that social ties are important more generally. They shape economic activity also in sectors where market relations guide firm behaviour and structure, precisely because they are at the origin of the shape that these firms and their market relations take (Granovetter 1990).

This kind of sociological analysis has been applied extensively to subjects of direct relevance to IPE. First, sociological institutionalists have employed their analysis of firms to explain broader political changes. Neil Fligstein (1991), for instance, explains the diversification strategies of large American firms by investigating power holders (management and shareholders) and their capacity to impose their views. Mintz and Schwartz (1990) explain the increasing influence of finance and insurance companies over firm strategies in terms of the changing corporate cultures. Finally, Charles Sabel (1995) argues that evolving discursive practices determines whether middle-level management resists or adopts flexible production strategies. This is in turn essential for understanding the extent to which there will be an overall shift to new flexible, post-Fordist forms of production.

Second, sociological institutionalism has been used to analyse how (changes in) the relationship between context and firms influence power relations in society. Thus, Boltanski (1981) shows the importance of the Cold War and a coalition of conservative politicians and the business elite for shifting management practices in France. He focuses on alterations in the worldview of the French business elite and its impact on their business strategies. He argues that they resulted in a reorganisation of the economy (and of the elite). Likewise, comparative work has underlined the importance of differences in socio-political contexts in shaping firm structures and strategy which in turn are directly linked to distributional issues in society. An excellent example is the work by Hamilton and Biggart on organisational forms in the Asian economies (Orrù *et al.* 1991; Hamilton and Woolsey Biggart 1992). They show the importance of cultural factors, including a shared Confucian culture, in shaping similarities and the significance of different histories, state interventions and political events in explaining differences in the overall structure of the private business sector and the strategies of firms. The relations between different social groups are correspondingly different. There is a wealth of excellent studies, focusing on the same issue in various countries (see e.g. Bugra 1991; Sadowski 1991; Bahout 1994; Szelényi *et al.* 1996).

IPE scholars have occasionally made use of sociological institutionalism. Work on foreign direct investment and the strategies of MNCs sometimes turns to it. Sally (1992) used a sociological institutional approach to study the behaviour of French and German multinationals in the chemical industry. He takes sectoral policies and state business relations as a basis for understanding the business culture, and consequently firm behaviour, in the two countries (see also Tavis 1988). Similarly, the approach has been used for studying the role of state institutions and policies in shaping firm structures and behaviour (Katzenstein and Tsujinaka 1992; Whitley 1998).

On the whole, however, the sociological institutionalist literature on firms is ignored. This is regrettable since sociological institutionalism could be used to break the trend which is making firm studies in IPE a branch of business studies and help those who try to use the study of firms to understand the international *political* economy.

## Conclusion

To sum up, sociological institutionalism could play the same role in IPE as constructivism does in IR. Both raise similar issues concerning the importance of intersubjective meaning in the construction of identities, politics, and the economy. However, unlike constructivism in IR, sociological institutionalism has not yet received the recognition it deserves. In IR constructivism has been noisy and visible; a self-proclaimed 'constructivist school' has triggered a new seminal discipline debate (between 'constructivists and rationalists') and this in turn has led to theoretical renewal and to the development of a whole range of new empirical research agendas. By contrast, as just shown, sociological institutionalism is only seeping into IPE slowly and selectively. In many areas, here exemplified by the study of firms, sociological institutionalism has developed outside of the IPE debate. In other areas where sociological institutionalism has influenced IPE very strongly, as in the debate around the state, sociological institutionalists have not flagged their specific contributions and the value of their presence. They have been absorbed, but remain invisible and undervalued. The argument here is that providing a higher profile to sociological institutionalism would allow IPE scholars to move forwards both theoretically and empirically.

An obvious question following from this is what explains the difference between IR and IPE: why is constructivism so assertive in IR and its kin in IPE so nebbish? The easy answer would be that IPE is more focused on economic phenomena and actors, and that the theoretical tool kit of economic approaches is best suited for the study of these. However, as underlined above, this is simply not true. A more interesting way to answer the question would be to apply sociological institutionalism reflexively to the field of IPE and to clarify why the strategies of IPE scholars have so far been constructed in a way which has largely excluded this kind of approach. Indeed, a further virtue of making the sociological institutionalism an explicit part of IPE would be that it paves the way for a treatment of reflexive issues, such as this one, and for attempts to make serious (and critical) sense of the future directions taken by our discipline.

## Notes

1   Special thanks to Tanja Boerzel, Bela Greskovits, Stefano Guzzini, Mihaly Laki, Jennifer Milliken and Ronen Palan for commenting extensively on an early version of this paper.
2   However, there can be very fruitful interchanges between sociological and rational choice institutionalism as illustrated by the collaboration between Pierre Bourdieu and James Coleman (Coleman and Bourdieu 1991) around the concepts of social and symbolic capital.
3   For an application of Bourdieu to the study of power in international relations, exemplified by a study of the second Gulf War, see Guzzini (1994: chap. 11 in particular).
4   Palan (1999) rightly points out that not all regulationists fit the following account. Some scholars have simply adopted a realist conception of the international and hence have failed to properly integrate the global into their accounts let alone theorise how this integration could be accomplished.
5   See Bourdie and Waquant (1998) for an elaboration on importance of US foundations in spreading the ideas. They fund both 'scientific' and NGO work on issues which are conceived according to the prevailing understanding of social and economic sciences.

# 13 Trends in development theory

*Jan Nederveen Pieterse*

This chapter maps out major trends in contemporary development thinking, centring on development theories as organized reflections on development, rather than on development *tout court*. I argue that the lineages of development are quite mixed. It includes the application of science and technology to collective organization, but also managing the changes that arise from the application of technology. Virtually from the outset development includes an element of reflexivity. It ranges from infrastructure works (railways, roads, dams, canals, ports) to industrial policy, the welfare state, new economic policy, colonial economics and Keynesian demand management.

A number of concerns and priorities are broadly shared across development stakeholders (such as globalization, poverty alleviation, gender awareness and environmental management). But development is intrinsically a field of multi-level negotiation and struggle among different stakeholders. Different stakeholders in the development field have different views on the meaning of development and how to achieve it. Consequently, generalizations about development are meaningless and one always needs to ask, whose development? In fact, not only are there a number of contending development theories, but each of these theories consist of shades of meaning and multiple layers determined by factors such as: context, explanation, epistemology, methodology, representation and future agendas.

The chapter opens with general observations on the different meanings of 'development' over time, which places the discussion of contemporary trends in a historical context. The next section juxtaposes these different understandings of development to changing patterns of global hegemony. Zeroing in on the contemporary setting, the different stakeholders and institutions in the development field are mapped out. Against this backdrop we turn to development trends over time, first long-term trends in theory and methodology, next policy changes and finally to likely futures of development.

## Antecedents of development theory

Over time 'development' has carried very different meanings. The term 'development' in its present sense dates from the post-war era of modern development thinking.[1] In hindsight, earlier practices have been viewed as antecedents of development policy, though the term development was not necessarily used at the time. Thus, Kurt Martin (1991) regards the classic political economists, from Ricardo to Marx, as development thinkers for they addressed similar problems of economic development. The turn of the century latecomers to industrialization in Central and Eastern Europe faced basic development questions, such as the appropriate relationship between agriculture and industry. In central planning, the Soviets found a novel instrument to achieve industrialization. During the Cold War years of rivalry between capitalism and communism, these were the two competing development strategies: Western development economics, on the one hand, and, on the other, some form of central planning (in Soviet, Chinese or Cuban varieties). In this general context, the core meaning of development was catching up with the advanced industrialized countries.

Cowen and Shenton uncover yet another meaning of development. In nineteenth-century England 'development', they argue, referred to a remedy for the maladies and shortcomings of progress. These involve questions such as population (according to Malthus), job loss (for the Luddites), the social question (according to Marx and others) and urban squalor. In this argument, progress and development (which are often viewed as a seamless web) are contrasted and development differs from and complements progress. Thus, for Hegel, progress is linear and development curvilinear (1996: 130). Accordingly, twentieth-century development thinking in Europe and the colonies had already traversed many terrains and positions and was a reaction to nineteenth-century progress and policy failures where industrialization left people uprooted and out of work, and social relations dislocated.

The immediate predecessor of modern development economics was colonial economics. Economics in the European colonies and dependencies had gone through several stages. In brief, an early stage of commerce by chartered companies followed by plantations and mining. In a later phase, colonialism took on the form of 'trusteeship', managing colonial economies not merely with a view to their exploitation for metropolitan benefit but allegedly also to develop the economies in the interest of the native population. Development, if the term was used at all, in effect referred mainly to resource management, first, to make the colonies cost-effective, and later to build up economic resources with a view to national independence. Industrialization was not part of colonial economics because the comparative advantage of the colonies was held to be the export of raw materials for the industries in the metropolitan countries. Indeed, there are many episodes, amply documented, when European or colonial interests destroyed native manufactures (textile manufacturing in India is the classic case) or sabotaged efforts at industrialization in the periphery (Egypt, Turkey, Persia are cases in point; Stavrianos 1981). This is a significant difference between the colonial economies and the latecomers in Central and Eastern Europe.

In modern development thinking and development economics, the core meaning of development was economic growth, as in growth theory and Big Push theory. In the course of time mechanization and industrialization became part of this, as in Rostow's *Stages of Growth*. When development thinking broadened to encompass modernization, economic growth was combined with political modernization, i.e. nation building, and social modernization, such as fostering entrepreneurship and 'achievement orientation'. In dependency theory, the core meaning of development likewise was economic growth, under the heading of accumulation. But in contrast to modernization theory, dependency theory postulated distorted forms of accumulation as dependent accumulation, which led to the theory of 'development of underdevelopment', and an intermediate form dubbed 'associated dependent development'. The positive goal shared by both modernization and dependency theory was national accumulation (or autocentric development). However, with the onset of alternative development thinking, new understandings of the term 'development' came to the fore focused on social and community development, or development as 'human flourishing' in John Friedmann's definition (1992). With human development in the mid-1980s came the understanding of development as capacitation, following Amartya Sen's work on entitlements and capacities. In this view the point of development, above all, is that it is enabling. Accordingly, the core definition of development in the Human Development Reports is 'the enlargement of people's choices'.

Two radically different perspectives on development came to the fore around the same time. Neoliberalism in its return to neoclassical economics eliminates the foundation of development economics, which is that developing economies represent a 'special case'. According to the neoliberal view, there is no special case. What matters is to 'get the prices right' and to let market forces do their work. Development in the sense of government intervention, in this perspective, is anathema for it means market distortion. The central objective of development, which neoliberals equate with economic growth, is to be achieved through structural reform, deregulation, liberalization, privatization – all of which are to roll back government and reduce market distorting interventions, and by the same token, in effect, annul 'development'. In other words, neoliberalism retains one of the conventional core meanings of 'development', i.e. economic growth, while the 'how to' of development switches from state to market. Accordingly, neoliberalism is essentially an anti-development perspective, not in terms of goals but in terms of means. Ironically, just like neoliberalism, post-development thinking also puts forth an anti-development position. But it does so more radically, for it applies not merely to the means (the state is accused of authoritarian engineering) but also to the goals (economic growth is repudiated) and the results (which are deemed a failure or disaster for the majority of the population) of traditional development theories (Rahnema and Bawtree 1997; discussed in Nederveen Pieterse 1998c).

How should we account for this shift of meanings of development over time? One view is to treat this kind of genealogy of development discourse as a deconstruction of development, i.e. as part of a development critique. Another is to treat it as part of the historical contextuality of development maintaining that it is quite sensible that development changes meaning in relation to changing circumstances and sensibilities. 'Development' then serves as a mirror of chang-ing economic and social capacities, priorities and choices. A third option is to recombine these different views as dimensions of development, i.e. to weave them all together as part of a development mosaic and thus to reconstruct development as a synthesis of components (e.g. Martinussen 1997, Chapter 3). Thus, if we consider each development theory as offering a Gestalt of development, a total picture from a particular angle, then the array of successive and rival development theories offers a kaleidoscopic view into the collective mirror. A fourth and related one is to treat the different meanings of development in the context of changing relations of power and hegemony. By any account, the different meanings of development relate to the social field.

## Development is struggle

Focusing exclusively on the evolution of development and development theory over time is incomplete, for in addition there are different dimensions to 'development' at any one time. To each developmnet theory there are various dimensions or layers of function and meaning. Accordingly, each development theory can be read on different levels including:

1    The historical context and political circumstances. Each perspective unfolds in a particular historical setting. Understanding development theory in context means understanding it as a reaction to problems, perspectives and arguments at the time.
2    Explanations or assumptions about causal relationships.
3    Epistemology or rules of what constitutes knowledge.
4    Methodology, or indicators and research methods.
5    Representation, of articulating and privileging particular political and class interests and cultural preferences.
6    Agenda-setting role of theory, as a set of policy implications and a future project.

To this we should add a third complicating factor, the relationship between knowledge and power. That every truth is a claim to power and every power is a centre of truth is the point of discourse analysis and part of a postmodern understanding of knowledge. This involves more or less subtle considerations. For instance, one can argue for a relationship between technological capacities and epistemology and politics. 'Heavy technology' such as the steam engine then correlates with an epistemology of determinism and a politics of hierarchy; whereas soft or light technology, such as touch-button tech, implies much subtler epistemologies and more horizontal relations (Mulgan 1994).

From this third perspective, while broadly speaking each development theory can be read as a hegemony or a challenge to hegemony, explanation is not always the most important function of theory. On the contrary, in line with the neocolonial intellectual division of labour in which 'theory' is generated in the West and data are supplied by the South, grand theories have typically been fashioned in the West and therefore articulate Western political interests and follow Western intellectual styles and priorities. Reading development theory then is also reading a history of hegemony and political and intellectual Eurocentrism (Amin 1989; Mehmet 1995; Nederveen Pieterse 1991).[2]

We can map, then, the main contours of development thinking in different periods and place them in the context of the pattern of hegemony in international relations and the structures of explanation prevalent at the time (Table 13.1). Thus, we relate the global relations of power or international hegemony to intellectual patterns of hegemony (in line with Gramscian international relations theory). The assumption in this schema is that the explanatory frameworks that inform development thinking are shaped by the paradigms that are available in the intellectual market at the time.

## The development field

Development thinking and policy, then, is a terrain of hegemony and counter-hegemony. In this contestation of interests there are many stakeholders and multiple centres of power and influence. Taking a closer look at the contemporary development field, we can schematically map the main actors and forces generating 'development theories' as shown in Table 13.2.

*Table 13.1*   Development theories in relation to global hegemony

| Development thinking | Historical context | Hegemony | Explanation |
|---|---|---|---|
| Progress, evolutionism | nineteenth century | British Empire | Social Darwinism, colonial anthropology |
| Classical development | 1890–1930s | Late comers, colonialism | Classical political economy |
| Modernization | Post-war | United States hegemony | Growth theory, structural functionalism |
| Dependency | Decolonization | Third World nationalism, NAM, G77 | Neo-Marxism |
| Neoliberalism | 1980s > | Finance and corporate capital | Neoclassical economics, monetarism |
| Human development | 1980s > | Rise of Asian and Pacific rim, big emerging markets | Capacity, entitlements, developmental state |

*Table 13.2*   Actors in development field (1990s): different stakeholders, different development

| Institutions | State | IFIs | UN system | Civil society |
|---|---|---|---|---|
| Structure | Governments, ministries North and South | IMF, World Bank | UN agencies | INGOs and NGOs |
| Infrastructure | Bureaucracies, interest groups, parties, factions, electorates | G7, central banks, international banks, MNCs, WTO, development banks | UN General Assembly, governments, ILO etc. | Social movements, trade unions, churches, donors |
| Locations | Capitals | Washington DC | New York, Geneva, Paris, Nairobi, etc. | Dispersed |
| Development thinking | Economics (Keynesian to neoclassical) and human development | Neoclassical economics, neoliberalism, monetarism | Human development | Alternative development |
| Disciplines | Economics, political science, sociology | Economics | Economics, political economy, IR, political science | Sociology, anthropology, ecology, gender, cultural studies |

To the surface structure of dispersed centres of influence we may add the infrastructure of behind-the-scenes forces, i.e. those forces whom the overt centres of influence themselves depend on or are following. Thus, what matters are not simply the World Bank or the IMF, but their Boards of Trustees and other significant forces who influence the parameters of policy. For instance, current analysis refers to the 'Treasury–Wall Street–IMF complex' as a successor to the military–industrial complex (Wade and Veneroso 1998). Further, at some remove (because these relations are not always clear-cut and straightforward), we may add the development thinking that would be congenial to these circles and the disciplines that typically inform their angle of vision. The dispersal of stakeholders in development to some extent roughly correlates with the disciplinary sprawl of development studies, so this fragmentation may have not only an intellectual basis in the academic division of labour but also an institutional basis

Table 13.2 is a schematic representation. Obvious provisos are that NGOs need to be broken down in various types, some of which are more aligned with GOs than others. In addition in the infrastructures of power different ideologies may prevail. For instance, among multinational corporations (MNCs), more radical forms of *laissez-faire*, and among social movements or disaffected intellectuals, post-development views may prevail.

From this mapping of the development field several points follow:

1   It is not really possible to generalize about development: the question is, whose development? Different stakeholders have different views of the meaning of development and how to achieve it. This is not a minor point but a fundamental circumstance. Development intrinsically is a field of multi-level negotiation and struggle among different stakeholders.
2   Schematic as it is, this outline may enable us to fine-tune thinking about the relationship between power and knowledge in development.
3   New concerns and priorities that are broadly shared across development stakeholders (such as globalization, poverty alleviation, gender awareness, environmental management) make for new combinations and partnerships that cross-cut 'boxes'.
4   Emergencies occur which make for cross-cutting alliances and approaches – such as complex human emergencies, humanitarian action, conflict prevention and post-conflict reconstruction. In this light this kind of map is already overtaken on the ground, which serves as a reminder that the map should not be mistaken for the territory.

## Trends in development theory

Due to the complexity of the development field, the selection and representation of contemporary trends are a tricky issue. If it is true that development is a mirror of the times, then a development trend report is caught in a double-bind of its own reflection. There is no methodology to achieve this in a neat and clean fashion. The format I adopted here is a concise profile of trends with limited references to sources. Because they are long-term changes (over fifty years or more) they have a certain degree of plausibility but we need to bear in mind that they are also rather general and of a high level of abstraction. Even so, a long-term perspective in a field dominated by short-termism may be welcome.

Arguably, long-term trends in development theory echo the general shifts in the social science from nineteenth-century to late twentieth-century episte-mologies. In the first place, this involves a shift from structuralist perspectives that emphasize the role of macro-structures towards more agency-oriented views, a change that can also be described as a change from deterministic to interpretative views (cf. Bauman 1992 on the changing role of the intel-lectual from legislator to interpreter) and from materialist and reductionist views to multidimensional and holistic views. Classical and modern develop-ment thinking was fundamentally structuralist, centring on the large-scale patterning of social realities by structural changes in the economy, the state and the social system. Such epistemologies were also applicable to critical development thinking at the time, which was informed by Marxism, which in its orthodox forms is basically structuralist. It further applies to the structuralist school associated with Raúl Prebisch, which preceded the emergence of dependency theory in Latin America, and to neo-Marxism, dependency theory, modes of production analysis, structuralist Althusserian Marxism and the regulation school.

The dominance of structuralist and functionalist epistemologies began to weaken in the social sciences under the growing influence of phenomenology (dating back to nineteenth-century antecedents) and a variety of orientations, such as existentialism (and its emphasis on individual responsibility), hermeneutics (involving a more complex epistemology), symbolic interactionism and ethnomethodology (in anthropology), new institutional economics and rational choice, social choice and capability (in economics), and feminism (e.g. standpoint theory). In Marxism, structuralist epistemologies have come under attack under the influence of Gramscian Marxism.

The same trend can be described differently as a shift from structuralism to constructivism, i.e. from an account of social realities as determined and patterned by macro-structures, to an account of social realities as being socially constructed. The lineages of constructivism include phenomenology – as in Schutz (1972) and Berger and Luckmann (1967) and Max Weber, with Giddens' structuration theory (1984) exemplifying the turn. Poststructuralism and postmodernism, taken in a methodological sense, are further expressions of this reorientation (Rosenau 1992).

In development studies, these broad changes involve various implications. One of the consequences of the emphasis on agency is that development thinking becomes spatialized and more local, or regional in orientation. Another implication is the growing concern for differentiation and diversity. Early and modern development thinking were fundamentally generalizing and homogenizing, reflecting the essentialist philosophy of structuralism. By contrast, the so called 'post-impasse' in development thinking highlights diversity and differentiation (Schuurman 1993; Booth 1994). Thus, concern shifts from, e.g., 'the South' to 'five different Souths' (Group of Lisbon 1995). Along with this comes a movement away from grand overall theories and big schema policies. General theories and recipes are discredited, and development policies are no longer viewed as relevant across countries and regions. The singular therefore makes way for the plural generally – development is no longer considered a legitimate field, the question becomes: what kind of development?; growth is no longer taken at face value, the question becomes: what kind of growth? Accordingly, a plurality of qualifications and caveats proliferate, exemplified by terms such as 'sustainable development', 'people-friendly growth', 'pro-poor growth', etc. While such qualifications had always figured in the critical literature; now they have entered mainstream discourse. Among the concrete expressions of the agency-orientation in development thinking are recent work on strategic groups, the actor-oriented approach (Long 1994) and the general emphasis on a participatory approach (e.g. Oommen 1998).

Concern with diversity and agency is introducing a new kind of tension:

what, then, is the relationship between the local and the global, between the internal and the external, the endogenous and exogenous, between micro and macro policies? The shift from structuralism to constructivism and from structure to agency is not complete but a matter of emphasis and perspective; one does not replace the other but complements it. There is no doubt that structural changes and macro-policies matter (such as Structural Adjustment lending and the Multilateral Agreement on Investments), but these issues no longer constitute the field of development theory, they are perceived as only part of the field. As a result there is a renewed sense of empowerment, as many actors actively negotiate politically and analytically, and feel they can do something about them. Indeed, the impact of these actors on public debate and policy-making can be measured (e.g. Clarke 1998). A step towards the democratization of development politics, constructivism, in this sense, can be interpreted as the methodological expression of a political transformation.

This perspective offers one angle on current trends in development thinking. Several ongoing trends in development are linked to these general changes, or follow them, without being reducible to them. Among these I would highlight the following:

### Interdisciplinarity

Traditionally sectoral theories have dominated development studies, with the resulting gap between economic development and social and political development theories. (Although, admittedly, grand theories such as modernization and dependency theory managed to bridge the gap to some extent.) Concerns with questions such as the embeddedness of economic and market activities in political institutions, social capital, cultural practices and social relations coupled with the introduction of methodologies such as social accounting, imply new combinations of disciplinary sensibilities.

### Discourse analysis

The origins of this methodology are in linguistics and literature studies, owing its influence to the general impact of poststructuralism. In this regard development studies follow a general trend in social science. Discourse analysis treats development as a story, a narrative and a text and has generated a wave of critiques of development texts or 'deconstructions of development' (e.g. Sachs 1992; Escobar 1995; Cowen and Shenton 1996; Nederveen Pieterse 1991). According to some recent literature, the power of development is the power of story telling (development is a narrative, myth or fairy tale) (Crush 1996; Rist 1997). By now discourse analysis has become an almost standard genre (a critical discussion is to be found in Grillo and Stirrat 1997).

In itself, discourse analysis is not remarkable; it is simply the 'linguistic turn' applied to development studies. Its contribution to development lies principally in instilling an awareness that development is never only a theory or policy. It forces development theory to step beyond the concept of ideology, or interest articulation, and pay attention to development texts and utterances, not merely as ideology but as epistemology.[3] Thus, it involves sociology of knowledge not only in terms of class interests (as in ideology critique) but also in terms of an inquiry into what makes up an underlying 'common sense'. Discourse analysis has been used in another way to argue that development theory is fictional, untrue, bogus, deceptive. That it is a form of Western modernism and scientific distortion that sets illusory goals of material achievement and in its pursuit wreaks havoc upon Third World people. Here, discourse analysis turns into anti- or post-development thinking (e.g. Escobar 1992; Sachs 1992) and in the process methodology turns into ideology – an instrument of analysis becomes an ideo- logical platform, a political position; so that politics of knowledge turns into knowledge of politics.[4] Likewise, such interpretation of discourse analysis involves the admixture of outside elements: an *esprit* of anti-modernism with romantic overtones (as in Ivan Illich) and/or post-Gandhian utopianism (as in Ashis Nandy 1989). Development as a discourse is presented then as alien to the Third World (Western), authoritarian (state, IMF), engineering (modern), controlling and steamrollering and perverting local culture, grassroots interests and perceptions: this development critique is the newest critical populism.

Discourse analysis is employed also in the sense of 'unmasking' develop- ment as 'myth' or 'fairy tale' (e.g. Rist 1990); i.e. development is 'only a story', a narrative, in fact a 'grand narrative'. But this is a rather contradictory argu- ment, for the very point of discourse analysis is that discourse matters, talk and representation matter, and representation is a form of power which in turn constructs social realities. Some analysts seem to want to have it both ways: development is a story and yet somehow it is 'only a story'. By doing so they confuse two different methodological dispositions: that of ideological critique (which measures ideology, as masked interests or false consciousness, to some yardstick of 'truth') and discourse analysis.

Notwithstanding, discourse analysis adds a level of reflexivity, theoretical refinement and sophistication to development studies, and thus opens the poli- tics of development to a more profound engagement. Its weakness and limitation – in development studies just as in literature criticism and cultural studies – are that it may skirt the actual issues of power and divert attention from development 'on the ground', so to speak. In that case, we risk slipping from determinism into discursivism, i.e. reading too much into texts, or textu- alism, and overrating the importance of discourse analysis as if by rearranging texts one could alter power relations. This amounts to an alternative struc- turalism: from social macro-structures to linguistic and epistemic structures; or, the order of language as a stand-in and code for the order of social relations.

The emergence of new fields of interest also shapes development studies. Gender, ecology, democratization, good governance, empowerment, culture, communication and globalization now figure prominently in development agendas. Ecology involves not just resource economics but novel syntheses such as ecological economics and ecological politics. Gender plays a fundamental role in development practice and discourse. 'Empowerment' and 'participation' are ubiquitous, also in development management. As well as active public administration, accountability, democracy and citizenship figure prominently. Globalization is a major vortex of change also in the development arena. These fields of interest generate new theoretical and policy angles but so far not necessarily new overall theoretical frameworks. Consequently, several themes that are not new in themselves appear but the emphasis they receive is novel. Or, some themes acquire a new significance over time. Thus, corruption has been a familiar theme in development work but at each turn of the wheel, it takes on a different meaning. In the context of modernization, it was presented as a residue of premodern, particularist leanings. In the dependency framework, corruption was a symptom of dependent development and of the comprador politics of the lumpen bourgeoisie. Kleptocracy, 'crony capitalism' and 'money politics' are variations on this theme. In the context of neoliberalism corruption is understood as rent seeking, an ominous sign of state failure and market distortion and 'a hazard to free trade and investment' (Leiken 1996: 55).

## Culture and development

Conventionally development has been a monocultural project as modernization and Westernization were virtually synonyms. As part of 'nation building' development was taken as a homogenizing project. In the context of decolonization struggles this began to change: along with the indigenization of politics and administration, indigenous culture and knowledge became an additional topos. Thus, for a while culture was incorporated into development studies but in a subsidiary fashion ('add culture and stir'). The critique of Eurocentrism generated a concern with polycentrism, cultural multipolarity (Amin 1989) and pluralism. The UNESCO-sponsored World Decade on Culture and Development also resulted in growing regard for cultural dimensions of development (Report of the World Commission on Culture and Development 1996). In the wake of the cultural turn in development (Nederveen Pieterse 1995) culture represents another dimension of development that can no longer be ignored or viewed as just an obstacle (as in orthodox modernization thinking). 'Culture' now figures in several ways. First, in terms of cultural diversity – obviously, in an age of ethnicity and religious resurgence this is not an entirely innocent theme. A second and related concern is cultural capital, both as a human capacity and a form of human capital, and as a political currency (both in ethnic and religious mobilization and as an asset in economic relations). A step further is to view cultural diversity itself as an engine of economic growth (Griffin 1996).

## The unit of development

From the classics to dependency theory the conventional unit of development was the nation. The key development statistics and measures used by the international institutions are still country statistics. However, while the nation remains the central domain of development it is no longer the only game in town.

Gradually development is becoming a multi-level, multi-scalar series of efforts, simultaneously taking place at levels smaller than the nation, at the national level, and at levels bigger than the nation.

Smaller than the national level are community development, local economic development (LED) and microregional development. Community development, a subsidiary theme in colonial times and for modernization theories, received a new emphasis with alternative development. Local development in its various forms connects with questions of rural/urban disparities, urban development, regional inequality, new regionalism, ethnic mobilization ('ethnodevelopment'), and new localism with a view to endogenous development and in reaction to globalization. Bigger than the nation are questions of macro-regional coopera-tion and global macroeconomic policies. Macro-regional cooperation concerns the conventional issues of economies of scale, increase of market size, regional standardization and interfirm cooperation as well as the horizons of the regional Development Banks. Besides country statistics another set of development statis-tics are regional, concerning 'Latin America', 'Africa', 'Asia', 'the Caribbean', etc. The region, in other words, is becoming almost as familiar a unit of develop-ment as the nation. A third scale of development action is the world: local, national and macro-regional decision-making interfaces with global macro-poli-cies on the part of international institutions and the UN system.

Hence, development policy is increasingly viewed in terms of decision-making dispersed over a wide terrain of actors, institutions and frameworks. Development theorizing, which is habitually centred on the state, needs to accommodate this widening radius. Development theory needs to be renewed by reconceptualizing development as multi-scalar public action. Contemporary development policy is incoherent because the different levels of development action – local, micro-regional, national, macro-regional, international, global – are not adequately articulated. Thus a comprehensive, holistic approach to development is not only multi-dimensional but also multi-scalar, such that devel-opment efforts at different levels would be cumulative and would interconnect.

## Intersectoral cooperation

After development thinking has been, more or less successively, state-led (classical political economy, modernization, dependency), market-led (neoliberalism) and society-led (alternative development), it is increasingly understood that develop-ment action needs to pay attention to all of these but in new combinations. New perspectives and problems (such as complex emergencies, humanitarian action) increasingly involve cooperation between government, civic and international organizations, and market forces. Human development, social choice, public action, urban development and LED all involve such intersectoral partnerships. For government at local and national levels, this increasingly involves a coordi-nating role as facilitator and enabler of intersectoral cooperation. The theme of development partnership at present serves an ideological role as part of a neolib-eral New Policy Framework which papers over contradictions and the rollback of government (e.g. Hearn 1998). However, the underlying significance is much more profound: just as sectoral approaches and disciplinary boundaries have been losing their relevance, sectoral agendas are now too narrow. The ideological use that is being made of this conjuncture should not obscure the significance of the trend itself.

International development cooperation has been changing in several ways. The emphasis has shifted from projects to programmes and from bilateral to multilateral cooperation. The trend is towards, on the one hand, formal channels (particularly multilateral cooperation through international and regional institutions) and, on the other, informal channels (NGOs) (Bernard *et al.* 1998).

## Futures of development

Whither development is a familiar question (e.g. McMichael 1996). Considering plausible future trends in development by way of trend extrapolation, even if it is a limited exercise, provides an opportunity to uncover background questions. What is likely first is that there will not be a single future trend. The current array of perspectives, which represents a dispersal in subjectivities and interest positions, is likely to continue in some fashion if only because these interest positions and subjectivities will continue. In other words, to each of the current development positions is a set of futures and options in facing challenges. Accordingly, futures are viewed through multiple lenses and from each angle, there are different options – many are prefigured in current debates and others are hypothetical or can be inferred by logic. The starting point is the existing set of development theories, each of which, as a framework or a sensibility, continues to attract adherents and to renew itself. What follows then is a précis of (1) perspectives on development according to the major existing development theories, (2) ongoing revisions and (3) future options (Table 13.3).

### *Modernization theory*

There are several current themes in relation to modernization theory:

1   Neomodernization theory already involves a more complex understanding of modernity and a revaluation of 'tradition', no longer as an obstacle but as a resource (So 1990).
2   A current theme that is likely to become a future trend is to view modernities in the plural. Specifically this means that developing countries no longer consider themselves merely as consumers of modernity (as in Lee 1994) but also as producers of modernity, generating new and different modernities (Pred and Watts 1992; Nederveen Pieterse 1998a). There is no lack of voices in the majority world, which are not merely critical but assert alternative modernities (e.g. Ibrahim 1997, Mohamad and Ishihara 1995).
3   Another trend may be a serious engagement with postmodernism – not merely as a condition (flexible specialization, post-Fordism, and urban and social complexity) but as a sensibility, a style and a philosophical disposition.

*Table 13.3*   Current trends in development theory

| Trend | Conventional and recent views | New themes |
|---|---|---|
| Differentiation | Grand theories | Middle range theories, local knowledge |
| Reflexivity, self-questioning | i Unreflexive use of language, indicators, models,<br><br>ii Discourse analysis | Development as social learning, social feedbacks, reflexive development |
| Interdisciplinarity | Sectoral theories. Gap between economic and social/ political development. (Multi) disciplinary case studies, policies. | Bridging approaches: embeddedness, new institutional economics, sociology of economics, social capital, social economy, holism |
| Intersectoral cooperation | State, market or society-led development | Intersectoral synergies. Public action |
| Social diversity | Homogenization, essentialism | Balance. Politics of difference |
| Human security | i Betting on the strong,<br>ii humanitarian assistance, from relief to development | Risks of polarization, transnational social policy, global social contract |
| Gender awareness | i Gender blind, ii WID (add women and stir) | Gender interests, gendering development |
| Environment | i Mastery over nature,<br>ii sustainable development (add environment and stir) | Green GDP, political ecology |
| Cultural turn | i Westernization,<br>ii homogenization vs. indigenization (add culture and stir) | i Cultural diversity, ii cultural capital, as political currency, iii as engine of growth |
| Unit of development | i Nation, ii local | Local, national, regional and world development and multi-scalar partnerships |

## *Dependency theory*

In relation to reworking dependency theory, a well-established trend is the analysis and critique of NICs. In the 1990s, key problems that were being revisited from a dependency point of view were neoliberalism and uneven global development (e.g. Cardoso 1993; Boyer and Drache 1996; Hoogvelt 1997). This takes the form of a general critique of uneven globalization (Amin 1997; Mittelman 1996). A crucial distinction that is rarely clearly drawn runs between globalization as a process and as a specific 'project' (as in McMichael 1996; Dessouki 1993), or, between globalization as a trend and neoliberal globalization policies (e.g. Bienefeld 1994; Brohman 1995). Analyses of globalization projects focus, for instance, on the World Trade Organization and global environmental management (e.g. Khor 1997). Rethinking dependency theory has taken innovative directions (e.g. Frank 1996 and 1998), including the renewal of structuralist analysis (Kay 1998). Other trends that involve a renewal of dependency thinking in a broad sense are 'new political economy' and international political economy.

### Neoclassical economics

From the point of view of neoliberalism and neoclassical economics, a major area of concern is the adjustment of Structural Adjustment policies. There have been attempts to implement Structural Adjustment 'with a human face', in combination with a safety net, and to somehow combine structural reform with poverty alleviation. Current concerns are to make structural adjustment policies country-specific and user-friendlier. The concern with good governance and an effective state (World Bank 1997) represents a further adjustment. Clearly, structural adjustment is not the end of development – as was believed some years ago – but rather an intermezzo. An area of concern that may grow in time is the regulation of international finance ('the architecture of the international financial system'). A different turn, which is prefigured in new institutional economics (Mehmet 1995), is the interest in the cultural and social dimensions of development (witness e.g. Fukuyama's work on trust 1995, 1996).

A broad question that underlies the futures of development concerns the character of capitalism. This is a question of global interest: what kind of capitalism? Presently different kinds of capitalism coexist – Rhineland capitalism, Anglo-American free enterprise capitalism, East Asian capitalism, the NICs, the rentier capitalism of the oil producing countries, etc. (cf. Albert 1993). The differences among them reflect levels of technology, historical itineraries, the timing of development, geographical locations, resource endowments, cultural capital and institutional differentiation (Nederveen Pieterse 1997b). From a sociological point of view this may be captured under the heading of 'different modernities', which then raises the question of the interaction of modernities. For a long time Anglo-American capitalism has been hegemonic. This is now being globally transmitted through the 'Washington consensus', the international financial institutions and the World Trade Organization, in part by default, in the absence of an alternative policy consensus. Arguably, more in line with the interests of other, majority forms of capitalism and modernity are proposals for global or transnational social policy and possibly global neo-2Keynesianism (e.g. Group of Lisbon 1995).

### Alternative development

Some of the keynotes of alternative development thinking, in particular participatory development, have become increasingly influential in mainstream development approaches. The strength of alternative development is local development. With this comes a concern with local project failure, cultural sensitivity and endogenous development (Carmen 1996). Oddly, the disaffection with the state in alternative development resonates with the neoliberal complaints about state failure, and this conjuncture has contributed to the great wave of 'NGO-ization' and informalization since the 1980s. For a long time alternative development has been strong on critique and weak on alternatives beyond the local, beyond decentralization. Increasingly, the attention now also includes global alternatives, or an alternative globalization 'beyond Bretton Woods' (e.g. Korten 1990; Arruda 1996).

One may argue that alternative development is not an appropriate heading now that it is no longer 'alternative' and that a different, more specific heading would be welcome. Options include 'popular development' (Brohman 1996) or grassroots development but the limitation of such headings is that the idea of global alternatives slips out of the picture. Alternatively, one can retain the commitment to alternative development but define its core elements (such as participation, empowerment) more sharply to distinguish alternative from main-stream approaches.

## Human development

The human development approach is being extended in different dimensions such as gender (as in the Gender Development Index) and political rights (as in the Freedom Development Index) (ul Haq 1995; UNDP 1997). It also extends to different regions, in the preparation of regional human development reports (e.g. ul Haq and Haq 1998). Merged with participatory development, it gives rise to new combinations, such as 'just development' (Banuri *et al.* 1997).

Substantively what may be a growth area for the human development approach is to examine the relationship between human capital (its original main concern) and social and cultural capital. Bourdieu (1976) has argued all along that these different forms of capital are interrelated and interchangeable. For Bourdieu, this served as an analysis of 'modes of domination'. What is on the agenda now is the significance and potential of these interrelations from an analytical and a programmatic and policy-oriented view. Social capital now figures in social and economic geography: 'institutional densities' and civic polit-ical culture emerge as significant variables in explaining regional economic success or failure. The success of micro-credit schemes may be explained by the fact that they make maximum use of people's social capital. Part of the cultural turn in development is regard for local cultural capital, for instance in the form of indigenous knowledge. Cultural diversity and the mingling of different cultural communities (diasporas, migrants, travellers) may be considered as a potent ingredient in economic innovation and growth (Griffin 1996). That participation has become a mainstream concern opens possibilities for wider cooperation. A way forward may be the exploration of development synergies, i.e. the relationship between civic organizations, local government and firms.

This may take the form of a concern with supply-side social development (Nederveen Pieterse 1997a).

The theme of human security refers to a new combination of concerns, a conjunction of conflict and development (e.g. Naqvi 1996). This finds expression in the new development problematic of humanitarian action and 'linking relief and development' (e.g. Nederveen Pieterse 1998b). Another current in human development, almost from the outset, has been a concern with global reform. This ranges from the role of the UN system in relation to the Bretton Woods institutions and the World Trade Organization (Singer and Jolly 1995) to macroeconomic regulation and global taxes (Cleveland *et al.* 1995; ul Haq 1995). This is likely to remain a major preoccupation. This ties in with the question of global governance in the sense of global managed pluralism (Falk 1994; Commission on Global Governance 1995).

### Anti-development

A major concern in anti-development approaches currently is 'resistance to globalization', such that anti-development and anti-globalization are becoming synonyms: globalization is viewed as the main form of developmentalism at the end of the millennium (Mander and Goldsmith 1996). Anti-development has all along been concerned with local autonomy, at times advocating local delinking (Sachs 1992). A further turn to this is a connection with ecological liberation movements (Peet and Watts 1997). The Zapatista rebellion in Chiapas is, according to some, concerned with land rights and local autonomy; but the Zapatistas also organize with a view to political reform in Mexico and global alliances of resistance and hope (Castells 1997). The major limitation of the post-development approach is that beyond local autonomy it offers no significant future perspectives, so that the most likely future of anti- or post-development is localism.

There are other changes affecting the development field that are not revealed by looking at the transformations of theories. One is the trend towards convergence of developed countries and NICs. In light of technological change, globalization, knowledge intensity, developed countries are presently developing much like LDCs, though starting from a higher base and more stable institutions. If we compare the developmental profiles of the United States with those of e.g. Korea and Brazil, we find a broadly similar agenda. In either, the emphasis is on innovation-driven growth, human capital, technopoles, industrial districts, R&D, and knowledge intensity (e.g. Connors 1997). This is a new form of 'betting on the strong', driven by the imperative of global competitiveness (Group of Lisbon 1995). Meanwhile the 'Asian crisis' since 1997 has shown the frailty of the 'emerging markets'. The net figures in terms of productivity and exports may line up with those of advanced countries, but the institutional settings are quite different. The common verdict on globalization and development is that while the gap between advanced countries and NICs is in some respects narrowing, the gap between both of these and the least developed countries is widening.

As well as the policy innovations concerning the least developed countries in the era of globalization, this development gap also points towards the global horizon. Combined and uneven globalization makes for global inequality as well as global risks. Ecological hazards, financial instability, technological change and conflict require global risk management. The challenge for a global development approach is to bring separate and opposing interests and constituencies together as part of a worldwide bargaining and process approach.

## Notes

1   I owe many thanks to Ranjit Dwivedi for comments on an earlier version of this chapter.
2   Notable exceptions are dependency theory (which was also informed by Marxism, i.e. originally a Western counter-hegemony), alternative development and human development thinking, which largely originate outside the West.
3   An effective use of discourse analysis is as an analytical instrument applied for example to development policy (e.g. Apthorpe and Gasper 1996; Rew 1997).
4   There have been similar agnostic moves in Foucault and Derrida's work.

# 14 The constructivist underpinnings of the new international political economy

*Ronen Palan*

Constructivism deserves attention for two reasons. First, and perhaps less important, constructivism, or more appropriately, one version of constructivism has gained tremendous popularity in International Relations during the past few years (see for instance, Adler 1997; Onuf 1989; Wendt 1992). The question, then, is to what extent constructivism is relevant to International Political Economy. Second, a sharp distinction is commonly drawn between economic and political economic theory, on the one hand, and poststructuralist, postmodernist theories, and more broadly 'cultural' theories, on the other. Indeed, many believe that political economy, including its international variant, stands as bulwark against the ephemeral, fashion conscious, if not reactionary tendencies of the 'posties' in the social sciences.

Recent developments in political economy, in particular the rise in popularity of evolutionary institutionalism (see chapters in this volume by Phillips, Nitzan and Bichler, Leander), on the one hand, and the rediscovery of the institutionalist tenets of Marxist thought on the other (see Dunford, Chapter 10 in this volume), have demonstrated that the relationship between political economy and the broader tradition of thought dubbed as the 'continental' or critical tradition of the social sciences is close if complex (Mirowski 1990; Silverman 1997, see also Ling, Chapter 16 in this volume). Modern institutionalist thought in particular is united in rejecting rationalist, progressivist and crude-materialist explanations of social processes and practices. Rather than adopt a simple ideas versus practice type of theory, they view 'the materiality of social institutions and their dynamics (as products) of evolving interrelated systems of institutions and discourse rather than as grounded in externalised and objective social realities' (Cameron and Palan 1999).

While rationalist thought is grounded, as Carlson (Chapter 8) and Spruyt (Chapter 9) remind us, in methodological individualism, the critical tradition takes the view that 'economic activity is socially constructed' (Wilkinson 1997: 309). This chapter seeks to clarify the relationship between constructivism and the critical wing of as Murphy and Tooze (1991) called it, the 'new' International Political Economy or Barry Gills and I described as neostructuralism (Palan and Gills 1994). I seek to demonstrate that constructivism is rooted in a theory of the subject as a 'paranoid construct', and this theory of the subject underpins the constructivist theory of discourse, institutions and social reflexivity.

## What is constructivism?

Terms such as constructivism, constructionism, constitutiveness are used by different people to describe different things. To complicate matters, Onuf excluded, constructivism in International Relations appears to draw primarily on a position which developed as an extension of 'Chicago-style' symbolic interactionist methodology (or latterly known better as ethnographic research) whose adherents do not describe themselves as constructivists (key texts include Blumer 1969; Mead 1934, Schutz 1972. For discussion see Charon 1998; Prus 1997).

To the best of my knowledge, the term constructivism was coined in the early 1920s by a group of Soviet artists and architects to describe a new artistic movement. Today constructivism is most commonly used to describe a well-defined epistemological position that bears little resemblance to Soviet constructivism. Credited to Vico, epistemological constructivism evolved in repudiation of the conventional view of knowledge appropriation maintaining that knowledge cannot be the result of passive receiving, but is inseparable from the processes of knowing (Glaserffeld 1984: 31). Constructivism may be defined therefore as an epistemological doctrine that rejects models of human knowledge that are premised on the strict separation between the observer and the observed. In particular, epistemological constructivism maintains that since knowledge is expressed in symbolic form (language, mathematics symbols, images, and so on), society must implicate our theories of knowledge.

In sociology, constructivism is used somewhat differently to denote the idea that reality is socially constructed. That is, 'humans see the world through perspectives, developed socially ... [and consequently] reality is social, and what we see "out there" (and within ourselves) is developed in interaction with others' (Charon 1998: 42). In other words, however real or factual our social environment may appear, it is nothing but a product of human endeavour and human imagination.

Constructivism varies from *radical constructivists* who deny an objective stand for knowledge, to mild constructivists who reject the separation between the observer and the observed. Constructivist tenets, whether radical or not, are found in all radical critiques of society, from left to right. For the simple reason that a theory that maintains that what takes place is a direct outcome of some objective human conditions, must accept limitations on the possibilities of change and hence must accept some limitation on its own critique. Radical critiques assume at the very least that what exists is one world among possibly many, hence what exists is an outcome of human belief and action and if those change, then the world we take for granted will change as well.

Constructivists are fascinated by orthodoxy because orthodoxy tends to represent itself as natural, self-evident or common sense. Indeed, constructivism comes into sharp relief when contrasted with conventional or positivist theory knowledge.[1] Conventionally, knowledge is viewed as a cumulative process. The assumption being that humanity began from a very low level of knowledge of itself and its surroundings, and gradually built up a body of solid information and understanding of itself. According to this view those people we call 'primitive' had a very crude and incorrect knowledge of themselves and of their surroundings. They substituted lack of knowledge and understanding by presumptions, speculations, superstitions and myths. The implication of that view is that modern society knows and understands itself better than the ancient or 'savages'. Since the 'discovery' of the scientific method in the sixteenth century, humanity has found a new and superior method for obtaining objective knowledge of itself and the world. The progressivist view of knowledge is closely associated then with the scientific revolution and the Enlightenment.

The spectacular success of the physical sciences attributed to the scientific method has had profound implications for the development of social philosophy and, in time, for the new disciplines of the social sciences. In a crude form, 'scientific' approaches to society produced theories that reduce humans to physical attributes. In the opening pages of the *Leviathan*, Thomas Hobbes asks:

> Why may we not say, that all automata (Engines that move themselves by springs and wheels as doth a watch) have an artificial life? For what is the Heart, but a Spring; and the Nerves, but so many Strings?
>
> (Hobbes 1951: 81)

Hobbes sought to develop the equivalent of Newton's laws of nature in society by formulating some immutable laws of politics (or political science). Human behaviour was deemed regulated 'by some desire' over which they had no control. Reflexivity, or the ability of humans to reflect on their action and the effect reflection has on their action did not enter the equation.

Still with us today is a second aspect of Hobbes's methodology, the idea that theory evolves as deduction from the first principle or, 'truths about how people are obliged to organise themselves socially and politically' (Hamilton 1996: 2). First principles are assumed or asserted: Hobbes began by assuming some basic laws which govern human behaviour. Similarly, modern rational choice theory assumes that behaviour is 'being intentionally brought about by human agents seeking goals and holding beliefs' (Ferejohn and Satz 1996: 74). Whatever the case, theory evolves as deduction from such first principles (see Carlson, Chapter 8 in this volume).

The scientific method is founded also on the understanding that knowledge must be *public*; an experiment or a rule is deemed to be true, if and only if it can be replicated under similar conditions by whoever wishes to replicate it. Max Weber argued that sociology 'seeks to formulate type concepts and generalized uniformities of *empirical process*' (1978: 19, my emphasis). To achieve that goal the social science must eschew hypothetical entities such as nation, society or class and focus, in contrast, only on knowledge of empirical facts or human action, which is the only publicly observable knowledge. The social sciences must begin therefore from those simple observable propositions, hence the close association between the 'scientific method' and methodological individualism.

Empiricism is often associated with positivism. Both assume a distinction between real facts and ideologies or fantasies. As Oakes observes: positivism is a particular view of science as a field of study that 'is concerned with the explanation of data, the status of which may be regarded as unproblematic and given. Thus the only interesting and important methodological issue is the question of the conditions that must be satisfied by the explanation of these data' (1988: 25). Conventional or non-constructivist approaches are deeply concerned with methodology, but have scant regard to question of epistemology (i.e., theories of knowledge appropriation), and of course, ontology (theory or theories of being or Heidegger's *Dasein*).

The implication (although not shared by Max Weber) is that the social world is governed by objective laws and rules and the role of science is to discover its laws and behaviour. Such methodological assumptions abound – although not always in rigorous form. For example, the realist position claims generalise upon a 'discovery', albeit a long time ago, of the basic laws that govern anarchical political systems. The theory identifies a 'first principle', such as the alleged states 'survival instinct' as in the case of Waltz (1979), or the pursuit of power and prestige as in the case of Morgenthau (1948), and then develop an entire theory of international affairs as extension of these principles.

The general pattern of theorising tends to be then:

1   Discover some universal laws that govern human behaviour.
2   The task of theory is then to model this reality. Models do not capture reality, however, theory captures an abstracted essence.
3   The observer is and should be detached from the observed.

Demonstrating that such a position is contradictory is not very difficult. The assumption that the subject's perception of the world does not change that world, on the contrary, the subject is situated in that world, is entirely legitimate. At the same time, certain social categories, such as the 'nation', the 'people', 'God', which are admittedly hypothetical entities in the sense that no one has seen them, are matters of faith rather than fact. And yet, it is impossible to deny that such hypothetical entities shape our social world to a considerable extent.

If such hypothetical entities shape the world, then can we simply relegate them to the realm of 'ideology' or false consciousness and then ignore them? In other words, if we accept that belief in God is pertinent to the nature of the society in which such beliefs prevail, then how far can we take an objectivist approach to social investigation? How do such hypothetical entities come about in the first place? Why and how do they shape the world?

Constructivists internalise these questions. Indeed, it is rarely recognised that like positivists, constructivists were equally impressed by the scientific revolution. Only they adopt a diametrically opposed interpretation of the implications of the scientific revolution to the study of human societies. In addition, rather than assume that other civilisations possess a false view of the world, constructivists are struck by the instrumental and functional roles played by different systems of knowledge in their unique context. Constructivists argue therefore that (a) all societies ascribe correct knowledge to themselves and false knowledge (or false gods) to others, consequently we must entertain the idea that our own theories of knowledge are not as objective we believe them to be; (b) if knowledge plays a constructive-functional role in other civilisations, then it probably plays a similar role in ours. Knowledge, then, cannot be divorced from the interest and the social position of the knower. Knowledge in other words cannot be divorced from power – meaning, the question of knowledge belongs to the realm of political economy as much as to the realm of philosophy and the two cannot remain separate.

Consequently, constructivists argue that political economy must internalise the problematic of knowledge and knowledge acquiring. Constructivists are far more interested in epistemology then methodology, believing that excessive concern with methodology in fact comes at the expense of the more critical and important epistemological questions. The social science must begin therefore not by assuming that humans are ultimately reducible to physical or biological organisms, but by confronting the complexities of the human psyche and deriving a theory of society from it.

## The subject, discourse and institutions

How, then, do we go about internalising this relationship between 'imagined' (or hypothetical) entities and human behaviour? How do we deal with the question of the real and the imaginary, acknowledging that both affect the subject of our investigation? Social philosophy has traditionally oscillated between two sets of answers: idealism and realism/materialism:

> [Idealism] refers to perspectives based on the assumption that ideas and spiritual values are the controlling factors in society, history, or the world as a whole. In idealism change beings as an idea ... in realism change beings as action, the action of many people, and is only expressed as an idea.
>
> (Wilden 1987: 83)

The salience and power of 'imagined' entities such as God or the nation are no problem for the idealists because they privilege the realm of ideas over matter. For the materialists, these 'imagined' entities are nothing but expressions of human alienation: they are the symbolic expressions by which society rationalises and legitimises power and exploitation.

Increasingly, however, the very dichotomy is viewed with suspicion, as behaviour or practice cannot be separated from ideas and perception. How can behaviour and action be detached from the dynamic process of perception and reflection? Where do our ideas and perception come from, if not from the 'reality' of our lives? Assuming even that 'reality' is only a pragmatic reality in

Peirce's sense, that is that 'knowledge is judged by how useful it is in defining the situation we enter. The more we can apply it to what we encounter in our world, the more we come to believe it' (Charon 1998: 29), how is correspondence established between such pragmatic reality and ideas? How can we say that the relationship between ideas and practice is dialectical without first artificially separating them? In fact, idealism and materialism are reflected in the Cartesian distinction between body and soul. Considered as two separated attributes of the subject, the body and soul distinction in itself is founded upon another dichotomy, the one that distinguishes the realm of the 'real' and the realm of ideas (soul). Constructivist theories try to eliminate such *a priori* dichotomies.

## The subject

Arguably the more interesting line of investigation that has tried to transcend the idealist–materialist divide, follows Kant through Hegel, Heidegger to Jacques Lacan. This version of 'constructivist' epistemology resolves the idealist–materialist divide by an unusual device: asserting the structural impossibility of reaching the 'real' (the 'material' in materialist discourse) because of the subjects' subordination to language. In other words, the dichotomy is transcended by questioning the concept of the real and by demonstrating that the 'real' is not an ontological realm separated from 'ideas'. It was Hegel who already argued that truth is of necessity 'inter-subjective' and hence the 'real' or 'reality' in common discourse is a fiction:

> All that I can express by language is a universal; even if I say 'this thing here' I am still expressing it by an abstraction, and I cannot attain the 'thing-itself' in speaking of it. Through the 'miracle' of the understanding, with its power of abstraction, it is the negation of the thing itself which provides it with a universal essence in the concept. And since the named thing is still a universal, so too, is the ich.
>
> (cited in Wilden 1968: 194)

Lacan expresses the same idea when he says that the subject (the individual) is subjected to an ontological 'splitting' as the 'real' can never be appropriated in other ways than language and images. René Magritte's painting, 'ceci n'est pas une pipe' illustrates the point. Margritte's painting is that of an image of a pipe, but the title of the painting is: 'this is not a pipe'. Meaning the image is only an image of a pipe and can never be a pipe. This is not due to the inadequacy of Magritte's rendition of the image, but it is a structural problem that any rendition, any image, is not and can never be the thing in itself. Concepts, words and images, the symbols and signs are the tools by which we represent what we take to be the Real, but they are never the real. The very utterance and thinking already imply the 'death' of the Real and the supremacy of the Imaginary and the Symbolic. This structural ordering is grounded in the very essence of language and hence knowledge.

In other words, since the object of knowledge, whether physical phenomenon or social are 'defined only through the medium of a particular logical and conceptual structure' (Cassirer 1955: 76), namely, language, we use signs and symbols to depict or 'capture' knowledge. The conventional assumption is that these sign and symbols are only mediums, and neutral at that, and therefore external to the reality (data) they are supposed to depict. Whereas the constructivist position maintains that 'the sign is no mere accidental cloak to the idea, but its necessary and essential organ ... Consequently, all truly strict and exact thought is sustained by the symbolic and semiotics on which it is based' (ibid.: 86.), meaning, rather than assume we are studying some reality 'out there', social scientific theories are in cultural science: we are studying politics and economics as forms of culture.

Therefore in Lacan's terminology humans inhabit an Imaginary order embedded in the symbolic structure. One way of introducing Lacan's ideas is through the structuralist theory of the development of the Self. The child is introduced into society through a process we call socialisation or, as Foucault calls it (showing his Lacanian credentials), more accurately 'normalisation'. Whereas socialisation assumes a gradual learning process by which the child is equipped to handle the adults' world, normalisation implies a forceful and psychologically violent act by which subjectivity (the ego) emerges. Socialisation is normally understood as the inculcation of the young in the dominant values. It is assumed that cohabitation in the family facilitates that transmission of attitudes and communal terms of reference. So that parents are constantly surveying their children and 'after a while an attitude of confidence develops and there is no need for constant surveillance' (Claval 1978: 47). In using the term normalisation, Foucault refers to the structuralist theory of the very act of discovery of the self as Other.

Structuralist psychology makes much of the 'mirror phase' in the development of the child. The significance of the phase is that the child's

> attempt to appropriate or control their own image in a mirror is that their actions are symptomatic of these deeper relationships. Through his perception of the image of another human being, the child discovers a form (Gestalt), a corporeal unity, which is lacking to him at this particular stage of his development ... the central concept is clear; this primordial experience is symptomatic of what makes the moi an Imaginary construct. The ego is an Idealich, another self, and the stade du miroir is the source of all later identifications.
> (Wilden 1968: 160)

In this way, 'the young child's entry into the symbolic order will fashion him in accordance with the structures proper to that order: the subject will be fashioned by the Oedipus and by the structures of language' (Lemaire 1970: 6).

Human behaviour therefore cannot be broken down simply into methodologically salient atomistic building blocks as Weber had suggested, but much of social interaction is believed to contain a number of explicit as well as subliminal messages about 'reality' which are then interpreted and provide additional contextual reference points in which 'action' is embedded. Action is embedded, in other words, in discourse.

## Between needs and desire

The difference between conventional and constructivist theories of the subject crystallises in what may appear as a semantic hair splitting: the distinction between the concept of human need and human desire. For empiricism humans join together into collectivities (or societies) because societies are the best guarantees for the fulfilment of certain fundamental needs such as food, shelter, security, and so on. The concept of 'human needs' may appear simple and straightforward, but it is not. In fact, the concept is philosophically driven. As Juranville points out, empiricism is a sceptical philosophy. It is a particular mode of discourse in which experience is opposed to the *a priori* logic of language in general. Consequently, for empiricism there is no truth. 'The unity of language confers on things not a real unity, but fictive or imaginary unity. Empiricism in this sense is essentially nominalist, in that the unity of things is only nominal.' Consequently, 'for empiricism there is nothing to desire, not even knowledge. Desire itself is conceived as an illusion. For empiricism there is nothing but need' (1996: 71, my translation).

Juranville describes Lacan as a theory of partial truth, a theory of pure desire. As Deleuze and Guattari explain:

> from the moment that we place desire on the side of acquisition, we make desire an idealistic (dialectical, nihilistic) conception, which causes us to look upon it as primarily a lack: a lack of an object, a lack of the real object … In point of fact, if desire is the lack of the real object, its very nature as a real entity depends upon an 'essence of lack' that produces the fantasised object. Desire thus conceived of as production … this means that the real object that desire lacks is related to an extrinsic natural or social production, whereas desire intrinsically produces an imaginary object that functions as a double of reality, as though there were a 'dream-of' object behind every real object' or a mental production behind the real production.
>
> (Deleuze and Guattari 1984: 25)

Deleuze and Guattari understand capitalism as a specific social system in which

> lack is created, planned, and organised in and through social production: production is never organised on the basis of a pre-existing need or lack … the deliberate creation of lack as a function of market economy is the art of a dominant class. This involved deliberately organising wants and needs amid an abundance of production; making all of desire teeter and fall victim to the great fear of not having one's needs satisfied.
>
> (1984: 28)

The idea of the creation of lack in the midst of abundance is found, albeit in different language, in Veblenian political economy (see Nitzan and Bichler, Chapter 5 in this volume).

Needs are pre-theoretical, the bestial aspect of humanity which is at the heart of neoclassical economics (Palan 1997), desire belongs to the realm of the imaginary – it is the imaginary created lack.

## *Discourse*

Now, if the distinction between what we take to be the 'real' and what we take to be ideas is not as absolute as we thought, then the distinction between the observer and the observed cannot be absolute as well. That does not mean that the observer 'shapes' the observed – which is an extreme idealist position that is generally rejected, but it means that the observer has no way of knowing the true nature of the observed – or to put it another way, the concept of an *objective* world is a particular observational technique, or a particular discourse.

In fact, Lacanian theory demonstrates the subjectivity and individuality emerges in discourse. The term discourse in the narrow sense means the formal description of words beyond the level of the sentence. More broadly, however, discourse has come to denote the entirety of an utterance. Discourse may be one of several types or genre; some of which are verbal some are not. When recorded it is called text. Discourse cannot be reduced to language. While 'language imposes structure and content on our relationship to our reality, and therefore on our relationship to reality, and therefore on our understanding of reality' (Wilden 1987: 132). Language should not be confused with discourse.

The force of discourse in the social is traceable to the Lacanian notion that 'it is on discourse that every determination of the subject depends' (Wilden 1968 : 178), including thought, affect, enjoyment, meaning, and even one's identity and sense of being. Discourse is a necessary structure that subsists in certain fundamental relations and thus conditions every speech act and the rest of our behaviour and actions as well.

Lacan points out that the constitutive role of discourse is most visible in fact in science. Science, as we know it, greatly surpasses anything that could result from just an effective understanding of things. Contrary to conventional wisdom, science therefore involves not a better understanding of the world but rather the *construction* of realties that we previously had no awareness of. 'What science constructs is not just a new model of the world, but a world in which there are new phenomena. And this constructed world occurs solely through the play of a logical truth, a strict combinatory' (Bracher 1994: 108). The same, of course, is true about the law, and in fact about every facet of social life.

If we think of society as a form of communication and exchange, then what is taken to be the natural order of things is now understood as a dominant discourse. But the dominant form is never absolute, in any society, we can expect to find dominant and subordinate discourses. The most universal is the dominance of the male discourse over the female discourse.

## A constructivist interpretation of the ancient city's political economy

A good example of a 'constructivist' interpretation is found in Fustel De Coulange's brilliant study of the ancient city. The ancient city, says De Coulange:

> looked upon death not as a dissolution of our being, but simply as a change of life ... [So that] According to the oldest belief of the Italians and Greeks, the soul did not go into a foreign world to pass its second existence; it remained near men, and continued to live underground.
>
> (1955: 15)

The dead were buried in the house and were recalled in an altar placed centrally in every household. The household obtained therefore for the ancient people imminent and transcendental value, as it was the visible link between the living and the dead, whereby the living had a moral duty to carry on the name and reputation of the household in the name of the dead. The house then attained as a sacred value for the living. The altar in the house, recalling the dead, became the focal point of family life. The central component of the ancient city was then the sacred household. Consequently, the ancient city was perceived as a community of families, each of which were a sovereign entity. The city therefore adopted a particular form of inter-familial democracy (as opposed to the modern bourgeois democracy). Similarly, although the ancient people accepted the notion of market, land, which was sacred because of the link with the dead, could not be exchanged. The ancient concept of private property was therefore different from ours. De Coulange's history of the ancient city demonstrates, then, how a foundational myth, the belief in the transmutation of the dead, defined the ancient people's relation to the household, the land, the family, private property, and to the city. In that way the ancients' cosmology served as the basis upon which the entire economic, social, religious and political character of the ancient city was constituted.

For De Coulange the character of ancient societies was structured around a foundational myth. The foundational myth of the ancestor is a pure construction in modern eyes. This foundational myth (or the master discourse in Lacanian language) served as the 'truth' for the ancient people. They found positive affirmation for their 'truth' in the sense that what the ancient people saw around them could only confirm the 'reality' of such foundational myth – although to us the myth of the ancestors is nothing but a myth. The idea of the myth structured practice, but the myth in turn was supported and maintained by practice. In addition, the ancients were subject to systems of penalties and rewards that supported this theoretical construction. De Coulange demonstrates to us that the foundational myth was in a pragmatic sense, the ancient people's truth. De Coulange depicts then a world that is entirely 'constructed' upon some imaginary myth. And yet for all this it is no less real for its participants. Consequently, a historical study of the ancient people is lacking if it does not place the foundational myth and its relationship of affirmation. In other words, we need to understand the ancients' discourse.

Constructivism maintains that not only the ancient city was structured as a discourse, but the modern world is equally constructed around foundational myths, for example, the myth of the 'imagined community', the nation. In fact, everything that we take to be the fundamentals of human life can be easily demonstrated to be 'myths' in De Coulange's rendering, namely, they have no stronger claim for reality or rationality then the ancient people's theories of the dead. For example, realists maintain that states seek to aggrandise their power and prestige. But what drives states to aggrandise their power and prestige? If we probe deeper into the reasons for their behaviour, we are likely to find no ultimate reason. Waltz, for example, maintains that the ultimate reason is the survival instinct of states, but who endowed states with a survival instinct? Do we have any proof that such instinct exists? Why do some states seem to be concerned with their survival and others apparently are not? Similarly, it is assumed that the profit motive reigns in the economy. The logic of maximising profits appears to be founded on a consumerist rationale: I would like to increase my profits so I could buy more consumer goods and services. But why, ask Nitzan and Bichler (1995), would a GM or an IBM like to raise profits? Surely, they are not consuming more as a result? The underlying logic of the entire capitalist system and modern instrumental and acquisitive rationality, as it is expressed in theories of the individual, the company or the state, are in fact a mystery. What drives capitalists to accumulate? Indeed, what is accumulation? (See Nitzan and Bichler, Chapter 5 in this volume.) There is no logic external to the very logic of the capitalist system and its myths; there is no logic outside of discourse.

Reading in such way it is difficult not to arrive at the conclusion that the fundamental unit of investigation is the myth itself. As Foucault suggests, we need to suspend the notion that social investigation is about some fundamental truths, and examine instead how historically specific constructs, historically contingent truth, produce certain social conditions. Social studies must take the 'myth' itself and the way by which it structures social life as the starting point.

De Coulange implicitly suggests that we can study cultural formation as a 'system of signs'. The importance of this insight, however, is that idea of the recurrence of systemic relations that give social formations their coherence. In other words, discourses are subject to their laws.

## Marxism and discourse

As already hinted in the discussion of the distinction between needs and desire, it is possible to re-read the Marxist theory of capital as discourse. The Marxian theory of exchange value is a theory clearly based on Imaginary relationships. Retrospectively, the Imaginary is clearly visible in Marx's notion of commodity fetishism:

The commodity-form, and the value-relation of the products of labour within which it appears, *have absolutely no connection with the physical nature of the commodity and the material relations arising out of it.* It is nothing but the definite social relations between men themselves which assumes here, for them, *the fantastic form of a relation between things.*

(1970: 165)

Marx was, after all, a pupil of Hegel. Marx's *Capital* opens with a paradox: how come, asked Marx, 'the wealth of societies in which the capitalist mode of production prevails *appears* as an immense collection of commodities' (1970: 125, my emphasis)? This is a multifaceted riddle that has fascinated the various branches of the critical tradition ever since. Why indeed, does wealth 'appear' as a collection of commodities?

In response, Marx begins an inquiry into the nature of the commodity. Not what it is but what it 'appears' to be:

The commodity is, first of all, an external object, a thing which through its qualities satisfies human needs of whatever kind. The nature of these needs, whether they arise, for example, from the stomach, or the imagination, makes no difference.

(Marx 1970: 125)

Marx then quotes, in an accompanying note, Nicholas Baron who says: 'Desire implies want; it is the appetite of the mind.' While the distinction of needs and desire was unfamiliar in the times of Marx, he is clearly groping for the modern concept of desire.

What gives Marxism – together with critical conservatives like Heidegger – their critical edge is precisely the notion that desire for commodities is not the 'need of the stomach' but the 'desire of the head'. It is not an idealistic, 'ontological' desire for acquisition – as found in neoclassical economics, rational choice and so on – it is in fact, for lack of a better word, a socially manufactured 'lack': it is an exploitative process, a process that exploits not only human labour, but equally the human soul, the Self.

These normative insights are then used by critical thinkers to begin and understand processes of exchange in terms of the cybernetics of human organisation. But it is not exchange that predominates. In contrast to Lévi-Strauss, society, say Deleuze and Guattari: 'is not first of all a milieu for exchange where the essential would be to circulate or to cause circulate, but rather a socius of inscription where the essential thing is to mark and to be marked' (1984: 142). They then demonstrate their contention by pointing out how primitive societies inscribed the socius, 'tattooing, excising, incising, carving, scarifying, mutilating, encircling, and initiating' (p.144). Capitalist society also 'inscribes' the socius, as it carves out the modern acquisitive sovereign individual, which is a mere representative and owner of commodity: 'Here the persons exist for one another merely as representatives and hence owners, of commodities' (Marx 1970: 179). The subject, the sovereign individual of liberal thought is understood here as a histor-ically specific innovation, inscribed in discourse. It becomes then possible to conceive of a history of subjectivity itself (Foucault 1970).

The relationship between capitalist economy and what Talcott Parsons (1951) calls the 'personality system' is well understood. But in the idealist/materialist debate one side was always privileged over the other, as if capitalism somehow preceded capitalist free labour or the other way around. A constructivist position as expressed in different work seeks to describe the concomitant change.

## Social institutions and constructivism

This theory of the subject and discourse produces a particular emphasis on insti-tutions. In conventional rendering, an individual's behaviour, action and thought are structured by something called the 'social structure'; the social structure being in effect the concept representing the 'immutable' laws of politics. To the constructivists, the term 'structure' has a specific hermeneutical meaning: struc-ture designates 'the configurations of the perceptual field, those wholes articulated by certain lines of force and giving every phenomenon its local value' (Merleau-Ponty 1964: 116). Structure is the horizon of knowing or the dominant discourse.

Discourses, however, are not produced in abstract. Discourses are further constrained by social institutions:

> institution differs from a conversation in that it always requires supplemen-tary constraints for statements to be declared admissible within its bounds. The constraints function to filter discursive potentials, interrupting possible connections in the communication networks ... they also privilege certain classes of statements whose predominance characterises the discourse of the particular institution.
>
> (Lyotard 1984: 17)

The relationship between different discourses is therefore not simply a 'battle of ideas'; discourses are rooted in a certain institutional structure which privileges certain discourses, and patterns of discourses, over others.

Inter-discursive or inter-institutional relationship is a point of weakness of institutionalist thought. Veblen presents a view of society as inter-related sets of institutions. On the one hand, institutions are ultimately structures around and maintain 'habits of thought'. The longer an institution exists, say, the institution of the family, the contract, sovereignty or private property, the more 'natural' they appear to be. These institutions prescribe and proscribe individual behaviour and thought. Social change takes place as institutional change and hence it is path-dependent

On the other hand, institutions are then submerged within totalising discourses. Institutionalists have great difficulties in articulating theories of social power and human exploitation. Poulantzas sought to resolve the problem by theorising that institutions are forms of institutionalised power. Any form of power for Poulantzas was essentially class power, but we can extend the notion to other forms of social power, the idea is that power institutionalises its gains in society. Institutions are then conceived not as simple neutral sites of discourse, but as sites of power struggles. Institutional change proceeds as form of mutations and re-articulation of existing institutional pattern, but the motive and direction of change are attributed to power.

Behind discourse therefore lies power. But how power and discourse work is a matter of debate. As Foucault said once, I understand who gains and who loses, it is power I do not understand.

## Conclusion

How important is the constructivist underpinning of the new IPE? My main thesis is that the 'new' or critical IPE is founded upon a theory of the subject as a 'paranoid construct' as opposed to standard economics which begins from the theory and ontology of the individual and their rights and duties. Here it is the opposite, the individual or subjectivity of liberalism is viewed as a hypothetical proposition and modern subjectivity is viewed as historically contingent.

How significant are these theories to IPE? On the one hand, it may be argued that an informed audience should be aware of the epistemological and ontological concepts upon which their theories rely. There is evidence for the profusion of 're-inventing the wheel' types of research as much of the new IPE struggles to articulate the ideas such as: what we take to be real is only historically contingent; dominant discourses are only dominant, they are not absolute; the state, the market and globalisation should be seen as 'totalising' rather than total. The Lacanian theory of the subject tells us that the new IPE insistence on the constructivist and historically contingent nature of modern society is not a moralising whim but is founded upon a theory of the subject.

But can we advance a stronger claim for the need of the new IPE to be aware of its 'constructivist' underpinnings? The question is whether there is something that modern IPE cannot say or articulate without the concomitant holistic theory. This is a question to which I have no answer.

## Note

1    There is, of course, an important debate as to the meaning of constructivism. Positivism here refers to the doctrine which can be characterised by two features:

> first, it is empiricist and positivist: there is knowledge only from experience, which rests on what is immediately given. This sets the limits for the context of legitimate science. Second, the scientific world conception is marked by the application of a certain method, namely, logical analysis. The aim of scientific effort is to reach the goal, unified science, by applying logical analysis to the empirical material.
>
> (Caldwell 1982: 13)

# 15 Historical sociology and global transformation

*Martin Shaw*

The social sciences are undergoing a major transformation at the beginning of the twenty-first century. The theoretical turmoil in international political economy (as in international relations) is one reflection of a wider crisis, which can be seen across the social sciences and indeed in all fields of knowledge. Fundamental intellectual challenges have arisen not just from within the disciplines themselves, but from historical turbulence and change.

It is generally the case that intellectual currents, however esoteric they sometimes seem, are deeply implicated in the social ferments which in turn they attempt to grasp. Any proposal for understanding the intellectual problems of the present, such as that which I make in this chapter, is itself necessarily a response – direct or indirect – to the historical situation. By naming the crisis in a certain way, we are also contributing to a particular direction within it, even to a certain kind of solution.

There is some agreement that at the beginning of the twenty-first century we are in a period of deep historical flux. Indeed, the question of when and how the twentieth century ended (in other than the strict chronological sense) is a key question of contemporary historiography. Eric Hobsbawm (1994) argued that the 'short twentieth century' actually came to an end around 1989. In this sense the twenty-first century is well under way: there was no need to wait for 1 January 2000.

Even in the 1980s, the idea that society was moving beyond the principal features of the modern age was widespread. A discourse of 'post-modernity' became fashionable in many fields, so that the specifically geopolitical turn – 'the post-Cold War era' of which many began to write in the early 1990s – had already been anticipated by many ideas of movement beyond modern conditions in culture and society. 'Post-' ideas of all kinds, however, indicated a loose, even nebulous sense of change rather than a definite content. Indeed, the point of post-modern thought was precisely the dissolution of certainty.

By the mid-1990s, however, one particular concept of change was becoming central to many social science fields, and was particularly influential in international political economy. This was the idea of 'globalisation', defined by Anthony Giddens (1990), one of its most influential proponents, as the worldwide stretching and intensification of social relations. In many versions, this kind of global change had an inexorable quality, linked to the rapid spread and speeding up of market relations, eliminating the possibilities of conscious social control.

While we are indeed in the midst of a fundamental historical transition, none of these widely diffused accounts adequately grasps its character. Indeed, there is a continuing incoherence at the heart of the 'globalisation' literature, in that the meaning of 'global' is often undefined. Where it is, it is identified with the essentially technical changes in communications, transportation and economic structure which have linked distant locales. In this sense, the social meaning of 'globality' (the name for the global as a condition: see Albrow 1996) is not grasped. This meaning should be located, I argue in this chapter, in the widespread recognition of a worldwide human commonality, or of world society as a whole as the framework of human action.

Global change, in this sense, is literally a revolutionary transformation, and of course a highly contested one. In this context, globalisation as commonly understood creates only some of the technical conditions for globality. The mechanisms of worldwide linkage, which are not all as novel as some 'globalisers' suppose, are necessary but not sufficient for global transformation in its full meaning. Globality is a conscious process or it is nothing: the key is the worldwide development of a *common* human consciousness, not as a simple abstract moral or intellectual affair, but deeply rooted in social struggles, and linked to social processes like democratic change which are commonly seen as discrete. In this sense a diffuse, uneven and unfinished global revolution – as well as many manifestations of anti-globalist counter-revolution – can be identified.

While globalisation has been identified as an economic and cultural process, global change in the broader sense is much more political. Global politics can be seen at work in the growth of democratic pluralism, environmentalism, gender politics and anti-racism, even if in their concrete forms these often have confused relationships to nationality and globality – many involve, for example, ideas of 'resistance' to 'globalisation'. Global politics has contradictory relationships, too, to transformations in the state-system, in particular the tendency towards the formation of a 'global state' from the dominant Western system of power.

Understanding the major historical change of our own times, therefore, involves us in understanding the links between economic, cultural and political transformations, and between markets, state institutions and social movements. If these can be considered tasks for international political economy, they obviously involve understanding the field in the broadest sense. They bring into question the relationship between international political economy and other disciplines.

In particular this proposal directs our attention towards the field's intersections with history and sociology. If global change is considered not just as a set of relatively discrete processes, but as a profound and all-embracing transformation, then it takes us back to the foundations of our understanding of the modern world as well as forward to new ways of thinking. We need to examine the history of social thought in order to understand its current dilemmas – and to see the relevance of the historical–sociological approach with which this chapter is concerned. I start in the first main section of this chapter with an account of the history of social thought, before turning in subsequent parts to the specific contributions of a historical sociology to understanding the state and international relations, and to contemporary global change.

## Sociology, history and political economy

International political economy can be considered a 'new' field of social science only in that it is the product of late twentieth-century attempts to bridge disciplinary boundaries between economics, politics and international relations. This does not mean, however, that the subject has no history – even less that the history of the social sciences can be considered irrelevant to the future of international political economy. On the contrary, classical debates, at the root of the modern social-scientific tradition, are of central relevance to contemporary international political economy. If historical sociology is a new approach in international political economy debates, it is nevertheless a synthesis of major classic traditions of understanding. To appreciate the contribution which a historical–sociological approach can make, we need first to understand something of these traditions and their background.

Classical political economy was one of the forms of thought which emerged in the revolutionary changes which created what we have come to think of as the modern world. In the eighteenth and early nineteenth centuries, Britain was in the forefront of industrial change, and Scottish writers like Adam Smith – seen today as the founder of economics – developed important insights into the relations of the market relations of the emerging industrial world.

In the other major European countries industrialism was slower to develop, but the French Revolution had stimulated the development of political theory and of philosophy. The greatest thinkers of the early nineteenth century were much more encyclopaedic than their successors in the twentieth-century social sciences. Among the greatest of the German philosophers, for example, Immanuel Kant was concerned with the conditions of world peace, and G.F.W. Hegel absorbed many of the critical insights of the new political economy.

In the mid- to late nineteenth century, however, fundamental changes occurred in the intellectual picture. With the consolidation of the increasingly industrial market economy, on the one hand, and of the modern bureaucratic state, on the other, the relationships between philosophy, economic thought and politics were transformed. On the one hand, the greatest of all polymaths, Karl Marx, synthesised the dialectical thought of Hegel with the political economy of Smith's principal successor, David Ricardo, and the emergent communist and socialist strand in the revolutionary politics of the time. On the other, the new disciplines of social-scientific thought emerged and eventually became institutionalised in the academy. Sociology was developed by writers like Auguste Comte, as a new form of social thought in which economic conditions were no longer seen as fundamental. Later, as a result of what was called the 'marginalist' revolution, economics developed as a discipline which no longer acknowledged social and political relations as theoretically central to the economy.

Marx presented his work as a *critique* of political economy, in the sense that it not only uncovered the historically specific social relations of labour and capital underlying the market economy – these had already been acknowledged in Ricardo's claim that labour was the source of value – but in that it showed how these would lead to the transcendence of political economy in practice. Marx understood his theory as pointing beyond philosophy, political economy and political theory as they had been understood previously, although it incorporated a 'critical' version of each of these. Overall, however, Marx has been seen as making a transition from philosophy to *historical social theory* (Korsch 1963). For Marx, social relations, understood as specific to a particular historical epoch, were the central problem in the understanding of economics, politics and philosophy.

Sociology represented a parallel but, initially at least, a radically opposed development. Not only did Comte proclaim a 'positive' scientific philosophy – hence 'positivism' – in opposition to Marx's continuation of Hegel's 'negative' or dialectical thought (Marcuse 1968), but for Comte, like his forerunner Henri de Saint-Simon, what was important about the new industrial society was not the contradictory social relations of the market, but the scientific idea through which a new sense of social solidarity would emerge.

This strand of sociology – opposed to political economy – which was developed further in the work of Émile Durkheim, became central to the functionalist theory of the 'social system' developed by Talcott Parsons (1951), which dominated American sociology in its mid-twentieth-century heyday. With Parsons, the main tradition of sociology became fundamentally idealist, locating the unity of society in its 'central value system'. It also became profoundly *a*historical, not only in the Marxist sense of neglecting the contradictory historical specificity of capitalist social relations, but in the more general sense of seeing broad transhistorical generalisations as its basic purpose, and any kind of historical difference as of secondary significance.

A more historical approach to sociology had been developed, however, by Max Weber (even if the historical dimension of his work was minimised by Parsons, who also claimed Weber's legacy). Not only has the significance of his huge, wide-ranging life's work often been compared to that of Marx's, but he has been seen as the 'bourgeois Marx', offering a fundamental alternative to the latter. In reality, Weber's work does not lend itself to such an easy ideological polarisation. Despite his famous investigation into the significance of Protestant religion for the rise of capitalism (1948), Weber does not offer a simple 'idealist' foil for Marx's 'materialism'. Just as Marx, the heir of Hegel, understood the significance of ideas, so did Weber emphasise material circumstances.

Weber's importance lay precisely in the breadth of his historical perspectives, centred on a comparative sociology of world civilisations, and the reasons why only the West had developed capitalist economic rationality. Weber (1964), like Marx, recognised the world-historic significance of capitalist modernity, but he defined capitalism more in terms of this rational logic of market relations than the specific social relation of wage-labour and capital, which Marx made central. This meant that he had a view of the future of capitalism which was simultaneously more closed and more open than Marx's.

On the one hand, Weber believed that the instrumental rationality ushered in by the capitalist market – even if originating partly in religious ideas – was becoming universal and all-pervasive. Weber believed that socialism, far from radically disrupting this process, would actually consolidate it. In this sense, there was no escape from the 'iron cage' of capitalist rationality. Rationalisation – which Weber also saw as implying bureaucratisation – was ineluctable, and history was in this sense 'closed' to any serious alternative to capitalism.

In another sense, however, Weber's approach appeared more open than Marx's. Capitalism was compatible, he recognised, with a variety of cultures and historical conditions. The defining class dialectics of Marx's understanding of capitalism, which in some hands became a deterministic view of the inevitability of socialism, were circumvented. Weber's historical method was looser than the more systematic approach to which Marx's concept of historic specificity lent itself.

As critical sociology developed a distinctive voice against the 1950s' supremacy of Parsons and other functionalists, writers like C. Wright Mills (1958) argued that the 'sociological imagination' needed to be historical – in a broad sense that owed more to Weber than to Marx. The late 1960s and early 1970s, however, saw the re-emergence of calls for sociology to be historical in distinctively Marxist senses: although even among Marxists, differences emerged between the structuralist followers of Louis Althusser (1972) and the others whose idea of history was more humanist (e.g. E.P. Thompson 1978). These Marxist divisions centred on the relationship between opposed concepts of history: as the succession of modes of production, or as the product of the agency of classes.

By the 1980s, these arguments were increasingly transcended in a sociology which was broadly Weberian, but also post-Marxist in the sense of having absorbed some important parts of Marx's and subsequent Marxist thought. Giddens (1981, 1984) had developed a 'contemporary critique of historical materialism', and attempted to resolve the dilemma of structure and agency in his theory of 'structuration'. Giddens' theory, even more than Weber's, was a sociology which was intrinsically historical but also made open-endedness and discontinuity principles of analysis (see Giddens 1985).

Despite this new synthesis gaining a dominant position, especially in Europe, much contemporary sociology remains very limited in scope – centred in partial analyses of present-day Western society. For this reason, Philip Abrams' *Historical Sociology* (1982) set a trend in seeing this as a specific sub-field of the discipline, and other major writers adopting a distinctively historical approach, like Theda Skocpol (1979) and Michael Mann (1986, 1993) have been regarded as 'historical sociologists'. Historical sociology has come to be seen as Weber-inspired, but like the Marxism from which it has also drawn, is characterised by a concern with macro-issues of the nature of large-scale historical phenomena.

At the beginning of the twenty-first century, therefore, historical sociology can be regarded as both a general theoretical tradition of the discipline, and increasingly a specific set of approaches within it. It is not particularly helpful to try to legislate away this dilemma, which is strongly rooted in the history and institutional embedding of these strands of social thought. Although the introduction of a historical–sociological approach into international relations has tended to rely on a relatively few works, concerned with a fairly well-defined set of issues (as we shall see in the next section), it also draws on this broader tradition of historical social thought, both Marxist and Weberian.

The core relevance of historical sociology to international political economy (and indeed to international relations) is therefore its potential to offer a richer pathway out of the classic dilemmas of social thought, than those offered by the political-science and economic roots of the field. Historical sociology offers the possibility of both transcending the narrow institutionalism of some mainstream 'IPE' and developing a broader-based historical alternative to Marxist-inspired work, with its own particular closures of historical perspective. Having explained the roots of the approach, we can now turn to some of the particular ways in which recent historical sociology has been developed, and how some have attempted to incorporate it into international political economy and international relations.

## The historical sociology of the state and international relations

A number of writers are currently cited in international studies as key figures of historical sociology. Steve Hobden, in an international relations-based critique of the field (1997), takes four as central: Skocpol and Mann, together with Charles Tilly and Immanuel Wallerstein. The latter he praises as the only one of the four to have a developed concept of the international system.

This is one way of recognising the difference between Wallerstein and the other writers, who are actually more representative of what would be considered by most scholars a historical–sociological approach. Wallerstein's 'world-systems theory' is clearly Marxist-derived, although often considered quite distinct from mainstream Marxism because of its emphasis on the world market rather than capitalist relations of production. Even more than more orthodox Marxists, however, Wallerstein is widely regarded as offering a one-dimensional approach. The overriding emphasis on the 'world system', like parallel structural systems-approaches in international relations (such as Waltz 1979), creates a particular closure in historical explanation, and tends to reduce the significance of agency.

Tilly, who is widely acknowledged as a founding writer in contemporary historical sociology, in contrast, comes from a more mainstream historiographical background. His trend-setting work (e.g. Tilly 1975) was less sharply informed by a distinctive theoretical position, but he adopted a broad comparative approach to questions of macro-historical change such as the origins of the nation-state in Europe, and the nature of revolutions. Tilly's work has had an agenda-setting role for other historical sociologists, as these issues have been central to the work of all the best-known contributors to the field.

In many ways, the pathbreaking work in the emergence of a distinct historical sociology was Skocpol's *State and Social Revolutions* (1979). In tackling the three key revolutions of modern times – France 1789, Russia 1917 and China 1949 – she not only examined upheavals in which Marxist doctrines had played defining roles, but addressed a field of historiography in which Marxists were dominant. Her critique of predominantly 'internal', class-based explanations was therefore a clear marker of the post-Marxist character of the new historical sociology, setting the scene in some ways for the more fundamental theoretical critique which Giddens (1984) was shortly to publish.

Skocpol defined some fundamental positions in the emergent sociology of the nation-state. Revolutions were defined as responses to instabilities of the international order (notably wars) as well as of social relations, and revolutions were seen as inherently – rather than incidentally – international events, with causes and consequences in international conflict. States, she argued, were 'Janus-faced', pointing both inwards towards 'their' societies and outwards towards other states in the international arena. States were also, as Evans, Rueschemayer and Skocpol (1985) argued, centres of interest distinct from those of dominant classes.

The importance of Giddens to the specific development of historical sociology rests mainly on *The Nation-state and Violence* (1985). This is both the fullest systematic historical articulation of his own perspective, and the most comprehensive theoretical exposition to date of a historical–sociological perspective on the nation-state in the context of war and international relations. (As such, its omission from the canon by Hobden is difficult to justify.) At the basis of Giddens' approach is his definition of four main institutional clusters of modernity, concerned with capitalism, industrialism, surveillance and warfare.

The nation-state is defined by Giddens, similarly to Skocpol, in terms of two sets of processes, inward-pointing surveillance and outward-pointing warfare. He argues that as surveillance has become more complete, and violence has been 'extruded' from the internal social relations of states, so it has become concentrated in their external relations. Giddens' account has been criticised, by more orthodox Marxists such as Bob Jessop (in Held and Thompson 1989) for its separations of capitalism, industrialism and state, and by the present writer (Shaw, in Held and Thompson 1989, 1994) for its neglect of more complex dialectics of war and 'internal' conflict.

Discussion of *The Nation-state and Violence* in international relations has suggested that it does not go far enough in challenging the bifurcation of domestic and international spheres. Justin Rosenberg (1990) argued that surveillance is not just a process within, but also between states. Faruk Yalvaç (in Banks and Shaw 1991) pointed out the irony that while international relations writers were moving away from realism, sociologists appeared to be adopting quasi-realist world views. Certainly Giddens does seem to conform to this pattern, but this is partly because he develops a broad historical perspective on the rise of the nation-state, rather than closely examining contemporary realities. Among other writers, John Hall (in Shaw 1984), who is influenced by Raymond Aron, probably came closest to an explicit realism, although Mann (in Shaw 1984; in Shaw and Creighton 1987) also argued for the importance of 'geopolitical' explanations.

Even granting the salience of Yalvaç's point, it would be a very serious mistake to see historical–sociological accounts as limited to the restatement of realism. At the very least, this school of work has provided far fuller, sociologically-rooted explanations of the important fact that, during the heyday of the nation-state and even in the Cold War, there *appeared* to be a rigid separation of intra- and inter-state social relations. Giddens and others have made it clear that the nation-state unit cannot be regarded as a given, as international realism has assumed. They have shown how the nation-state has been socially constructed, and how this affects its international role. In this sense, there has been a fundamental advance on realism.

In the most developed work of the new historical sociology, Mann's *The Sources of Social Power*, and especially its second volume on major nineteenth-century states (1993), any tendency towards realism was clearly transcended. Mann argues that modern sociology has oscillated between civilisational and national definitions of society. His own approach examines the significance of nations within what he calls the 'multi-power actor' civilisation of the West. In his closely argued study of the nineteenth century, he demonstrates the complex articulation of the development of state power with the (contemporaneous) creation of both nation and class as major categories of social action. In an approach based on the idea of 'power networks' – which include what international theorists have called both state and 'non-state' actors – Mann shows the interaction of societal and state forces in the production of 'international' outcomes (which involve of course also distinct societal results) like the First World War.

In Mann's work, what he has called 'empirical theory' (Mann 1988) vindicates a broadly Weberian approach to historical sociology. Capitalism is not analytically prioritised, as it is by Marxists, and instead the major forms of power – in Mann's terms, economic, political, military and ideological – are analysed in terms of their historical changing forms and relationships. Not surprisingly, it is this approach which has inspired a second tier of researchers, and some important new work on the relationship between states and economic development (Weiss and Hobson 1995; Hobson 1997).

Although I have noted the concern among international scholars about the apparent (in reality very partial) congruence of some historical sociology with realist assumptions, in general the trends in sociology which we have discussed have provoked positive reactions in critical areas of international relations. As we saw, Giddens' *The Nation-state and Violence* produced responses in the international literature. More generally, Fred Halliday, for example, has seen the integration of sociological concerns as part of the new agenda in international relations. He has particularly emphasised the international–national–international circuit of revolutionary change, in work which interweaves the issues raised by Skocpol (Halliday 1999; in Banks and Shaw 1991).

The broadly Weberian approach has also found echoes in historical work by international scholars. Notable among these are Spruyt's (1994) account of how the sovereign state saw off its main competitors to emerge as the dominant modern political form and Halperin's (1997) comparative historical studies of European development. The point which was made earlier, that historical sociology is, however, broader than Weber, is emphasised not only by Spruyt's critique of neo-Weberianism (1994: 19–21), but by the more clearly Marxist-inspired work of Rosenberg (1994).

The increasing body of the new historical sociology has led to an attempt by John Hobson (1998) to systematise its contribution to international relations. He identifies six principles of its approach to states and the international system:

1   *History and change*: state forms are not 'a natural product of an alleged liberal social contract', but are 'forged … in the heat of battle and warfare'. Nor indeed, he argues, 'should the anarchic system of sovereign states be regarded as natural'.
2   *Multi-causality*: the claim that there is more than one source of power, so that reductionism is rejected.
3   *Multi-spatiality*: societies are 'constituted by multiple overlapping and inter-secting sociospatial networks of power' (Mann).
4   *Partial autonomy*: 'power forces and actors' constantly 'interact and shape each other in complex ways' and hence are not 'wholly autonomous and self-constituting'.
5   *Complex change*: historical sociology understands 'both societies and interna-tional politics' as 'immanent orders of change' (Norbert Elias); it emphasises 'discontinuity' (Giddens); it indicates moments of 'tracklaying' and 'converting to a new gauge' (Mann).
6   *A 'non-realist' concept of state autonomy*: historical sociology introduces the important notion of state embeddedness within society, developed particu-larly in Hobson's own work (1997).

Hobson's summary is very useful in pointing up key differences between histor-ical sociology and more mainstream international relations approaches. In particular it indicates clearly why the simple conflation of historical sociology with realism is inappropriate. However, the limitations of his approach are indi-cated by his presentation of state embeddedness, for example, as a means of understanding 'foreign policy and international relations', and 'the spatial trini-tarian approach' (Halliday's conception of an 'international–national–international' chain of causality) providing 'an alternative perspective for understanding *tradi-tional IR concerns*'.

In these phrases, Hobson indicates a problem of his approach, which to some extent represents a difficulty in historical–sociological work as a whole. Although the school clearly presents a distinctive and powerful *explanatory framework*, it has largely accepted the *categories* of traditional international relations. Hobson's historical sociology is rooted in the old international, pre-global categories of realism. Thus Hobson seeks to incorporate historical sociology into 'interna-tional' relations, and does not recognise the extent to which the categories of the national and international have become problematic in critical global theorising.

The way the broader potential of the historical sociology approach is restricted by Hobson is indicated by his collapsing of Mann's idea of *multi*-spatiality into the idea of the *dual* reflexivity of the 'international' and 'domestic' spheres. Hobson assumes the relationships of *a* state and *a* society, of *the* state to *its* society. The dualism of state and society is tackled but its sister error, the dualism of national and international, remains firmly in place. Hobson thus confines historical sociology to a world in which the international and national (domestic) are the two main spatial dimensions. But in the emerging global world these are intersected by many others – conventionally described as local, regional, transnational, world-regional and global, although these terms only partially capture contemporary 'sociospatial networks of power'.

A serious problem here is the rootedness of the major historical–sociological works in the nineteenth- and early twentieth-century world order. Tilly studied the origins of the nation-state system; Skocpol's major study was of classic revolutions; Giddens' work focused on the consolidation of the nation-state; Mann's study of power has so far reached only the First World War and (in ongoing research) fascism. No major work has yet tackled the historical present. Although Giddens (e.g. 1990, 1991) has written extensively about globalisation, he has presented it as fundamentally continuous with modernity, and has not presented a fully historical account of its development. While Mann (1997) has accepted some of the novelty of contemporary global change, he remains cautious as to its significance. This may be correct: but it cannot be assumed, as it appears to be in Hobson's account of historical sociology.

This difficulty is clearly critical if historical sociology is to be taken seriously in international political economy. Much of the impetus to the development of the field has come from dissatisfaction with the traditional concerns of international relations. International political economists have developed our understanding of the contemporary significance of trans- as well as inter-national relations, and of global and regional developments. It is true that the field has not resolved its own dilemmas over the relations of internationality and globality – indeed, 'international' and 'global' are often used interchangeably to name it. Nevertheless the sense that the world has changed in ways which move beyond traditional international categories has been at the centre of debate (see e.g. Strange 1994).

If historical sociology is to be relevant to international or global political economy, it too needs to address these issues. The most obvious developments of historical sociology to date are in quite fundamental senses insufficiently radical and contemporary. Indeed, they sometimes appear to have hardly kept up with critical trends in either international or sociological theory, since they almost completely ignore the emergence of global theorising of all kinds (except for world-system theory).

## The historical sociology of contemporary global change

Historical sociology cannot simply be the study of the past, where the present is acknowledged only through the prism of prior ages and the possibility of a radically different future is absent. For Marx and Weber, it was axiomatic that a historical approach involved engaging with the novelty of contemporary forms, and with the definition of possible futures. Marx claimed that the distinctiveness of his approach lay not in the identification of the class struggle in history, but in the conclusions he drew about the possibility of proletarian revolution. Weber's practical concerns – like his view of historical possibility – were more limited, but he too was politically involved, for example in the consolidation of national-democratic forms in Germany after the First World War.

The decisive issue for historical sociology at the beginning of the twenty-first century is to understand – and to contribute to shaping – the character of today's 'global' transition. We need a new development of the approach, with a sense of contemporary discontinuities – the moments of 'tracklaying' we are currently living through. We need to recognise that historical change is disrupting the very categories which international relations has taken as constitutive. Power actors can no longer be characterised in any simple way by the domestic–international distinction. Increasingly states as much as firms, movements and communication networks take global and regional forms. 'Nation-states' are embedded not merely in 'their' societies but in the multi-layered socio-spatial networks of an emergent global society. Some networks may be only residually national-and-international in character. In breaking free from national–international dualisms, we can begin to understand the transformations of the emerging 'global age' (Albrow 1996).

There are two partial, and ultimately inadequate, theoretical responses to these transformations. One is represented by many strands of international political economy which downplay the classic military context of state power and argue that realism has overstated its significance. While such political-economic approaches have analysed the changing economic and juridical aspects of the state – the 'competition' state (Cerny 1991), the 'offshore' state (Palan 1998b) etc. – they have neglected the changed relations of violence in the emerging global period, in the context of which these economic and juridical changes have developed.

The other flawed response, however, is a continuing Weberian characterisation of the nation-state as a monopolist of violence, presented as though the changes of the last half-century have not occurred. Accounts of state–society relations in the nineteenth and early twentieth centuries cannot be offered as models for contemporary international relations. The global must be clearly in view. Historical sociology cannot examine the variables of the old order – states, state systems, the international economy and social forces – at the expense of those of the new – globalised authority networks, globally legitimated policing, global markets, global communications and global social movements.

What we need today are theoretical approaches which go beyond traditional international relations concerns. We need sociological approaches, historical in character, which address the fundamental transition towards a different world order which is underway in our times. Many of the ideas of a neo-Weberian historical sociology can be integrated, with critical transformation, into a new globalist historical sociology, which extends the debate in international political economy. However, it is as much a question of exploring the rich, general legacy of historical social theory as of developing the more specific tradition of analysis which has been developed in recent years.

Thus we should take on board accounts which are broadly historical and sociological in approach but which do not come with the label 'neo-Weberian historical sociology'. The application of classic Marxist ideas to international relations by Rosenberg (1994), mentioned above, is relevant here. Another direction from which such an approach has developed is 'neo-Gramscian' theory (discussed more fully elsewhere in this volume), which has begun to translate the problem of hegemony from the statist terms of realist debate into the broader terms of class economic, cultural and ideological dominance (see e.g. Cox 1987; Gill 1990). However, as Germain and Kenny (1998) have pointed out, a key problem of this literature is its failure to develop the concept of the internationalised state, to correspond to the emerging 'global civil society' which they posit. As I have argued in a more extended discussion of the state in international relations (Shaw 1999), the underdevelopment of an alternative concept of the state is a key weakness of most critical, post-realist international relations.

The contribution of historical sociology to global theory should extend the understanding of the state developed by writers like Giddens, Mann and Skocpol, and show how the state of the global era has developed beyond the nation-state which has hitherto been at the centre of both historical sociology and international theory. In other recent work (Shaw 1997), I have analysed, in outline, the rise and development of the integrated, transatlantic Western state from around 1940 and its transformation into the core of a global state from about 1990.

The historical sociology of globalism also needs to examine the mutual constitution of the globalised state and the economic, social and cultural forms of 'globalisation'. At its centre will be the question of how the Western state created conditions for economic, social and cultural globalisation, as well as the more commonly discussed issue of how the transformation of states is increasingly conditioned by rapid economic, social and cultural changes.

This historical sociology will need to examine the contribution of various forms of agency to global transformation. The dominant concept of globalisation in international political economy, as in other fields, is that of the inexorable progress of market forces, and the dominance of transnational corporate interests. What need to be brought into our understanding are not only the role of state elites, but the extent to which global political change is the work of cosmopolitan democratic forces worldwide. The end of the Cold War, for example, has been understood primarily as the outcome of elite processes, in the USA as well as the Soviet Union. In this way, the contribution of democratic movements to political change has tended to be explained away.

A historical sociology of the current transformation needs to encompass its contradictory character. It is clear that, on the one hand, global change involves major steps towards the universalisation of market relations in all fields of social activity and territorial jurisdictions. On the other, however, it involves processes of integration of state forms, in which borders of violence between states are replaced by new borders between the globalised Western state conglomerate and some secondary centres of state power.

On one hand, global change involves the increased subordination of political power to market imperatives. On the other, it involves stronger global norms of human rights and the beginnings of some new forms of international law enforcement. On one hand, democratic movements have achieved significant political change across many states and regions. On the other, an anti-globalist counter-revolution of nationalist parties and authoritarian movements has carried out horrific genocidal massacres.

An all-encompassing understanding of the current global transformation, which understands how these contradictions can be resolved, is easier to demand than to achieve. Nevertheless historical sociology enables us to raise this question: to look at the relations between economics, politics, military power and culture in the context of broad historical trends and periodisation. Although in some senses current changes continue long historic processes of change – such as the universalisation of market relations – in others they are much more revolutionary – notably in the formation of a much more unified global set of authority relations radiating through more integrated state institutions.

To global political economy, historical sociology offers the promise of studying global change as this contradictory set of political processes, in the context of change in the social relations surrounding state power as well as the forms that this power takes. It lays the foundations for a broader programme, in which the analysis of contemporary trends is brought into contact with theoretical perspectives deeply rooted in the history of social thought. By integrating the understanding of a transformed historical sociology, global political economy can play a role in the transformation of the social sciences as they respond to current changes.

# 16 Global passions within global interests: race, gender, and culture in our postcolonial order

*L.H.M. Ling*

## Introduction

An underlying economism reaches across liberal-critical divides in theorising about the global political economy.[1] It stresses macro-structural, 'objective', interest-driven factors over those considered micro-personal, 'subjective', or passion-based such as racism and sexism. What results is a 'rational pursuit of interest' that implicitly reinforces the values, norms, institutions, and practices of those who have always been on top and aim to stay there (Murphy and de Ferro 1995: 63). Feminists alone differ by directly linking the macro-structural with the micro-personal,[2] the objective with the subjective,[3] and interest with passion.[4] But these works remain marginalised in a field that valorises 'hard' facts over 'soft' or 'unreliable' domains of inquiry.

As with most myths of social science, this one needs debunking. This chapter underscores that interest reflects and sustains passion, just as objectivity often inverts subjectivity, and the macro-structural a cover for the micro-personal. For evidence, I review current discussions of globalisation. Their apparent 'econocentrism' (Turim 1997: 145) cannot stamp out colonial power relations of old where 'the global' stands for the 'masculinised Western Self'; and 'the local', the 'backward, irrational Native Other'. Indeed, this colonial resilience puzzles given that many in the core of globalisation today echo sentiments of celebration or despair similar to those voiced by formerly colonised subjects during their struggles for modernisation and independence in face of Westernisation.

This chapter argues that global political economy, as a field of study and practice, needs more honest theorising. Not only is theory always for someone, for some purpose, as Robert Cox (1995a: 31) has noted famously, but it is also about someone, about some purpose. Only by understanding the context of theorising can we explain why certain interests are always upheld while others remain lost and never found.

## Globalisation as passion and interest

Four layered narratives underlie current discussions of globalisation. Each recalls earlier relations between a colonial Self and its native Other:

1 **First narrative: globalism vs. localism, Self vs. Other.** Like their colonial predecessors, globalists today view globalisation from above: that is, as a macro-structural, border-crossing, knowledge-intensive juggernaut of big capital, technology, trade, and/or finance integrating with one another to serve up ever bigger, more profitable market shares.[5] In so doing, globalists counterpose two developmental opposites: the global and the local. The global exudes a masculinised agency that builds empires ('McWorld'); the local remains mired in a feminised state of arrested development, reactionary fascism, structural victimisation, and/or cultural peripheralisation ('Jihad') (Barber 1996). Thus 'the global' serves as code for the masculinised, progressive Western Self of colonial lore; and 'the local', the feminised, backward native Other. Even the same normative asymmetries apply: civilisation vs. barbarism, objectivity vs. irrationality, law and order vs. insurrection and chaos.

2 **Second narrative: global penetration/conquest of the local, Western penetration/conquest of the native Other.** A second narrative emphasises the global's penetrative, conquering impact on the local. Some openly embrace this capitalist engulfment, hailing a 'borderless world' (Ohmae 1990) though history may 'end' (Fukuyama 1989) and the state be 'hollowed out' (Thrift 1992). Critics disagree on globalisation's effects, especially its lack of collusion with the capitalist state (Panitch 1994). Nevertheless, they, too, fall back on a similar economism that projects the rise of 'global classes' under the aegis of a 'world-hegemony' of liberal capitalism (Cox 1987). This second narrative of global penetration and conquest echoes of nineteenth-century rationalisations of colonialism as rape. 'Colonisation', declared one seventeenth-century French philosopher, 'is the expansive force of a people; it is its power of reproduction; *it is its enlargement and its multiplication through space*; it is the subjection of the universe or a vast part of it to that people's language, customs, ideas, and laws' (my emphases, quoted in Said 1979: 219).

3 **Third narrative: failure of global penetration, failure of Western control.** And yet, an increasing anxiety besets those in the core of globalisation. Where do these 'Jihads' come from – and why do they persist – despite the global transformations of 'McWorld'? Simply identifying local 'fragmentations' due to globalisation begs the issue (Clark 1997). Neither does attributing one to be the dialectical product of the other suffice (Barber 1996). That localities survive, not to mention reformulate, the globalisation process belies its grandiose claims (Escobar 1995; Niederveen Pieterse 1994; Appadurai 1990). Accordingly, some openly flag racist and sexist propaganda in the guise of preparing for a 'new world order' (Fukuyama 1998; Huntington 1996). This third narrative of anxiety recalls stories of the 'yellow peril' and other intractable Others who refuse to succumb to or obey the Western Self's enlightened dictates. Those ultimate symbols of the alien Other – Fu Manchu, Dracula, the Mummy, just to name a few – always manage to escape imperial law and order to return and disturb 'civilisation' another day (Ling 2000).

4    **Fourth narrative: illicit desire and repulsion.** A fourth and most significant narrative of this global/colonial talk conveys hidden desires and
repulsions.

Globalism's gendered and racialised undertones surface most prominently in
discussions of global culture. For Stephen Gill (1995a: 399), globalisation produces a
'neoliberal civilisation' that consists of 'affluent minorities in the OECD [as well as]
the urban elites and new middle classes in the Third World'. These neoliberals affirm
a Westernised, industrialised, and masculinised outlook despite the fact that they live
in different parts of the globe, practice different religions and beliefs, and operate
from different historical-political contexts. Remarkably, the 'affluent minorities' of
the global economy resemble a late modern masculine identity attributed to men in
the West: that is, a 'world that is ahistorical, economistic, materialistic, "me-oriented",
short-termist, and ecologically myopic' (ibid.). Gill's neoliberals also escape all those
concerns usually associated with pre-capitalist traditions and the feminised household: e.g., interpersonal/family relationships, bodily care, sensuality, self-sacrifice
especially for the collective, and nurturing future generations.

Even descriptions of a globalised lifestyle sound a colonial theme. Cosmo-
politanism, according to Ulf Hannerz (1990: 239), requires 'an orientation, a
willingness to engage with the Other. It is an intellectual and aesthetic stance of
openness toward divergent cultural experiences, a search for contrasts rather
than uniformity'. Hannerz's cosmopolitan straddles cultures with a 'competence'
that stems from 'a sense of mastery' even when 'surrender[ing]' to alien environments. The cosmopolitan need not 'negotiate' with these different cultures, only
accept them as a 'package deal', thereby affirming a 'personal autonomy' that
allows the cosmopolitan to 'exit' at will. The cosmopolitan, at times a 'self-made
m[a]n' and most likely an 'intellectual', still manages a certain cultural playful-
ness: dissatisfied with the 'frontstage spectacle' of formal culture, he wants to
'sneak backstage' to experience its less inhibited offerings.

Clearly, Hannerz's Cosmopolitan Man (is there any doubt as to gender here?)
is used to taking charge and has the resources to do so. He basks in competence,
mastery, autonomy, self-made-ness, intellectual acumen. His relationship to other
cultures, moreover, patterns after other colonial/imperial encounters, most typically between plantation or harem masters and their concubines: e.g., not
'negotiating' even while 'surrendering' to Others, yet always ready to 'exit at
will'. Cosmopolitan Man evokes, also, a certain class background as he saunters
'backstage' to savour delights titillated by 'frontstage' spectacles. Who among us
can presume to 'sample' cultures at will? Who among us wants to?

Recent studies of imperialism reveal an underlying desire to such colonial
conquests. British geneticists of the Victorian era, for example, could not refrain
from eroticising native Others even while denouncing them as 'disgusting',
'repulsive', or 'hideously ugly'. Note this passage of unrequited desire in the
guise of scientific interest:

> There are in Africa, to the north of the line, certain Nubian nations, as
> there are to the south of the line certain Caffre tribes, whose figures, nay

even whose features, might in point of form serve as models for those of an Apollo. Their stature is lofty, their frame elegant and powerful. Their chest open and wide; their extremities muscular and yet delicate. They have foreheads arched and expanded, eyes full, and conveying an expression of intelligence and feeling: high narrow noses, small mouths and pouting lips. Their complexion indeed still is dark, but it is the glossy black of marble or of jet, conveying to the touch sensations more voluptuous even than those of the most resplendent white.

(quoted in Young 1995: 96–97)

Another twist to imperial machismo comes from its use of rape as metaphor during times of political instability. Officers of the empire did not hesitate to compare local revolts to rape of a white woman by black or brown men. Such feminisation of glorious, manly empire satisfied two goals at once (Sharpe 1993). Embodying empire in the bourgeois white woman underscored its 'civilising' mission; hence, any revolt against empire, especially by black and brown men, amounted to a violation of the natural order. Such 'transformation of subjectivity' was possible through colonialism's ability to reconfigure the colonising Self as a 'servant of an imperial destiny [that] it masterfully manufacture[d]' (Bivona 1990: 123).

Real-life people bore real-life consequences for such inversions of master and slave. T.E. Lawrence, that manly British imperialist extraordinaire, revealed in his autobiography a 'shattering' incident in the Deraa desert where, confused for a white Circassian Arab, he was raped and whipped by Britain's colonial Other who was also the Arab's conquering Self, a Turkish officer. From this point on, Lawrence found himself 'irrevocably lost' to empire, to Arabia, to himself – and yet, he confessed to a sensation of 'delicious warmth, probably sexual … swell[ing] through [his] body' even as it 'divided into parts [which] debated [whether] their struggle might be worthy, but the end foolishness and a rebirth of trouble' (quoted in Dawson 1994: 199).

What accounts for such insistence on imperial, global interest despite the slavish, local passions that roil underneath? Albert O. Hirschman (1977) and Michel Foucault (1990) have offered two paradigmatic explanations.

## Passions vs. interests in the West

From his succinct history of Enlightenment thought, Hirschman concluded that the West has always sought to curb, counter, or subvert passion with interest. Steeped in Christian doctrine, philosophers from St Augustine down regarded passion as a source of chaos, mystery, and danger. In contrast, interest promised order, science, and security. Many tried to root out passion with interest but where that failed, both intellectually and practically, interest became reformulated as a kinder, gentler version of passion such as *le douce commerce*. Hirschman (1977: 134) quoted Samuel Johnson, that exemplar of eighteenth-century pragmatism, that '[i]t is better that a man should tyrannise over his bank balance than over his fellow-citizens: and whilst the former is sometimes denounced as being but a means to the latter, sometimes at least it is an alternative'.

To Hirschman, tradition matters. Many who complain about the alienation and anomie of modern capitalism forget its philosophical and religious origins:

> for capitalism was precisely expected and supposed to repress certain human drives and proclivities and to fashion a less multifaceted, less unpredictable, and more 'one-dimensional' human personality. This position, which seems so strange today, arose from extreme anguish over the clear and present dangers of a certain historical period, from concern over the destructive forces unleashed by the human passions with the only exception, so it seemed at the time, of 'innocuous' avarice. *In sum, capitalism was supposed to accomplish exactly what was soon to be denounced as its worst feature.*
>
> (original emphasis, Hirschman 1977: 132)

Hirschman's study itself reflects this tradition. It construes passion and interest as opposed conditions, with each potentially displacing the other. Accordingly, Hirschman himself accepted the imposition of interest over passion even while recognising its stultifying effects. Here, he followed a venerable tradition from Sigmund Freud to Max Weber to Karl Marx. Each believed that the rise of Western civilisation stemmed from an industrialised, bureaucratised economy with no other outlet for the human soul than material accumulation. Foucault, however, disputed this tradition. Western bourgeois society not only failed to douse passion ('sex' to him) with interest, but intensified it instead with a discourse of repression: 'What is peculiar to modern societies, in fact, is not that they consigned sex to a shadow existence, but that they dedicated themselves to speaking of it *ad infinitum*, while exploiting it as *the* secret' (original emphasis, Foucault 1990: 35).

A pleasure-pinching rationale resulted. It tried to save 'labor' by 'avoid[ing] any useless "expenditure", any wasted energy'; in part, it aimed 'to ensure ... reproduction', otherwise known as 'the regulated fabrication of children' (ibid.: 114). But it also 'relie[d] ... on a multiple channeling [of passion/sex] into the controlled circuits of the economy' through 'a hyperrepressive desublimation' (ibid.: 114). In this sense, Foucault anticipated our contemporary era of globalised, Internet-facilitated sex where technology satiates the triple requirement of control, desire, and *secrecy*.

Despite their opposing views, Hirschman and Foucault both agreed that capitalism exiles passion/sex to satisfy Christianity's demand for a self-abnegating work ethic. Put differently, Western, bourgeois capitalism successfully camouflages its passion as interest by exporting it overseas through colonialism.

Note, for example, Admiral Alfred Thayer Mahan of the US Navy and author of *The Influence of Sea Power upon History* (1890). Combining social Darwinism with the Protestant ethic, Mahan designated Asia as the other side of America's manifest destiny where naval supremacy would ensure America's 'virile' and 'civilized' endowments (Takaki: 265). Mahan, true to Foucault's critique of Western love as labour's lost, likened America's surging prominence in world affairs to a steam engine, with *self-control* as key:

Emotion harnessed and guided is steam controlled in a boiler, with pipes connecting to the engine which it is to drive. The steam is no less a force if it be allowed to escape; it simply becomes a force wasted unimproved.

(quoted in Takaki 1990: 270)

Toward this end, Mahan preached a 'New Navy' to provide a 'sanctuary of American scepticism' for the preservation of 'asceticism, violence, and masculinity' (Takaki 1990: 272). A good life led, in short, is a good life devoted to empire. Yet despite all this good living, Mahan suffered from constant and debilitating headaches. Ronald Takaki speculated why given this letter from Mahan to a former classmate:

I lay in bed last night, dear Sam, thinking of the gradual rise and growth of our friendship. My first visit even to your room is vividly before me, and how as I went up there from night to night I could feel my attachment to you growing and see your own love for me showing itself more and more every night. After all, what feeling is more delightful than that of loving and being loved, even though it be only man's love for man? ... One night in particular; it has perhaps escaped your recollection, but I remember it as yesterday and prize the recollection most dearly. The happiness that I felt that night I will never forget.

(Mahan quoted in Takaki, 1990: 270–271)

What superhuman effort Mahan must have exerted to ensure that such 'steam' would not escape, to become 'wasted unimproved'! All this love, caring, and poignant sentimentality gushing towards the forbidden Self, only to be damned up by America's 'iron cages' of republicanism and industrialism – which, as Ronald Takaki (1990) argued, released a passionate 'demonism' onto the all-too-available Other. Indeed, as noted by Michael Hunt (1987), US foreign policy from its very beginnings had justified a simultaneous conquest of the Other both internally (Indians) and externally (Asia, Latin America) with an ordered, missionary priority of whites on top and everyone else below.

Neither Hirschman nor Foucault, moreover, included Europe's vociferous expansion into conquest and desire during their common period of study: the sixteenth to the twentieth centuries. In a footnote, Foucault mentioned a nexus of sex and power provided by servants in the bourgeois household but failed to extend it to the role of slaves and other colonised peoples in 'saving' European labour/love.

Indeed, Foucault himself unreflexively rehearsed a Western Self vs. native Other. He consigned to 'China, Japan, India, Rome, the Arabo-Moslem societies' an unencumbered, openly enjoyed 'ars erotica' where the Oriental master bestowed upon his disciple such privileges as 'an absolute mastery of the body, a singular bliss, obliviousness to time and limits, the elixir of life, the exile of death and its threats' (Foucault 1990: 57–58). In contrast, Foucault (1990: 54) sneered, the West logged a cold, calculating 'scientia sexualis' that split pleasure into 'two distinct orders of knowledge: a biology of reproduction ... and a medicine of sex'.

Both Hirschman and Foucault demonstrated, each in his own way, the enduring legacy of colonial power relations in the global political economy: that is, interest not only exiles passion but also masters it. Globalisation furthers this fiction by selling sex, race, and culture in the name of global business.

## Sex, race, and culture: a global business

M.I. Franklin (2000) has examined two recent advertisements for global telecom companies. One promotes Britain's Cable & Wireless; a second, Deutsche Telekom. The first ad consists of five identical world maps, accurately drawn with continents and oceans. To the side of each map appears a slogan, 'The WORLD according to …'. Names of the industry's 'big four' – British Telecom, Deutsche Telekom, France Telecom, AT&T, in addition to Cable & Wireless – fill in the blanks. The ad suggests that Cable & Wireless, unlike the other companies, allows consumers to 'pick and choose' in 'a world of difference':

> to wit 'global communications' will be authentic (federalist and so 'free') and not nationally identifiable (and so, again 'free'). In short, not only is the Cable & Wireless Federation truly democratic but it also truly represents (transgendered and transcultural) 'you'. The point here is that the very map representing said 'world of difference' is in fact the modernist representation of the world … albeit one centred nostalgically on Asia and the Pacific Ocean … Here, the same post-colonial 'funny old world' is visually recycled to (mis)represent not only the current but also the projected telecommunications hierarchy.
>
> (Franklin 2000)

Indeed, the world map drawn in territorial, 'realist' terms invokes that era of the 'Great Game' when white men tromped through the world, warring and profiteering to their privileged delight. Today's telecom giants, this ad hints, now replace yesteryear's 'great powers'.

A second ad, from rival Deutsche Telekom, underscores this point. Three male hands, stretching from business-suit sleeves, grasp one another by the wrist. The ad states that 'Real international understanding starts here'. One sleeve bears the stars and stripes of the American flag; the fabric of the other two is less discernible. The ad, Franklin observed, seeks to convey that:

> a 'truly global dimension', 'truly global basis' of business communication is synonymous to 'worldwide', 'international' 'consortiums' and 'partnerships'. [But it] is the traditional international relations' representation of the world as a state-centred, male domain that is called upon and reiterated in this quaint conflation of 'global' with the European Union ('the world's single largest market place') and the 'global dimension' with the USA and the 'Pacific Rim'.
>
> (Franklin 2000)

The racial, gender, and class underpinnings of such 'international cooperation' sharpen further into focus with another advertisement for another product but targeted at a related market. A beer ad depicts three men in a crowded bar. Two are Asian and one European. The two Asian men have on three-piece suits with ties while the European lounges in an unbuttoned polo shirt. They are laughing and sharing a toast of beer. The slogan claims: 'The sign of *real* friendship' (original emphasis). International cooperation, in short, means a common investment in masculine, global interests.

But what are the rewards of such globe-straddling, business-hammering interest? Capitalism, paraphrasing Robert Young (1995) on colonialism, produces a 'machine of desire'. With consumption as its ultimate goal, capitalist desire fixates most commonly and directly on its most visible target: the body. As the first site of disparate power relations, the body rehearses those privileges enjoyed by coloniser over colonised, West over non-West, masculine over feminine. Accordingly, capitalist desire invariably conveys the reward of global business/interest in bodily terms: i.e., sexual conquest by (Western) Cosmopolitan Man over (non-Western) Native Woman.

Note, for example, this ad for a hotel chain in Asia. It features a young woman sitting with her slender, naked back to the viewer. Her long black hair, a stereotyped feature assigned to Asian women, is swept to one side. Large print to the right of this picture coos: 'Come to the Banyan Tree with your wife and leave with a different woman'. Playing with the subtext that the viewer/customer must be a well-off executive burdened with global business interests, the ad recommends a recuperative stay at this resort which could include untold, exotic transformations of the executive's wife. A second, subliminal message suggests that if the wife proves inadequate or unavailable, sexual partners trained in Foucault's school of Oriental 'ars erotica' may be of service.

## Consequences: violations of Self and Other

So what, one may ask, that globalisation discourse contains these implicit contradictions, conflicts, and inconsistencies? After all, isn't this true of all cultures, including those that discourse on globalisation? Colonial power relations, I would argue, deserve special attention. Ashis Nandy (1988) has shown us that they inflict four, system-wide pathologies: (1) a denigration of the feminine that justifies 'a limited role for women – and femininity – by holding that the softer side of human nature is irrelevant to the public sphere'; (2) a false cultural homogeneity that 'blur[s] the lines of social divisions by opening up alternative channels of social mobility in the colonies ... through colonial wars of expansion'; (3) an 'underdeveloped heart' that 'trigger[s] "banal" violence' due to an 'isolation of cognition from affect'; and (4) an empty potency that 'promise[s] to liberate man from his daily drudgery' but which, with the decline of empire, unleashes a 'racist underside' and 'wholesale Westernisation'. Colonial Self-delusion, in short, violates the Self as well as the Other.

Such pathologies suffuse today's global political economy. They surface more clearly when paired: the first and last together since each accounts for the other; the second and third, as reflections or derivations of the first two.

### Denigration of the feminine

Globalisation as the latest version of capitalist interest/passion denigrates the feminine ideologically, structurally, and bodily. Elsewhere, I demonstrate how firms market globalisation as a lucrative playground for the young, masculinised, educated, technically-proficient, and Westernised (Ling 1996). Race configures along gender and class lines as 'native' urban, educated males work in solidarity with 'international' (translation: white) urban, educated males. But 'traditional' (translation: rural, uneducated, native) men shuffle in that corner designated as 'undeveloped', along with 'traditional' women. All women, whether urban and educated or rural and illiterate, serve men for purposes of reproduction, production, entertainment, or combinations of all three. Asia's 'miracle' economies, for example, have historically maximised upon the economic utility and social dispensability of their female labour in the name of serving the 'benevolent' family-state (Truong 1999).

Furthermore, structural adjustment policies imposed by international financial institutions like the World Bank press underemployed young men and women into another line of feminised service: domestic work. Located within the private home and historically identified with women, domestic service enacts a 'regime of labour intimacy' (e.g., raising children, cooking food, cleaning house, washing clothes) that renders possible the adventures of 'techno-muscular capitalism' usually identified with globalisation (Chang and Ling 2000). Recent data confirm that women, mostly from the poorer economies in Asia (e.g., Philippines, Indonesia, Sri Lanka, India), now predominate international migration flows primarily to work as domestics or 'entertainers' (often a euphemism for prostitutes) in wealthier economies, either within the region (e.g., Hong Kong, Japan, Singapore) or outside (e.g., Middle East, Europe, US) (Gulati 1997).

A seemingly neutral, economistic language also obscures race, gender, and class from globalising processes like the North American Free Trade Agreement (NAFTA). Marianne Marchand (1996) has noted, for example, that the overall category of 'labour' used by economists to consider NAFTA's policy implications subsumes the fact that mostly poor, working-class women of particular racial backgrounds are affected. For this reason, she concluded, feminists have little recourse or political space from which to mobilise action.

As Jan Jindy Pettman (1996) has observed, an 'international political economy of sex' now traffics exclusively in female bodies through migrant labour, mail-order brides, sex tourism, and militarised prostitution. Typically the first sector to 'internationalise', it services the manly state and its equally masculinised partner, global capital, in the form of politicians, soldiers, businessmen, tourists, police, tribal chiefs, and so on (Lim 1998). Prostitution booms especially in postsocialist or transitional economies like China, Vietnam, and Kampuchea as they 're-integrate' into the global capitalist economy.[6]

## Racist underside and wholesale Westernisation

A reactionary 'hypermasculinity' (also Nandy's term) accounts for this denigration of the feminine. It projects onto men all those 'magical feelings of omnipotence and permanence' (Nandy 1988: 35) that valorise power, aggression, and competition over anything smacking of women and the household, including emotionality, homosexuality, intellectual activity, and social welfare. Initially a Western colonial construct, hypermasculinity now infects the native Other as a reaction to his cultural, political, and economic emasculation by Western imperialism. Indeed, orders of hypermasculinity spiral over time and space. The West re-hypermasculinises against the product of its own creation, the hypermasculine Other, which subsequently goads more of the same in the Other and the cycle continues.

One example is Samuel P. Huntington's *The Clash of Civilizations and the Remaking of World Order* (1996). In it, Huntington cautioned against two 'anti-Western' civilisations, the Confucian and Islamic. In defying and refuting Western norms, goals, and aspirations, he declared, they compel the West to ally with other, more 'compatible' civilisations. Huntington's racism, however, does not end at the water's edge. The 'real clash', he admitted towards the end of his book, concerns what's 'out there' trying to enter 'in here' (Huntington 1996: 307). And, clearly, what's involved are not fancy 'civilisations' like Confucianism or Islam but, more basically, whites vs. non-whites. Recalling the empire-as-rape-victim metaphor, Huntington breathlessly conjured up a future scenario when Hispanics would come to power in the US because 'large segments of the American public blame the severe weakening of the United States on the narrow Western orientation of WASP elites' (ibid.: 316). China, Japan, and 'most of Islam' now combat the US, Europe, Russia, and India in a third world war. Benefitting from such holocaust would be 'those Latin American countries which sat out the war' and Africa, 'which has little to offer the rebuilding of Europe [other than to] disgorg[e] hordes of socially mobilised people to prey on the remains' (ibid.: 315–316).

Francis Fukuyama's (1998) latest screed on women and world politics responds to such racialised politics in America by further victimising the victim. *La différence*, Fukuyama claimed, accounts for why men should stay in control of international relations and women, not. Genetically more aggressive, hierarchical, and violent, men are better equipped to handle 'politics and warfare' because they are more aggressive, hierarchical, and violent – and so on. Women, Fukuyama continued, are genetically peaceful, emotional, and social; therefore, they should support men and not seek to 'control' them through feminism and the like. Still, Fukuyama differentiated among specific types of men: i.e., those who erect a democratic, capitalist 'zone of peace' vs. those who degenerate into murderous politics like the 'chimps at Gombe' (Fukuyama 1998: 33). Not coincidentally, the former comes from (white) Europe and America; the latter, the non-white world of 'Muslims and Serbs in Bosnia, Hutus and Tutsis in Rwanda, or militias from Liberia and Sierra Leone to Georgia and Afghanistan' (ibid.: 33). Fukuyama added that people from agricultural societies, as opposed to those in 'advanced countries', value life less given their 'surpluses of young, hotheaded men' (ibid.: 38). In short, Fukuyama's gender politics swears allegiance to globalised white-male rule by ostensibly subordinating women – but really, non-white men as well – in order to elide both racial and gender subalterities in a world he helps to make: Huntington's America.

### Banal violence

With racism and sexism theorised at the global level, there should be little surprise at the persistence of banal violence practiced in daily life. Whether labelled 'gang warfare' at home or 'ethnic rivalry' abroad, they reflect a continued 'isolation of cognition from affect' that prohibits any cure for hypermasculinity's 'underdeveloped heart'. For this reason, eruptions of ethnic and gender violence in Indonesia induced by its economic crisis and the Los Angeles rebellion/riot of 1992 after the first Rodney King trial highlight a common phenomenon: frustration, anger, and resentment against unresolved Self/Other relations.

David Palumbo-Liu (1994) has theorised about a 'white absence' in the Los Angeles rebellion/riot. He used as metaphor an oft-printed picture taken during the outbreak of violence. It shows a Korean-American male, wearing a Malcolm X T-shirt, while holding a gun ostensibly directed against rampaging blacks:

> A hierarchy of presence is significant here: an Asian body occupies the foreground in this narrative; blacks are present as second-level images (Malcolm X on the T-shirt) – however, whites are invisible, somehow not part of 'this' America. Thus what is missing in the narrative implicated by this photo-text is any inquiry into the structure of an economic system that historically has pitted Asians against blacks and Latinos, and which exploits that antagonism in order to construct a displaced rehearsal of a simplified white/black, purely 'racial' antagonism.
>
> (Palumbo-Liu 1994: 370)

Removed from view and therefore public consciousness is the white gaze. Cast in terms of an inter-ethnic rivalry, the riot/rebellion transforms into a morality play about 'defending one's property' rather than 'racial justice':

> If white America was repulsed by the image of the anti-black violence of the King beating, it could by contrast react positively, immediately, and with ethical purity when viewing Asian-Americans defending themselves against black and Latino looters ... [While, at the same time] there is a hard residue of old-style orientalism – the notion that Asians have no concept of the sanctity of human life.
>
> (Palumbo-Liu 1994: 374–375)

Similarly, an ideological amnesia erases the role of international capital from Indonesia's financial collapse. The International Monetary Fund (IMF) and other repositories of global capital indict Indonesia for its 'crony capitalism', 'non-transparency', and other macro-managerial distortions incapable of resolving ethnic strife that was always ready to explode anyway. Conveniently overlooked are thirty years of collaboration with the same 'crony capitalists' who made themselves and other global capitalists too rich to care. As for ethnic and gender violence, it invokes that 'hard residue of old-style orientalism' that these backward Asians 'have no concept of the sanctity of human life'. Consequently, they need greater education in human rights, law, democracy, and so on.

A rash of suicides among young, rural women in China qualifies as perhaps the most tragic, yet banal, type of violence given its meaninglessness. *The New York Times* reports that China now has the highest suicide rate in the world with 56 per cent of all female suicides, amounting to approximately 500 per day, occuring in the Chinese countryside (Rosenthal 1999). A minor, even trivial, event could trigger the suicide. Rural women are downing poisonous pesticides by the droves in inchoate protest against a world that increasingly values what they are not: urban, educated, capital-rich, upwardly-mobile, and hypermasculine.

### *Colonial wars of expansion*

Colonies in the old, territorial sense may no longer exist to offer 'channels of social mobility', but new, non-territorial ones in the form of 'global market share' do. Many believe that Asia's economic crisis, for example, signals 'a reassertion of western hegemony' through the imposition of new rules that curtail competitiveness, 'bailouts' of local banks/companies by foreign ones, and heightened dependency of local governments on international (Western) financial institutions and Western governments (Breman 1998). South Korea may be a case in point. Touted as one of Asia's 'miracle' economies just a few years ago, it vows today not to deviate from IMF conditionalities even 'by one percent'.[7] Critics emphasise that over-supply of capital from 'the north' combined with under-capacity of absorption in Asia caused the cash-flow short-fall (DN 1998). But the latter remains burdened with the consequences while the former escapes scot-free, creating a 'moral hazard' in global finance. Indeed, Malaysia's Prime Minister Mohammed Mahathir voices publicly what many in Asia feel privately: Western financial institutions are imposing a 'new imperialism' in the global political economy. Just as Mahathir's cry of 'foul play!' resonates in Asia, so it will also in other parts of the world that feel undermined by globalisation (e.g., Russia). If so, globalisation's 'colonial expansion' through the world market may ignite more than one occasion of instability, crisis, and chaos.

### A postcolonial subjectivity for globalists

But there are internal reasons, as well, to redress globalisation's Self/Other dichotomy. Many in the core of globalisation today voice hopes and fears that echo those of formerly colonised subjects in the throes of their processes of internationalisation/globalisation.

Like postcolonial Others in the past, Scott Lash and John Urry celebrate a 'reflexive individualism' under modernisation/internationalisation/globalisation. They accord to globalisation today what colonised peoples had sought through nationalism: an 'open[ing] up [of] many positive possibilities for social relations – for intimate relations, for friendship, for work relations, for leisure and for consumption' (Lash and Urry 1994: 31). Globalisation also induces 'a process of de-traditionalisation [to] "set free" from the heteronomous control or monitoring of social structures in order to be self-monitoring or self-reflexive' (original emphases, ibid.: 5) – a process that many postcolonials saw as their only hope for 'catching up' with the West.

There are also those who, like revolutionaries of the past, reject internationalisation/globalisation for its 'fragmenting' effects. David Harvey (1990), in particular, has found that globalisation compresses Enlightenment-inherited notions of time, space, and general well-being. This sentiment echoes those revolutionary Others who castigated internationalisation as another onslaught of Westernisation, deracination, and de-culturalisation. Indeed, Harvey's 'shell-shocked, blasé, or exhausted' late modern subject invokes the postcolonial modern one as both 'bow down before the overwhelming sense of how vast, intractable, and outside any individual or even collective control everything is' (Harvey 1990: 350).

Still, there are those who, like Anthony Giddens (1995), remain ambivalent. Like a certain class of favoured colonial subjects of the past, they enjoy the benefits of Westernisation and modernisation. But they, like Giddens, also fear that globalisation's detraditionalising effects would 'eat into [and] attack local customs and traditions, local ways of doing things … in our personal lives at the same time as they do so at the level of the nation-state, and larger systems, too' (Giddens 1995: 10–11). In particular, Giddens worried about a 'democratisation of family life' (e.g., women's liberation) that would hearken a comparable 'hollowing out' of the state (e.g., patriarchal authority), thereby requiring fundamental changes 'in personal life, in business and in the state' (ibid.: 13). Accordingly, Giddens advised for today what postcolonials had preached in the past: individuals (e.g., men) need to rally against 'a passive acceptance of fixed roles, fixed economics systems – of work for life and all the rest of it' (ibid.: 13). Ambivalent progressives like Giddens acknowledge that detraditionalisation may 'produc[e] enormous anxieties for all of us [but it] also produc[es] some very interesting new opportunities' (ibid.: 15).

Globalisation, in short, blurs the boundaries not only between states and markets, but also Self and Other. Indeed, one necessarily leads to the other.

## Towards a GPE of passions and interests

It is in all of our interests, then, to recognise the role of passion in the global political economy. In this chapter, I emphasise the need to redress underlying colonial power relations that still permeate our thinking and theorising about the global political economy. Some initial steps towards this end may include: (1) exposing hypermasculinity and denigration of the feminine on a global scale; (2) refusing to allow racism/sexism/culturalism in the guise of 'New World Order' double talk; (3) identifying the global context to 'banal violence' rather than leaving it to individualist or segmented events; and (4) understanding that new, 'virtual' colonies for expansion victimise the Self as well as the Other.

Indeed, a simultaneous but uncoordinated movement towards passion-based theorising appears underway. Neta Crawford (1998), for example, has argued that the very foundation of traditional theorising in international relations – fear and insecurity – compels attention to emotions and how they affect decision-making. This pertains especially to foreign policy where cultural differences may distort readings of emotional expression, thereby leading to unintended catastrophes. As a start, Crawford suggested twelve preliminary hypotheses to research emotions and emotional relationships in international relations. Contemporaneously, Stephen Chan (1998) has called for a greater awareness of and sensitivity to subjectivity in international relations. To him, international relations represents a 'humourless, depersonalised' discipline that 'labours rationally to build the stone-by-stone wall of objective truth ... [that assumes to] substitut[e] uniformity for a true universality' (Chan 1998: 2). In so doing, it deadens any understanding of the grief, love, hatred, or revenge that daily confound our world. Chan recommended attention to narratives, either classical (e.g., myths) or popular (e.g., stories), to explain, in a manner of speaking, the passions that drive men mad. These works extend earlier critiques of a 'techo-rational' bias in theorising about international relations and international political economy such as Richard Ashley's (1983) 'three modes of economism'.

I hope this chapter furthers their insights by underscoring the lack of innocence, not to mention neutrality, that prevails in theory and theory-building. This postcolonial understanding of the global political economy explicitly acknowledges that passions motivate interests, multiplicity inheres within the Self as well as the Other, and global-local complicities must ensue to enable 'globalisation'.

## Notes

1 The author thanks Neta Crawford and M.I. Franklin for their helpful comments on this chapter.
2 See, for example, Maria Mies' (1986) linkage of global accumulation with 'housewifisation'.
3 See, for example, Aihwa Ong's (1987) study of Fordism and 'mass hysteria' among Malaysian women workers.
4 See, for example, my own examination of globalisation and 'hypermasculinity' (Ling 1999).
5 There are, of course, exceptions such as Agnew and Corbridge (1995).
6 Prostitutes in China range from urban college graduates to rural illiterates; in fact, party cadres are their most frequent clients given official access to and authority over dancing halls, karaoke lounges, saunas, and cafés. Average age for prostitutes in Asia is dropping drastically. Fear of AIDS raises a premium on virgins and very young girls, some pre-pubescent, are considered most eligible. Child prostitution, accordingly, is increasing. Nicholas Kristof (1996) reports finding an ad for a 6-year-old Cambodian prostitute for $3.
7 President Kim Dae Jung made this announcement in 1997 (Young 1998).

# Bibliography

Abercrombie, N. (1986) 'Knowledge, order and human interests', in J. Hunter and S. Ainlay (eds) *Making Sense of Modern Times*, London: Routledge and Kegan Paul.

Abrams, P. (1982) *Historical Sociology*, Milton Keynes: Open University Press.

Abrams, R. (1980) *Foundations of Political Analysis: An Introduction to the Theory of Collective Choice*, New York: Columbia University Press.

Adler, E. (1997) 'Imagined (security) communities: cognitive regions in international relations', *Millennium* 26, 2.

AFL-CIO (1997) Testimony of David A. Smith, Public Policy Director of the AFL-CIO to the House Committee on International Relations on Global Climate Negotiations, 24 July.

AFL-CIO (1998) 'The Kyoto Protocol', *AFL-CIO Executive Council Statement* 30 January.

Aglietta, M. (1979 [1976]) *A Theory of Capitalist Regulation: The U.S. Experience*, London: Verso.

—— (1998) 'Capitalism at the turn of the century: regulation theory and the challenge of social change', *New Left Review*, 232: 41–90.

Agnew, J. and Corbridge, S. (1995) *Mastering Space: Hegemony, Territory and International Political Economy*, London: Routledge.

Albert, M. (1993) *Capitalism Against Capitalism*, London: Whurr.

Albrow, M. (1996) *The Global Age*, Cambridge: Polity Press.

Allison, G. (1972) *The Essence of Decision*, Boston: Little, Brown.

Alt, J.E., Calvert, R.L. and Humes, B.D. (1988) 'Reputation and hegemonic stability: a game-theoretic analysis', *American Political Science Review*, 82, 2: 445–466.

Althusser, L. (1972) *For Marx*, Harmondsworth: Penguin.

Althusser, L. and Balibar, E. (1968) *Lire le Capital*, Paris: Maspéro.

Altvater, E. and Mahnkopf, B. (1997) 'The world market unbound', *Review of International Political Economy* 4, 3: 448–471.

Amin, A. (ed.) (1994) *Post-Fordism: A Reader*, Oxford: Basil Blackwell.

Amin, A. and Palan, R. (unpublished) 'Not so rationalist international political economy'.

Amin, A., Palan, R. and Taylor P. (1994) 'Forum for heterodox international political economy', *Review of International Political Economy* 1: 1–12.

Amin, S. (1989) *Eurocentrism*, London: Zed.

—— (1997) *Capitalism in the Age of Globalization*, London: Zed.

Amineh, M.P. (1998) *Die globale kapitalistische Expansion und Iran – Eine Studie der iranischen politischen Ökonomie (1500–1980)*, Frankfurt A/M: IKO Verlag.

Anderson, P. (1977) 'The antinomies of Antonio Gramsci', *New Left Review* 100, November–December, 5–80.

Andreff, W. (1976) *Profits et structures du capitalisme mondial*, Paris: Calmann-Lévy.

Andrews, D.M. and Willett, T.D. (1997) 'Financial interdependence and the state: international monetary relations at century's end', *International Organisation* 51, 3 (Summer): 479–511.

Antonelli, C. (1988a) 'A new industrial organization approach', in C. Antonelli (ed.) *New Information Technology and Industrial Change: The Italian Case,* London: Kluwer Academic Publishers.

—— (1988b) 'The emergence of the network firm', in C. Antonelli (ed.) *New Information Technology and Industrial Change: The Italian Case*, London: Kluwer Academic Publishers.

Antonelli, C., Petit, P. and Tahar, G. (1992) *The Economics of Industrial Modernization*, London: Academic Press.

Apeldoorn, B. Van (1999) 'Transnational capitalism and the struggle over European order', doctoral dissertation, European University Institute, Florence.

Appadurai, A. (1990) 'Disjuncture and difference in the global cultural economy', in M. Featherstone (ed.) *Global Culture: Nationalism, Globalization and Modernity*, Newbury Park: Sage Publications.

Apthorpe, R. and Gasper, D. (eds) (1996) *Arguing Development Policy: Frames and Discourses*, London: Frank Cass.

Aron, R. (1962) *Paix et la guerre entre les nations*, Paris: Calmann-Lévy.

Arrighi, G. (1994) *The Long Twentieth Century: Money, Power and the Origins of Our Times*, London: Verso.

—— (1998) 'Globalization and the rise of East Asia: lessons from the past, prospects for the future', *International Sociology* 13, 1: 59–78.

Arruda, M. (1996) *Globalization and Civil Society: Rethinking Cooperativism in the Context of Active Citizenship*, Rio De Janeiro: PACS: Alternative Policies for the Southern Cone.

Ashley, R. (1983) 'Three modes of economism', *International Studies Quarterly* 27: 463–496.

—— (1986) 'The poverty of neorealism', in R. Keohane (ed.) *Neorealism and Its Critics*, New York: Columbia University Press.

Ashley, R.K. (1989) 'Imposing international purpose: notes on a problematique of governance', in E.-O. Czempiel and J. Rosenau (eds) *Global Changes and Theoretical Challenges: Approaches to World Politics for the 1990s*, Lexington, MA: Lexington Books, pp. 251–290.

Auerbach, P. (1988) *Competition: the Economics of Industrial Change*, Oxford: Basil Blackwell.

Augelli, E. and Murphy, C. (1988) *America's Quest for Supremacy and the Third World: A Gramscian Analysis*, London: Pinter.

Auspitz, J.L. (1976) 'Individuality, civility, and theory: the philosophical imagination of Michael Oakeshott', *Political Theory*, 4, 2: 261–352.

Auster R.D and Silver, M. (1979) *The State as a Firm: Economic Forces in Political Development*, Boston: Martin Nijhoff.

Avant, D. (1994) *Political Institutions and Military Change: Lessons from Peripheral War*, Ithaca, NY: Cornell University Press.

Axelrod, R. (1981) 'The emergence of cooperation among egoists', *American Political Science Review* 75: 306–318.

—— (1984) *The Evolution of Cooperation*, New York: Basic Books.

Axelrod, R. and Keohane, R.O. (1986) 'Achieving cooperation under anarchy: strategies and institutions', in K. Oye (ed.) *Cooperation Under Anarchy*, Princeton, NJ: Princeton University Press.

Bacharach, P. and Baratz, M.S. (1970) *Power and Poverty: Theory and Practice*, New York: Oxford University Press.

Bahout, J. (1994) *Les Entrepreneurs syriens*, Beyrouth: CERMOC.

Balconi, M. (1993) 'The notion of industry and knowledge bases: the evidence of steel and mini-mills', *Industrial and Corporate Change* 2, 3: 471–507.

Baldwin, D.A. (1985) *Economic Statecraft*, Princeton, NJ: Princeton University Press.

—— (1989) *Paradoxes of Power*, Oxford: Blackwell.

—— (ed.) (1993) *Neorealism and Neoliberalism: The Contemporary Debate*, New York: Columbia University Press.

Ballance, R. (1987) *International Industry and Business: Structural Change, Industrial Policy and Industry Strategies*, London: Allen & Unwin.

Banks, M. and Shaw, M. (eds) (1991) *State and Society in International Relations*, Hemel Hempstead: Harvester-Wheatsheaf.

Banuri, T., Shahruck R.K. and Mahmood, M. (eds) (1997) *Just Development: Beyond Adjustment with a Human Face*, Karachi: Oxford University Press.

Baran, P.A. (1957) *The Political Economy of Growth*, New York: Monthly Review Press.

Baran, P.A. and Sweezy, P.M. (1968) *Monopoly Capital. An Essay on the American Economic and Social Order*, New York: Monthly Review Press.

Barber, B. (1996) *Jihad Vs. Mcworld*, New York: Ballantine Books.

Barbon, N. (1690, 1905) *A Discourse of Trade*, ed. J.H. Hollander, Reprints of Economic Tracts, Baltimore: The Johns Hopkins University Press.

Barry, B. (1978) *Sociologists, Economists, and Democracy*, Chicago: The University of Chicago Press.

—— (1988 [1987]) *The Uses of Power in Democracy, Power and Justice*, Oxford: Clarendon Press.

Bauman, Z. (1992) *Intimations of Postmodernity*, London: Routledge.

Becattini, G. (1989) 'Sectors and/or districts: some remarks on the conceptual foundations of industrial economics', in E. Goodman and J. Bamford (eds) *Small Firms and Industrial Districts in Italy*, London: Routledge.

Bendor, J. and Moe, T. (1985) 'An adaptive model of bureaucratic politics', *The American Political Science Review* 79: 755–774.

Ben-Porath, Y. (1980) 'The F-connection: families, friends, and firms in the organization of exchanges', *Population and Development Review* 6, 1: 1–30.

Berg, G.C. (1996) 'An economic interpretation of "like-product"', *Journal of World Trade* 30(2): 195–209.

Berg, M. van Den (1995) 'Culture as ideology in the conquest of modernity: the historical roots of Japan's regional regulation strategies', *Review of International Political Economy* 2, 3, Summer, 371–393.

Berger, P. and Luckmann, T. (1967) *The Social Construction of Reality*, London: Allen Lane.

Berki, R.N. (1971) 'On Marxian thought and the problem of international relations', *World Politics* 24, 1: 80–105.

Bernard, A., Helmich, H. and Lehning, P.B. (eds) (1998) *Civil Society and International Cooperation*, Paris: OECD.

Bettali, S. (1972) 'Machiavelli e la politica esterna fiorentina', in P. Gilmore Myron (ed.) *Studies on Machiavelli*, Florence: G.C. Sinorsi editore.

Bichler, S. and Nitzan, J. (1996a) 'Military spending and differential accumulation: a new approach to the political economy of armament – the case of Israel', *Review of Radical Political Economics*, 28, 1: 52–97.

—— (1996b) 'Putting the state in its place: US foreign policy and differential accumulation in Middle-East "energy conflicts"', *Review of International Political Economy*, 3,4: 608–661.

—— (1999) 'The rise and decline of Israeli inflation: a case study of differential accumulation', paper presented at the Union of Radical Political Economy Section, ASSA Annual Meetings in New York, January.

Bickerman, E.J. (1972) 'Mesopotamia', in J.A. Garraty and P. Gay (eds) *The Columbia History of the World*, New York: Harper & Row.

Bieler, A. (1998) 'Austria's and Sweden's accession to the European Community: a comparative neo-Gramscian case study of European integration', doctoral dissertation, University of Warwick.

Bieling, H-J, and Deppe, F. (1996) 'Gramscianismus in der internationalen politischen Ökonomie', *Das Argument* 38, 217: 729–740.

Bieling, H-J, Deppe, F. and Tidow, S. (1998) 'Soziale Kräfte und hegemoniale Strukturen in der internationalen politischen Ökonomie', 'Introduction' in R.W. Cox (1998) *Weltordnung und Hegemonie – Grundlagen der 'Internationalen Politischen Ökonomie'*, Marburg: Forschungs der University Presse Europäische Gemeinschaften, Philipps-Universität, Studie 11, 7–27.

Bienefeld, M. (1989) 'The lessons of history', *Monthly Review* 3: 9–41.

—— (1994) 'The new world order: echoes of a new imperialism', *Third World Quarterly*, 15, 1: 31–48.

Binmore, K. (1990) *Essays on the Foundations of Game Theory*, Oxford: Basil Blackwell.

Bivona, D. (1990) *Desire and Contradiction*, Manchester: Manchester University Press.

Blaug, M. (1980) *The Methodology of Economics*, Cambridge: Cambridge University Press.

Block, F.L. (1977) *The Origins of International Economic Disorder: A Study of United States Monetary Policy from World War II to the Present*, Berkeley, CA: University of California Press.

Blumer, H. (1969) *Symbolic Interactionism*, Englewood Cliffs, NJ: Prentice-Hall.

Böhm-Bawerk, E.V. (1891, 1971) *The Positive Theory of Capital*, trans. with a Preface and analysis by W. Smart, Freeport, NY: Books for Libraries Press.

Boltanski, L. (1981) 'America, America … Le plan Marshall et l'importation du management', *Actes de la Recherche en Sciences Sociales* 38: 19–41.

Booth, D. (ed.) (1994) *Rethinking Social Development*, Harlow: Longman.

Borrus, M. (1997) *Left For Dead: Asian Production Networks and the Revival of US Electronics*, BRIE Working Paper 100, Berkeley, CA: University of California Press, April.

Borrus, M. and Zysman, J. (1997a) *You Don't Have to Be a Giant: How the Changing Terms of Competition in Global Markets are Creating New Possibilities for Danish Companies*, BRIE Working Paper 96A, Berkeley, CA: University of California Press, February.

—— (1997b) *Wintelism and the Changing Terms of Global Competition: Prototype of the Future?*, BRIE Working Paper 96B, Berkeley, CA: University of California Press, February.

Bourdieu, P. (1976) 'Les Modes de domination', *Actes de la Recherche en Sciences Sociales*, 2 (2–3): 122–132.

—— (1979) *La distinction: critique du jugement sociale*, Paris: Les Éditions de Minuit.

—— (1980) *Le Sens pratique*, Paris: Éditions Minuit.

—— (1982) *Ce que parler veut dire. L'Économie des Échanges Linguistiques*, Paris: Fayard.

—— (1984) *Homo Academicus*, Paris: Les Éditions de Minuit.

—— (1989) *La Noblesse d'État*, Paris: Les Éditions de Minuit.

Boyer, R. (1990) *The Regulation School: A Critical Introduction*, New York: Columbia University Press.

—— (1996) 'The seven paradoxes of capitalism ... or is a theory of modern economies still possible?', seminar given at the University of Wisconsin-Madison, 18–19 November.

Boyer, R. and Drache, D. (eds) (1996) *States Against Markets: The Limits of Globalization*, London: Routledge.

Boyer R. and Durand, J.-P. (1993) *L'après Fordisme*, Paris: Syros.

Boyer, R. and Hollingsworth, R.J. (eds) (1997) *Contemporary Capitalism*, Cambridge: Cambridge University Press.

Bracher, M. (1994) 'On the Psychological and Social Functions of Language: Lacan's Theory of the Four Discourses', in M. Bracher (ed.) *Lacanian Theory of Discourse: Subject, Structure, and Society*, New York: New York University Press.

Braudel, F. (1982) *The Wheels of Commerce. Civilization and Capitalism 15th–18th Century*, vol. 2, trans. S. Reynolds, New York: Harper & Row Publishers.

Braunmühl, C. von (1973) 'Weltmarktbewegung des Kapitals, Imperialismus und Staat', *Gesellschaft* 1, 11–61.

Brawley, M.R. (1998) *Turning Points: Decisions Shaping the Evolution of International Political Economy*, Toronto: Broadview Press.

Breman, J. (1998) 'The end of globalisation?,' *Economic and Political Weekly* 14 February: 333–389.

Brewer, A. (1980) *Marxist Theories of Imperialism*, London: Routledge.

Brohman, J. (1995) 'Economism and critical silences in development studies: a theoretical critique of neoliberalism', *Third World Quarterly* 16, 2: 297–318.

—— (1996) *Popular Development: Rethinking the Theory and Practice of Development*, Oxford: Blackwell.

Brubaker, R. (1985) 'Rethinking classical theory: the sociological vision of Pierre Bourdieu', *Theory and Society* 14, 6: 745–774.

Brucan, S. (1978) *The Dialectic of World Politics*, New York: The Free Press.

Brunhoff, S. de (1976) *État et Capital: Recherches sur la Politique Économique*, Grenoble: Presses Universitaires de Grenoble.

Buckley, P.J. and Casson, M. (1988) 'A theory of cooperation in international business', in Contractor, F.J. and Lorange, P. (eds) *Cooperative Strategies in International Business*, Lexington: D.C. Heath, pp. 31–54.

Bugra, A. (1991) 'Political sources of uncertainty in business life', in M. Heper (ed.) *Strong State and Economic Interest Groups: The Post-1980 Turkish Experience*, Berlin and New York: Walter de Gruyter, pp. 151–161.

Bukharin, N. (1972 [1917]) *Imperialism and World Economy*, London: Merlin.

Bull, H. (1977) *The Anarchical Society: A Study of Order in World Politics*, London: Macmillan.

Burchill, S. and Linklater, A. (1996) *Theories of International Relations*, London: Macmillan, with R Devetak, M. Paterson and J. True.

Burnham, P. (1991) 'Neo-Gramscian hegemony and the international order', *Capital and Class* 45, Autumn, 73–94.

—— (1994) 'Open Marxism and vulgar international political economy', *Review of International Political Economy*, 1, 2: 221–232.

Busch, K. (1974) *Die multinationalen Konzerne. Zur Analyse der Weltmarktbewegung des Kapitals*, Frankfurt: Suhrkamp.

Cafruny, A. (1995) 'Class, state and world systems: the transformation of international maritime relations', *Review of International Political Economy* 2, 2 (Spring): 285–314.

Caldwell, B.J. (1982) *Beyond Positivism: Economic Methodology in the Twentieth Century*, London: George Allen and Unwin.

Cameron, A. and Palan, R. (1999) 'The imagined economy: mapping transformations in the contemporary state', *Millennium* 28, 2: 267–289.

Cameron, M., Lawson, R. and Tomlin, B. (eds) (1998) *To Walk Without Fear: The Global Movement to Ban Landmines*, Toronto: Oxford University Press.

Caporaso, J.A. (1978) 'Introduction to the special issue on dependence, dependency and power in the global system: a structural and behavioural analysis', *International Organization* 32, 1 (Winter): 2–43.

Cardoso, F.H. (1993) 'North–South relations in the present context: a new dependency?', in M. Carnoy, M. Castells, S.S. Cohen and F.H. Cardoso (eds) *The New Global Economy in the Information Age*, University Park, PA: Pennsylvania State University Press.

Carmen, R. (1996) *Autonomous Development: Humanizing The Landscape*, London: Zed.

Cassirer, E. (1955) *The Philosophy of Symbolic Forms: vol. 1. Language*, Yale and London: Yale University Press.

Casson, M. (1987) *Multinationals and World Trade: Vertical Integration and the Division of Labour in World Industries*, London: Allen and Unwin.

Castells, M. (1989) *The Informational City: Information Technology, Economic Restructuring, and the Urban-Regional Process*, Oxford: Basil Blackwell.

—— (1993) 'The informational economy and the new international division of labor', in M. Carnoy, M. Castells, S.S. Cohen and F.H. Cardoso (eds) *The New Global Economy in the Information Age*, University Park: Pennsylvania State University Press, pp. 15–44.

—— (1996) *The Rise of the Network Society*, Oxford: Blackwell.

—— (1997) *The Power of Identity*, Oxford: Blackwell.

Cerny, P. (1991) *The Changing Architecture of Politics*, London: Macmillan.

—— (1994) 'The infrastructure of the infrastructure? Towards embedded financial orthodoxy in the international political economy', in R.P. Palan and B. Gills (eds) *Transcending the State–Global Divide: A Neostructuralist Agenda in International Relations*, Boulder, CO: Lynne Reinner, pp. 223–249.

—— (1999) 'Globalization and the erosion of democracy', *European Journal of Political Research*, 35, 5 (July/August): pp. 1–26.

—— (2000) 'The dynamics of political globalization: towards an actor-centered approach', (in preparation).

Cerny, P.G. and Evans, M. (1999) 'New Labour, globalization and the competition state', working paper no. 70, Center for European Studies, Harvard University.

—— (2000) 'Political agency in a globalizing world: toward a structurational approach', paper presented at the annual convention of the International Studies Association, Los Angeles, 14-18 March.

Champernowne, D. (1953–4) 'The production function and the theory of capital: a comment', *Review of Economic Studies*, 21, 2: 112–135.

Chan, S. (1998) 'Redeeming the shield of Achilles: on behalf of stories and subjectivity in I.R.', paper presented at the ISA-ECPR conference, Vienna, 16–19 September.

Chandler, A. (1977) *The Visible Hand*, Cambridge, MA: Harvard University Press.

Chang, K. and Ling, L.H.M. (forthcoming) 'Globalisation and its intimate other: Filipina domestic workers in Hong Kong', in M. Marchand and A.S. Runyan (eds) *Feminist Sightings of Global Restructuring: Conceptualizations and Reconceptualizations*, London: Routledge.

Charon, J.M. (1998) *Symbolic Interactionism: An Introduction, An Interpretation, An Integration*, 6th edn. Simon & Schuster.

Chesnais, F. (1988) 'Technical cooperation agreements between firms', *STI Review* 4: 51–119.

Chossudovsky, M. (1997) *The Globalisation of Poverty. Impacts of IMF and World Bank Reforms*, Penang: Third World Network.

Christensen, C. (1977) 'Structural power and national security', in K. Knorr and F.N. Trager (eds) *Economic Issues and National Security*, Kansas: Regents Press for the National Security Education Program.

Ciborra, C. (1991) 'Alliances as learning experiments: cooperation, competition and change in high-tech industries', in L.K. Mytelka (ed.) *Strategic Partnerships in the World Economy*, London: Pinter Publishers.

Clark, I. (1997) *Globalization and Fragmentation*, Oxford: Oxford University Press.

Clark, J.B (1899, 1965) *The Distribution of Wealth*, New York: Augustus M. Kelley.

Clarke, G. (1998) 'Non-governmental organizations and politics in the developing world', *Political Studies* 46: 36–52.

Clarke, S. (1978) 'Capital, fractions of capital and the state', *Capital and Class* 5: 32–77.

Clarke, T. and Barlow, M. (1997) *MAI: The Multilateral Agreement on Investment and the Threat to Canadian Sovereignty*, Toronto: Stoddart.

Claudín, F. (1975) *The Communist Movement: From Comintern To Cominform*, Harmondsworth: Penguin Books.

Claval, P. (1978) *Espace et pouvoir*, Paris: PUF.

Clayton, R. and Pontusson, J. (1998) 'Welfare state retrenchment revisited: entitlement cuts, public sector restructuring, and inegalitarian trends in advanced capitalist societies', *World Politics* 51, 1 (October): 67–98.

Cleveland, H., Henderson, H. and Kaul, I. (eds) (1995) *The United Nations: Policy and Financing Alternatives*, New York: Apex Press.

Coase, R. (1937) 'The nature of the firm', *Economica* 4: 386–405.

Cohen, B.J. (1998) *The Geography of Money*, Ithaca, NY: Cornell University Press.

Coleman, W. D. (1994) 'Keeping the shotgun behind the door: performance and control of economic factors', in R. J. Hollingsworth, W. Streeck and P. C. Schmitter (eds) *Governing Capitalist Economies*, New York: Oxford University Press, pp. 244–300.

Collier, P. and Horowitz, D. (1976) *The Rockefellers. An American Dynasty*, New York: Holt, Rinehart and Winston.

Commission on Global Governance (1995) *Report of the 1995 Our Global Neighbourhood*, New York: Oxford University Press.

Common, J. (1934) *Institutional Economics*, Madison, WI: University of Wisconsin Press.

Commons, J. (1959 [1924]) *The Legal Foundations of Capitalism*, Madison, WI: University of Wisconsin Press.

Compa, L. and Hinchliffe-Darricàre, T. (1995) 'Enforcing international labor rights through corporate codes of conduct', *Columbia Journal of Transnational Law* 33: 663–689.

Connors, M. (1997) *The Race to the Intelligent State: Charting the Global Information Economy in the 21st Century*, Oxford: Capstone.

Conybeare, J.A.C. (1984) 'Public goods, Prisoner's Dilemmas, and the international political economy', *International Studies Quarterly* 28: 5–22.

—— (1985) 'Trade wars: a comparative study of Anglo-Hanse, Franco-Italian, and Hawley-Smoot conflicts', *World Politics* 38: 147–172.

—— (1987) *Trade Wars*, New York: Columbia University Press.

Council of Economic Advisors (1994) *Economic Report of the President*, Washington: United States Government Printing Office.

Cowen, M.P. and Shenton, R.W. (1996) *Doctrines of Development*, London: Routledge.

Cowhey, P. (1993) 'Domestic institutions and the credibility of international commitments: Japan and the United States', *International Organization* 47: 299–326.

Cox, G. (1997) *Making Votes Count*, New York: Cambridge University Press.

Cox, R.W. (1977) 'Labor and hegemony', *International Organization* 31, 3, (Summer): 385–424.

—— (1981) 'Social forces, states, and world orders: beyond international relations theory', *Millennium: Journal of International Relations*, 10, 2 (Summer): 126–155.

—— (1983) 'Gramsci, hegemony, and international relations: an essay in method', *Millennium: Journal of International Relations*, 12, 2 (Summer): 162–175.

—— (1987) *Production, Power and World Order: Social Forces in the Making of History*, New York: Columbia University Press.

—— (1989) 'Middlemanpowership, Japan, and future world order', *International Journal*, 44(4): 823–862.

—— (1992) 'Towards a post-hegemonic conceptualization of world order: reflections on the relevancy of Ibn Khaldun', in J.N. Rosenau and E.-O. Czempiel (eds) *Governance Without Government: Order and Change in World Politics*, Cambridge: Cambridge University Press.

—— (1994) 'Global perestroika', in R. Miliband and L. Panitch (eds) *Socialist Register*, London: Merlin Press.

—— (1995a) 'Critical political economy', in B. Hettne (ed.) *International Political Economy*, London: Zed Press.

—— (1995b) 'Civilizations: encounters and transformations', *Studies in Political Economy* 47 (Summer): 7–31.

—— (1996) 'Civilisations in world political economy', *New Political Economy* 1, 2: 141–156.

—— (ed.) (1997) *The New Realism. Perspectives on Multilateralism and World Order*, London: Macmillan.

—— (1998) *Weltordnung und Hegemonie – Grundlagen der 'Internationalen Politischen Ökonomie'*, Marburg: Forschungs der University Presse Europäische Gemeinschaften, Philipps-Universität, Studie 11.

—— (1999) 'Civil society at the turn of the millennium: prospects for an alternative world order', *Review of International Studies* 25, 1 (January): 3–28.

Cox, R.W. and Sinclair, T.J. (1996a) *Approaches to World Order*, Cambridge: Cambridge University Press.

Crane, G.T. and Amawi, A. (1997) *The Theoretical Evolution of International Political Economy: A Reader*, 2nd edn, Oxford: Oxford University Press.

Crawford, N.C. (1998) 'The passion of world politics: hypotheses on emotions and emotional relationships', paper presented at the American Political Science Association Conference, Boston, August.

Crouch, C. and Streeck, W. (eds) (1997) *The Political Economy of Modern Capitalism: Mapping Convergence and Diversity*, London: Sage.

Crozier, M. and Friedberg, E. (1977) *L'Acteur et le système: les contraintes de l'action collective*, Paris: Éditions du Seuil.

Crush, J. (ed.) (1996) *The Power of Development*, London: Routledge.

Curtin, P. (1984) *Cross-Cultural Trade in World History*, New York: Cambridge University Press.

Dacey, R. (1994) 'Inducing fair trade out of hegemonic trade', *Synthese* 100: 497–504.

—— (1995) 'A general model of international interactions and peace economics', *International Interactions* 21, 2: 155–180.

—— (1999) 'A general model of international interactions and peace economics' http:www.-uidaho.edu/rdacey/dtnotes/

Dahl, R. (1961) *Who Governs? Democracy and Power in an American City*, New Haven: Yale University Press.

Dahmén, E. (1988) 'Development blocks in industrial economics', *Scandinavian Economic History Review* 36,1: 3–14.

Dasgupta, P. and David, P. (1987) 'Information disclosure and the economics of science and technology', in G. Feiwal (ed.) *Arrow and the Ascent of Modern Economic Theory*, New York: New York University Press.

—— (1988) *Priority, Secrecy, Patents and the Socio-Economics of Science and Technology*, Research Paper 127, Stanford, CA: Stanford University, March.

—— (1991) *Resource Allocation and the Institutions of Science*, mimeo, CEPR, Stanford, CA: Stanford University.

Dassbach, C. (1994) 'The social organization of production, competitive advantage and foreign investment', *Review of International Political Economy* 1, 3 (Autumn): 489–517.

Dawson, G. (1994) *Soldier Heroes*, London: Routledge.

Debnam, G. (1984) *The Analysis of Power: A Realist Approach*, London: Macmillan.

De Coulanges, F. and Denis, N. (1955) *The Ancient City: A Study on the Religion, Laws, and Institutions of Greece and Rome*, New York: Doubleday Anchor Books.

De Leo, F. (1994) 'Understanding the roots of your competitive advantage: from product/market competition to competition as a multiple-layer game', in G. Hamel (ed.) *Competence-Based Competition*, Chichester: John Wiley & Sons, pp. 35–55.

Deleuze, G. and Guattari, F. (1984) *Anti-Oedipus: Capitalism and Schizophrenia*, London: The Athlone Press.

Denemark, R. and O'Brien, R. (1997) 'Contesting the canon: IPE at US and UK universities', *Review of International Political Economy* 5, 2 (Spring).

Dessouki, A.E.H. (1993) 'Globalization and the two spheres of security', *The Washington Quarterly* 16, 4: 109–117.

Dezalay, Y. and Garth, B. (1998) 'Le "Washington Consensus" ', *Actes de la Recherche en Sciences Sociales* March, 121/122: 3–21.

DN (1998) 'End of catch-up industrialisation: notes on South-East and East Asian crisis', *Economic and Political Weekly* 16 May: 1163–1166.

Doremus, P., Keller, W., Reich, S. and Pauly, L. (1998) *The Myth of the Global Corporation*, Princeton, NJ: Princeton University Press.

Dosi, G. (1988) 'The nature of the innovation process', in G. Dosi, C. Freeman, R. Nelson, G. Silverberg and L.U.C. Soete (eds) *Technical Change and Economic Theory*, London: Pinter Publishers, pp. 221–238.

Dougals, M. (1992) *Essays in Cultural Theory*, London: Routledge

Dowding, K. (1991) *Rational Choice and Political Power*, Hants: Edward Elgar.

—— (1996) *Power*, Minneapolis: University of Minnesota Press.

Drainville, A. (1994) 'International political economy in the age of open Marxism', *Review of International Political Economy* 1, 1 (Spring): 105–132.

Dunleavy, P.J. (1994) 'The globalisation of public services production: can government be "best in world"?', *Public Policy and Administration* 9, 2 (Summer): 36–64.

Dunning, J. (1981) *International Production and the Multinational Enterprise*, London: Allen and Unwin.

—— (1988) *Explaining International Production*, London: Unwin Hyman.

—— (1995) 'Reappraising the eclectic paradigm in an age of alliance capitalism', *International Journal of Business Studies* 26, 3: 461–491.

—— (1997) 'Governments and the macro-organization of economic activity: an historical and spatial perspective', *Review of International Political Economy* 4, 1: 42–86.

Eden, L. (1991) 'Special section: sovereignty at bay', *Millennium* 20, 2 (Summer).

Eggertsson, T. (1990) *Economic Behavior and Institutions*, New York: Cambridge University Press.

Elster, J. (1989) *Nuts and Bolts for the Social Sciences*, Cambridge: Cambridge University Press.

Emmanuel, A. (1972) *Unequal Exchange: A Study of the Imperialism of Trade*, New York: Monthly Review Press.

Engels, F. (1890) 'Letter to Conrad Schmidt in Berlin, 5 August 1890', in K. Marx and F. Engels, *Brieven Over Het Historisch Materialisme* ('Letters on Historical Materialism'), Amsterdam: Pegasus (1978), pp. 30–32.

Enloe, C. (1989) *Bananas, Beaches and Bases: Making Feminist Sense of International Relations*, London: Pandora.

Ernst, D. (1994) *Carriers of Regionalization: The East Asian Production Networks of Japanese Electronics Firms*, BRIE Working Paper 73, Berkeley, CA: University of California Press.

—— (1997) *From Partial to Systemic Globalization: International Production Networks in the Electronics Industry*, BRIE Working Paper 98, Berkeley, CA: University of California Press, April.

Escobar, A. (1992) 'Reflections on "development": grassroots approaches and alternative politics in the Third World', *Futures* June: 411–436.

—— (1995) *Encountering Development*, Princeton, NJ: Princeton University Press.

Esping-Andersen, G. (1996) 'After the golden age? Welfare state dilemmas in a global economy', in G. Esping-Andersen, *Welfare States in Transition: National Adaptations in Global Economies*, London: Sage, pp. 1–31.

Evans, M. and Davies, J. (1999) 'Understanding policy transfer: a multi-level, multi-disciplinary perspective', *Public Administration* (forthcoming).

Evans, P. (1995) *Embedded Autonomy*, Princeton, NJ: Princeton University Press.

—— (1997) 'The eclipse of the state?', *World Politics* 50 (October): 6–87.

Evans, P., Rueschemayer, D. and Skocpol, T. (1985) *Bring The State Back In*, Cambridge: Cambridge University Press.

Evans, P.B., Jacobson, H.K. and Putnam, R.D. (1993a) 'Double-edged diplomacy: exploitation, public goods, and free rides', *International Studies Quarterly*.

—— (1993b) *Double-Edged Diplomacy: International Bargaining and Domestic Politics*, Berkeley, CA: University of California Press.

Falk, R. (1994) *On Humane Governance: Towards A New Global Politics*, Cambridge: Polity.

Fearon, J. D. (1997) 'Signaling foreign policy interests: tying hands versus sinking costs', *Journal of Conflict Resolution* 41, 1: 68–90.

Feaver, P. (1998) 'Crisis as shirking: an agency theory explanation of the souring of American civil–military relations', *Armed Forces and Society* 24: 407–434.

Ferejohn, J. and Satz, D. (1996) 'Unification, universalism and rational choice theory', in J. Friedman (ed.) *The Rational Choice Controversy: Economic Models of Politics Reconsidered*, New Haven, CN: Yale University Press.

Ferge, Z. (unpublished) 'What are the state functions neoliberalism wants to get rid of?'

Ferguson, C. and Morris, C. (1993) *Computer Wars: How The West Can Win in A Post IBM World*, New York: Times Books.

Ferguson, C.E. (1969) *The Neoclassical Theory of Production and Distribution*, Cambridge: Cambridge University Press.

Finnemore, M. (1993) 'International organizations as teachers of norms: the United Nations Educational, Scientific, and Cultural Organization science policy', *International Organization* 47: 565–597.

—— (1996) *National Interests in International Society*, Ithaca, NY: Cornell University Press.

Finnemore, M. and Sikkink, K. (1998) 'International norm dynamics and political change', *International Organization* 52, 4 (Autumn): 887–917.

Fligstein, N. (1991) 'The structural transformation of American industry: an institutional account of the causes of diversification in the largest firms, 1919–1979', in W. Powell and P. Dimaggio (eds) *The New Institutionalism: An Organizational Analysis*, Chicago: University of Chicago Press, pp. 311–336.

Foray, D. (1991) 'The secrets of industry are in the air: industrial cooperation and the organizational dynamics of the innovative firm', *Research Policy* 20: 393–405.

Foray, D. and Garrouste, P. (1993) 'The pertinent levels of analysis in industrial dynamics', in G. Hodgson and E. Screpanti (eds) *Rethinking Economics: Markets, Technology and Economic Evolution*, Aldershot: Edward Elgar.

Forcese, C. (1997) *Commerce With Conscience?: Human Rights and Corporate Codes of Conduct*, Montreal: International Centre For Human Rights and Democratic Development.

Foss, N. (1996) 'Higher-order industrial capabilities and competitive advantage', *Journal of Industrial Studies* 3, 1: 1–20.

Foss, N. and Knudsen, C. (eds) (1996) *Towards A Competence Theory of the Firm*, London: Routledge.

Foucault, M. (1970) *The Order of Things*, London: Tavistock.

—— (1977) *Discipline and Punish*, London: Allen Lane.

—— (1990 [1976]) *The History of Sexuality*, vol. I, New York: Vintage Books.

Frank, A.G. (1967) *Capitalism and Underdevelopment in Latin America*, New York: Monthly Review Press.

—— (1996) 'The underdevelopment of development', in S. Chew and R. Denemark (eds) *The Underdevelopment of Development*, London: Sage.

—— (1998) *Reorient: Global Economics in the Asian Age*, Berkeley, CA: University of California Press.

Franklin, M.I. (2000) 'Sewing up the globe: ICTs and dematerialised gender–power relations', in B. Saunders and M. Foblets (eds) *Changing Genders in Intercultural Perspective*, Oxford: Berg.

Freeman, C. (1995) 'The "national system of innovation" in historical perspective', *Cambridge Journal of Economics* 19, 1: 5–25.

Freeman, C. and Perez, C. (1988) 'Structural crises of adjustment: business cycles and investment behaviour', in G. Dosi, C. Freeman, R. Nelson, G. Silverberg and L. Soete (eds) *Technical Change and Economic Theory*, London: Pinter Publishers.

Frey, B. S. (1997) 'The public choice view of international political economy', in G.T. Crane and A. Amawi (eds) *The Theoretical Evolution of International Political Economy: A Reader*, 2nd edn, Oxford: Oxford University Press, pp. 227–239.

Frieden, J. (1991) 'Invested interests: the politics of national economic policies in a world of global finance', *International Organization* 45, 4: 425–452.

—— (1994) 'International investment and colonial control: a new interpretation', *International Organization* 48: 559–594.

Friedmann, J. (1992) *Empowerment: The Politics of Alternative Development*, Oxford: Blackwell.

Fukuyama, F. (1990) 'The end of history?', *The National Interest* 16: 3–18.

—— (1995) 'Social capital and the global economy', *Foreign Affairs* 74, 5: 89–103.

—— (1996) *Trust: Social Virtues and the Creation of Prosperity*, London: Penguin.

—— (1998) 'Women and the evolution of world politics', *Foreign Affairs* September/October: 25–41.

Galbraith, J.K. (1958) *The Affluent Society*, Boston: Houghton Mifflin Company.

—— (1967) *The New Industrial State*, London: Hamish Hamilton.

Galtung, J. (1971) 'A structural theory of imperialism', *Journal of Peace Research* 8, 1: 81–117.

Gereffi, G. (1989) 'Rethinking development theory: insights from Latin America and East Asia', *Sociological Forum* 4, 4: 505–533.

Gerlach, M. (1992) *Alliance Capitalism: The Social Organization of Japanese Business*, Berkeley, CA: University of California Press.

Germain, R. (1997) *The International Organization of Credit*, Cambridge: Cambridge University Press.

Germain, R. and Kenny, M. (1998) 'Engaging Gramsci: international relations theory and the new Gramscians', *Review of International Studies* 24: 3–21.

Giddens, A. (1981) *A Contemporary Critique of Historical Materialism*, London: Macmillan.

—— (1984) *The Constitution of Society*, Cambridge: Polity.

—— (1985) *The Nation-State and Violence*, Cambridge: Polity.

—— (1990) *The Consequences of Modernity*, Cambridge: Polity

—— (1991) *Modernity and Self-Identity*, Cambridge: Polity.

—— (1995) 'The new context of politics', *Democratic Dialogue* 1: 8–23.

Gill, S. (1988) *The Global Political Economy*, Brighton: Harvester Wheatsheaf.

—— (1990) *American Hegemony and the Transnational Commission*, Cambridge: Cambridge University Press.

—— (1992) 'Economic globalization and the internationalization of authority: limits and contradictions', *Geoforum* 23, 3: 269–283.

—— (ed.) (1993) *Gramsci, Historical Materialism and International Relations*, Cambridge: Cambridge University Press.

—— (1995a) 'Globalization, market civilisation, and disciplinary neoliberalism', *Millennium* 24, 3: 399–423.

—— (1995b) 'The global Panopticon? The neoliberal state, economic life, and democratic surveillance', *Alternatives* 2: 1–49.

—— (ed.) (1997) *Globalization, Democratization and Multilateralism*, London: Macmillan.

—— (1998) 'European governance and new constitutionalism: economic and monetary union and alternatives to disciplinary neoliberalism in Europe', *New Political Economy* 3,1: 5–26.

Gill, S. and Law, D. (1988) *The Global Political Economy: Perspectives, Problems and Policies*, Baltimore: The Johns Hopkins University Press.

—— (1989) 'Global hegemony and the structural power of capital', *International Studies Quarterly* 33: 475–499.

Gill, S. and Mittelman, J.H. (eds) (1997) *Innovation and Transformation in International Studies*, Cambridge: Cambridge University Press.

Gills, B.K. (1987) 'Historical materialism and international relations theory', *Millennium: Journal of International Studies* 16, 2: 265–272.

Gilpin, R. (1975) *US Power and Multinational Corporations: The Political Economy of Foreign Direct Investment*, New York: Basic Books.

—— (1981) *War and Change in World Politics*, Cambridge: Cambridge University Press.

—— (1987) *The Political Economy of International Relations*, Princeton, NJ: Princeton University Press.
Glaserffeld, E. (1984) 'An introduction to radical constructivism', in P. Watzlawick (ed.) *The Invented Reality: How Do We Know What We Believe We Know? Contributions To Constructivism*, New York and London: W.W. Northon.
Gomes-Casseres, B. (1996) *The Alliance Reution: The New Shape of Business Rivalry*, London: Cambridge University Press.
Gowa, J. (1986) 'Anarchy, egoism, and the third images: the evolution of cooperation and international relations', *International Organization* 40, 1: 167–186.
—— (1989a) 'Bipolarity, multipolarity, and free trade', *American Political Science Review* 83, 4: 1245–1256.
—— (1989b) 'Rational hegemons, excludable goods, and small groups: an epitaph for Hegemonic Stability Theory?', *World Politics* 41: 307–324.
Gowa, J. and Mansfield, E.D. (1993) 'Power politics and international trade', *American Political Science Review* 87, 2: 408–420.
Gramsci, A. (1971) *Selections from the Prison Notebooks*, New York: International Publishers.
Granovetter, M. (1990) *Entrepreneurship, Development and the Emergence of Firm*, Berlin: Wissenschaftszentrum Berlin für Sozialforschung.
—— (1992) 'Economic action and social structure: the problem of embeddedness', in M. Granovetter and R. Swedberg (eds) *The Sociology of Economic Life*, Boulder, San Francisco, Oxford: Westview Press, pp. 53–81.
—— (1995) 'Coase revisited: business groups in the modern economy', *Industrial and Corporate Change*, 4,1: 93–130.
Green, D. and Shapiro, I. (1994) *Pathologies of Rational Choice Theory*, New Haven, CN: Yale University Press.
Greif, A. (1992) 'Institutions and international trade: lessons from the commercial revolution', *The American Economic Review* 82: 128–133.
Grieco, J.M. (1988a) 'Realist theory and the problems of international cooperation', *Journal of Politics* 50, 3: 577–599.
—— (1988b) 'Anarchy and the limits of cooperation: a realist critique of the new liberal institutionalism', *International Organization* 42, 4: 485–508.
Griffin, K. (1996) *Culture, Human Development and Economic Growth*, University of California, Riverside: Working Paper in Economics 96–17.
Grillo, R.D. and Stirrat, R.L. (eds) (1997) *Discourses of Development*, Oxford: Berg.
Grimwade, N. (1989) *International Trade: New Patterns of Trade and Investment*, London: Routledge.
Grossman, G.M. and Helpman, E. (1994) 'Protection for sale', *American Economic Review* 84: 833–850.
—— (1995) 'Trade wars and trade talks', *Journal of Political Economy* 103: 675–708.
Group of Lisbon (1995) *Limits To Competition*, Cambridge, MA: MIT Press.
Grunberg, I. (1996) *Rival States, Rival Firms: How Do People Fit In?* Discussion Papers Series 4, New York: UNDP Office of Development Studies.
Guéhenno, J-M. (1995) *The End of the Nation-State*, Minneapolis: University of Minnesota.
Gulati, L. (1997) 'Asian women in international migration with special reference to domestic work and entertainment', *Economic and Political Weekly* 22 November: 3029–3035.
Guzzini, S. (1993) 'Structural power: the limits of neorealist power analysis', *International Organization* 47, 3: 443–78.
—— (1994) 'Power analysis as a critique of power politics: understanding power and governance in the Second Gulf War', PhD dissertation. Florence: European University Institute.
—— (1998) *Realism in International Relations and International Political Economy: The Continuing Story of a Death Foretold*, London and New York: Routledge.
—— (2000) 'A reconstruction of constructivism in international relations', *European Journal of International Relations*, 6, 2 (June).
Haas, P. (1992) 'Knowledge, power and international policy coordination', special issue of *International Organization*, 46, 1.
Hagedoorn, J. and Schakenraad, J. (1990) 'Inter-firm partnerships and co-operative strategies in core technologies', in C. Freeman and L. Soete (eds) *New Explorations in the Economics of Technical Change*, London: Pinter, pp. 3–37.
Haggard, S. (1990) *Pathways from the Periphery: The Politics of Growth in the Newly Industrializing Countries*, Ithaca, NY: Cornell University Press.
Hall, J. (1996) *International Orders*, Cambridge: Polity.
Hall, P. and Taylor, R.C.R. (1996) 'Political science and the three new institutionalisms', *Political Studies* XLIV: 936–957.

Hall, P.A. (1997) 'The political economy of adjustment in Germany', in F. Naschold, D. Soskice, B. Hancké and U. Jürgens (eds) *Ökonomische Leistungsfähigkeit und institutionelle Innovation: Das deutsche Produktions- und Politikregime in globalen Wettbewerb*, WZB-Jahrbuch, Berlin: Edition Sigma.

Hall, R.B. (1997) 'Moral authority as power resource', *International Organization* 51, 4: 591–622.

Halliday, F. (1987) 'State and society in international relations', *Millennium* 16, 2: 215–229.

—— (1994) *Rethinking International Relations*, London: Macmillan.

—— (1999) *Revolutions and International Relations*, London: Macmillan.

Halperin, S. (1997) *In The Mirror of the Third World: Capitalist Development in Modern Europe*, Ithaca, NY: Cornell University Press.

Hamel, G. and Heene, A. (eds) (1994) *Competence-Based Competition*, Chichester: John Wiley & Sons.

Hamilton, G. G. and Woolsey Biggart, N. (1992) 'Markets, culture, and authority: a comparative analysis of management and organization in the Far East', in M. Granovetter and R. Swedberg (eds) *The Sociology of Economic Life*, Boulder, San Francisco, Oxford: Westview Press, pp. 233–263.

Hamilton, P. (1996) *Historicism*, London and New York: Routledge.

Hannerz, U. (1990) 'Cosmopolitans and locals in world culture', *Theory, Culture, and Society* 7, 2–3: 237–251.

Hansenclever, A., Mayer, P. and Rittberger, V. (1997) *Theories of International Regimes*, Cambridge: Cambridge University Press.

Haq, M. Ul (1995) *Reflections on Human Development*, New York: Oxford University Press.

Haq, M. Ul and Haq, K. (1998) *Human Development in South Asia: The Education Challenge*, Karachi: Oxford University Press.

Harcourt, G.C. (1969) 'Some Cambridge controversies in the theory of capital', *Journal of Economic Literature*, 7, 2: 369–405.

—— (1972) *Some Cambridge Controversies in the Theory of Capital*, Cambridge: Cambridge University Press.

Hardin, R. (1982) *Collective Action*, Baltimore: Johns Hopkins University Press.

Hardt, M. and Negri, A. (1994) *Labor of Dionysus: A Critique of State-Form*, Minneapolis: University of Minnesota Press.

Harmes, A. (1998) 'Institutional investors and the reproduction of neoliberalism', *Review of International Political Economy* 5, 1: 92–121.

Harris, N. (1986) *The End of the Third World*, Harmondsworth: Penguin.

Harrod, J. (1987) *Power, Production and the Unprotected Worker*, New York: Columbia University Press.

—— (1997) 'Social forces and international political economy: joining the two IRs', in S. Gill and J. Mittleman (eds) *Innovation and Transformation in International Studies*, Cambridge: Cambridge University Press.

Harshé, R. (1997) *Twentieth Century Imperialism. Shifting Contours and Changing Conceptions*, New Delhi: Sage.

Harvey, D. (1990) *The Condition of Postmodernity*, Oxford: Blackwell Publishers.

Haus, L. (1995) 'Openings in the wall: transnational migrants, labor unions and U.S. immigration policy', *International Organization* 49, 2 (Spring): 285–313.

Hearn, J. (1998) 'The "NGO-Isation" of Kenyan society: USAID and the restructuring of health care', *Review of African Political Economy*, 75: 89–100.

Held, D. and Thompson, J. (eds) (1989) *The Social Theory of Modern Societies: Anthony Giddens and His Critics*, Cambridge: Cambridge University Press.

Helleiner, E. (1994) *States and the Reemergence of Global Finance*, Ithaca, NY: Cornell University Press.

—— (1998) 'State power and the regulation of illicit activity in global finance', in R. Friman and P. Andreas (eds) *The Illicit Global Economy and State Power*, Lanham, MD: Rowman and Littlefield.

Hennings, K.H. (1987) 'Capital as a factor of production', in J. Eatwell, J.M. Milgate and P. Newman (eds) *The New Palgrave*, vol. 1, London: Macmillan.

Herod, A. (1997) 'Labor as an agent of globalization and as a global agent', in K. Cox (ed.) *Spaces of Globalization*, New York: Guilford Press.

Hettne, B. (ed.) (1995) *International Political Economy: Understanding Global Disorder*, London: Zed Books.

Hicks, J. (1973) *Capital and Time. A Neo-Austrian Theory*, Oxford: Clarendon Press.

Hilferding, R. (1910 [1981]) *Finance Capital: A Study of the Latest Phase in Capitalist Development*, London: Routledge & Kegan Paul.

Hirsch, P., Michaels, S. *et al.* (1990) 'Clean models vs. dirty hands: why economics is different from sociology', in S. Zukin and P. DiMaggio (eds) *Structures of Capital: The Social Organization of the Economy*, Cambridge: Cambridge University Press, pp. 39–57.

Hirschman, A. O. (1967) *Development Projects Observed*, Washington, DC: The Brookings Institution.

—— (1977) *The Passions and the Interests*, Princeton, NJ: Princeton University Press.

—— (1981) *The Rise and Decline of Development Economics. Essays in Trespassing: Economics to Politics and Beyond*, Cambridge: Cambridge University Press.

Hirst, P. and Thompson, G. (1996) *Globalisation in Question*, London: Polity.

Hobbes, T. (1951) *Leviathan*, ed. C.B. Macpherson, Harmonsworth: Penguin.

Hobday, M. (1998) 'Product complexity, innovation and industrial organisation', *Research Policy* 26(6–7): 689–710.

Hobden, S. (1997) 'Four authors in search of a system' (unpublished paper).

Hobsbawm, E.J. (1994) *Age of Extremes: The Short Twentieth Century, 1914–1991*, London and New York: Michael Joseph.

Hobson, J.A. (1902) *Imperialism: A Study*, London: Allen and Unwin.

Hobson, J. M. (1997) *The Wealth of States: A Comparative Sociology of International Economic and Political Change*, Cambridge: Cambridge University Press.

—— (1998) 'The historical sociology of the state and the state of historical sociology in international relations', *Review of International Political Economy* 5, 2: 284–320.

Hodgson, G.M. (1994) 'Some remarks on "economic imperialism" and international political economy', *Review of International Political Economy* 1, 1.

—— (1997) 'The fate of the Cambridge capital controversy', in P. Arestis, G. Palma and M. Sawyer (eds) *Capital Controversy, Post-Keynesian Economics and the History of Economic Thought*, London and New York: Routledge.

Hoedeman, O. with Balanya, B., Doherty, A., Ma'anit, A. and Wesselius, E. (1998) 'Maigalomania: the new corporate agenda', *The Ecologist* 28, 3: 154–161.

Hollingsworth, R. J. (1998) 'New perspectives on the spatial dimensions of economic coordination: tensions between globalization and social systems of production', *Review of International Political Economy* 5, 3 (Autumn): 482–507.

Holloway, J. and Picciotto, S. (eds) (1978) *State and Capital: A Marxist Debate*, London: Edward Arnold.

Holman, O. (ed.) (1992) 'European unification in the 1990s: myth and reality', *International Journal of Political Economy* 22, 1: 3–22.

—— (1996) *Integrating Southern Europe. EC Expansion and the Transnationalization of Spain*, London: Routledge.

Holman, O. and van der Pijl, K. (1996) 'The capitalist class in the European Union', in G.A. Kourvetaris and A. Moschonas (eds) *The Impact of European Integration: Political, Sociological and Economic Changes*, Westport, CN: Praeger.

Holman, O., Overbeek, H.W. and Ryner, M. (eds) (1998) 'Neoliberal hegemony and European restructuring', *International Journal of Political Economy* 28, 1 and 2.

Hoogvelt, A. (1997) *Globalisation and the Post Colonial World: The New Political Economy of Development*, London: Macmillan.

Hoogvelt, A. and Yuasa, M. (1994) 'Going lean or going native?' *Review of International Political Economy* 1, 2 (Summer): 281–303.

Howard, M.C. and King, J.E. (1992) *A History of Marxian Economics. Volume II, 1929–1990*, Princeton, NJ: Princeton University Press.

Huber, E. and Stephens, J.D. (1998) 'Internationalization and the Social Democratic Model', *Comparative Political Studies* 31, 3: 353–397.

Hume, D. (1752) *Political Discourses* (Edinburgh: printed by R. Fleming, for A. Kincaid and A. Donaldson).

Hunt, E.K. (1992) *History of Economic Thought. A Critical Perspective*, 2nd edn, New York: HarperCollins Publishers.

Hunt, M. (1987) *Ideology and U.S. Foreign Policy*, New Haven, CN: Yale University Press.

Huntington, S.P. (1996) *The Clash of Civilizations and the Remaking of World Order*, New York: Simon and Schuster.

Ibrahim, A. (1996) *The Asian Renaissance*, Singapore: Times Books.

ICFTU (1995) 'Rethinking the role of the IMF and World Bank: ICFTU proposals to the annual meetings of the board of governors of the IMF and World Bank', Washington 10–12 October.

IHT (1998a) 'Korean unions reluctantly agree to layoffs', *International Herald Tribune* 7–8 February, 1.

—— (1998b) 'World Bank targets the next Asian danger: growing social unrest', *International Herald Tribune* 2 February, 4.

Iida, K. (1993) 'When and how do domestic constraints matter? Two-level games with uncertainty', *Journal of Conflict Resolution* 37: 403–426.

Imai, K. and Baba, Y. (1991) 'Systemic innovation and cross-border networks, transcending markets and hierarchies to create a new techno-economic system', in *Technology and Productivity: The Challenges for Economic Policy*, Paris: OECD.

Imai, K. and Itami, H. (1984) 'Interpenetration of organisation and market: Japan's firm and market in comparison with US', *International Journal of Industrial Organization*, 2: 285–310.

Immergut, E.M. (1998) 'The theoretical core of the new institutionalism', *Politics and Society* 26, 1 (March): 5–24.

Ingham, G. (1994) 'States and markets in the production of world money: sterling and the dollar', in S. Corbridge, R. Martin and N. Thrift (eds) *Money, Power and Space*, London: Blackwell.

Inkpen, A. (1996) 'Creating knowledge through collaboration', *California Management Review* 39: 123.

Ismi, A. (1998) 'World Bank: plunder with a human face', *Z Magazine* February: 9–12.

Jensen, M. and Meckling, W. (1976) 'Theory of the firm: managerial behavior, agency costs and ownership structure', *Journal of Financial Economics*, 14: 305–360.

Jessop, B. (1997) 'Capitalism and its future: remarks on regulation, government and governance', *Review of International Political Economy* 4, 3: 561–581.

Jevons, W.S. (1871, 1931) *The Theory of Political Economy*, London: Macmillan.

Johnson, C. (1982) *M.I.T.I. and the Japanese Miracle: The Growth of Industrial Policy, 1925–1975*, Stanford, CA: Stanford University Press.

Jorde, T. and Teece, D. (eds) (1992) *Antitrust, Innovation, and Competitiveness*, Oxford: Oxford University Press.

Josephson, M. (1934) *The Robber Barons. The Great American Capitalists, 1861–1901*, New York: Harcourt, Brace and Company.

Juranville, A. (1996) *Lacan et la philosophie*, Paris: Presses Universitaires de France.

Kaldor, M. (1990) *The Imaginary War: Understanding the East–West Conflict*, Oxford: Blackwell.

Kaldor, N. (1972) 'The irrelevance of equilibrium economics', *The Economic Journal*, 82, 328: 1237–1255.

Kanbur, R. (1998) *Aid, Conditionality, and Debt in Africa*, Cornell: Institute for African Development.

Katzenstein, P. J., Keohane, R.O. *et al.* (1998) 'Special Issue: International Organization at its golden anniversary', *International Organization* 52, 4.

Katzenstein, P. J. and Tsujinaka, Y. (1992) ' "Bullying" vs. "Buying": U.S.– Japanese Transnational Relations and Domestic Structures', Annual Meeting of the American Political Science Association.

Kautsky, K. (1914) 'Ultra-imperialism', translated in *New Left Review* 59: 1970.

Kay, C. (1998) *Relevance of Structuralist and Dependency Theories in the Neoliberal Period: A Latin American Perspective*, The Hague: Institute of Social Studies Working Paper, no. 281.

Keck, M. and Sikkink, K. (1998) *Activists Beyond Borders; Advocacy Networks in International Politics*, Ithaca, NY: Cornell University Press.

Kemp, T. (1967) *Theories of Imperialism*, London: Dobson.

Keohane, R.O. (1984) *After Hegemony: Cooperation and Discord in the World Political Economy*, Princeton, NJ: Princeton University Press.

—— (1986) 'Theory of world politics: structural realism and beyond', in R.O. Keohane (ed.) *Neorealism and Its Critics*, New York: Columbia University Press.

—— (1997) 'Problematic lucidity – Stephen Krasner's "state power and the structure of international trade" ', *World Politics* 50, 1: 150.

Keohane, R.O. and Milner, H. (eds) (1996) *Internationalization and Domestic Politics*, Cambridge: Cambridge University Press.

Keohane, R.O. and Nye, J. (eds) (1971) 'Transnational relations and world politics', *International Organization* 25, 3 (Summer), re-published by Harvard University Press in 1972.

—— (1977) *Power and Interdependence: World Politics in Transition*, Boston: Little Brown.

Khor, M. (1995) 'Countering the North's new trade agenda', *Third World Network*, 9 November.

—— (1997) 'Effects of globalisation on sustainable development after UNCED', *Third World Resurgence*, 81/82, May–June: 5–11.

Kindleberger, C.P. (1973) *The World in Depression 1929–1939*, Berkeley, CA: University of California Press.

—— (1979) *The Monopolistic Theory of Direct Foreign Investment. Transnational Corporations and World Order*, San Francisco: G.A. Modelski.

—— (1981) 'Dominance and leadership in the international economy: exploitation, public goods, and free rides', *International Studies Quarterly* 25: 242–254.

Kline, S. and Rosenberg, N. (1986) 'An overview of innovation', in R. Landau and N. Rosenberg (eds) *The Positive Sum Strategy*, Washington, DC: National Academy Press.

Knight, F. H. (1921[1965]) *Risk, Uncertainty and Profit*, Boston: Houghton Mifflin.

Knorr, K. (1973) *Power and Wealth: The Political Economy of International Power*, London: Macmillan.
Koc, M. (1994) 'Globalization as a discourse', in A. Bonnano, L. Busch, W. Friedland, L. Gouveia and E. Mingione (eds) *From Columbus to Conagra. The Globalization of Agriculture and Food*, Lawrence: University Press of Kansas.
Korpi, W. (1992) *Halkar Sverige Efter?*, Stockholm: Carlssons.
Korsch, K. (1963) *Karl Marx*, New York: Russell & Russell.
Korten, D. C. (1990) *Getting to the 21st Century: Voluntary Action and the Global Agenda*, West Hartford, CN: Kumarian Press.
Kotz, D. M., McDonough, T. and Reich, M. (eds) (1994) *Social Structures of Accumulation. The Political Economy of Growth and Crisis*, Cambridge: Cambridge University Press.
Krasner, S.D. (1976) 'State power and the structure of international trade', *World Politics* 28: 317–347.
—— (1982) 'Regimes and the limits of realism: regimes as autonomous variables', *International Organization* 36, 2 (Spring): 497–510.
—— (1985) *Structural Conflict: The Third World Against Global Liberalism*, Berkeley, CA: University of California Press.
—— (1988) 'Sovereignty: an institutional perspective', *Comparative Political Studies* 21, 1: 66–94.
—— (1994) 'International political economy: abiding discord', *Review of International Political Economy* 1, 1: 13–19.
Kratochwil, F. (1996) 'Is the ship of culture at sea or returning?', in Y. Lapid and F. Kratochwil (eds) *The Return of Identity and Culture in IR Theory*, Boulder, CO: Lynne Rienner, pp. 201–222.
Kratochwil, F.V. and Ruggie, J.G. (1986) 'International organization: a state of the art and an art of the state', *International Organization* 40, 4: 753–775.
Krippendorff, E. (1975) *Internationales System Als Geschichte. Einführung in Die Internationalen Beziehungen 1*, Frankfurt A/M: Campus Verlag.
—— (1977) *Internationale Beziehungen als Wissenschaft. Einführung 2*, Frankfurt/M.: Campus Verlag.
Kristof, L. (1969) 'The nature of frontiers and boundaries', in C.R.E. Kasperson and J.V. Minghi (eds) *The Structure of Political Geography*, Chicago: Aldison Publishing Co.
Kristof, N.D. (1996) 'Asian brothels enslaving tens of thousands', *Seattle Times* 14 April: A8.
Krugman, P. (1996) 'What economists can learn from evolutionary theorists': a talk given to the European Association for Evolutionary Political Economy, November.
Krugman, P. and Lawrence, R. (1994) 'Trade, jobs and wages', *Scientific American* (April): 22–27.
Krugman, P.R. and Obstfeld, M. (1991) *International Economics*, New York: HarperCollins Publishers.
Kubálkové, V. and Cruickshank, A. (1980) *Marxism-Leninism and Theory of International Relations*, London: Routledge & Kegan Paul.
Kuhn, H.W. (1953) 'Extensive games and the problem of information', in H.W. Kuhn and A.W. Tucker (eds) *Contributions to the Theory of Games II*, Annuals of Mathematics Studies Series 28, Princeton, NJ: Princeton University Press.
Laitin, D. (1991) 'The national uprisings in the Soviet Union', *World Politics* 44: 139–177.
Lake, D.A. (1988) *Power, Protection, and Free Trade: The International Sources of American Commercial Strategy*, New York: Columbia University Press.
—— (1993) 'Leadership, hegemony, and the international economy: naked emperor or tattered monarch with potential?', *International Studies Quarterly* 37: 459–489.
Lam, A. (1997) 'Embedded firms, embedded knowledge: problems of collaboration and knowledge transfer in global cooperative ventures', *Organization Studies* 18, 6: 973–996.
Lambert, R. and Caspersz, D. (1995) 'International labour standards: challenging globalization ideology?' *The Pacific Review* 8, 4: 569–588.
Langois, R. and Foss, N. (1997) *Capabilities and Governance: The Rebirth of Production in the Theory of Economic Organization*, DRUID Working Paper 97–2, Copenhagen: Danish Research Unit For Industrial Dynamics, January.
Lasch, C. (1995) *The Return of the Elites and the Betrayal of Democracy*, New York: W.W. Norton & Company.
Lash, S. and Urry, J. (1994) *Economies of Signs and Space*, London: Sage Publications.
Lasswell, H.D. (1977) *On Political Sociology*, ed. D. Marvick, Chicago and London: Chicago University Press.
Latham, A. and Hooper, N. (eds) (1995) *The Future of the Defence Firm: New Challenges, New Directions*, Dordrecht and London: Kluwer Academic.
Lauderdale, J.M. Earl of (1804) *An Inquiry into the Nature and Origin of Public Wealth, and into the Means and Causes of Its Increase*, Edinburgh: printed for Arch. Constable & Co. and London: T.N. Longman & O. Rees.

Leary, V. (1996) 'Workers rights and international trade: the social clause (GATT, ILO, NAFTA, US Laws)' in J. Bhagwati and R. Hudec (eds) *Fair Trade and Harmonization: volume 2, Legal Analysis*, Cambridge, MA: MIT Press.

Lebaron, F. (1997) 'Les fondements sociaux de la neutralité économique: le conseil de la politique monétaire de la Banque de France', *Actes de la Recherche en Sciences Sociales* 116/117: 69–90.

Lee, R.L.M. (1994) 'Modernization, postmodernism and the Third World', *Current Sociology* 42, 2.

Lei, D. and Slocum, J. (1992) 'Global strategy, competence-building and strategic alliances', *California Management Review* 35,1: 81–97.

Leiken, R. (1996) 'Controlling the global corruption epidemic', *Foreign Policy* 105: 55–73.

Lemaire, A. (1970) *Jaques Lacan*, London: RKP.

Lenin, V.I. (1917 [1978]) *Imperialism: The Highest Stage of Capitalism*, Moscow: Progress.

Lezuech, G. (1998) 'L'Internationalisation des grandes écoles françaises', *Actes de la recherche en sciences sociales* 121/122: 66–67.

Lijphart, A. (1994) *Electoral Systems and Party Systems*, Oxford: Oxford University Press.

Lim, L.L. (ed.) (1998) *The Sex Sector*, Geneva: International Labour Office.

Ling, L.H.M. (1996) 'Democratization under internationalization: media constructions of gender identity in Shanghai', *Democratization* 3, 2: 140–157.

—— (1999) 'Sex machine: global hypermasculinity and images of the Asian woman in modernity', *Positions: East Asia Cultures Critique* 72, 2: 1–30.

—— (2000) 'Globalisation and the spectre of Fu Manchu: white man's burden as dark irony', in J.S. Fritz and M. Lensu (eds) *Value Pluralism, Normative Theory and International Relations*, London: Macmillan.

Linklater, A. (1990) *Beyond Realism and Marxism. Critical Theory and International Relations*, London: Macmillan.

Lipietz, A. (1989) *Towards a New Economic Order: post-Fordism, ecology and democracy*, Cambridge: Polity Press.

—— (1996a) 'Social Europe: the post-Maastricht challenge', *Review of International Political Economy* 3, 3: 369–379.

—— (1996b) *La Société en sablier: le partage du travail contre le déchirure sociale*, Paris: Editions la Découverte.

—— (1997) 'The post-Fordist world: labour relations, international hierarchy and global ecology', *Review of International Political Economy* 4, 1: 1–41.

Lipschutz, R. (1992) 'Reconstructing world politics: the emergence of global civil society', *Millennium* 21, 3 (Winter): 389–420.

Long, N. (1994) 'From paradigm lost to paradigm regained? The case for an actor-oriented sociology of development', in N. Long and A. Long (eds) *Battlefields of Knowledge*, London: Routledge.

Loureiro, M. R. (1998) 'L'Internationalisation des milieux dirigeants au Brazil', *Actes de la recherche en sciences sociales* 121/122: 42–52.

Luce, D.R. and Raiffa, H. (1957) *Games and Decisions*, New York: J. Wiley & Sons, Inc.

Lukauskas, A. (1997) *Regulating Finance*, Ann Arbor, MI: The University of Michigan Press.

Lukes, S. (1974) *Power: A Radical View*, London: Macmillan.

Lundvall, B.A. (ed.) (1992) *National Systems of Innovation: Towards a Theory of Innovation and Interactive Learning*, London: Pinter.

Luxemburg, R. (1913 [1951]) *The Accumulation of Capital*, London: Routledge & Kegan Paul.

Lynn, L., Reddy, N. and Aram, J. (1996) 'Linking technology and institutions: the innovation community framework', *Research Policy*, 25,1: 91–106.

Lyotard, J.F. (1984) *The Postmodern Condition: A Report on Knowledge*, trans. G. Bennington and B. Massumi, Minneapolis: University of Minnesota Press.

McCubbins, M. and Sullivan, T. (eds) (1987) *Congress: Structure and Policy*, New York: Cambridge University Press.

McGinnis, M.D. (1986) 'Issue linkage and the evolution of international cooperation', *Journal of Conflict Resolution* 30, 1: 141–170.

Machin, H. and Wright, V. (eds). (1985) *Economic Policy and Policy-Making under the Mitterand Presidency, 1981–1984*, London: Frances Pinter.

Maclean, J. (1988) 'Marxism and international relations: a strange case of mutual neglect', *Millennium: Journal of International Studies* 17, 2 (Summer): 295–320.

McMichael, P. (1987) 'State formation and the construction of the world market', in M. Zeitlin (ed.) *Political Power and Social Theory*, Greenwich, CT: JAI Press.

—— (1995) 'The "new colonialism": global regulation and the restructuring of the inter-state system', in D. Smith and J. Borocz (eds) *A New World Order? Global Transformations in the Late Twentieth Century*, Westport, CN: Greenwood Press.

—— (1997) 'Rethinking globalization: the agrarian question revisited', *Review of International Political Economy* 4, 4 (Winter): 630–662.

—— (2000) *Development and Social Change. A Global Perspective*, 2nd edn, Thousand Oaks, CA: Pine Forge Press.

Magdoff, H. (1969) *The Age of Imperialism*, New York: Monthly Review Press.

Maier, C. (1977) 'The politics of productivity: foundations of American international economic policy after World War II', *International Organization* 31: 607–633.

Malmberg, A. and Maskell, P. (1995) 'Localised learning and industrial competitiveness', *BRIE Working Paper 80*, Berkeley: University of California.

—— (1997) 'Towards an explanation of regional specialization and industry agglomeration', *European Planning Studies* 5: 25–41.

Mandel, E. (1962) *Marxist Economic Theory*, London: Merlin Press.

—— (1968) *Die EWG und die Konkurrenz Europa-Amerika*, Frankfurt: Europäische Verlagsanstalt; trans. in English as *Europe Vs America*, London: New Left Books, 1970.

—— (1972) *Der Spätkapitalismus*, Frankfurt: Suhrkamp, trans. in English as *Late Capitalism*, London: New Left Books, 1975.

Mander, J. and Goldsmith, E. (eds) (1996) *The Case Against the Global Economy, and for a Turn Toward the Local*, San Francisco: Sierra Club Mander.

Mann, M. (1986, 1993) *The Sources of Social Powers*, vols I and II, Cambridge: Cambridge University Press.

—— (1988) *States, War and Capitalism*, Oxford: Blackwell.

—— (1997) 'Has globalization ended the rise and rise of the nation-state?', *Review of International Political Economy*, 4, 3: 472–96.

Marazzi, C. (1995) 'Money in the world crisis: the new basis of capitalist power', in W. Bonefeld and J. Holloway (eds) *Global Capital, the National State and the Politics of Money*, London: St. Martin's Press.

March, J. and Olsen, J. (1989) *Rediscovering Institutions*, New York: The Free Press.

Marchand, M. (1996) 'Selling NAFTA: gendered metaphors and silenced gender implications', in E. Kofman and G. Youngs (eds) *Globalization*, London: Pinter.

Marcuse, H. (1964) *One Dimensional Man. Studies in the Ideology of Advanced Industrial Society*, Boston: Beacon Press.

—— (1968) *Reason and Revolution*, London: Routledge & Kegan Paul.

Marshak, J. (1950) 'Rational behavior, uncertain prospects, and measurable utility', *Econometrica* 18, 2: 111–114.

Marshall, A. (1920) *Principles of Economics. An Introductory Volume*, 8th edn, London: Macmillan (first published in 1890).

Martin, K. (1991) 'Modern development theory', in K. Martin (ed.) *Strategies of Economic Development*, London: Macmillan.

Martin, L. and Simmons, B. (1998) 'Theories and empirical studies of international institutions', *International Organization* 52: 729–758.

Martinussen, J. (1997) *Society, State and Market: A Guide to Competing Theories of Development*, London: Zed.

Marx, K. (1867; 1906) *Capital: A Critique of Political Economy, vol. 1. The Process of Capitalist Production*, Chicago: Charles H. Kerr & Company.

—— (1967) *Capital*, vol. 1, Moscow: Progress Publishers.

—— (1973) *The Revolution of 1848*, Harmondsworth: Penguin.

—— (1979) *Capital* ,vol. 3, Harmondsworth: Penguin.

Marx, K. and Engels, F. (1974) *De Duitse Ideologie Deel 1*, Nijmegen: SUN.

Maskell, P., Eskelinen, H., Hannibalsson, I., Malmberg, A. and Vatne, E. (1998) *Competitiveness, Localised Learning and Regional Development*, London: Routledge.

Maskell, P. and Malmberg, A. (1995) *Localised Learning and Industrial Competitiveness*, BRIE Working Paper 80, Berkeley, CA: University of California Press, October.

Mayer, A.J. (1981) *The Persistence of the Old Regime: Europe to the Great War*, London: Croom Helm.

Mead, G.H. (1934) *Mind, Self and Society*, ed. C.W. Morris, Chicago: University of Chicago Press.

Mehmet, O. (1995) *Westernizing the Third World: The Eurocentricity of Economic Development Theories*, London: Routledge.

Meier, G.M. (1990) 'Trade policy, development, and the new political economy', in R.W. Jones and A.O. Krueger (eds) *The Political Economy of International Trade: Essays in Honor of Robert E. Baldwin*, Oxford: Basil Blackwell.

Meinecke, F. (1962) *Machiavellism: The Doctrine of Raison D'état and its Place in Modern History*, London: Routledge & Kegan Paul.

Merleau-Ponty, M. (1964) *Signs*, Evanston, IL: Northwestern University Press.

Mészáros, I. (1995) *Beyond Capital: Towards a Theory of Transition*, London: Merlin Press.

Metcalfe, J.S. (1995) 'Technology systems and technology policy in an evolutionary framework', *Cambridge Journal of Economics* 19, 1: 25–46.

Metz, K.H. (1982) 'The politics of conflict: Heinrich von Treitschke and the idea of Realpolitik', *History of Political Thought* 3:1, Spring.

Michalet, C. (1991a) 'Strategic partnerships and the changing internationalization process', in L.K. Mytelka (ed.) *Strategic Partnerships and the World Economy*, London: Pinter Publishers.

—— (1991b) 'Global competition and its implications for firms', in *Technology and Productivity: The Challenges for Economic Policy*, Paris: OECD.

Mies, M. (1986) *Patriarchy and Accumulation on a World Scale: Women in the International Division of Labour*, London: Zed Press.

Miliband, R. (1973) *The State in Capitalist Society. The Analysis of the Western System of Power*, London: Quartet Books.

Miller, G. (1992) *Managerial Dilemmas*, New York: Cambridge University Press.

Mills, C.W. (1958) *The Sociological Imagination*, Harmondsworth: Penguin.

Milner, H. (1997) *Interests, Institutions and Information: Domestic Politics and International Relations*, Princeton, NJ: Princeton University Press.

Milner, H. and Rosendorff, B. (1997) 'Trade negotiations: elections and divided government as constraints on trade liberalization', *Journal of Conflict Resolution*, 41, 1: 117–146.

Mintz, B. and Schwartz, M. (1990) 'Capital flows and the process of financial hegemony: structures of capital', in S. Zukin and P. DiMaggio (eds) *The Social Organization of the Economy*, Cambridge: Cambridge University Press, pp. 203–227.

Mirowski, P. (1990) 'The philosophical bases of intitutionalist economics', in D. Lavoie (ed.) *Economics and Hermeneutics*, London: Routledge.

Mitchell, W. and Singh, K. (1992) 'Incumbents' use of preentry alliances before expansion into new technical subfields of an industry', *Journal of Economic Behavior and Organization* 18: 347–372.

—— (1996) 'Survival of businesses using collaborative relationships to commercialize complex goods', *Strategic Management Journal* 17, 3: 169–195.

Mittelman, J.H. (ed.) (1996) *Globalization: Critical Reflections*, Boulder, CO: Lynne Rienner.

—— (ed.) (1997) *Globalization. Critical Reflections, International Political Economy Yearbook 9*, Boulder, CO: Lynne Rienner.

—— (1998) 'Coxian historicism as an alternative perspective in international studies', *Alternatives* 23: 63–92.

Mo, J. (1994) 'The logic of two-level games with endogenous domestic coalitions', *Journal of Conflict Resolution* 38: 402–422.

Moe, T. (1984) 'The new economics of organization', *American Journal of Political Science* 28: 739–777.

Mohamad, M. and Ishihara, S. (1995) *The Voice of Asia*, Tokyo: Kodansha International.

Money, J. (1997) 'No vacancy: the political geography of immigration control in advanced industrial countries', *International Organization* 51, 4 (Autumn): 685–720.

Moody, K. (1997) *Workers in a Lean World: Unions in the International Economy*, London: Verso.

Moore, J. (1993) 'Predators and prey – a new ecology of competition', *Harvard Business Review* 71, 3: 75–86.

—— (1996) *The Death of Competition: Leadership and Strategy in the Age of Business Ecosystems*, New York: Harperbusiness.

Moravcsik, A. (1993) 'Introduction: integrating international and domestic theories of international bargaining', in P.B. Evans, H.K. Jacobson and R.D. Putnam (eds) *Double-Edged Diplomacy: International Bargaining and Domestic Politics*, Berkeley, CA: University of California Press, pp. 3–42.

—— (1998) *The Choice for Europe: Social Purpose and State Power from Messina to Maastricht*, Ithaca, NY: Cornell University Press.

Morgan, K. and Sayer, A. (1987) *Microcircuits of Capital: 'sunrise' industry and uneven development*, Cambridge: Polity Press.

Morgenthau, H.J. (1948) *Politics Among Nations: The Struggle for Power and Peace*, New York: Knopf.

Morriss, P. (1987) *Power: A Philosophical Analysis*, Manchester: Manchester University Press.

Morrow, J.D. (1994) *Game Theory for Political Scientists*, Princeton, NJ: Princeton University Press.

—— (1997) 'When do "relative gains" impede trade?', *Journal of Conflict Resolution* 41, 1: 12–37.

Mulgan, G. (1994) *Politics in an Antipolitical Age*, Cambridge: Polity.

Mumford, L. (1967) *The Myth of the Machine: Techniques and Human Development*, New York: Harcourt, Brace & World, Inc.

—— (1970) *The Myth of the Machine: The Pentagon of Power*, New York: Harcourt, Brace Jovanovich Inc.

Murphy, C. (1994) *International Organization and Industrial Change. Global Governance Since 1850*, Oxford: Polity Press.

—— (1998) 'Understanding IR: understanding Gramsci', *Review of International Studies* 24: 417–425.

Murphy, C.N. and Rojas De Ferro, C. (1995) 'The power of representation in international political economy', *Review of International Political Economy* 2, 1: 63–183.

Murphy, C.N and Tooze, R. (eds) (1991) *The New International Political Economy*, Boulder, CO: Lynne Rienner Publishers.

Murray, E.A. and Mahon, J.F. (1993) 'Strategic alliances: gateway to the new Europe', *Long Range Planning* 26, 4: 102–111.

Mydans, S. (1997) 'Asian bloc's anniversary celebration becomes a plea for outside help', *New York Times* 17 December: D6.

Mytelka, L.K. (1988) 'New modes of competition in the textile and clothing industry: some consequences for third world exporters', in J. Niosi (ed.) *Technology and National Competitiveness: Oligopoly, Technological Innovation and International Competition*, London: McGill Queen's University Press, pp. 225–246.

—— (1993) 'Transfer et maîtrise de la technologie: les cas des industries textiles en Afrique', manuscript.

—— (1995) 'Dancing with wolves: oligopolies and strategic partnerships', in J. Hagedoorn (ed.) *Technical Change and the World Economy*, Aldershot: Edward Elgar.

Mytelka, L.K. *et al.* (1985) *Les politiques d'industrialisation du tiers-monde face aux complexes industriels transnationalisés*, Paris: University of Nanterre.

Nandy, A. (1988) *The Intimate Enemy*, Delhi: Oxford University Press.

—— (1989) 'Shamans, savages and the wilderness: on the audibility of dissent and the future of civilizations', *Alternatives* 14: 263–277.

Naqvi, N. (ed.) (1996) *Rethinking Security, Rethinking Development*, Islamabad: Sustainable Development Policy Institute.

Nash, J. (1951) 'Noncooperative games', *Annals of Mathematics* 54: 289–295.

Nederveen Pieterse, J. (1991) 'Dilemmas of development discourse: the crisis of developmentalism and the comparative method', *Development and Change* 22,1: 5–29.

—— (1994) 'Globalization as hybridization', *International Sociology* 9, 2: 161–184.

—— (1995) 'The cultural turn in development: questions of power', *European Journal of Development Research* 7, 1: 176–192.

—— (1997a) 'Growth and equity revisited: a supply-side approach to social development', *European Journal of Development Research* 9, 1: 128–149.

—— (1997b) 'Going global: futures of capitalism', *Development and Change* 28, 2: 367–382.

—— (1998a) 'Hybrid modernities: mélange modernities in Asia', *Sociological Analysis*, 1 3: 75–86.

—— (1998b) 'Humanitarian intervention and beyond', in J. Nederveen Pieterse (ed.) *World Orders in the Making: Humanitarian Intervention and Beyond*, London: Macmillan.

—— (1998c) 'My paradigm or yours? Alternative development, post-development, reflexive development', *Development and Change* 29, 2: 343–373.

—— (1999) 'Critical holism and the tao of development', *European Journal of Development Research*, 8 (forthcoming).

Nee, V. and Peng Lian (1994) 'Sleeping with the enemy: a dynamic model of declining political commitment in state socialism', *Theory and Society* 23: 253–296.

Nelson, R. (1992) 'The role of firms in technical advance', in G. Dosi, R. Giannetti and P.A. Toninelli (eds) *Technology and Enterprise in a Historical Perspective*, Oxford: Clarendon Press.

Neumann, J. Von and Morgenstern, O. (1947) *Theory of Games and Economic Behavior*, 2nd edn, Princeton, NJ: Princeton University Press.

Neusüss, C. (1972) *Imperialismus und Weltmarktbewegung des Kapitals*, Erlangen: Politladen.

Nicholls-Nixon, C.L. and Jasinski, D. (1995) 'The blurring of industry boundaries: an explanatory model applied to telecommunications', *Industrial and Corporate Change*, 4, 4: 755–768.

Nitzan, J. (1992) 'Inflation as restructuring: a theoretical and empirical account of the U.S. experience', unpublished PhD dissertation, Department of Economics, McGill University, Montreal.

—— (1998) 'Differential accumulation: toward a new political economy of capital', *Review of International Political Economy* 5, 2: 169–216.

—— (1999) 'Regimes of differential accumulation: "breadth" and "depth" in capitalist development', paper presented at the International Studies Association Meetings in Washington, March.

Nitzan, J. and Bichler, S. (1995) 'Bringing capital accumulation back in: the weapondollar-petrodollar coalition – military contractors, oil companies and Middle-East "energy conflicts"', *Review of International Political Economy* 2, 3: 446–515.

—— (1996) 'From war profits to peace dividends – the new political economy of Israel', *Capital and Class*, 60: 61–94.

—— (1997) 'From depth to breadth in differential accumulation: the great u-turn in South Africa and Israel', paper presented at the International Studies Association Meetings in Toronto, March. Forthcoming in *The Review of Radical Political Economics*.

Nollen, S. and Quin, D. (1994) 'Free trade, fair trade, strategic trade and protectionism in The US Congress 1987–88', *International Organization* 48,3 (Summer): 491–525.

North, D. (1990) *Institutions, Institutional Change and Economic Performance*, New York: Cambridge University Press.

Nye, J.S., Jr. (1990) 'Soft power', *Foreign Policy* 80: 153–171.

Oakes, G. (1988) *Weber and Rickert: Concept Formation in the Cultural Sciences*, Cambridge, MA: MIT Press.

Oakeshott, M. (1976) 'On misunderstanding human conduct: a reply to my critics', *Political Theory* 4, 2: 353–367.

O'Brien, R. (1998) 'Shallow foundations: labour and the selective regulation of free trade', in G. Cook (ed.) *The Economics and Politics of International Trade*, London: Routledge.

O'Brien, R., Goetz, A., Scholte, J. and Williams, M. (2000) *Contesting Global Governance: Multilateral Economic Institutions and Global Social Movements*, Cambridge: Cambridge University Press.

OECD (1992) *Technology and the Economy: The Key Relationships*, Paris: OECD.

—— (1995) *Historical Statistics 1960–95*, Paris: OECD.

—— (1997) *Historical Statistics 1960–93*, Paris: OECD.

Ohmae, K. (1990) *The Borderless World: Power and Strategy in the Global Marketplace*, London: Collins.

Olson, M. (1965) *The Logic of Collective Action: Public Goods and the Theory of Groups*, Cambridge, MA: Harvard University Press.

—— (1982) *The Rise and Decline of Nations. Economic Growth, Stagflation and Social Rigidities*, New Haven and London: Yale University Press.

Ong, A. (1987) *Spirits of Resistance and Capitalist Discipline*, Albany, NY: State University of New York.

Onuf, N.G. (1989) *World of Our Making: Rules and Rule in Social Theory and International Relations*, Berkeley: University of South California Press.

Oommen, T.K. (1998) 'Changing paradigms of development: the evolving participatory society', *Journal of Social and Economic Development* 1: 35–45.

Orrù, M., Biggart Woolsey, N. *et al.* (1991) 'Organizational isomorphism in East Asia', in W. Powell and P. DiMaggio (eds) *The New Institutionalism in Organizational Analysis*, Chicago: University of Chicago Press, pp. 361–389.

Orwell, G. (1949) *Nineteen Eighty-Four*, London: Secker & Warburg.

Osborn, R. and Hagedoorn, J. (1997) 'The institutionalization and evolutionary dynamics of inter-organizational alliances and networks', *Academy of Management Journal* 40, 2: 261–278.

Osborne, D. and Gaebler, T. (1992) *Reinventing Government: How the Entrepreneurial Spirit is Transforming the Public Sector, from Schoolhouse to Statehouse, City Hall to the Pentagon*, Reading, MA: Addison-Wesley.

Ostrom, V., Tiebout, C.M. and Warren, R. (1961) 'The organization of government in metropolitan areas: a theoretical inquiry', *American Political Science Review*, 55, 3 (September): 831–842.

Ouchi, W. (1991) 'Markets, bureaucracies and clans', in G. Thompson (ed.) *Markets, Hierarchies, and Networks*, Newbury Park, CA: Sage.

Overbeek, H.W. (1990) *Global Capitalism and National Decline. The Thatcher Decade in Perspective*, London: Unwin Hyman.

—— (ed.) (1993) 'Restructuring hegemony', in *The Global Political Economy: the Rise of Transnational Neo-Liberalism in the 1980s*, London: Routledge.

Oye, K. (ed.) (1986) *Cooperation Under Anarchy*, Princeton, NJ: Princeton University Press.

Oye, K. A. (1996) 'The condition for cooperation in world politics', in R.C. Art and R. Jervis (eds) *International Politics: Enduring Concepts and Contemporary Issues*, 4th edn, New York: HarperCollins College Publishers.

Pahre, R. (1997) 'Endogenous domestic institutions in two-level games and parliamentary oversight of the European Union', *Journal of Conflict Resolution* 41, 1: 147–174.

Pahre, R. and Papayoanou, P.A. (1997) 'Using game theory to link domestic and international politics', *Journal of Conflict Resolution* 41, 1: 4–11.

Palan, R. (1997) 'Ontological consternation and the future of international political economy', *Economies et Sociétés, Relations Économiques Internationales* 4: 101–115.

—— (1998a) 'Les fantômes du capitalisme mondial: l'économie politique internationale et l'école française de la régulation', *L'Année de la Régulation: Économie, Institutions, Pouvoirs*, 2: 63–87.

—— (1998b) 'Trying to have your cake and eating it: how and why the state system has created offshore', *International Studies Quarterly* 42: 625–644.

—— (1999) 'Susan Strange 1923–1998: a great international relations theorist', *Review of International Political Economy* 6: 2.

Palan, R. and Abbott, J. (1996) *State Strategies in the Global Political Economy*, London: Pinter.

Palan, R. and Blair, B. (1993) 'On the idealist origins of the realist theory of international relations', *Review of International Studies* 19: 385–399.

Palan, R. and Gills, B. (eds) (1994) *Transcending the State–Global Divide. A Neostructuralist Agenda in International Relations*, Boulder, CO: Lynne Rienner.

Palloix, C. (1973) *Les firmes multinationales et le procès d'internationalisation*, Paris: Maspéro.

Palumbo-Liu, D. (1994) 'Los Angeles, Asians, and perverse ventriloquisms: on the functions of Asian America in the recent American imaginary', *Public Culture* 6: 365–381.

Panitch, L. (1994) 'Globalisation and the state', in R. Miliband and L. Panitch (eds) *Between Globalism and Nationalism*, London: Merlin Press.

—— (1998) '"The state in a changing world": social-democratizing global capitalism?', *Monthly Review* 50, 5: 11–22.

Parsons, T. (1951) *The Social System*, Glencoe, ILL: Free Press.

Pasinetti, L.L. and Scazzieri, R. (1987) 'Capital theory: paradoxes', in J. Eatwell, M. Milgate and P. Newman (eds) *The New Palgrave*, vol. 1, London: Macmillan.

Patel, P. and Pavitt, K. (1997) 'The technological competencies of the world's largest firms: complex and path-dependent, but not much variety', *Research Policy* 26, 2: 141–156.

Pavitt, K. (1993) 'What do firms learn from basic research?', in D. Foray and C. Freeman (eds) *Technology and the Wealth of Nations: The Dynamics of Constructed Advantage*, London: Pinter Publishers, pp. 29–40.

Peet, R. and Watts, M.J. (eds) (1996) *Liberation Ecologies: Environment, Development, Social Movements*, London: Routledge.

Penrose, E. (1995) *Theory of the Growth of Firms*, New York: Oxford University Press.

Pettman, J.J. (1996) 'International political economy of sex', in E. Kofman and G. Youngs (eds) *Globalization*, London: Pinter.

PGA (1997) *First Conference of The Peoples' Global Action Against 'Free' Trade and the World Trade Organisation*, Philippines: PGA Secretariat.

Picciotto, S. (1991) 'The internationalisation of the state', *Capital and Class* 43: 43–63.

—— (1998) 'Globalisation, liberalisation, regulation', paper presented to RIPE Globalization, State and Violence Conference, University of Sussex, April.

Picot, A., Rippengen, T. and Wolff, B. (1996) 'The fading boundaries of the firm: the role of information and communication technology', *Journal of Institutional and Theoretical Economics*, 152, 1: 373–385.

Pijl, K. van der (1978) *Een Amerikaans Plan Voor Europa*, Amsterdam: SUA.

—— (1979) 'Class formation at the international level', *Capital and Class* 9, (Autumn): 1–22.

—— (1984) *The Making of an Atlantic Ruling Class*, London: Verso.

—— (ed.) (1989) 'Transnational relations and class strategy', *International Journal of Political Economy* 19, 3, Fall.

—— (1993) 'State socialism and passive revolution', in S. Gill (ed.) *Gramsci, Historical Materialism and International Relations*, Cambridge: Cambridge University Press.

—— (1996a) *Vordenker der Weltpolitik. Einführung in die internationale Politik aus Ideengeschichtlicher Perspektive*, Opladen: Leske+Budrich.

—— (1996b) 'A theory of transnational revolution: universal history according to Eugen Rosenstok-Huessy and its implications', *Review of International Political Economy* 3, 2: 287–318.

—— (1997) 'The history of class struggle: from original accumulation to neoliberalism', *Monthly Review* 49, 1: 28–44.

—— (1998) *Transnational Classes and International Relations*, London: Routledge.

Piore, M. and Sabel, C. (1984) *The Second Industrial Divide*, New York: Basic Books.

Pocock, J.G.A. (1975) *The Machiavellian Moment: Florentine Political Thought and the Atlantic Republican Tradition*, Princeton, NJ: Princeton University Press.

Polanyi, K. (1944, 1957) *The Great Transformation: The Political and Economic Origins of Our Time*, Boston: Beacon Press.

Polsby, N.W. (1980) *Community, Power and Political Theory*, New Haven, CN: Yale University Press.

Porter, M. (1980) *Competitive Strategy*, New York: Free Press.

—— (1985) *Competitive Advantage*, New York: Free Press.

—— (1990) *The Competitive Advantage of Nations*, New York: Free Press.

Porter, M. and Fuller, M.B. (1986) 'Coalitions and global strategy', in *Competition in Global Industries*, Boston: Harvard Business Review Press, p. 581.

Poulantzas, N. (1968) *Pouvoir politique et classes sociales*, Paris: Maspéro.

—— (1973) *Political Power and Social Classes*, London: Verso.

—— (1974) *Les Classes sociales dans le capitalisme aujourd'hui*, Paris: Le Seuil.

Powell, R. (1993) 'Guns, butter, and anarchy', *American Political Science Review*, 87, 1: 115–132.

Powell, W. and Dimaggio, P. (eds) (1991) *The New Institutionalism in Organizational Analysis*, Chicago: University of Chicago Press.

Power, M. (1997) *The Audit Society: Rituals of Verification*, Oxford: Oxford University Press.

Prahalad, C. and Hamel, G. (1990) 'The core competence of the corporation', *Harvard Business Review*, 3: 79–91.

Pratt, J. and Zeckhauser, R. (eds) (1985) *Principals and Agents: The Structure of Business*, Boston: Harvard Business School Press.

Pred, A. and Watts, M.J. (1992) *Reworking Modernity: Capitalisms and Symbolic Discontent*, New Brunswick, NJ: Rutgers University Press.

Prencipe, A. (1997) 'Technological competencies and product's evolutionary dynamics: a case study from the aero-engine industry', *Research Policy*, 25, 8:1261-1276.

Prus, R. (1997) *Subcultural Mosaics and Intersubjective Reality: An Ethnographic Research Agenda for Pragmatizing the Social Sciences*, New York: State University of New York Press.

Przeworski, A. (1990) *The State and the Economy under Capitalism*, Chur: Hardwood.

Putnam, R.D. (1988) 'Diplomacy and domestic politics: the logic of two-level games', *International Organization* 42: 427–460.

—— (1993) 'Diplomacy and domestic politics: the logic of two-level games', in P.B. Evans, H.K. Jacobson, and R.D. Putnam (eds) *Double-Edged Diplomacy: International Bargaining and Domestic Politics*, Berkeley, CA: University of California Press.

Pye, L. (1988) 'The new Asian capitalism: a political portrait', in P.L. Berger and H-H. M. Hsia (eds) *In Search of an East Asian Development Model*, Oxford: Transaction Books.

Radice, H. (1998) 'Globalization and national differences', *Competition and Change* 3, 4.

Radosh, R. (1969) *American Labour and United States Foreign Policy*, New York: Random House.

Rahnema, M. and Bawtree, V. (eds) (1997) *The Post-Development Reader*, London: Zed.

Rapoport, A., Guyer, M.J. and Gordon, D.G. (1976) *The 2 X 2 Game*, Ann Arbor, MI: The University of Michigan Press.

Rasmusen, E. (1989) *Games and Information: An Introduction to Game Theory*, Cambridge: Basil Blackwell.

Reding, A. (1994) 'Chiapas is Mexico', *World Policy Journal* XI, 1 (Spring): 11–25.

Reich, R. (1992) *The Work of Nations: Preparing Ourselves for 21st-Century Capitalism*, New York: Knopf.

Reich, R.B. (1983) *The Next American Frontier*, New York: Times Books.

Rew, A. (1997) 'The donors' discourse: official social development knowledge in the 1980s', in R.D. Grillo and R.L. Stirrat (eds) *Discourses of Development*, Oxford: Berg.

RIPE (1994) 'Editorial: forum for heterodox international political economy', *Review of International Political Economy* 1, 1 (Spring): 1–12.

Risse-Kappen, T. (ed.) (1995) *Bringing Transnational Relations Back in: Non-State Actors, Domestic Structures and International Institutions*, Cambridge: Cambridge University Press.

Rist, G. (1990) ' "Development" as part of the modern myth: the western socio-economic dimension of "development" ', *European Journal of Development Alternatives* 2,1: 10.

—— 1997) *The History of Development from Western Origins to Global Faith*, London and New York: Zed.

Ritzer, G. (1996) *The Mcdonaldization of Society*, Thousand Oaks, CA: Pine Forge Press.

Rizvi, S.A.T. (1994) 'The microfoundations project in general equilibrium theory', *Cambridge Journal of Economics* 18, 4: 357–377.

Robinson, J. (1953–4) 'The production function and the theory of capital', *Review of Economic Studies* 21, 2: 81–106.

—— (1971, 1977) 'The relevance of economic theory', in J. Schwartz (ed.) *The Subtle Anatomy of Capitalism*, Santa Monika: Goodyear.

Rodrik, D. (1997) *Has Globalization Gone Too Far?*, Washington, DC: Institute for International Economics.

Roeder, P. (1993) *Red Sunset*, Princeton, NJ: Princeton University Press.

Rogowski, R. (1989) *Commerce and Coalitions*, Princeton, NJ: Princeton University Press.

Rose, R. (1981) 'Ungovernability: is there fire behind the smoke?', *Political Studies* 27: 351–370.

Rosenau, J. (1980) 'Capabilities and control in an interdependent world', in J. Rosenau (ed.) *The Study of Global Interdependence: Essays on the Transnationalisation of World Affairs*, London: Frances Pinter.

Rosenau, P. (1992) *Postmodernism and the Social Sciences*, Princeton, NJ: Princeton University Press.

Rosenberg, J. (1990) 'A non-realist theory of sovereignty? Giddens' The Nation-State and Violence', *Millenium*, 17, 2: 249–259.

——— (1994) *The Empire of Civil Society. A Critique of the Realist Theory of International Relations*, London: Verso.

Rosenthal, E. (1999) 'Suicides reveal bitter roots of China's rural life', *New York Times* 24 January.

Röttger, B. (1997) *Neoliberale Globalisierung und eurokapitalistische Regulation. Die politische Konstitution ses Marktes*, Münster: Westfälisches Dampfboot Verlag.

Rowthorn, B. (1971) 'Imperialism in the 1970s – unity or rivalry?', *New Left Review* 69: 31–51.

Ruggie, J.G. (1982) 'International regimes, transactions and change: embedded liberalism in the postwar economic order', *International Organization* 36: 397–415.

——— (1998) *Constructing the World Polity. Essays on International Institutionalization*, London: Routledge.

Rugman, A. (1986) 'New theories of the multinational enterprise: an assessment of internalization theory', *Bulletin of Economic Research* 38, 2: 101–118

Ruigrok, W. and Van Tulder, R. (1996) *The Logic of International Restructuring*, London: Routledge.

Rupert, M. (1995a) *Producing Hegemony: The Politics of Mass Production and American Global Power*, Cambridge: Cambridge University Press.

——— (1995b) '(Re)politicizing the global economy: liberal common sense and ideological struggle in the US NAFTA debate', *Review of International Political Economy* 2: 658–692.

——— (1998) '(Re-)engaging Gramsci: a response to Germain and Kenny', *Review of International Studies* 24: 427–434.

——— (forthcoming) *Ideologies of Globalization*, London: Routledge.

Sabel, C.F. (1995) 'Bootstrapping reform: rebuilding firms, the welfare state and unions', *Politics and Society* 23, 1: 5–48.

Sabel, C.F. and Prokop, J.E. (1996) 'Stabilization through reorganization: some preliminary implications of Russia's entry into world markets in the age of discursive quality standards', in. R. Frydman, C. W. Gray and A. Rapaczinski (eds) *Corporate Governance in Central Europe and Russia*, Budapest: CEU Press.

Sachs, W. (ed.) (1992) *The Development Dictionary: A Guide to Knowledge as Power*, London: Zed.

Sadowski, Y. M. (1991) *Political Vegetables: Businessman and Bureaucrat in the Development of Egyptian Agriculture*, Washington, DC: The Brookings Institution.

Said, E. (1979) *Orientalism*, New York: Vintage Books.

Sakamoto, Y. (ed.) (1994) *Global Transformation: Challenges to the State System*, Tokyo: United Nations University Press.

Sally, R. (1992) *States and Firms: The Political Economy of French and German Multinational Enterprises in International Competition*, London: London School of Economics and Political Science.

——— (1994) 'Multinational enterprises, political economy and institutional theory: domestic embeddedness in the context of internationalization', *Review of International Political Economy* 1, 1 (Spring): 161–192.

Samuelson, P. (1957) 'Wages and interest: a modern dissection of Marxian economic models', *American Economic Review* 47, 6: 884–912.

——— (1962) 'Parable and realism in capital theory: the surrogate production function', *Review of Economic Studies*, 29, 3: 193–206.

——— (1998) 'Global capitalism, R.I.P.?', *Newsweek* 14 September: 40–42.

Sandmo, A. (1989). 'Public goods', in J. Eatwell, M. Milgate and P. Newman (eds) *Allocation, Information, and Markets*, New York: W.W. Norton.

Sassen, S. (1996) *Losing Control? Sovereignty in an Age of Globalization*, New York: Columbia.

Savage, L.J. (1954) *The Foundations of Statistics*, New York: J. Wiley and Co.

Sayer, A. and Walker, R. (1992) *The New Social Economy: Reworking the Division of Labor*, Cambridge, MA: Blackwell.

Schaeffer, R. (1995) 'Free trade agreements: their impact on agriculture and the environment', in P. McMichael (ed.) *Food and Agrarian Orders in the World-Economy*, Westport, CT: Greenwood Press.

Schmidt, V.A. (1996) *From State to Market? The Transformation of French Business and Government*, Cambridge: Cambridge University Press.

Schumpeter, J.A. (1951) *Imperialism and Social Classes*, Kelley: New York.

——— (1954) *History of Economic Analysis*, ed. from manuscript by E.B. Schumpeter, New York: Oxford University Press.

Schutz, A. (1972 [1932]) *The Phenomenology of the Social World*, London: Heinemann.

Schuurman, F. (1993) (ed.) *Beyond the Impasse: New Directions in Development Theory*, London: Zed.

Scott, A. and Storper, M. (1992) 'Regional development reconsidered', in H. Ernste and V. Meier (eds) *Regional Development and Contemporary Industrial Response. Extending Flexible Specialisation*, London: Belhaven Press.

Screpanti, E. (1990) 'Capitalist forms and the essence of capitalism', *Review of International Political Economy* 6: 1.

Senior, N. (1872, 1938) *An Outline of the Science of Political Economy*, London: Allen & Unwin.

Sève, L. (1975) 'De Methode in De Ekonomiese Wetenschap', *Te Elfder Ure* 17, 671–690 (translated from the French original in *La Nouvelle Critique* 71, February 1974, 27–36).

Shaikh, A. (1990) 'Capital as a social relation', in J. Eatwell, M. Milgate and P. Newman (eds) *The New Palgrave. Marxian Economics*, New York and London: W.W. Norton & Company.

Sharpe, J. (1993) *Allegories of Empire*, Minneapolis: University of Minnesota Press.

Shaw, M. (ed.) (1984) *War, State and Society*, London: Macmillan.

—— (1994) *Global Society and International Relations*, Cambridge: Polity.

—— (1997) 'The state of globalization', *Review of International Political Economy*, 4, 3: 497–513.

—— (1999) 'The state of international relations', in S.B. Owen (ed.) *State and Identity in International Relations*, London: Macmillan.

Shaw, M. and Creighton, C. (eds) (1987) *The Sociology of War and Peace*, London: Macmillan.

Silverman, H.J. (1997) *Inscriptions: After Phenomenology and Structuralism*, Evanston, IL: Northwestern University Press.

Simon, H. (1947) *Administrative Behavior*, New York: Macmillan.

—— (1955) 'A behavioral model of rational choice', *Quarterly Journal of Economics* 69: 99–118.

Sinclair, T. (1994) 'Passing judgement: credit rating processes as regulatory mechanisms of governance in the emerging world order', *Review of International Political Economy*, 1, 1: 133–160.

—— (1996) 'Beyond international relations theory: Robert W. Cox and approaches to world order', in R.W. Cox, with T.J. Sinclair, *Approaches to World Order*, Cambridge: Cambridge University Press.

Singer, H.W. and Jolly, R. (eds) (1995) 'Fifty years on: the UN and economic and social development', *IDS Bulletin*, 26, 4.

Sklair, L. (1997) 'Social movements for global capitalism: the transnational capitalist class in action', *Review of International Political Economy* 4, 3: 514–538.

Skocpol, T. (1979) *State and Social Revolutions*, Cambridge: Cambridge University Press.

Smith, A. (1776, 1937) *An Inquiry into the Nature and Causes of The Wealth of Nations*, ed. with an Introduction by E. Cannan, New York: The Modern Library.

Snidal, D. (1985a) 'The limits of hegemonic stability theory', *International Organization*, 39: 579–614.

—— (1985b) 'Coordination versus prisoners' dilemma: implications for international cooperation and regimes', *American Political Science Review* 79, 4: 923–942.

—— (1986) 'The game theory of international politics', in K. Oye (ed.) *Cooperation Under Anarchy*, Princeton, NJ: Princeton University Press, pp. 25–57.

—— (1991) 'Relative gains and the pattern of international cooperation', *American Political Science Review* 85: 701–726.

Snyder, G.H. and Diesing, P. (1977) *Conflict Among Nations: Bargaining, Decisionmaking and System Structure in International Crises*, Princeton, NJ: Princeton University Press.

So, A.Y. (1990) *Social Change and Development*, London: Sage.

Solnick, S. (1996) 'The breakdown of hierarchies in the Soviet Union and China: a neoinstitutional perspective', *World Politics* 48: 209–238.

—— (1997) *Stealing the State*, Cambridge, MA: Harvard University Press.

Soros, G. (1997) 'The capitalist threat', *The Atlantic Monthly* 279, 2: 45–58.

Spruyt, H. (1994) *The Sovereign State and Its Competitors: An Analysis of Systems Change*, Princeton, NJ: Princeton University Press.

Sraffa, P. (1960) *Production of Commodities by Means of Commodities: prelude to a Critique of Economic Theory*, Cambridge: Cambridge University Press.

Stark, D. and Bruszt, L. (eds) (1998) *Post Socialist Pathways: Transforming Politics and Property Rights in East Central Europe*, Cambridge: Cambridge University Press.

Stavrianos, L.S. (1981) *Global Rift: The Third World Comes of Age*, New York: Morrow.

Steedman, I. (1975) 'Positive profits with negative surplus value', *Economic Journal*, 85: 114–123.

—— (1977) *Marx After Sraffa*, London: New Left Books.

Stein, A. (1984) 'The hegemon's dilemma', *International Organization* 38: 355–386.

Stiglitz, J. (1987) 'Principal and agent', in J. Eatwell, M. Milgrave, and P. Newman (eds) *The New Palgrave*, vol. 3, London: Macmillan.

Stone, D. (1999) 'Learning lessons, transferring policy and the international movement of ideas', conference paper WS/63, European University Institute, Florence, 25–26 March.

Stone, R. (1996) *Satellites and Commissars*, Princeton, NJ: Princeton University Press.

Stopford, J. and Strange, S. (1991) *Rival States, Rival Firms*, Cambridge: Cambridge University Press.

Storper, M. and Harrison, B. (1991) 'Flexibility, hierarchy and regional development: the changing structure of industrial production systems and their form of governance in the 1990s', *Research Policy* 20: 407–422.

Strange, S. (ed.) (1984) *Paths to International Political Economy*, London: George Allen & Unwin.

—— (1985) 'International political economy: the story so far and the way ahead', in W. Ladd Hollist and F. Lamond Tullis (eds) *The International Political Economy*, Boulder, CO: Westview Press.

—— (1988) *States and Markets: An Introduction to International Political Economy*, New York: Basil.

—— (1990) 'The name of the game: sea changes', in N. Rizopoulos (ed.) *American Foreign Policy in a World Transformed*, New York and London: Council on Foreign Relations Press, pp. 238–274.

—— (1991) 'Big business and the state', *Millenium*, 20, 2: 245–251.

—— (1993) 'Big business and the state', in L. Eden and E.H. Potter (eds) *Multinationals in the Global Economy*, New York: St. Martin's Press.

—— (1994) 'Wake up Krasner! The world has changed', *Review of International Political Economy* 1, 2: 209–220.

—— (1995) '1995 Presidential Address', *International Studies Quarterly* 39, 3 (September): 287–295.

—— (1996) *The Retreat of the State: The Diffusion of Power in the World Economy*, Cambridge: Cambridge University Press.

—— (1998a) *Mad Money*, Manchester: Manchester University Press.

—— (1998b) 'Finance in politics: an epilogue to mad money', mimeo, University of Warwick.

Streeck, W. and Schmitter, P.C. (1985) 'Community, market, state and associations? The prospective contribution of interest governance to social order', in W. Streeck and P. C. Schmitter (eds) *Private Interest Government: Beyond Market and State*, London: Sage, pp. 1–29.

Strom, N. (1998) 'Taking stock of NGO activity on MAI', *ICDA Journal* 6, 1: 60–64.

Sturgeon, T. (1997a) *Turnkey production networks: a new American model of industrial organization?*, BRIE Working Paper 92A, Berkeley, CA: University of California, August.

—— (1997b) *Does Manufacturing Still Matter? The Organizational Delinking of Production from Innovation*, BRIE Working Paper 92B Berkeley, CA: University of California, August.

Swedberg, R., Himmelstrand, U. *et al.* (1987) 'The paradigm of economic sociology', *Theory and Society* 16: 169–213.

Sweezy, P.M. (1942, 1970) *The Theory of Capitalist Development. Principles of Marxian Political Economy*, New York and London: Modern Reader Paperbacks.

Szelényi, I., Eyal, G. *et al.* (1996) 'Post-Communist Managerialism: The Remaking of the Economic Institutions and the Changes in the Social Structure during Post-Communist Transformation', Central European University Departmental Seminar, Budapest.

Takaki, R. (1990) *Iron Cages*, Oxford: Oxford University Press.

Tassey, G. (1991) 'The functions of technology infrastructure in a competitive economy'. *Research Policy* 20, 4: 345–361.

—— (1992) *Technology Infrastructure and Competitive Position*, Massachusetts: Kluwer Academic Press.

Taylor, M. (1976) *Anarchy and Cooperation*, New York: Wiley.

Taylor, P.J. (1996) *The Way the Modern World Works. World Hegemony to World Impasse*, Chichester: John Wiley & Sons.

Teece, D. (1986) 'Transaction cost economics and the multinational enterprise: an assessment', *Journal of Economic Behavior and Organization* 7: 21–47.

—— (1988) 'Technological change and the nature of the firm', in G. Dosi, C. Freeman, R. Nelson, G. Silverberg and L. Soete (eds) *Technical Change and Economic Theory*, London: Pinter Publishers, pp. 256–281.

—— (1992) 'Competition, cooperation, and innovation: organizational arrangements for regimes of rapid technological progress', *Journal of Economic Behavior and Organization* 18, 1: 1–25.

Teeple, G. (1995) *Globalization and the Decline of Social Reform*, Atlantic Highlands, NJ: Humanities Press.

Thiele, L. (1993) 'Making democracy safe for the world: social movements and global politics', *Alternatives* 18, 3 (Summer): 273–305.

Thompson, E.P. (1978) *The Poverty of Theory and Other Essays*, London: Merlin.

Thrift, N. (1992) 'Muddling through: world orders and globalization', *The Professional Geographer* 44: 3–7.

Tilly, C. (ed.) (1975) *The Formation of National States in Western Europe*, Princeton, NJ: Princeton University Press.

Tomaschewski, D.G. (1973) *Die Leninschen Ideen und die Internationalen Beziehungen der Gegenwart*, Berlin: Staatsverlag der DDR.

Tooze, R. (1984) 'Perspectives and theory: a consumer's guide', in S. Strange (ed.) *Paths to International Political Economy*, London: George Allen & Unwin, pp. 1–22.

—— (1990) 'Understanding the global political economy: applying Gramsci', *Millennium: Journal of International Studies* 19, 2: 273–280.

Travis, L.A. (ed.) (1988) *Multinational Managers and Host Government Interactions*, Notre Dame, IN: University of Notre Dame Press.

Treitschke, H. von (1916) *Politics*, London: Constable and Co.

Trentmann, F. (1998) 'Political culture and political economy: interest, ideology and free trade', *Review of International Political Economy* 5, 2: 217–251.

Trumbore, P.F. (1998) 'Public opinion as a domestic constraint in international negotiations: two-level games in the Anglo-Irish peace process', *International Studies Quarterly* 42: 545–565.

Truong, T.D. (1999) 'The underbelly of the tiger: gender and the demystification of the Asian miracle', *Review of International Political Economy* 6, 2: 133–165.

Turim, M. (1997) 'Specificity and culture', in A. King (ed.) *Culture, Globalisation and the World System*, Minneapolis: University of Minnesota Press.

Underhill, G.R.D. (1994) 'Introduction: conceptualizing the changing global order', in R. Stubbs and G.R.D. Underhill (eds) *Political Economy and the Changing Global Order*, Toronto: McClelland & Stewart Inc.

—— (1997) *The New World Order in International Finance*, London: Macmillan.

UNDP (1996, 1997, 1998) *Human Development Report*, New York: Oxford University Press.

UNESCO (1996) *Our Creative Diversity*, Report of The World Commission on Culture and Development, Paris: UNESCO Publishing.

US Department of Commerce (1986) *The National Income and Product Accounts of the United States, 1929–82, Statistical Tables*, Washington, DC: GPO (September).

Veblen, T. (1898) 'The beginning of ownership', reprinted in T. Veblen (1934) *Essays in Our Changing Order*, New York: The Viking Press.

—— (1899) 'The barbarian status of women', reprinted in T. Veblen (1934) *Essays in Our Changing Order*, New York: The Viking Press.

—— (1904, 1975) *The Theory of Business Enterprise*, Clifton, NJ: Augustus M. Kelley, Reprints of Economics Classics.

—— (1908a) 'Fisher's capital and income', reprinted in T. Veblen (1934) *Essays in Our Changing Order*, New York: The Viking Press.

—— (1908b) 'On the Nature of Capital. I: The Productivity of Capital Goods', reprinted in T. Veblen (1919) *The Place of Science in Modern Civilisation and Other Essays*, New York: Russell & Russell.

—— (1908c) 'On the Nature of Capital. II: Investment, Intangible Assets, and the Pecuniary Magnate', reprinted in T. Veblen (1919) *The Place of Science in Modern Civilisation and Other Essays*, New York: Russell & Russell.

—— (1908d) 'Professor Clark's economics', reprinted in T. Veblen (1919) *The Place of Science in Modern Civilisation and Other Essays*, New York: Russell & Russell.

—— (1909) 'Fisher's rate of interest', reprinted in T. Veblen (1934) *Essays in Our Changing Order*, New York: The Viking Press.

—— (1919, 1961) *The Place of Science in Modern Civilisation and Other Essays*, New York: Russell & Russell.

—— (1923, 1967) *Absentee Ownership and Business Enterprise in Recent Times. The Case of America*, with an Introduction by Robert Leckachman, Boston: Beacon Press.

—— (1934) *Essays in Our Changing Order*, ed. L. Ardzrooni, New York: The Viking Press.

Vogel, S.K. (1996) *Freer Markets, More Rules: Regulatory Reform in Advanced Industrial Countries*, Ithaca, NY: Cornell University Press.

Wade, R. (1996) 'Globalization and its limits: reports of the death of the national economy are greatly exaggerated', in S. Berger and R. Dore (eds) *National Diversity and Global Capitalism*, Ithaca, NY: Cornell University Press, pp. 60–89.

Wade, R. and Veneroso, F. (1998) 'The Asian crisis: the high debt model versus the Wall Street-Treasury-IMF Complex', *New Left Review* 228: 3–24.

Walker, R.J.B. (1994) *Inside/Outside International Relations as Political Theory*, Cambridge: Cambridge University Press.

Wallerstein, I. (1974) *The Modern World-System*, New York: Academic Press.

Waltz, K. N. (1979) *Theory of International Politics*, Reading, MA: Addison-Wesley.

—— (1986) 'A response to my critics', in R.O. Keohane (ed.) *Neorealism and Its Critics*, New York: Columbia University Press, pp. 322–345.

—— (1990) 'Realist thought and neorealist theory', *Journal of International Affairs* 44, (Summer): 21–38.

Wapner, P. (1995) 'Politics beyond the state: environmental activism and world civic politics', *World Politics* (April): 311–340.

Waterman, P. (1998) *Globalization, Social Movements and the New Internationalisms*, London: Mansell.

Weber, M. (1948) *The Protestant Ethic and the Spirit of Capitalism*, London: Allen & Unwin.

—— (1964) *The Theory of Social and Economic Organization*, New York: Free Press.

—— (1978) *Economy and Society*, vol. II, ed. G. Roth and C. Wittich, Berkeley, CA: University of California Press.

Weiss, L. (1997) 'Globalization and the myth of the powerless state', *New Left Review* 225: 327.

—— (1998) *The Myth of the Powerless State: Governing the Economy in a Global Era*, Cambridge, Polity Press.

Weiss, L. and Hobson, J. (1995) *States and Economic Development: A Comparative Analysis*, Cambridge: Polity.

Wells, D. (1998) 'Building transnational coordinative unionism', in H. Nunez and S. Babson (eds) *Confronting Change: Auto Labor and Lean Production in North America*, Detroit: Wayne State University Press.

Wendt, A. (1987) 'The agent-structure problem in international relations theory', *International Organization* 41, 3: 335–350.

—— (1992) 'Anarchy is what states make of it: the social construction of power politics', *International Organization* 46, 2: 397, n. 21.

—— (1995) 'Constructing international politics', *International Security* 20, 1: 71–81.

Wernerfelt, B. (1984) 'A resource-based view of the firm', *Strategic Management Journal* 5: 171–180.

Whitley, R. (ed.) (1995) *European Business Systems. Firms and Markets in Their National Contexts*, London: Sage Publications.

—— (1998) 'Internationalization and varieties of capitalism: the limited effects of cross-national coordination of economic activities on the nature of business systems', *Review of International Political Economy* 5, 3: 445–481.

Wicksell, K. (1935) *Lectures on Political Economy, 1, General Theory*, 2nd edn, trans. from the Swedish by E. Classen and edited with an Introduction by L. Robbins, London: George Routledge & Sons, Ltd.

Wilden, A. (1968) 'Lacan and the Discourse of the Other', in *Lacan, Jacques: the Language of the Self*, Baltimore: John Hopkins Press.

—— (1987) *The Rules Are No Game: The Strategy of Communication*, London and New York. RKP.

Wilkinson, J. (1997) 'A new paradigm for economic analysis?', *Economy and Society* 26, 3: 305–339.

Williamson, O. (1975) *Markets and Hierarchies: Analysis and Antitrust Implications*, New York: The Free Press.

—— (1985) *The Economic Institutions of Capitalism*, New York: The Free Press.

—— (1986) *Economic Organization*, New York: New York University Press.

WIP (1998) *Work in Progress*, Washington: AFL-CIO, 9 February.

Wolfers, A. (1962) *Discord and Collaboration: Essays on International Politics*, Baltimore and London: The Johns Hopkins University Press.

Wood, A. (1995) 'How trade hurt unskilled workers', *Journal of Economic Perspectives* 9, 3 (Summer): 57–80.

World Bank (1995) *Workers in an Integrating World*, New York: Oxford University Press.

—— (1997) *The State in a Changing World: World Development Report 1997*, New York: Oxford University Press.

—— (1998) 'Report and recommendation of the President of the International Bank for Reconstruction and Development to the executive directors on a proposed structural adjustment loan in an amount equivalent to US$2.0 billion to the Republic of Korea', March 19.

Wright, E.O. (1977) 'Alternative perspectives in Marxist theory of accumulation and crisis', in J. Schwartz (ed.) *The Subtle Anatomy of Capitalism*, Santa Monika: Goodyear.

Yarborough, B. and Yarborough, R. (1987) 'Cooperation in the liberalization of international trade: after hegemony what?', *International Organization* 41: 1–26.

—— (1990) 'International institutions and the new economics of organization', *International Organization* 44: 235–259.

—— (1992) *Cooperation and Governance in International Trade*, Princeton, NJ: Princeton University Press.

Yeung, H. (1998) 'The social–spatial constitution of business organizations: a geographical perspective', *Organization*, 5, 1: 101–128.

Young, R. (1995) *Colonial Desire*, London: Routledge.

Young, S. (1998) 'Korea's financial crisis: causes and prospects, a note', paper presented to ABD-OECD Forum on Asian Perspectives, Paris, 3 June.

Zysman, J. (1983) *Governments, Markets, and Growth: Financial Systems and the Politics of Industrial Change*, Ithaca, NY: Cornell University Press.

—— (1996) 'The myth of the global economy: enduring national foundations and emerging regional realities', *New Political Economy* 1, 1 (Summer): 157–184.

# Index